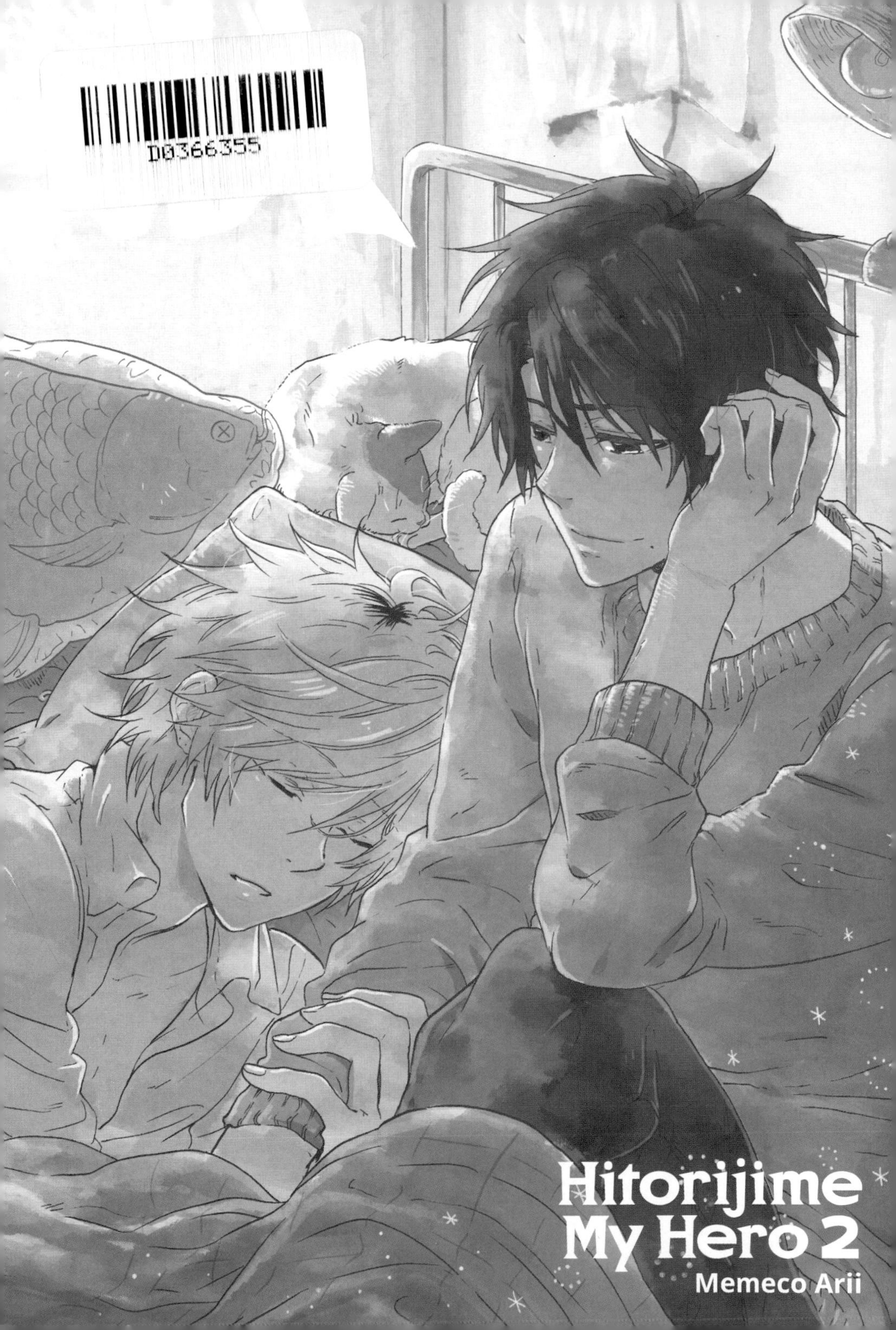
Hitorijime
My Hero 2
Memeco Arii

Hitorijime My Hero
CONTENTS

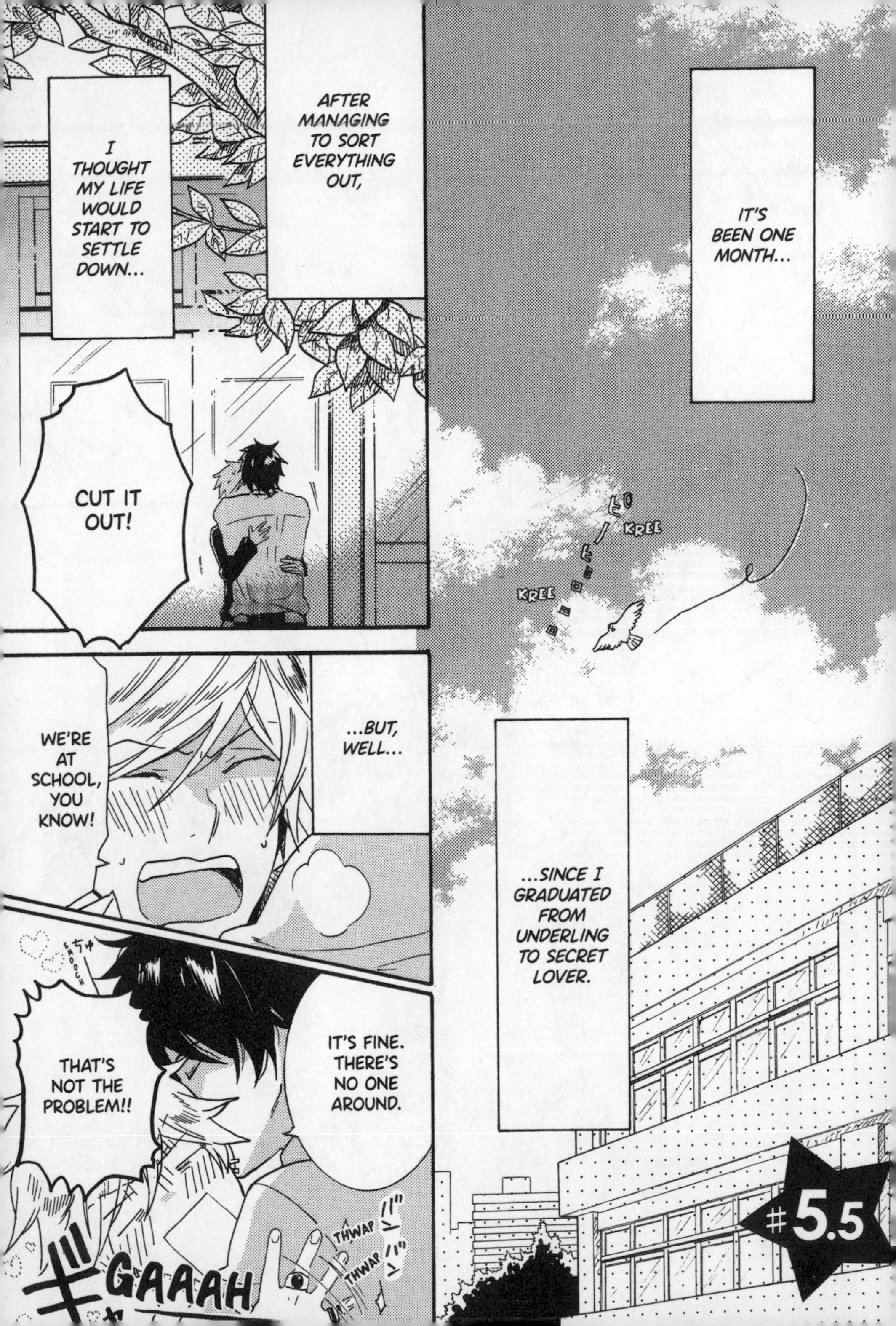
IT'S BEEN ONE MONTH...
KREE
KREE
...SINCE I GRADUATED FROM UNDERLING TO SECRET LOVER.
#5.5
AFTER MANAGING TO SORT EVERYTHING OUT,
I THOUGHT MY LIFE WOULD START TO SETTLE DOWN...
CUT IT OUT!
...BUT, WELL...
WE'RE AT SCHOOL, YOU KNOW!
SMOOCH
IT'S FINE. THERE'S NO ONE AROUND.
THAT'S NOT THE PROBLEM!!
THWAP
THWAP
GAAAH

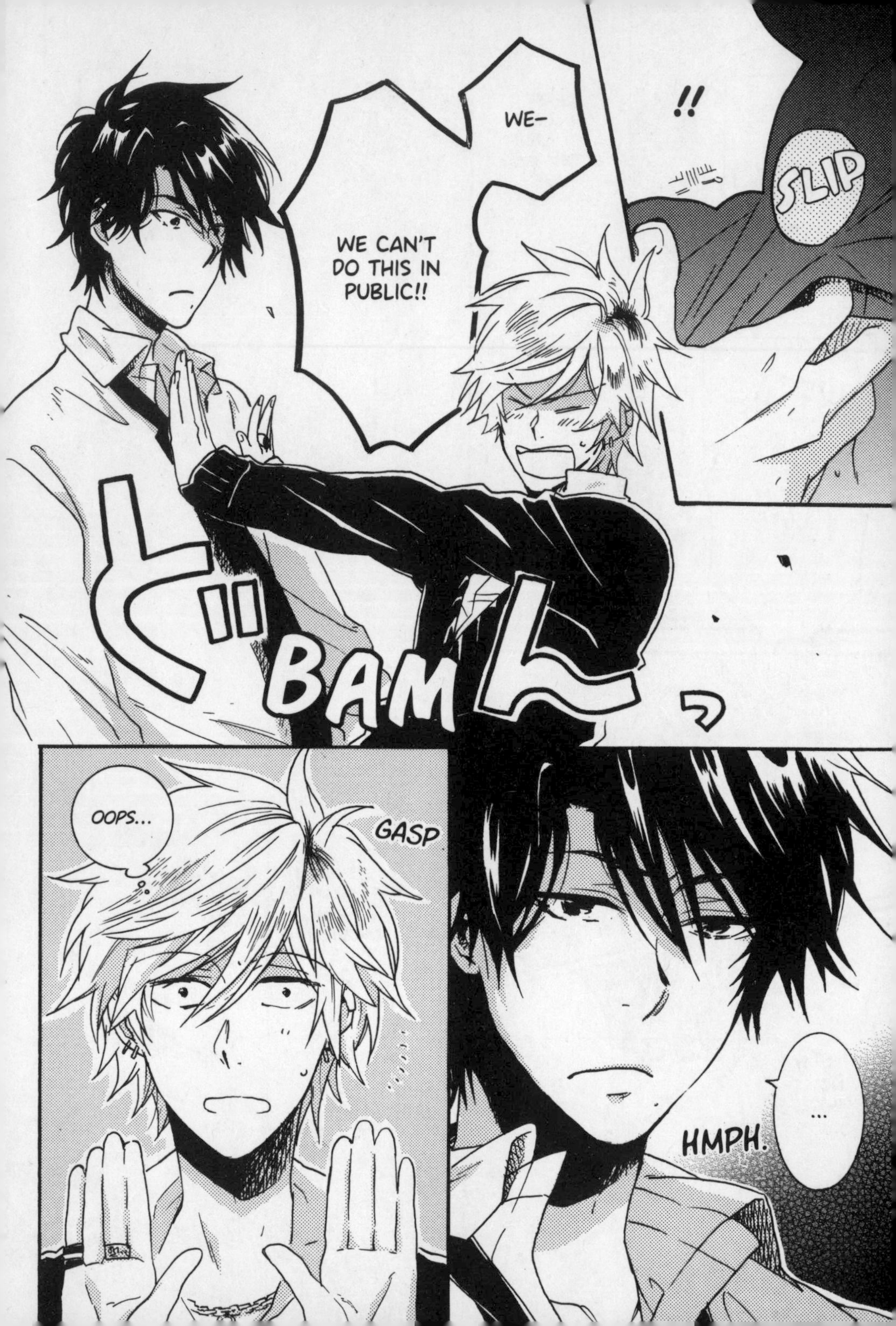
!!
SLIP
WE-
WE CAN'T DO THIS IN PUBLIC!!
BAM
...
HMPH.
OOPS...
GASP

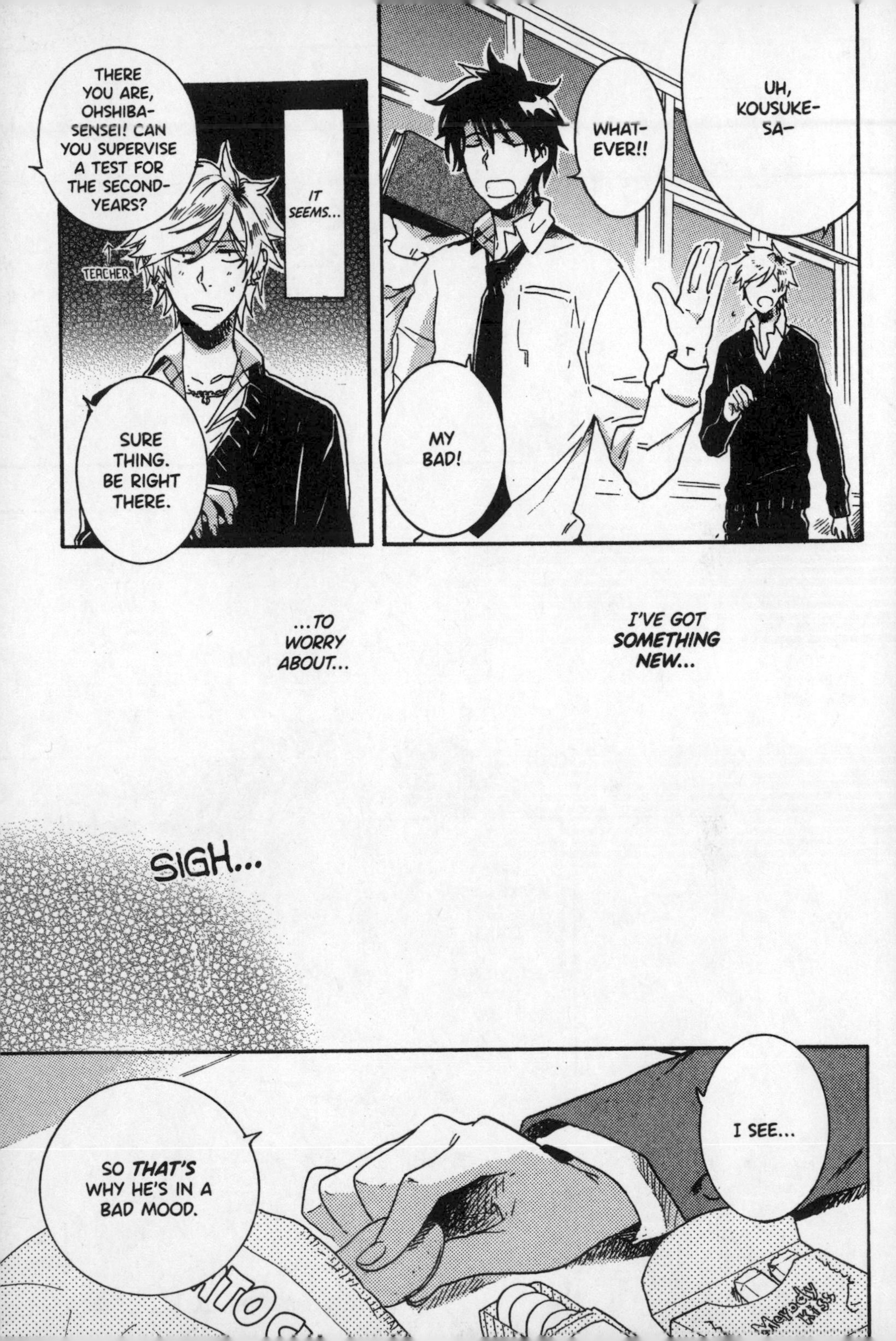
UH, KOUSUKE-SA—
WHAT-EVER!!
MY BAD!
IT SEEMS...
THERE YOU ARE, OHSHIBA-SENSEI! CAN YOU SUPERVISE A TEST FOR THE SECOND-YEARS?
TEACHER
SURE THING. BE RIGHT THERE.
I'VE GOT SOMETHING NEW...
...TO WORRY ABOUT...
SIGH...
I SEE...
SO *THAT'S* WHY HE'S IN A BAD MOOD.

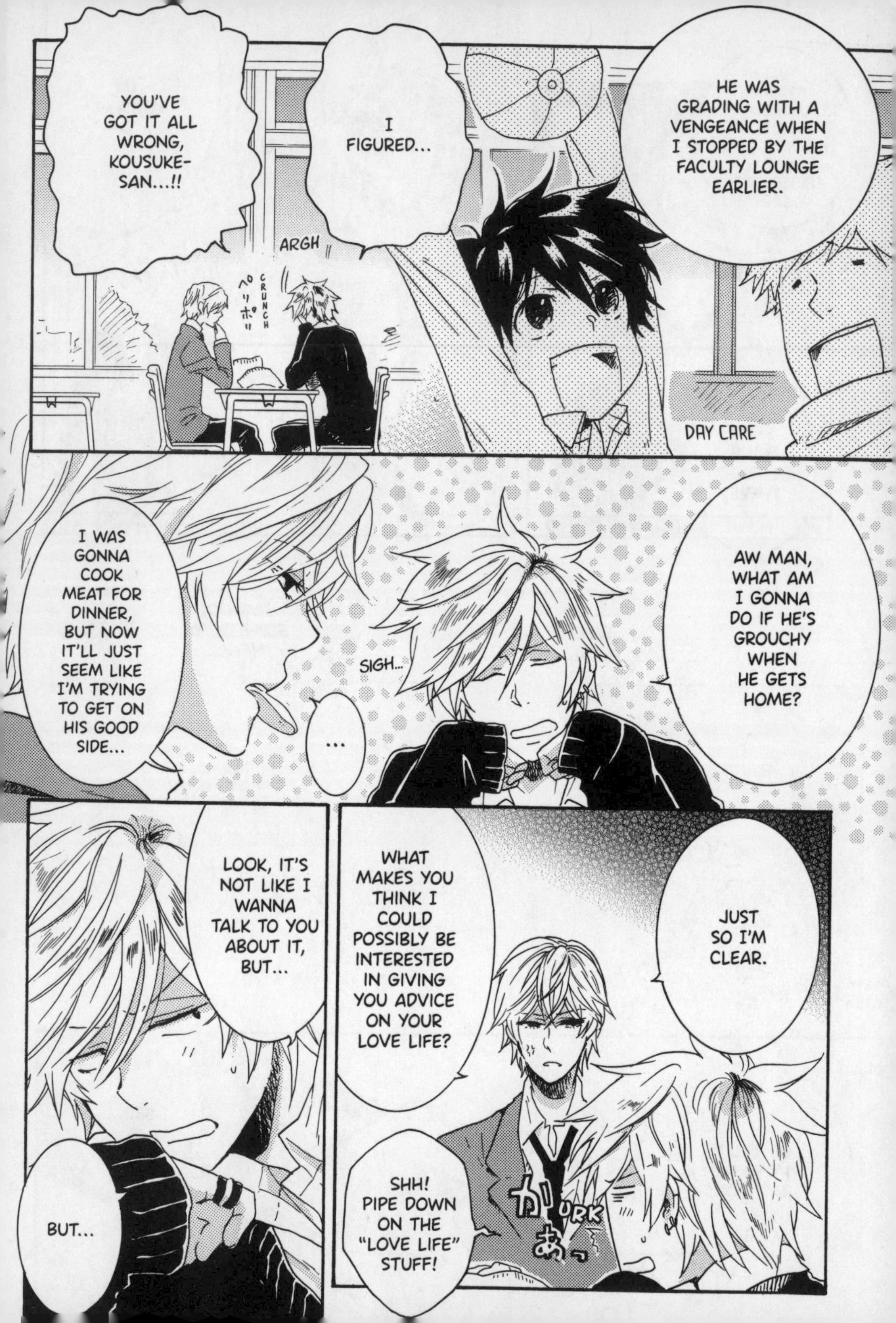
HE WAS GRADING WITH A VENGEANCE WHEN I STOPPED BY THE FACULTY LOUNGE EARLIER.
DAY CARE
I FIGURED...
ARGH
ペリポリ
CRUNCH
YOU'VE GOT IT ALL WRONG, KOUSUKE-SAN...!!
AW MAN, WHAT AM I GONNA DO IF HE'S GROUCHY WHEN HE GETS HOME?
SIGH...
...
I WAS GONNA COOK MEAT FOR DINNER, BUT NOW IT'LL JUST SEEM LIKE I'M TRYING TO GET ON HIS GOOD SIDE...
JUST SO I'M CLEAR.
WHAT MAKES YOU THINK I COULD POSSIBLY BE INTERESTED IN GIVING YOU ADVICE ON YOUR LOVE LIFE?
SHH! PIPE DOWN ON THE "LOVE LIFE" STUFF!
か URK あっ
LOOK, IT'S NOT LIKE I WANNA TALK TO YOU ABOUT IT, BUT...
BUT...

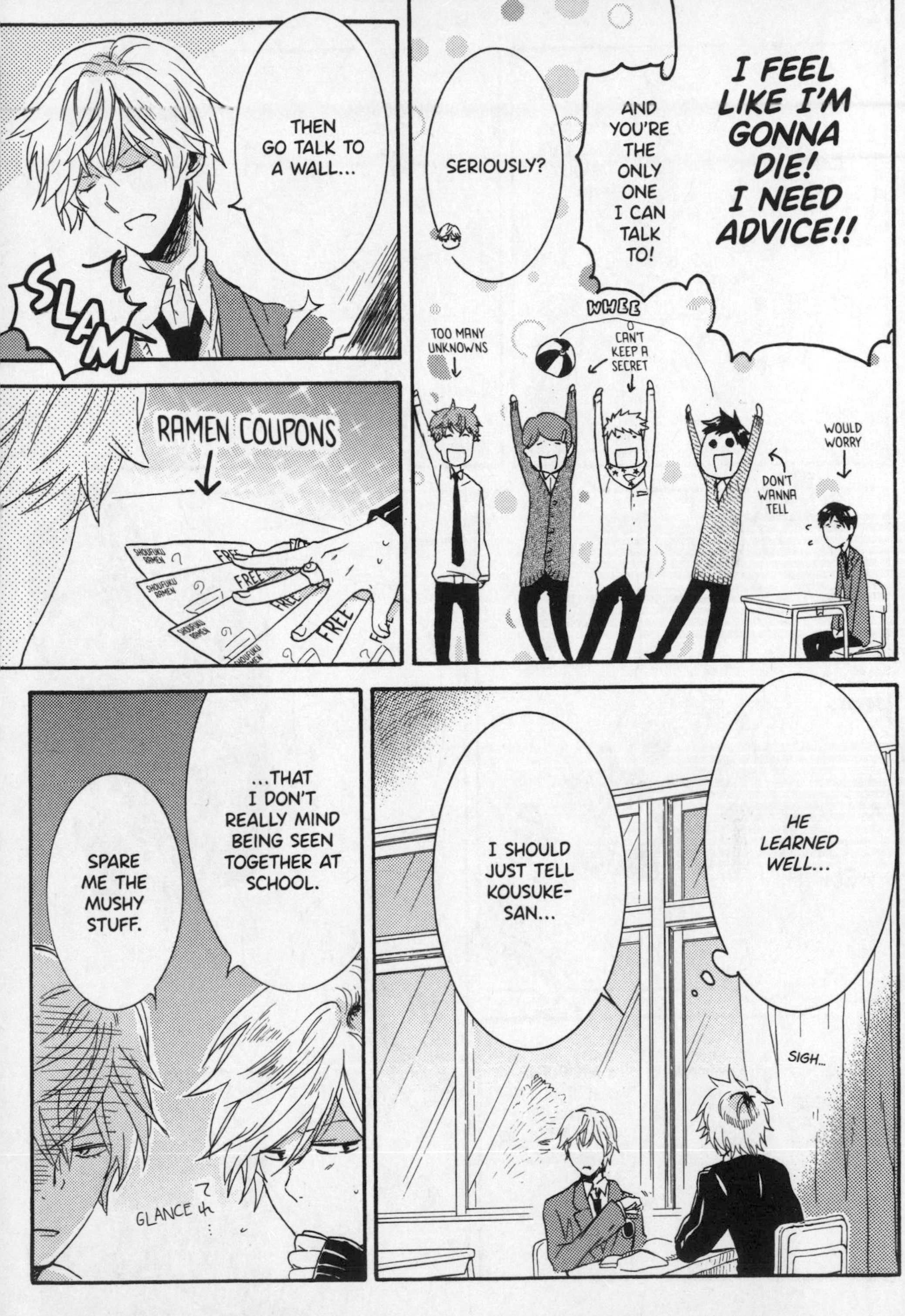
I FEEL LIKE I'M GONNA DIE! I NEED ADVICE!!
AND YOU'RE THE ONLY ONE I CAN TALK TO!
SERIOUSLY?
WHEE
WOULD WORRY
DON'T WANNA TELL
CAN'T KEEP A SECRET
TOO MANY UNKNOWNS
THEN GO TALK TO A WALL...
SLAM
RAMEN COUPONS
SHOUFUKU RAMEN
FREE
HE LEARNED WELL...
I SHOULD JUST TELL KOUSUKE-SAN...
SIGH...
...THAT I DON'T REALLY MIND BEING SEEN TOGETHER AT SCHOOL.
SPARE ME THE MUSHY STUFF.
GLANCE

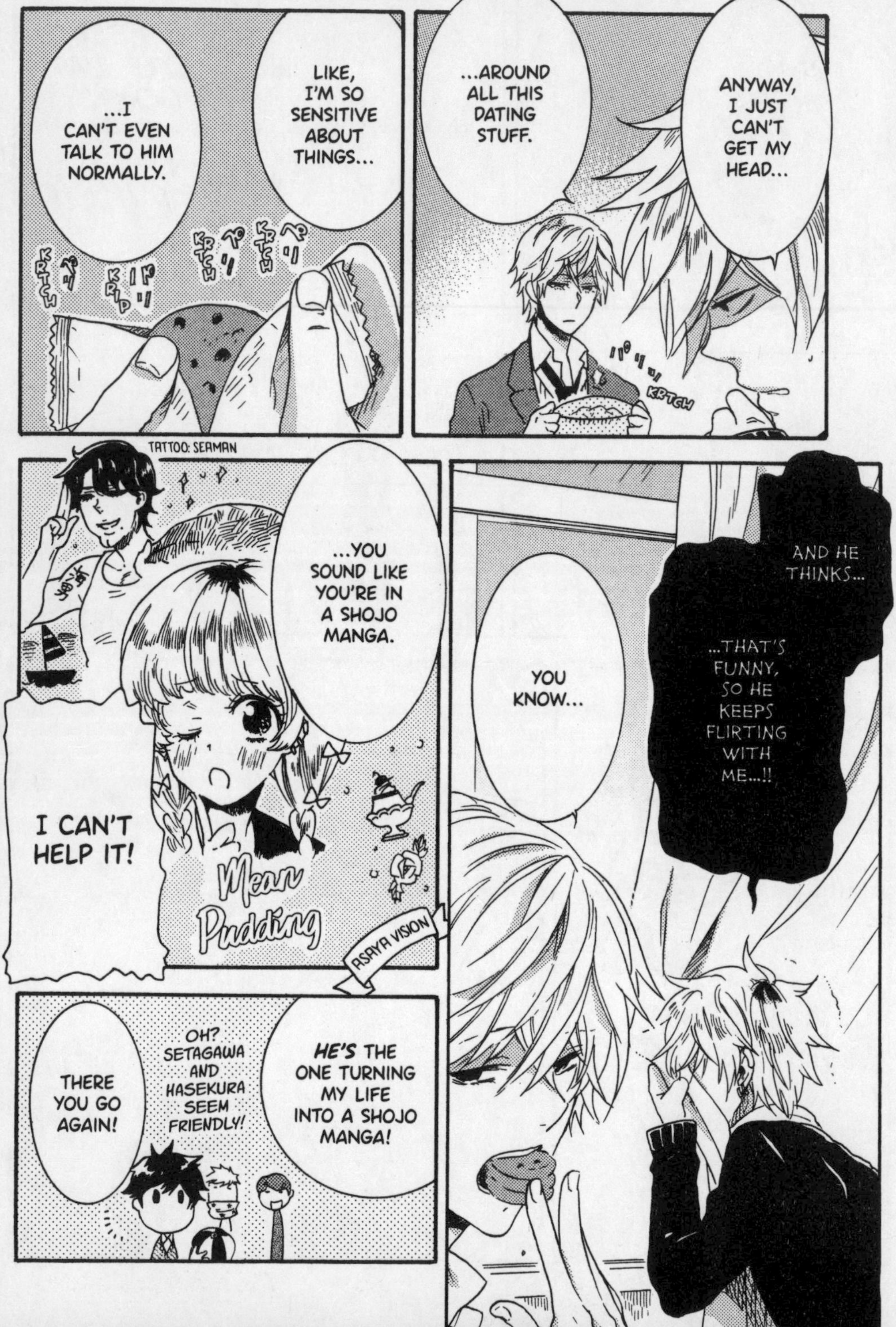
ANYWAY, I JUST CAN'T GET MY HEAD...
...AROUND ALL THIS DATING STUFF.
KRTCH
LIKE, I'M SO SENSITIVE ABOUT THINGS...
...I CAN'T EVEN TALK TO HIM NORMALLY.
KRTCH
KRTCH
KRIP
KRTCH
AND HE THINKS...
...THAT'S FUNNY, SO HE KEEPS FLIRTING WITH ME...!!
YOU KNOW...
...YOU SOUND LIKE YOU'RE IN A SHOJO MANGA.
TATTOO: SEAMAN
I CAN'T HELP IT!
Mean Pudding
ASAYA VISION
HE'S THE ONE TURNING MY LIFE INTO A SHOJO MANGA!
OH? SETAGAWA AND HASEKURA SEEM FRIENDLY!
THERE YOU GO AGAIN!

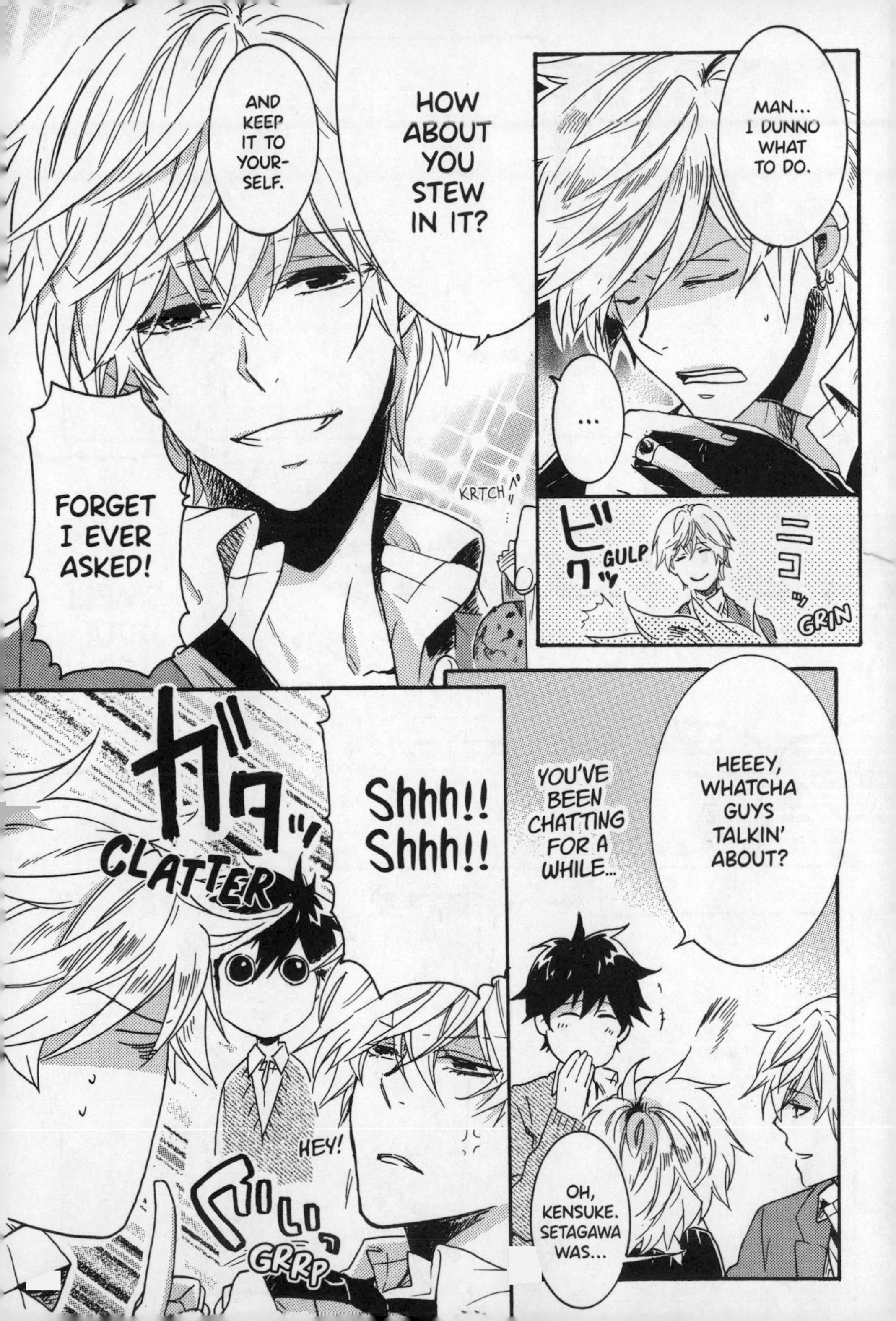
MAN... I DUNNO WHAT TO DO.
...
ビクッ
GULP
ニコッ
GRIN
HOW ABOUT YOU STEW IN IT?
AND KEEP IT TO YOURSELF.
KRTCH
FORGET I EVER ASKED!
HEEEY, WHATCHA GUYS TALKIN' ABOUT?
YOU'VE BEEN CHATTING FOR A WHILE...
OH, KENSUKE. SETAGAWA WAS...
Shhh!! Shhh!!
ガタッ
CLATTER
HEY!
GRRP

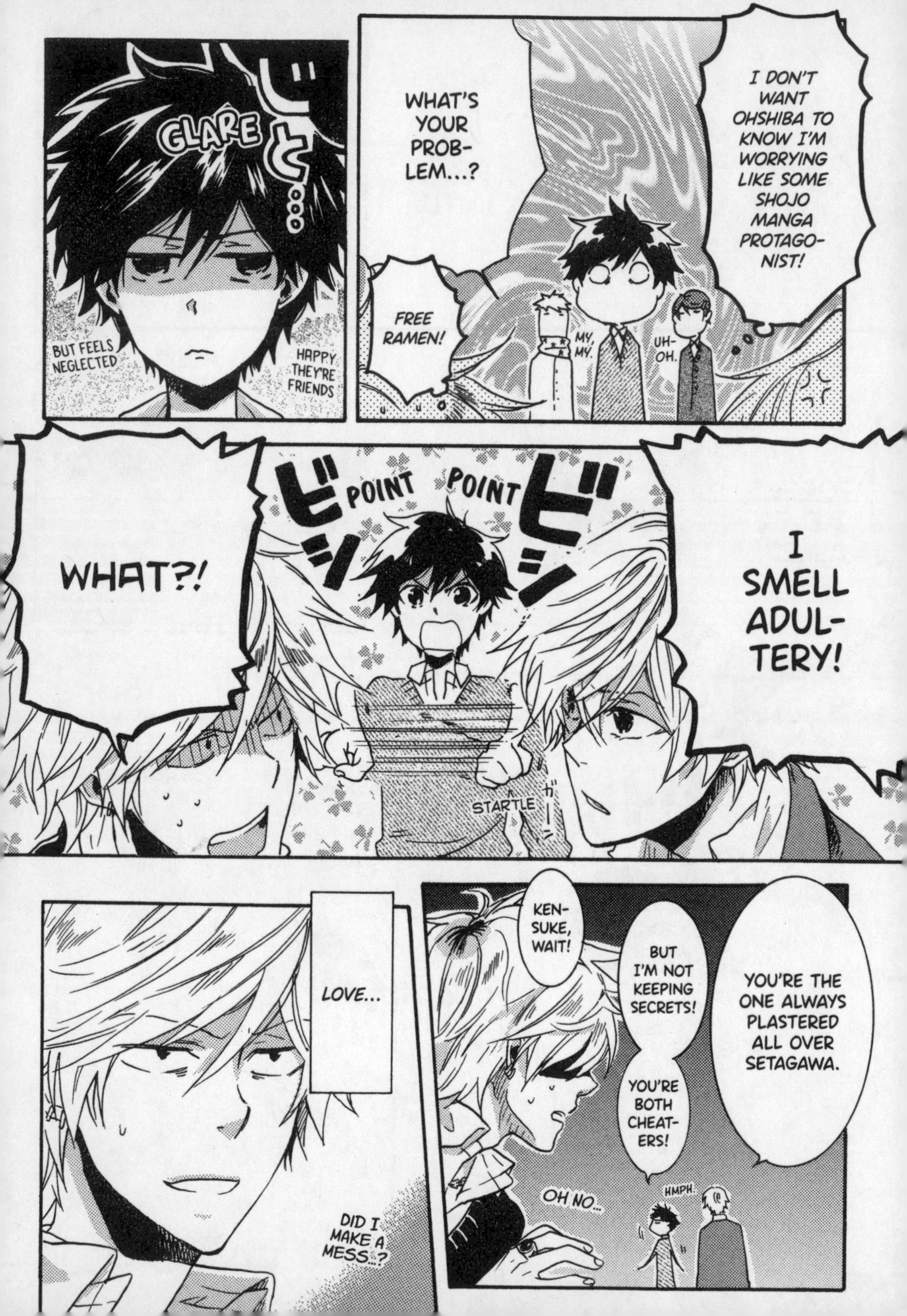

I DON'T WANT OHSHIBA TO KNOW I'M WORRYING LIKE SOME SHOJO MANGA PROTAGONIST!
WHAT'S YOUR PROB-LEM...?
UH-OH.
MY, MY.
FREE RAMEN!
じと
GLARE
HAPPY THEY'RE FRIENDS
BUT FEELS NEGLECTED
I SMELL ADUL-TERY!
ビシ
POINT
ビシ
POINT
STARTLE
WHAT?!
YOU'RE THE ONE ALWAYS PLASTERED ALL OVER SETAGAWA.
BUT I'M NOT KEEPING SECRETS!
YOU'RE BOTH CHEAT-ERS!
KEN-SUKE, WAIT!
HMPH.
OH NO..
LOVE...
DID I MAKE A MESS..?

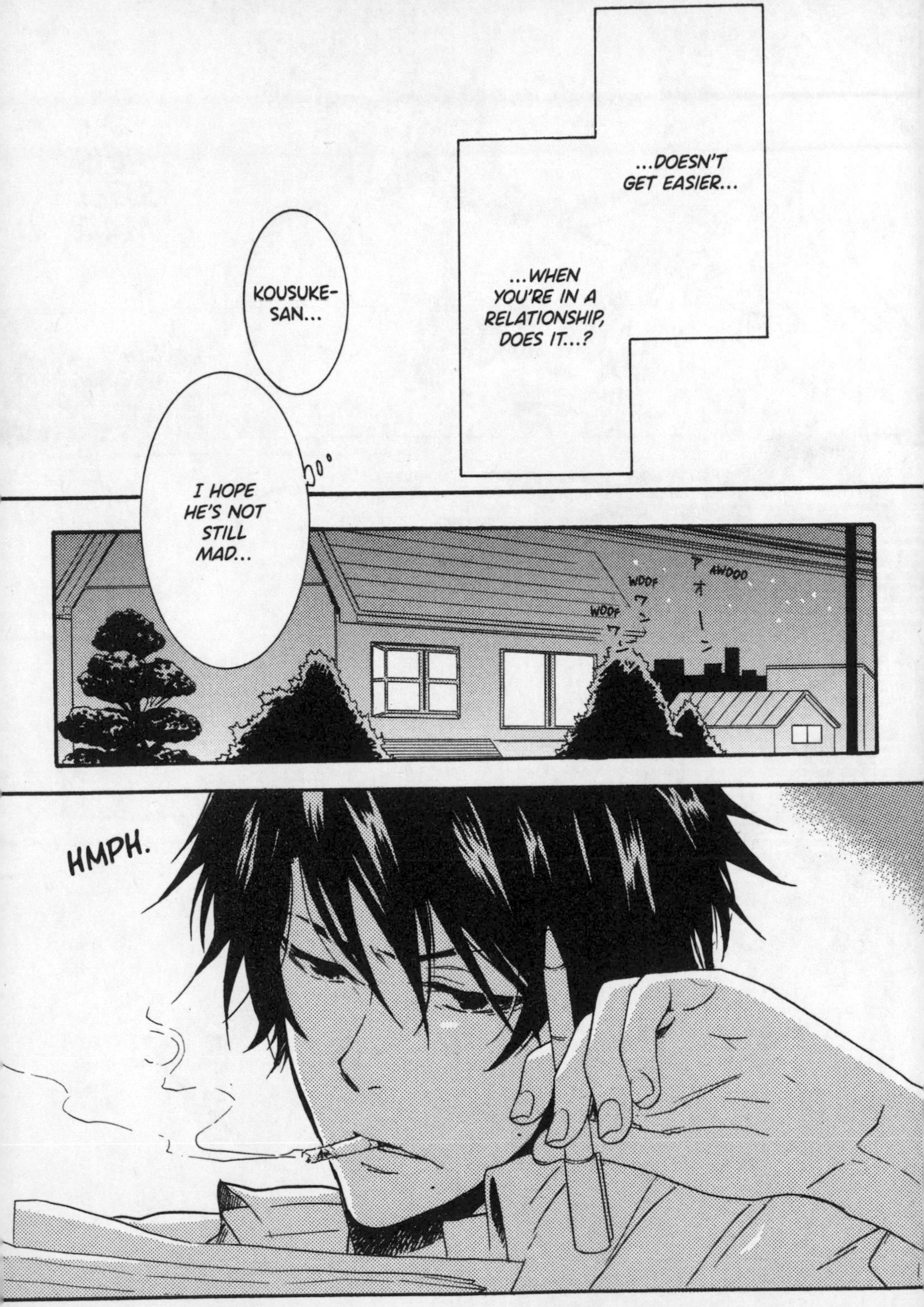
...DOESN'T GET EASIER...
...WHEN YOU'RE IN A RELATIONSHIP, DOES IT...?
KOUSUKE-SAN...
I HOPE HE'S NOT STILL MAD...
AWOOO
WOOF
WOOF
HMPH.

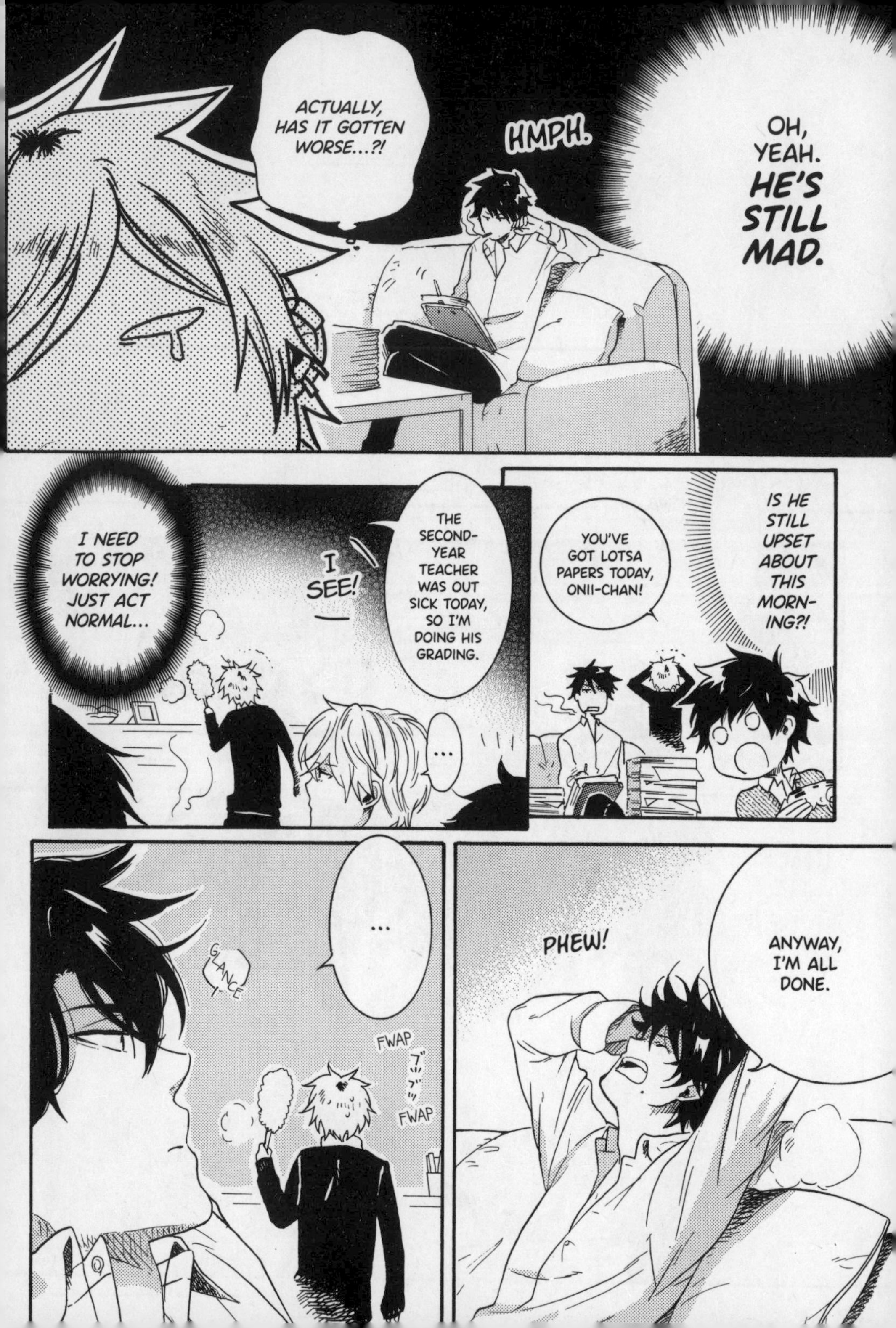
OH, YEAH. HE'S STILL MAD.
HMPH.
ACTUALLY, HAS IT GOTTEN WORSE...?!
IS HE STILL UPSET ABOUT THIS MORNING?!
YOU'VE GOT LOTSA PAPERS TODAY, ONII-CHAN!
THE SECOND-YEAR TEACHER WAS OUT SICK TODAY, SO I'M DOING HIS GRADING.
I SEE!
I NEED TO STOP WORRYING! JUST ACT NORMAL...
...
ANYWAY, I'M ALL DONE.
PHEW!
...
GLANCE
FWAP
FWAP

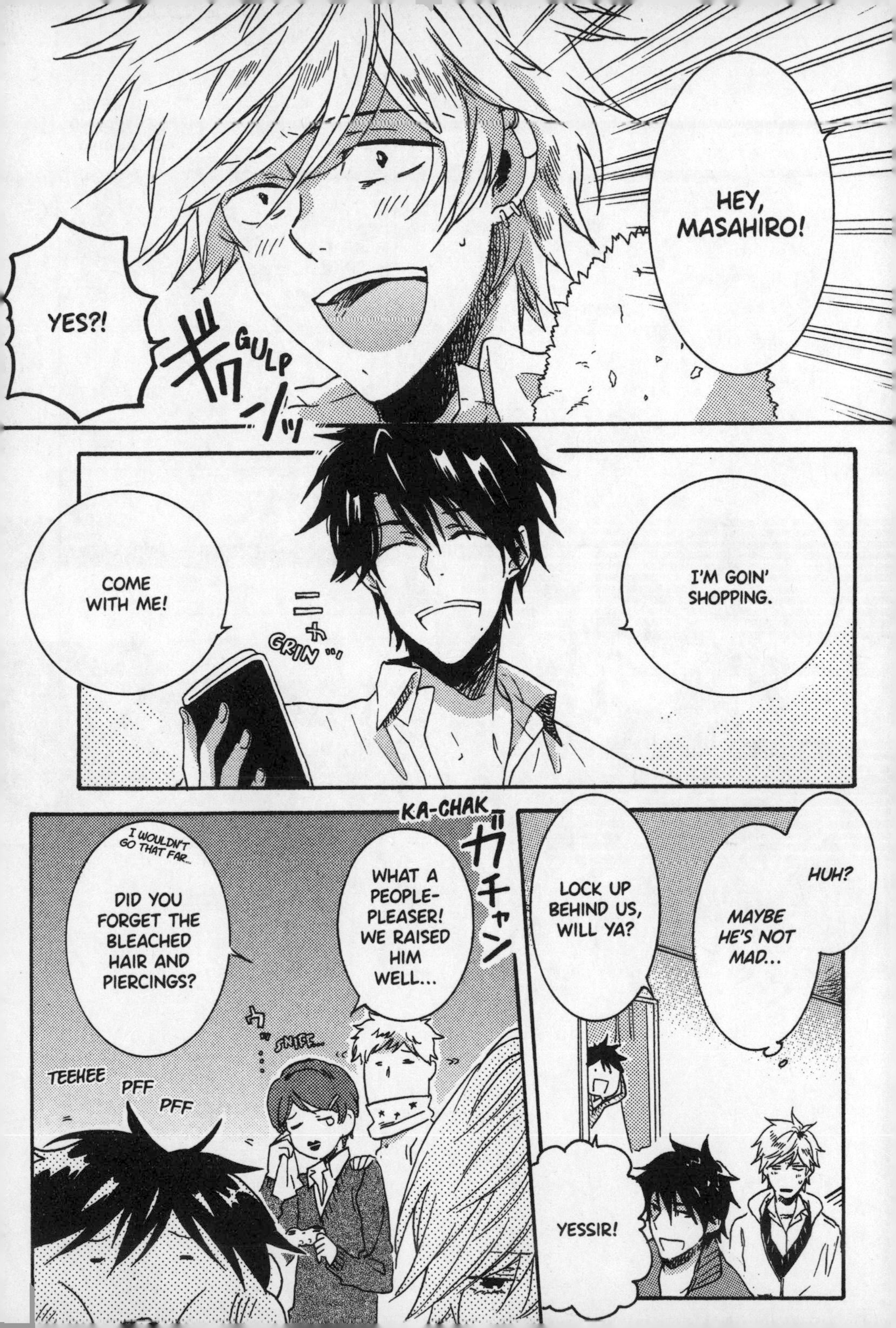
HEY, MASAHIRO!
YES?!
GULP
I'M GOIN' SHOPPING.
COME WITH ME!
GRIN
HUH?
MAYBE HE'S NOT MAD...
LOCK UP BEHIND US, WILL YA?
YESSIR!
KA-CHAK
ガチャン
WHAT A PEOPLE-PLEASER! WE RAISED HIM WELL...
SNIFF...
DID YOU FORGET THE BLEACHED HAIR AND PIERCINGS?
I WOULDN'T GO THAT FAR...
TEEHEE
PFF
PFF

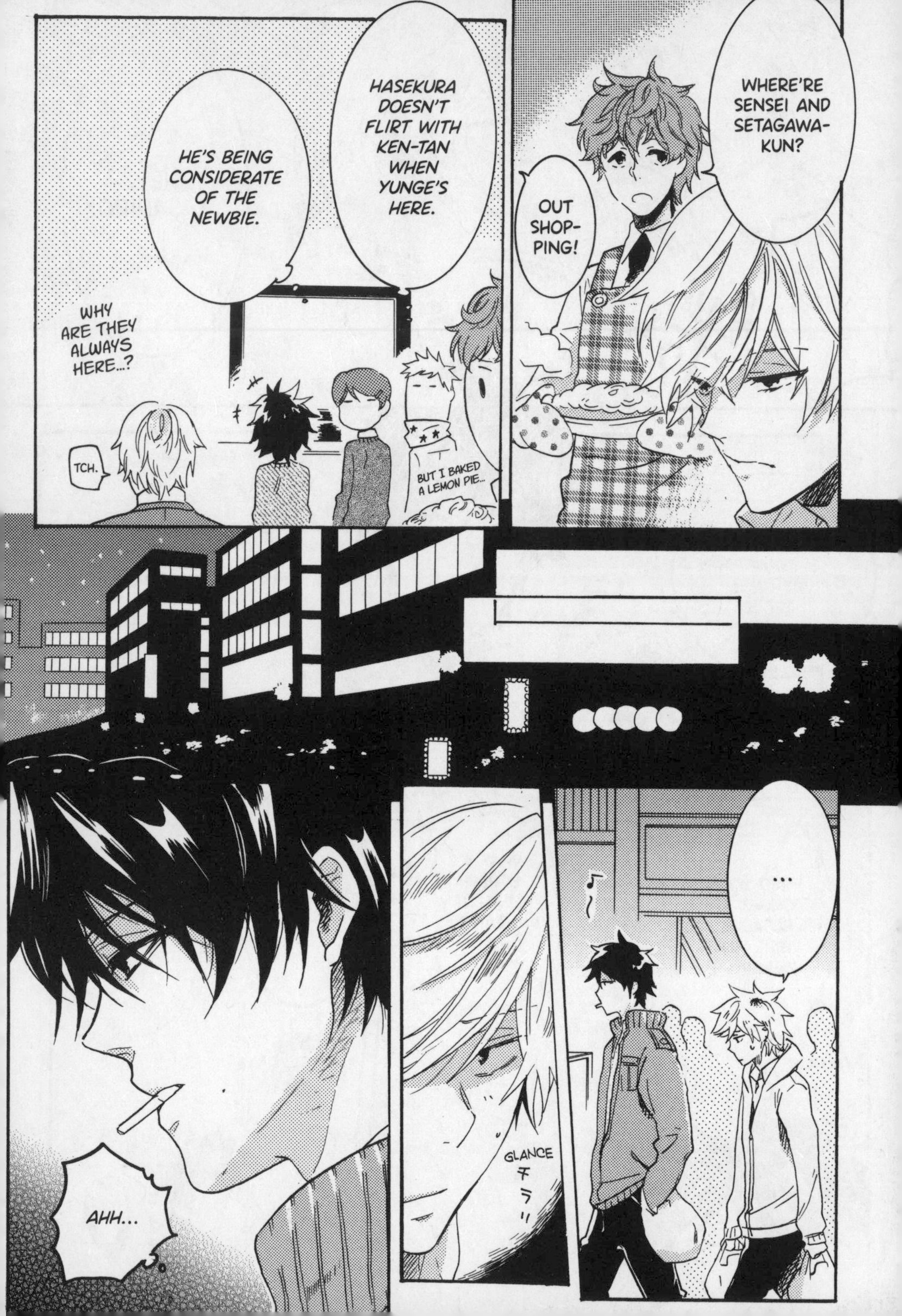
WHERE'RE SENSEI AND SETAGAWA-KUN?
OUT SHOP-PING!
HASEKURA DOESN'T FLIRT WITH KEN-TAN WHEN YUNGE'S HERE.
HE'S BEING CONSIDERATE OF THE NEWBIE.
WHY ARE THEY ALWAYS HERE...?
BUT I BAKED A LEMON PIE...
TCH.
...
GLANCE
チラッ
AHH...

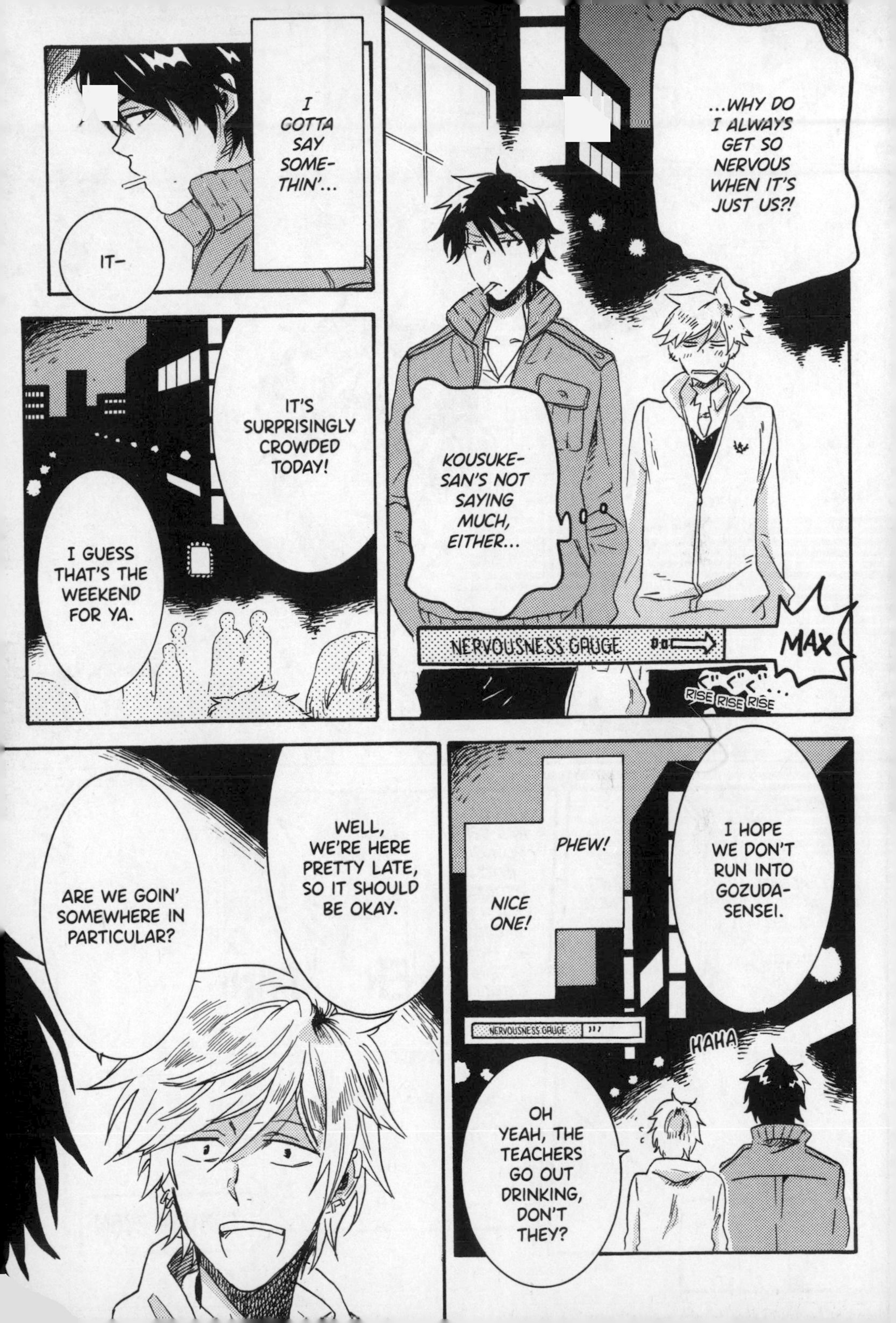
...WHY DO I ALWAYS GET SO NERVOUS WHEN IT'S JUST US?!
KOUSUKE-SAN'S NOT SAYING MUCH, EITHER...
NERVOUSNESS GAUGE
MAX
RISE RISE RISE
I GOTTA SAY SOMETHIN'...
IT-
IT'S SURPRISINGLY CROWDED TODAY!
I GUESS THAT'S THE WEEKEND FOR YA.
I HOPE WE DON'T RUN INTO GOZUDA-SENSEI.
PHEW!
NICE ONE!
NERVOUSNESS GAUGE
HAHA
OH YEAH, THE TEACHERS GO OUT DRINKING, DON'T THEY?
WELL, WE'RE HERE PRETTY LATE, SO IT SHOULD BE OKAY.
ARE WE GOIN' SOMEWHERE IN PARTICULAR?

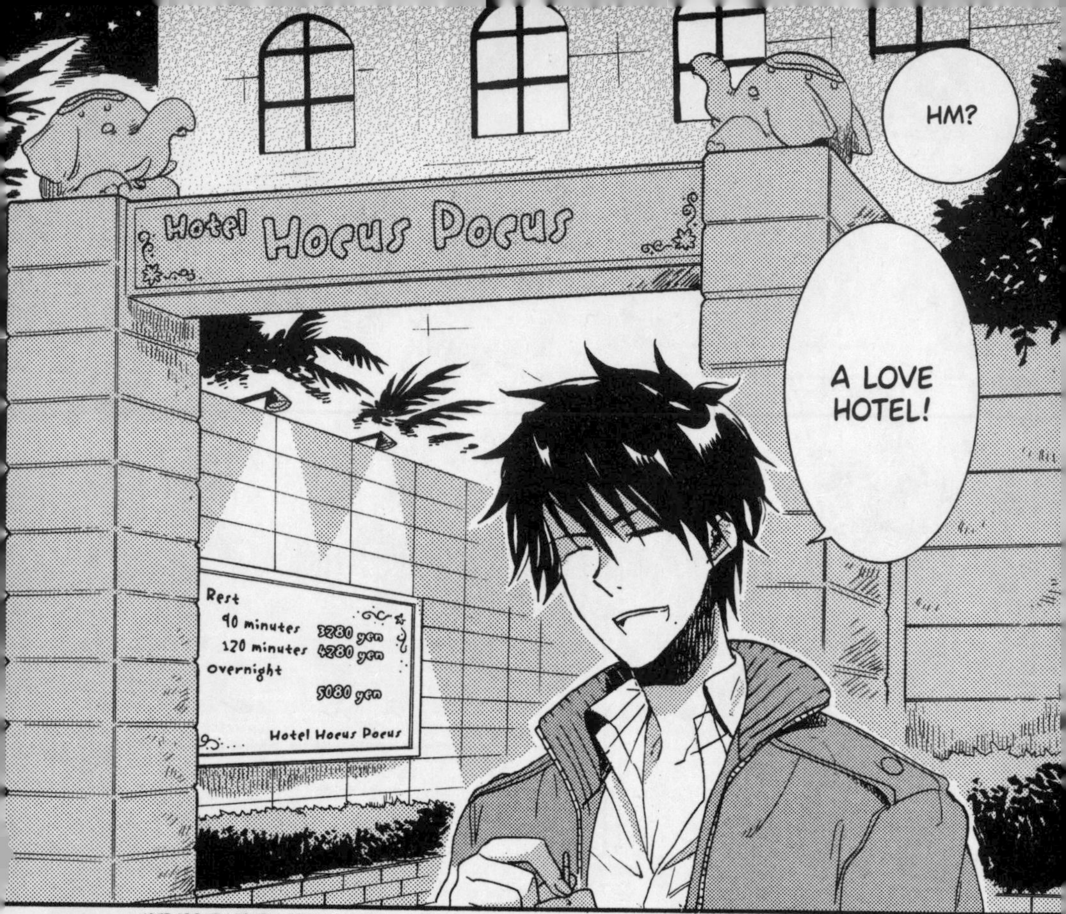
HM?
A LOVE HOTEL!
Hotel Hocus Pocus
Rest
90 minutes 3280 yen
120 minutes 4280 yen
overnight
5080 yen
Hotel Hocus Pocus

NOTE: 100 YEN EQUALS APPROXIMATELY 1 USD.

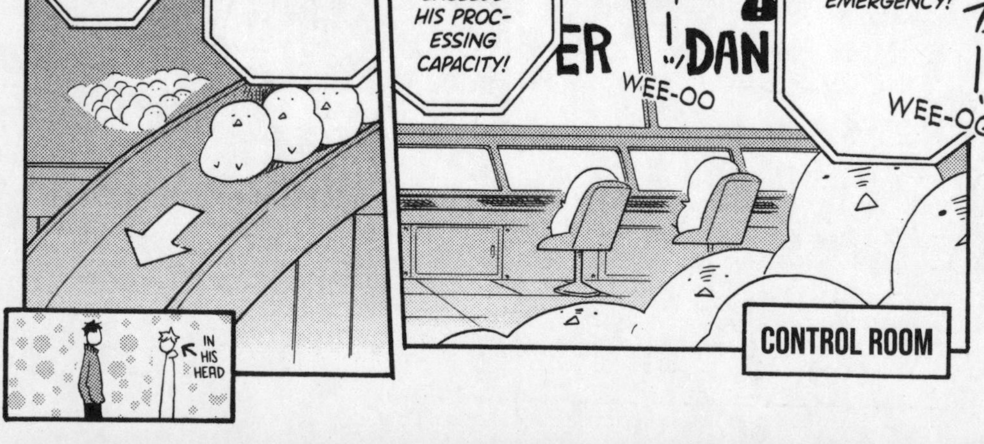
WEE-OO
EMERGENCY! EMERGENCY!
WEE-OO
WEE-OO
MASAHIRO HAS BEEN PLUNGED INTO A SITUATION WHICH FAR EXCEEDS HIS PROCESSING CAPACITY!
WEE-OO
CONTROL ROOM
SELF-DESTRUCT SEQUENCE INITIATED.
ALL UNITS EVACUATE IMMEDIATELY!
IN HIS HEAD

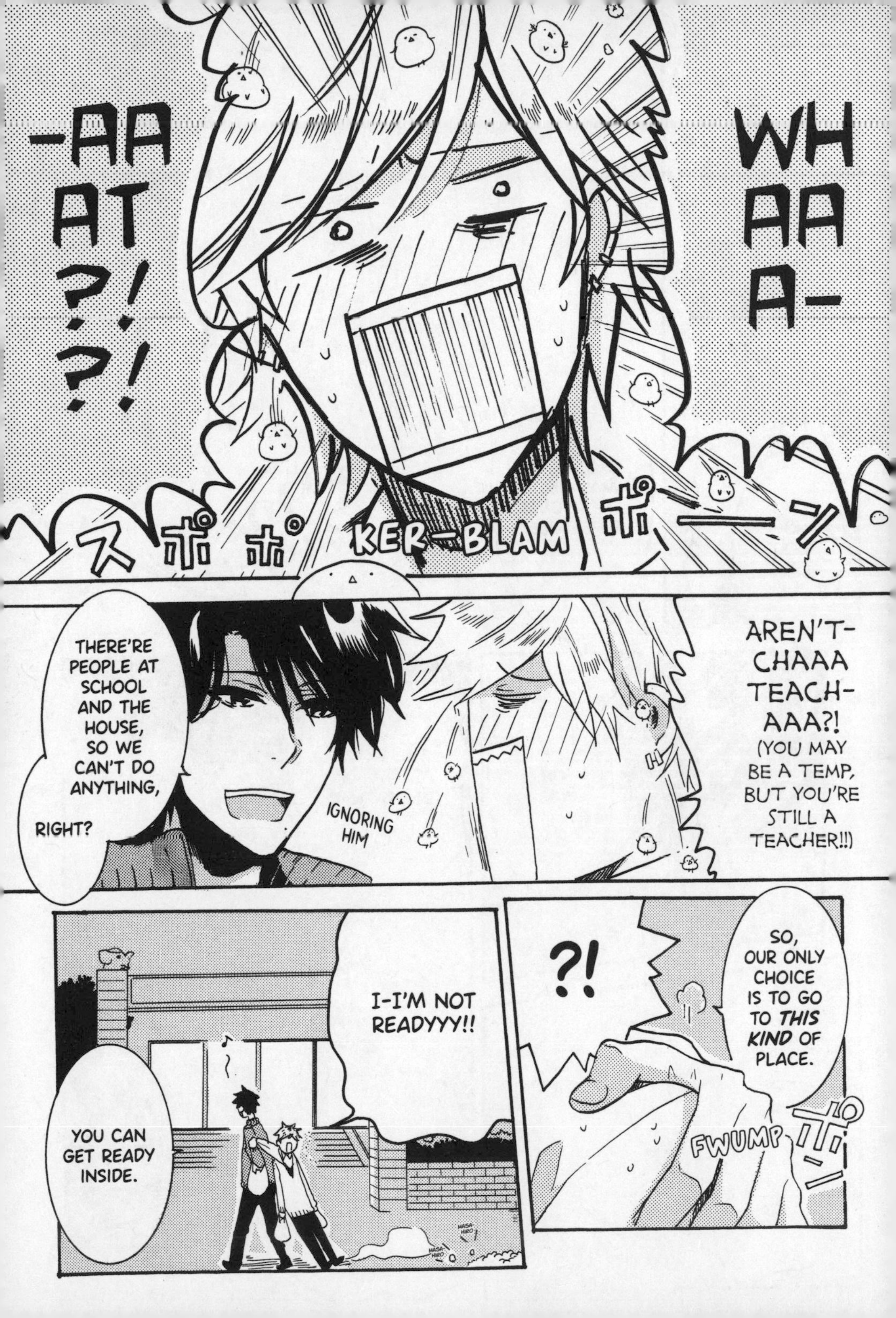
WHAAAA-
-AAAT?!?!
スポポ
KER-BLAM
ポーーン
AREN'T-CHAAA TEACH-AAA?!
(YOU MAY BE A TEMP, BUT YOU'RE STILL A TEACHER!!)
IGNORING HIM
THERE'RE PEOPLE AT SCHOOL AND THE HOUSE, SO WE CAN'T DO ANYTHING,
RIGHT?
SO, OUR ONLY CHOICE IS TO GO TO *THIS KIND* OF PLACE.
?!
FWUMP
ポン
I-I'M NOT READYYY!!
YOU CAN GET READY INSIDE.

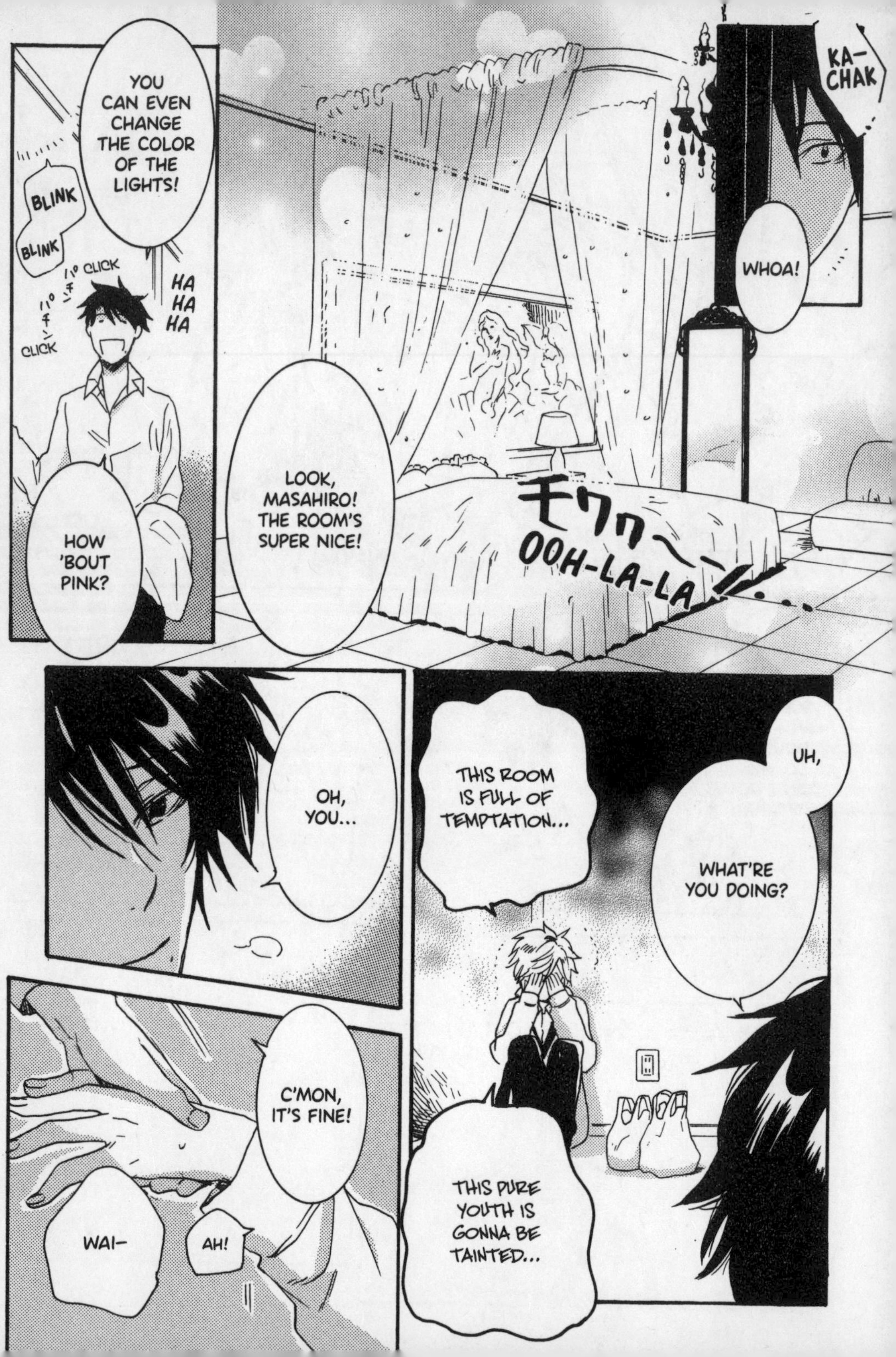
KA-CHAK
WHOA!
LOOK, MASAHIRO! THE ROOM'S SUPER NICE!
OOH-LA-LA...
YOU CAN EVEN CHANGE THE COLOR OF THE LIGHTS!
BLINK
BLINK
CLICK
CLICK
HA HA HA
HOW 'BOUT PINK?
UH,
WHAT'RE YOU DOING?
THIS ROOM IS FULL OF TEMPTATION...
THIS PURE YOUTH IS GONNA BE TAINTED...
OH, YOU...
C'MON, IT'S FINE!
AH!
WAI-

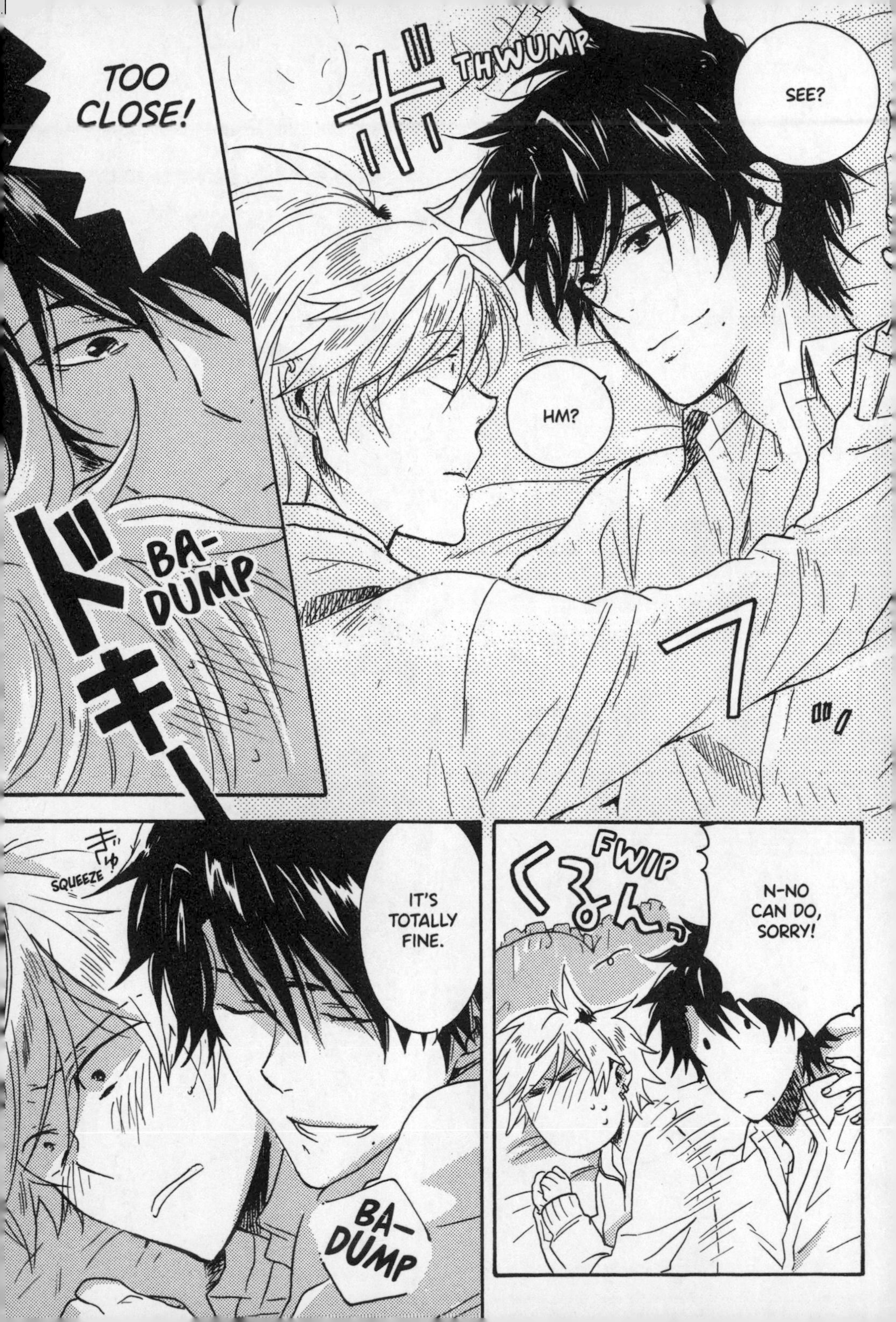
THWUMP
SEE?
HM?
TOO CLOSE!
BA-DUMP
FWIP
N-NO CAN DO, SORRY!
IT'S TOTALLY FINE.
SQUEEZE
BA-DUMP

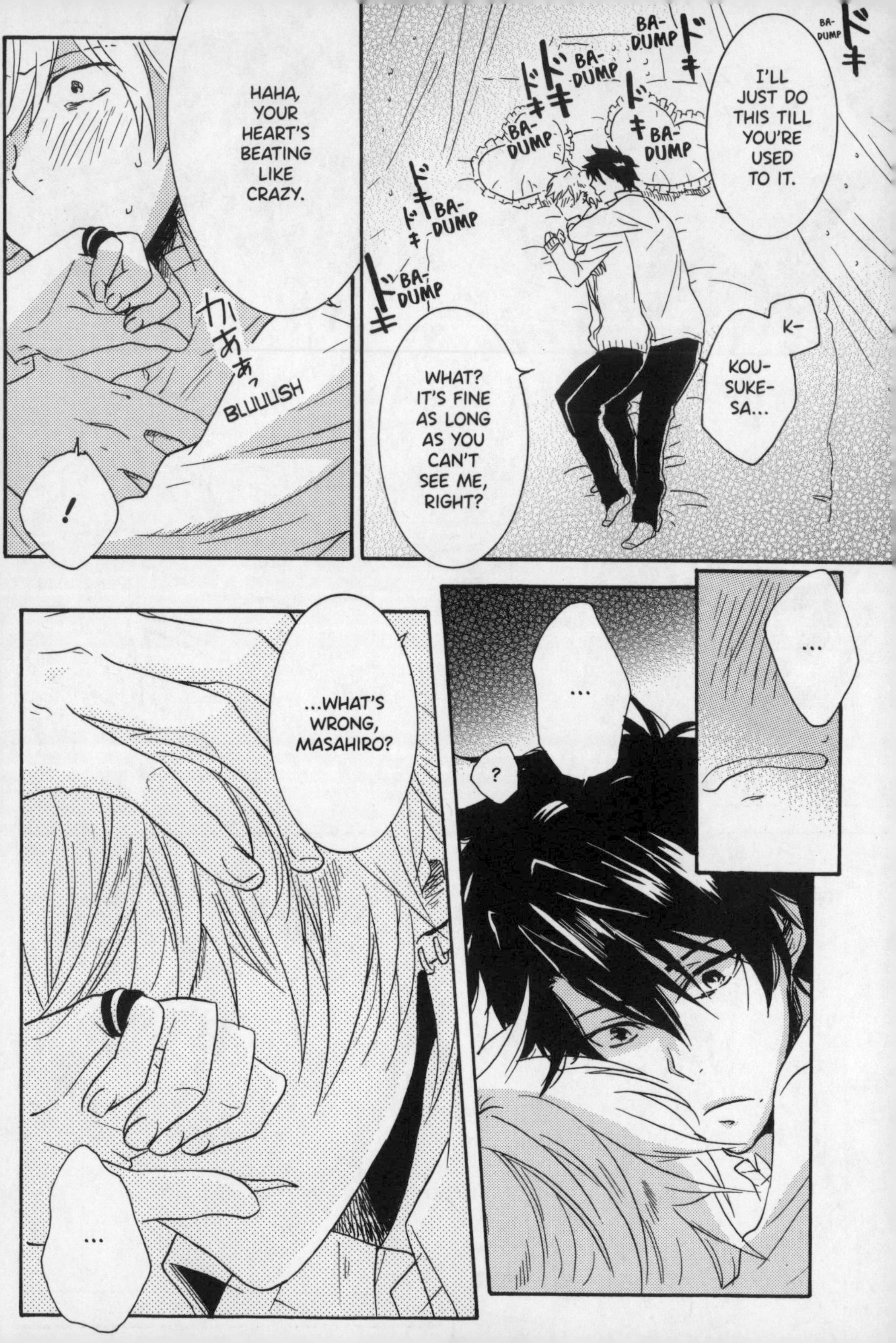
BA-DUMP
ドキ
I'LL JUST DO THIS TILL YOU'RE USED TO IT.
BA-DUMP
ドキ
BA-DUMP
ドキ
BA-DUMP
ドキ
BA-DUMP
ドキ
BA-DUMP
ドキ
BA-DUMP
ドキ
BA-DUMP
ドキ
K- KOU-SUKE-SA...
WHAT? IT'S FINE AS LONG AS YOU CAN'T SEE ME, RIGHT?
HAHA, YOUR HEART'S BEATING LIKE CRAZY.
かぁぁっ
BLUUUSH
!
...
...
?
...WHAT'S WRONG, MASAHIRO?
...

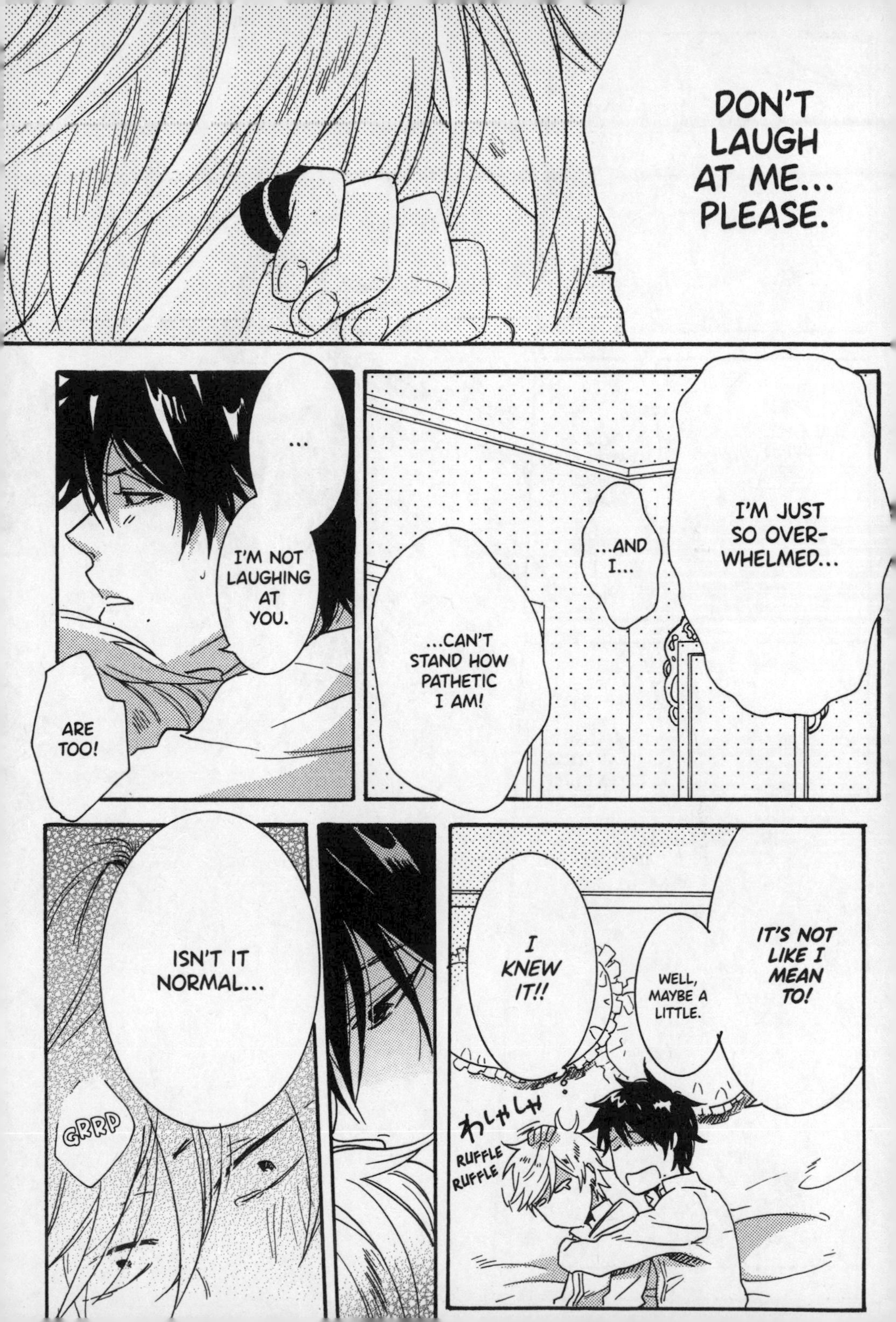
DON'T LAUGH AT ME... PLEASE.
I'M JUST SO OVER-WHELMED...
...AND I...
...CAN'T STAND HOW PATHETIC I AM!
...
I'M NOT LAUGHING AT YOU.
ARE TOO!
IT'S NOT LIKE I MEAN TO!
WELL, MAYBE A LITTLE.
I KNEW IT!!
RUFFLE RUFFLE
ISN'T IT NORMAL...
GRRP

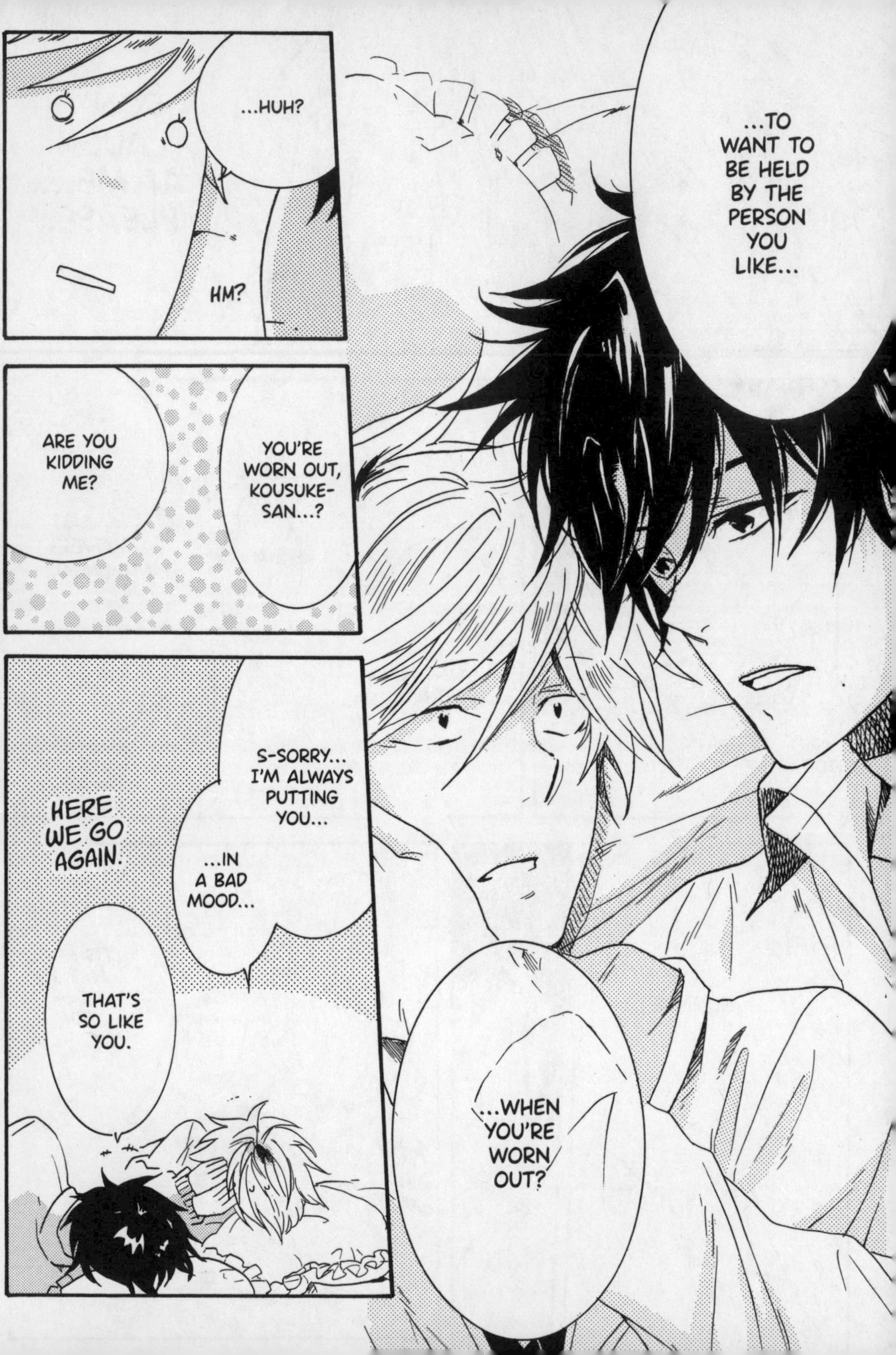
...TO WANT TO BE HELD BY THE PERSON YOU LIKE...
...WHEN YOU'RE WORN OUT?
...HUH?
HM?
YOU'RE WORN OUT, KOUSUKE-SAN...?
ARE YOU KIDDING ME?
S-SORRY... I'M ALWAYS PUTTING YOU...
...IN A BAD MOOD...
HERE WE GO AGAIN.
THAT'S SO LIKE YOU.

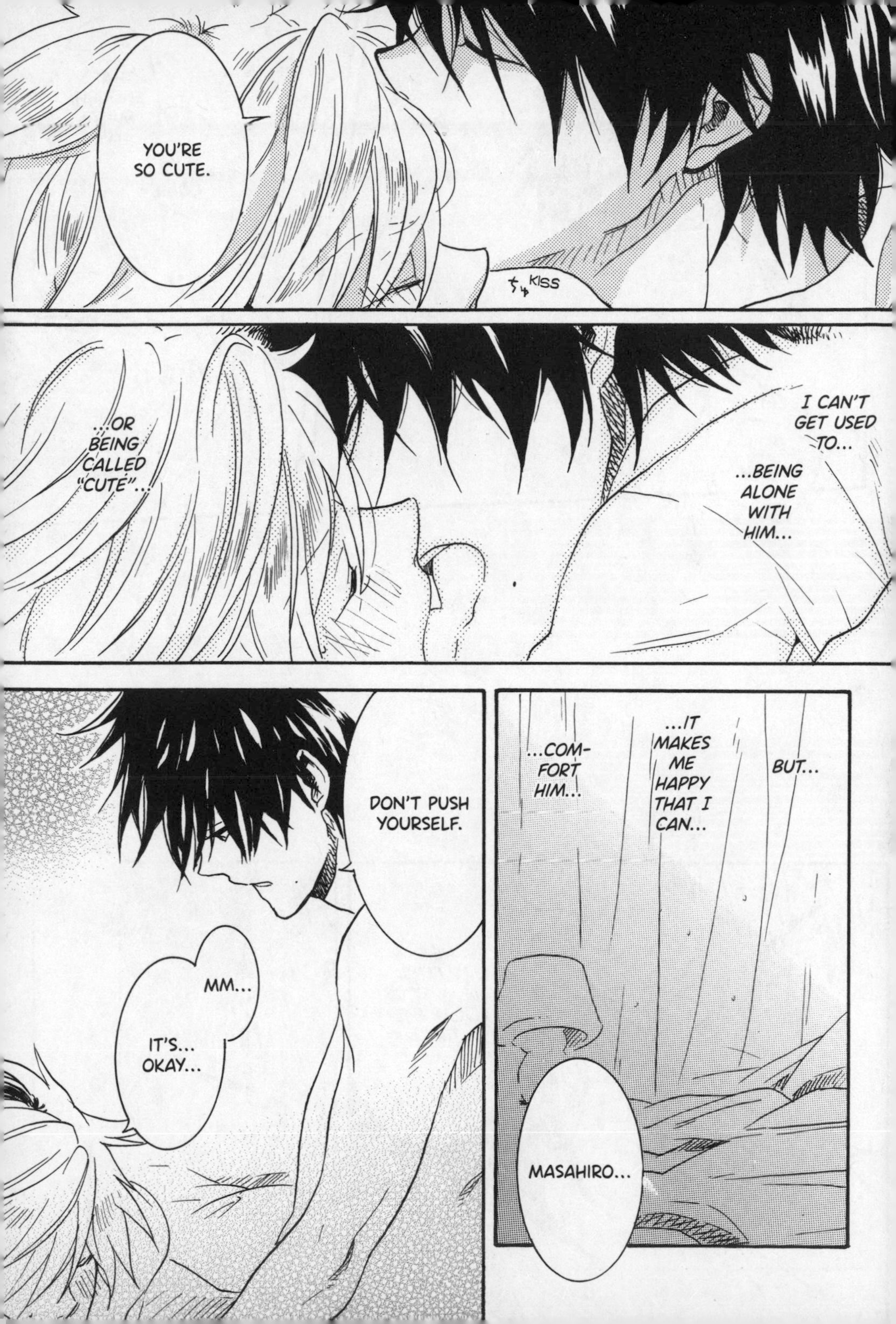
YOU'RE SO CUTE.
KISS
I CAN'T GET USED TO...
...BEING ALONE WITH HIM...
...OR BEING CALLED "CUTE"...
BUT...
...IT MAKES ME HAPPY THAT I CAN...
...COMFORT HIM...
MASAHIRO...
DON'T PUSH YOURSELF.
MM...
IT'S... OKAY...

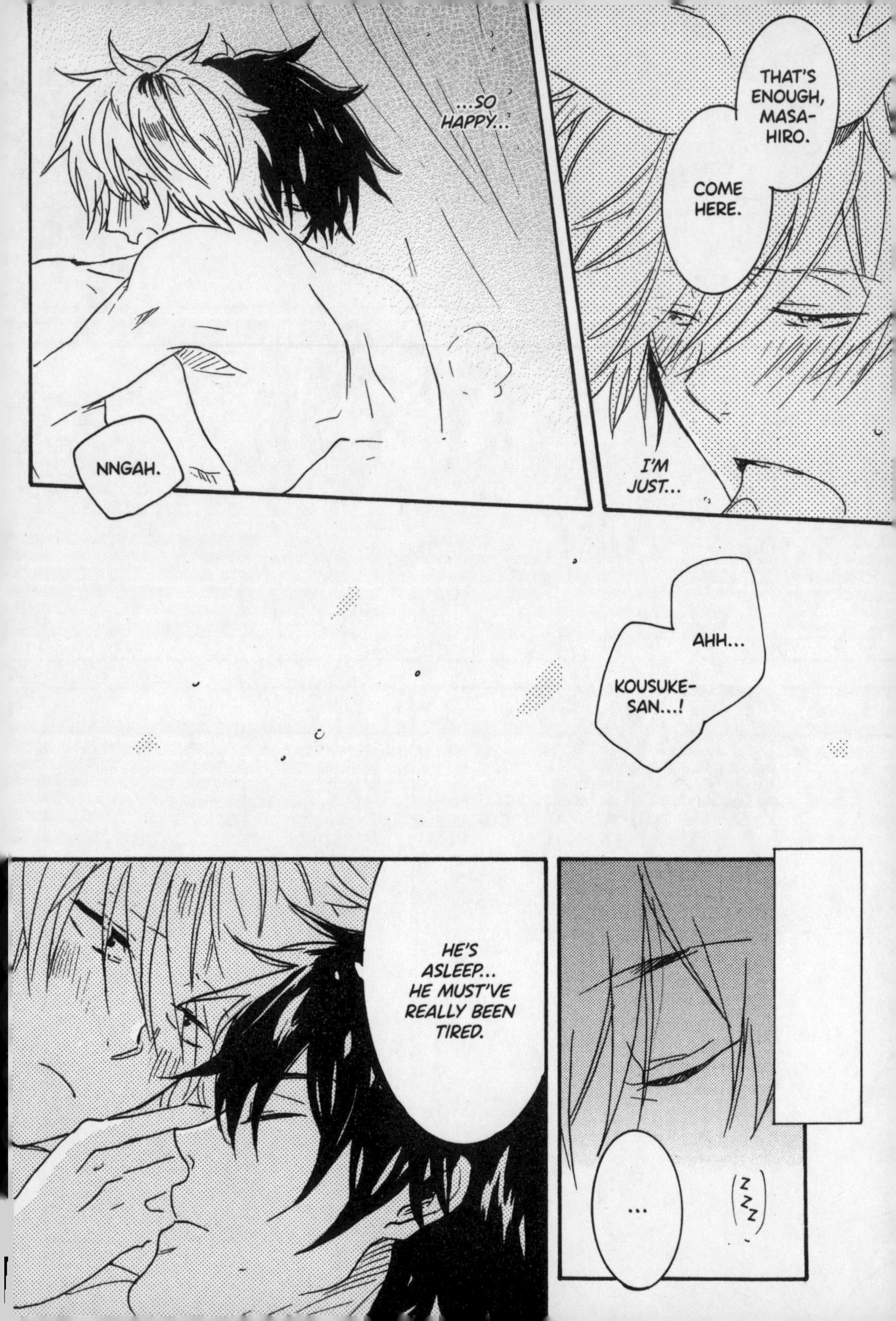
THAT'S ENOUGH, MASA-HIRO.
COME HERE.
I'M JUST...
...SO HAPPY...
NNGAH.
AHH...
KOUSUKE-SAN...!
...
ZZZ
HE'S ASLEEP... HE MUST'VE REALLY BEEN TIRED.

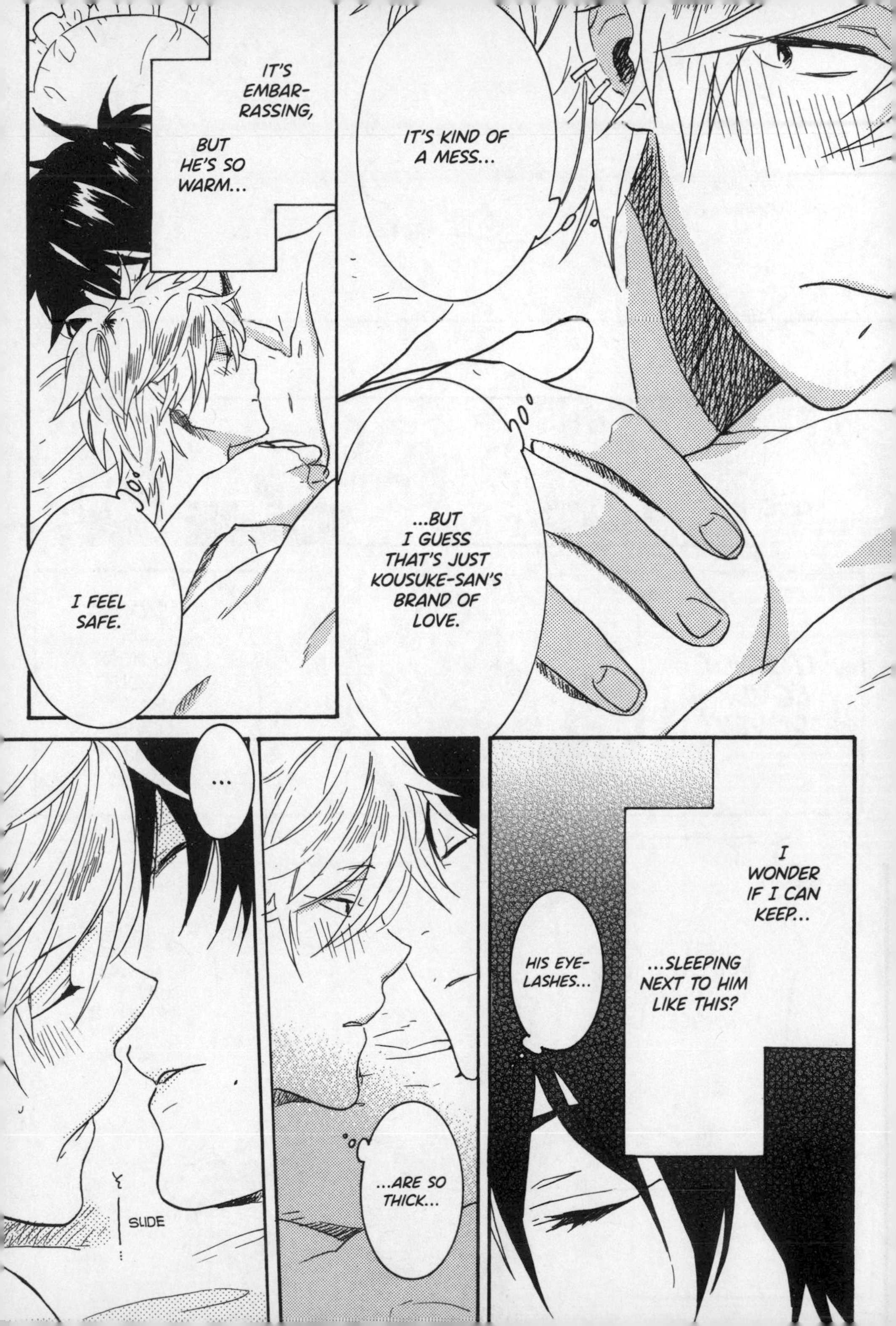
IT'S KIND OF A MESS...
...BUT I GUESS THAT'S JUST KOUSUKE-SAN'S BRAND OF LOVE.
IT'S EMBARRASSING,
BUT HE'S SO WARM...
I FEEL SAFE.
I WONDER IF I CAN KEEP...
...SLEEPING NEXT TO HIM LIKE THIS?
HIS EYE-LASHES...
...ARE SO THICK...
...
SLIDE

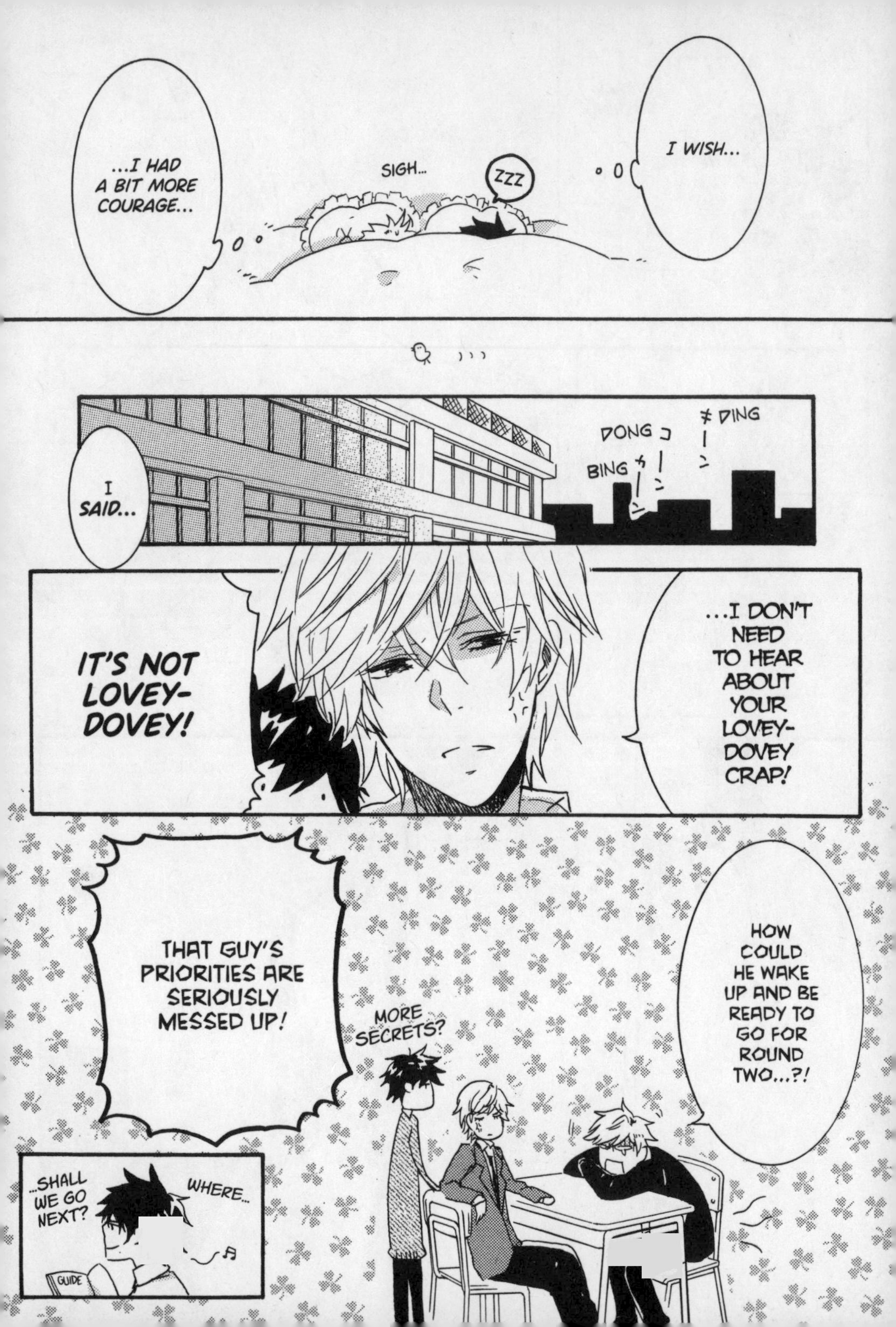
I WISH...
ZZZ
SIGH...
...I HAD A BIT MORE COURAGE...
DING
DONG
BING
I SAID...
...I DON'T NEED TO HEAR ABOUT YOUR LOVEY-DOVEY CRAP!
IT'S NOT LOVEY-DOVEY!
HOW COULD HE WAKE UP AND BE READY TO GO FOR ROUND TWO...?!
THAT GUY'S PRIORITIES ARE SERIOUSLY MESSED UP!
MORE SECRETS?
WHERE...
...SHALL WE GO NEXT?
GUIDE

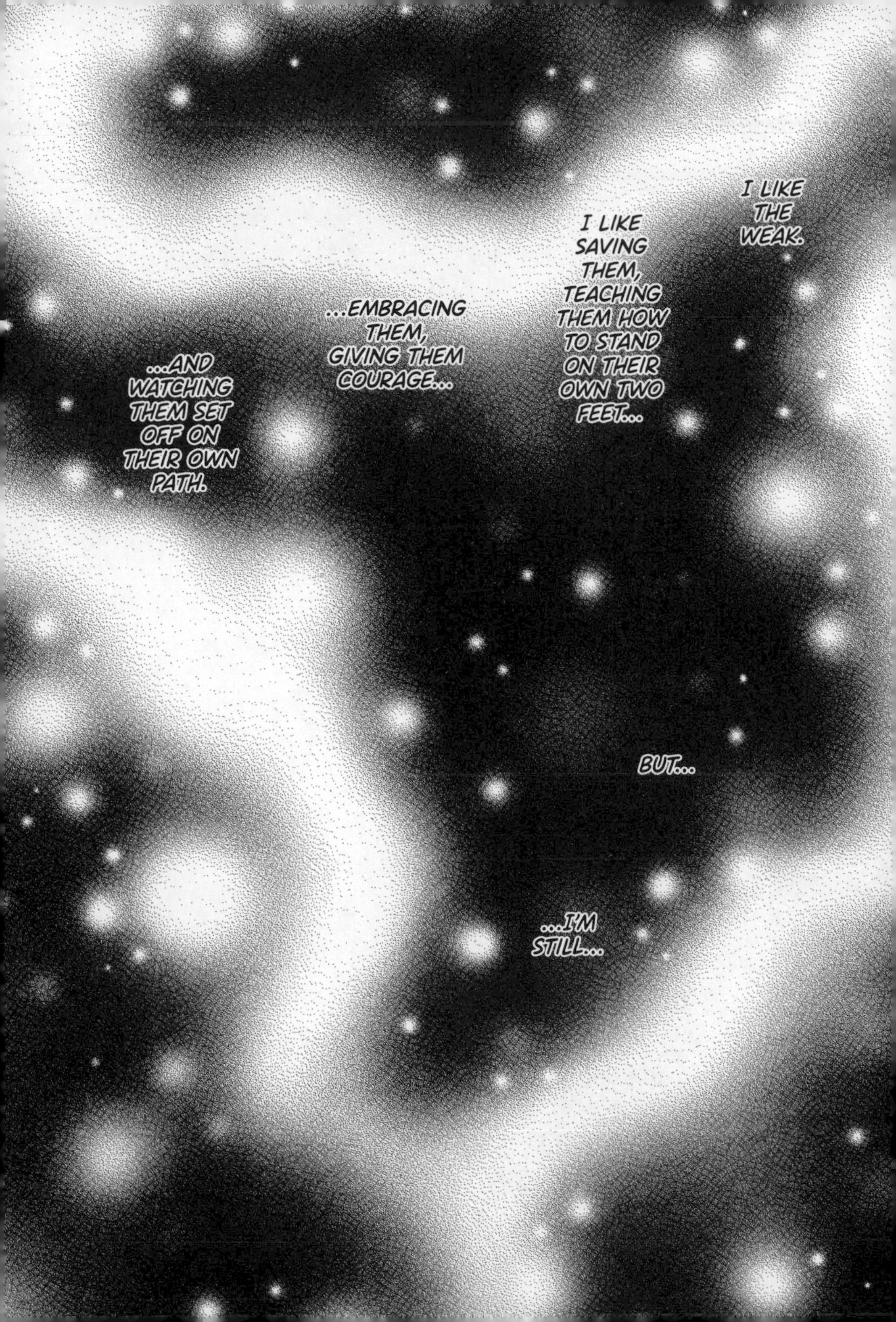
I LIKE THE WEAK.
I LIKE SAVING THEM, TEACHING THEM HOW TO STAND ON THEIR OWN TWO FEET...
...EMBRACING THEM, GIVING THEM COURAGE...
...AND WATCHING THEM SET OFF ON THEIR OWN PATH.
BUT...
...I'M STILL...

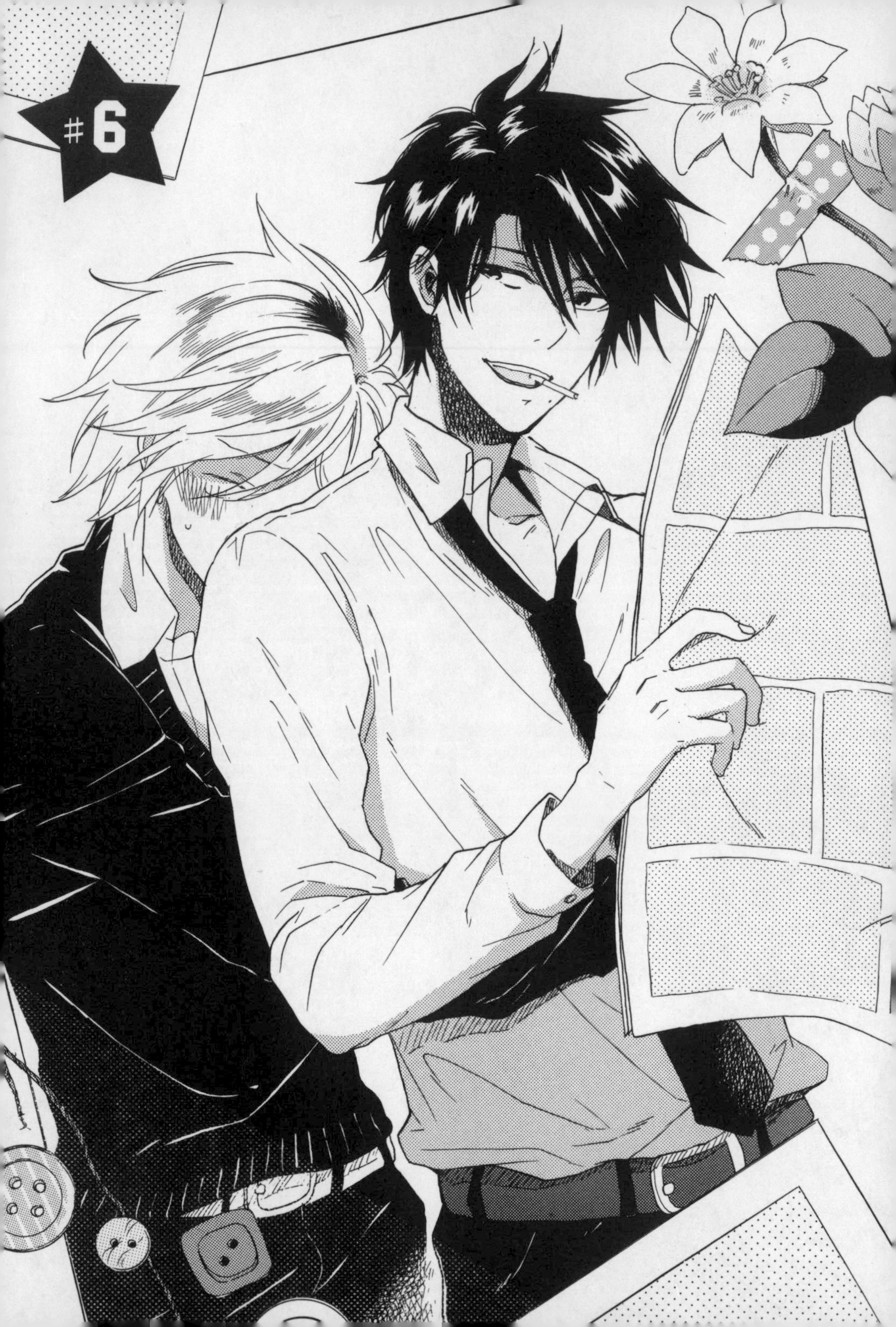
#6

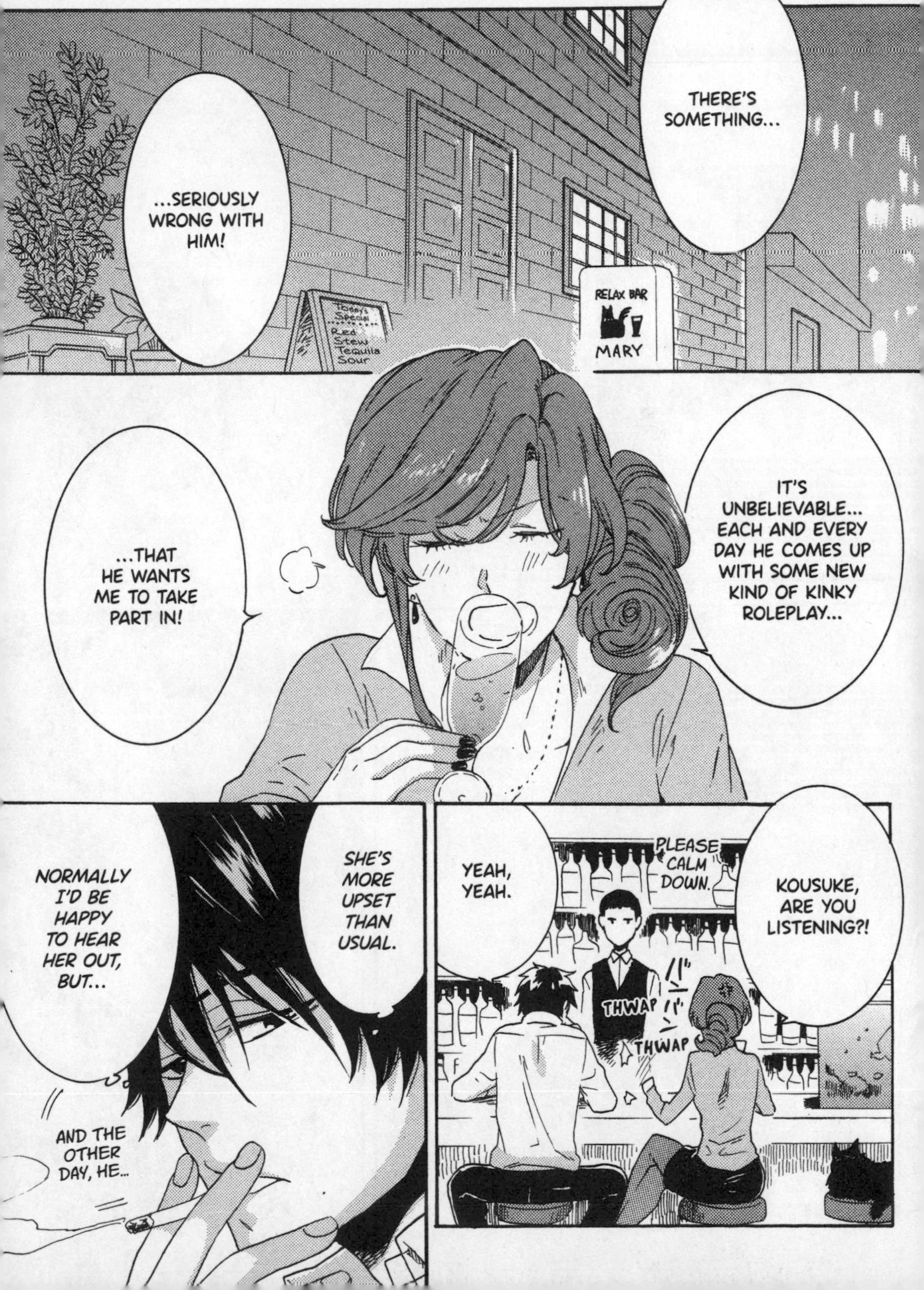
THERE'S SOMETHING...
...SERIOUSLY WRONG WITH HIM!
RELAX BAR MARY
Today's Special Red Stew Tequila Sour
IT'S UNBELIEVABLE... EACH AND EVERY DAY HE COMES UP WITH SOME NEW KIND OF KINKY ROLEPLAY...
...THAT HE WANTS ME TO TAKE PART IN!
KOUSUKE, ARE YOU LISTENING?!
PLEASE CALM DOWN.
THWAP
THWAP
YEAH, YEAH.
SHE'S MORE UPSET THAN USUAL.
NORMALLY I'D BE HAPPY TO HEAR HER OUT, BUT...
AND THE OTHER DAY, HE...

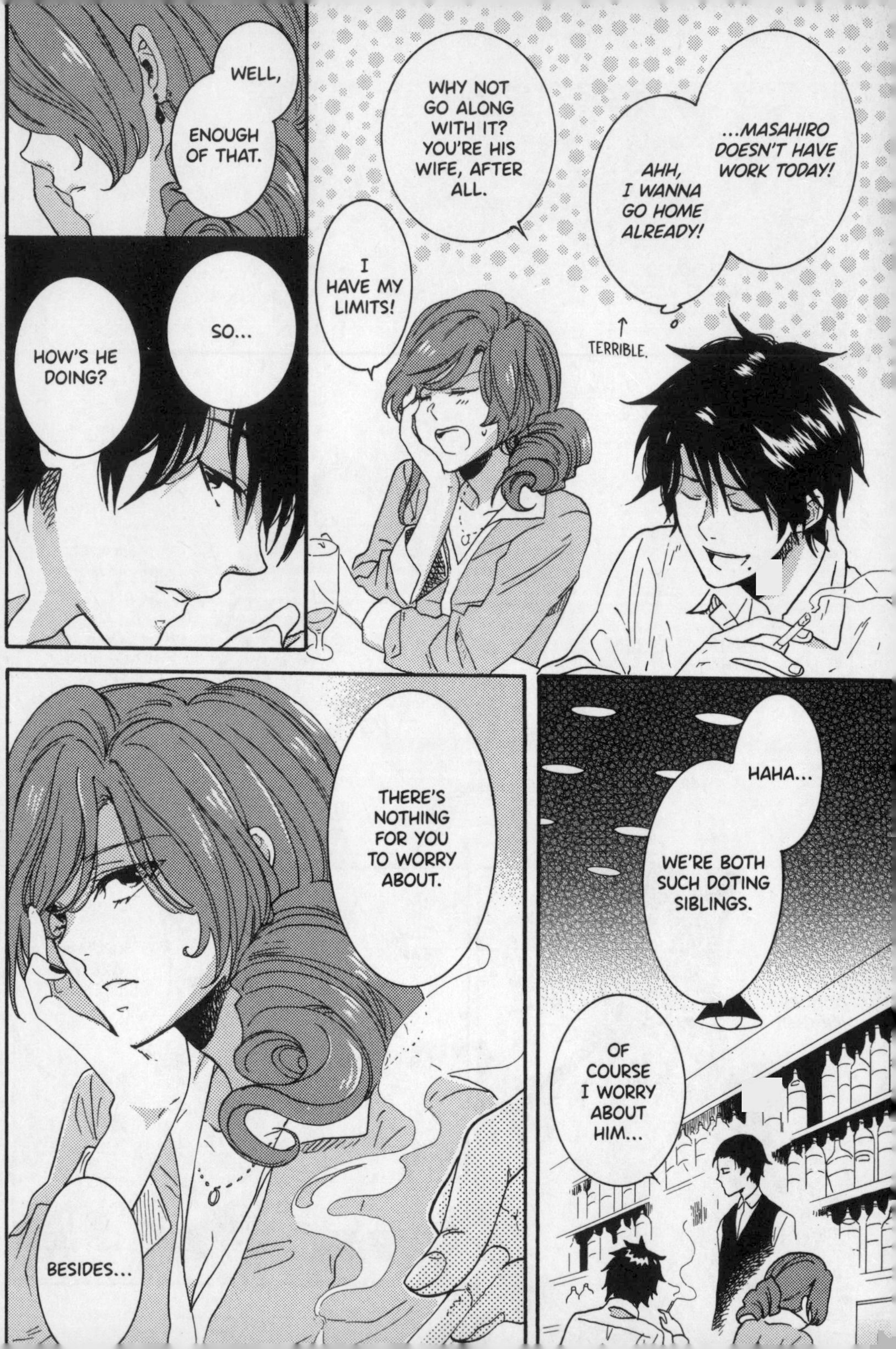
...MASAHIRO DOESN'T HAVE WORK TODAY!
AHH, I WANNA GO HOME ALREADY!
TERRIBLE.
WHY NOT GO ALONG WITH IT? YOU'RE HIS WIFE, AFTER ALL.
I HAVE MY LIMITS!
WELL,
ENOUGH OF THAT.
SO...
HOW'S HE DOING?
HAHA...
WE'RE BOTH SUCH DOTING SIBLINGS.
OF COURSE I WORRY ABOUT HIM...
THERE'S NOTHING FOR YOU TO WORRY ABOUT.
BESIDES...

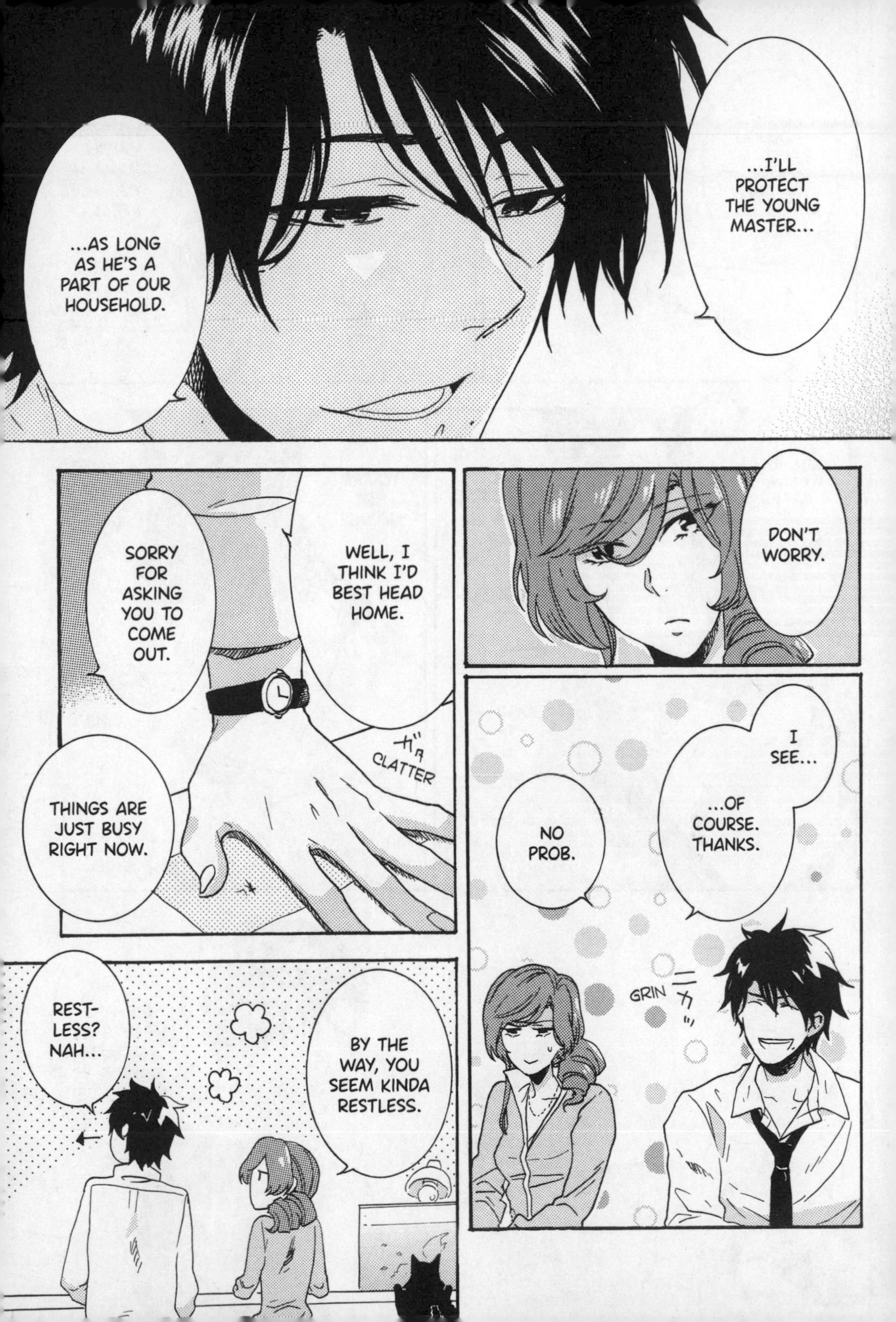

...I'LL PROTECT THE YOUNG MASTER...
...AS LONG AS HE'S A PART OF OUR HOUSEHOLD.
DON'T WORRY.
WELL, I THINK I'D BEST HEAD HOME.
SORRY FOR ASKING YOU TO COME OUT.
CLATTER
THINGS ARE JUST BUSY RIGHT NOW.
I SEE...
...OF COURSE. THANKS.
NO PROB.
GRIN
BY THE WAY, YOU SEEM KINDA RESTLESS.
REST-LESS? NAH...

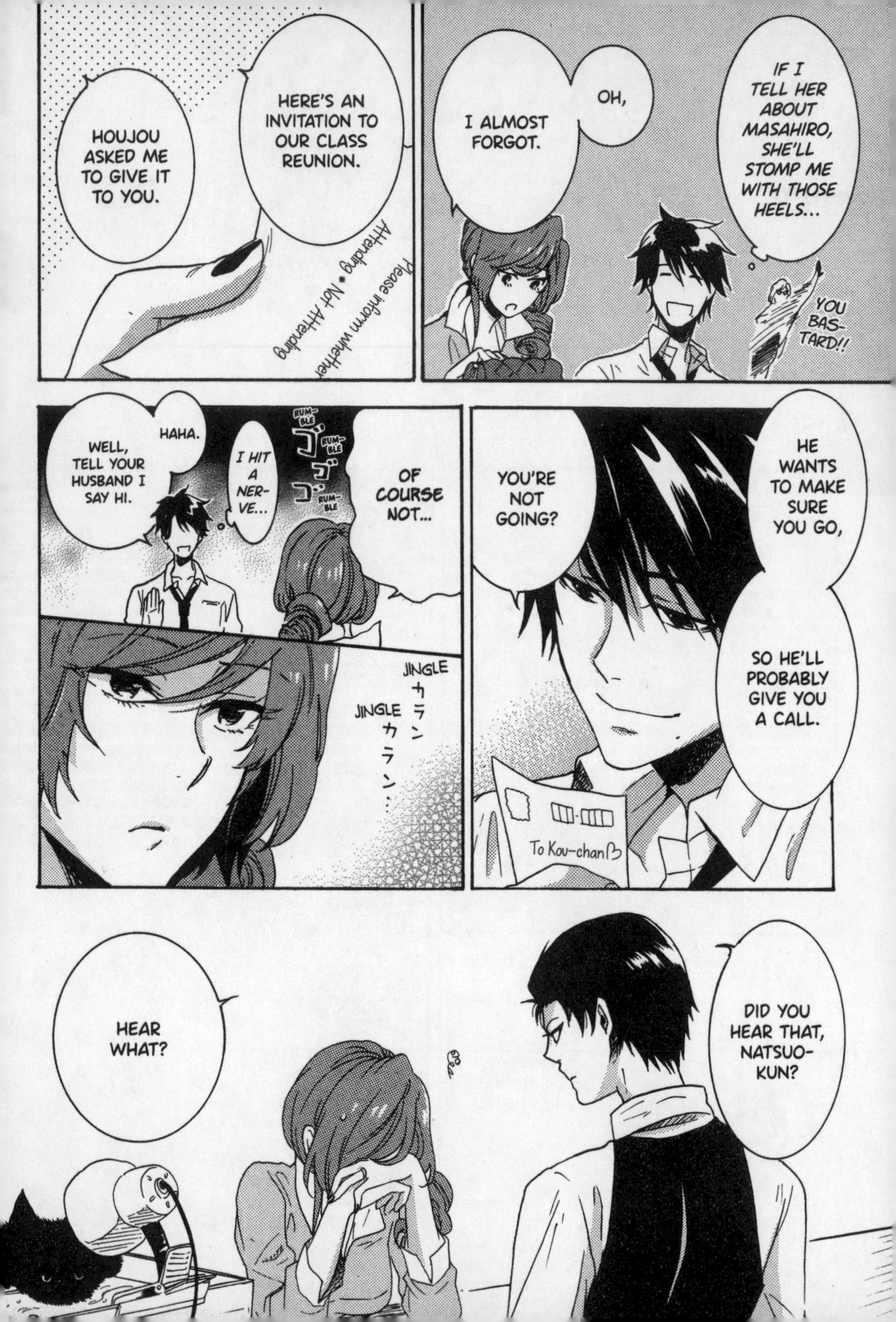
IF I TELL HER ABOUT MASAHIRO, SHE'LL STOMP ME WITH THOSE HEELS...
YOU BAS-TARD!!
OH,
I ALMOST FORGOT.
HERE'S AN INVITATION TO OUR CLASS REUNION.
HOUJOU ASKED ME TO GIVE IT TO YOU.
Please inform whether Attending * Not Attending
HE WANTS TO MAKE SURE YOU GO,
SO HE'LL PROBABLY GIVE YOU A CALL.
YOU'RE NOT GOING?
To Kou-chan
OF COURSE NOT...
RUMBLE ゴ RUMBLE ゴ RUMBLE ゴ
I HIT A NERVE...
HAHA.
WELL, TELL YOUR HUSBAND I SAY HI.
JINGLE カラン
JINGLE カラン…
DID YOU HEAR THAT, NATSUO-KUN?
HEAR WHAT?

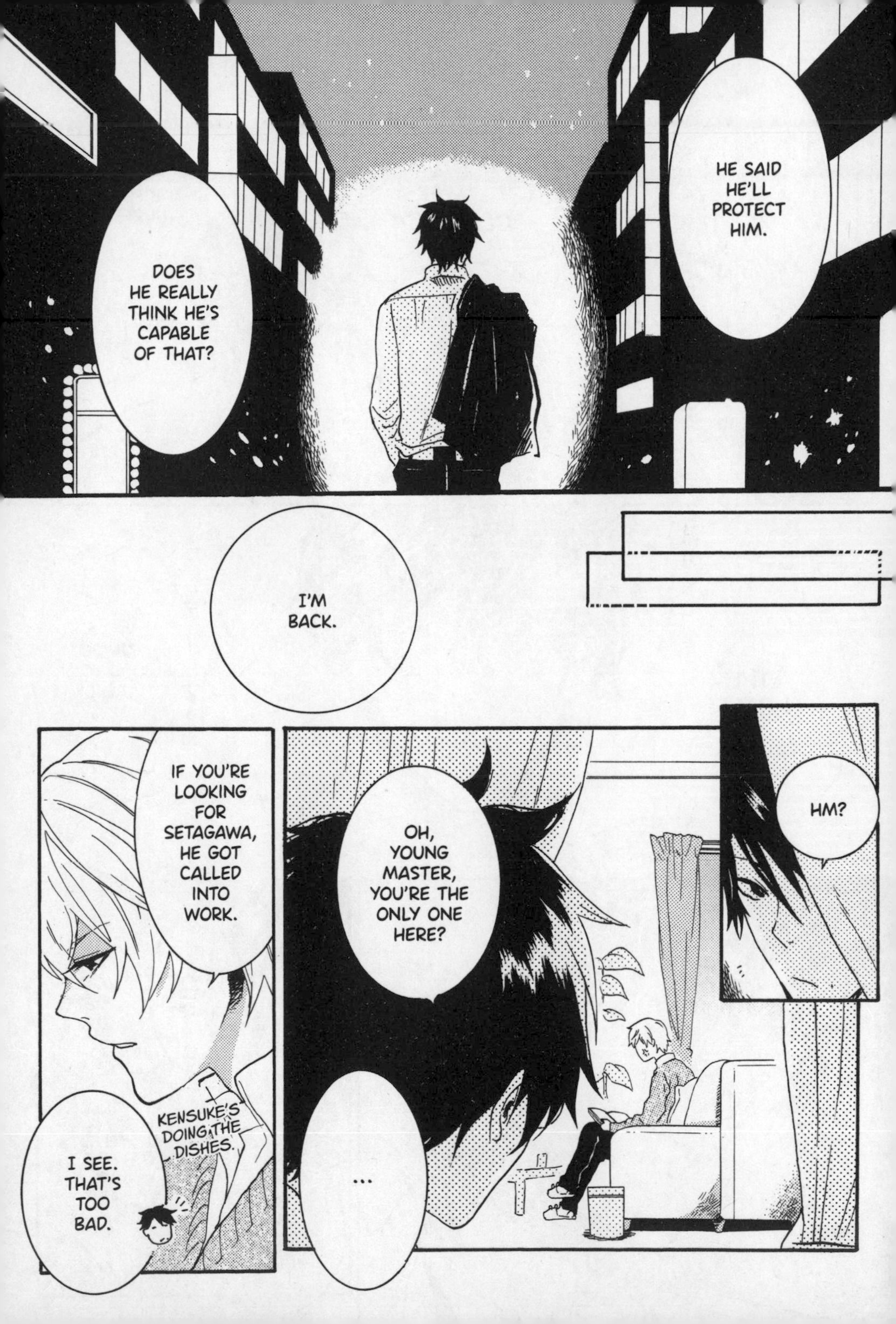
HE SAID HE'LL PROTECT HIM.
DOES HE REALLY THINK HE'S CAPABLE OF THAT?
I'M BACK.
HM?
OH, YOUNG MASTER, YOU'RE THE ONLY ONE HERE?
...
IF YOU'RE LOOKING FOR SETAGAWA, HE GOT CALLED INTO WORK.
KENSUKE'S DOING THE DISHES.
I SEE. THAT'S TOO BAD.

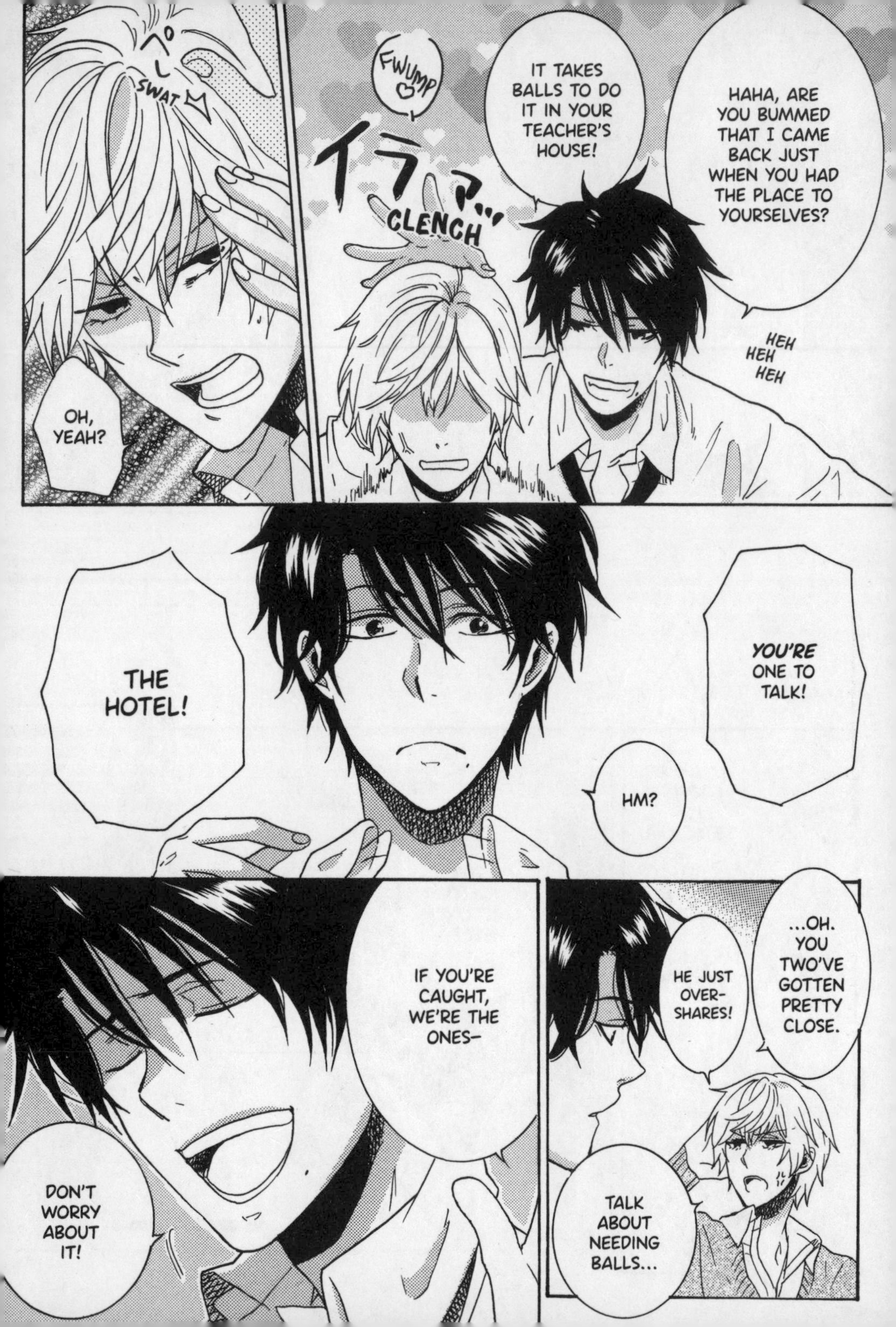
HAHA, ARE YOU BUMMED THAT I CAME BACK JUST WHEN YOU HAD THE PLACE TO YOURSELVES?
IT TAKES BALLS TO DO IT IN YOUR TEACHER'S HOUSE!
FWUMP ♡
イラァ…
CLENCH
HEH HEH HEH
ぺし
SWAT
OH, YEAH?
YOU'RE ONE TO TALK!
HM?
THE HOTEL!
...OH. YOU TWO'VE GOTTEN PRETTY CLOSE.
HE JUST OVER-SHARES!
TALK ABOUT NEEDING BALLS...
IF YOU'RE CAUGHT, WE'RE THE ONES–
DON'T WORRY ABOUT IT!

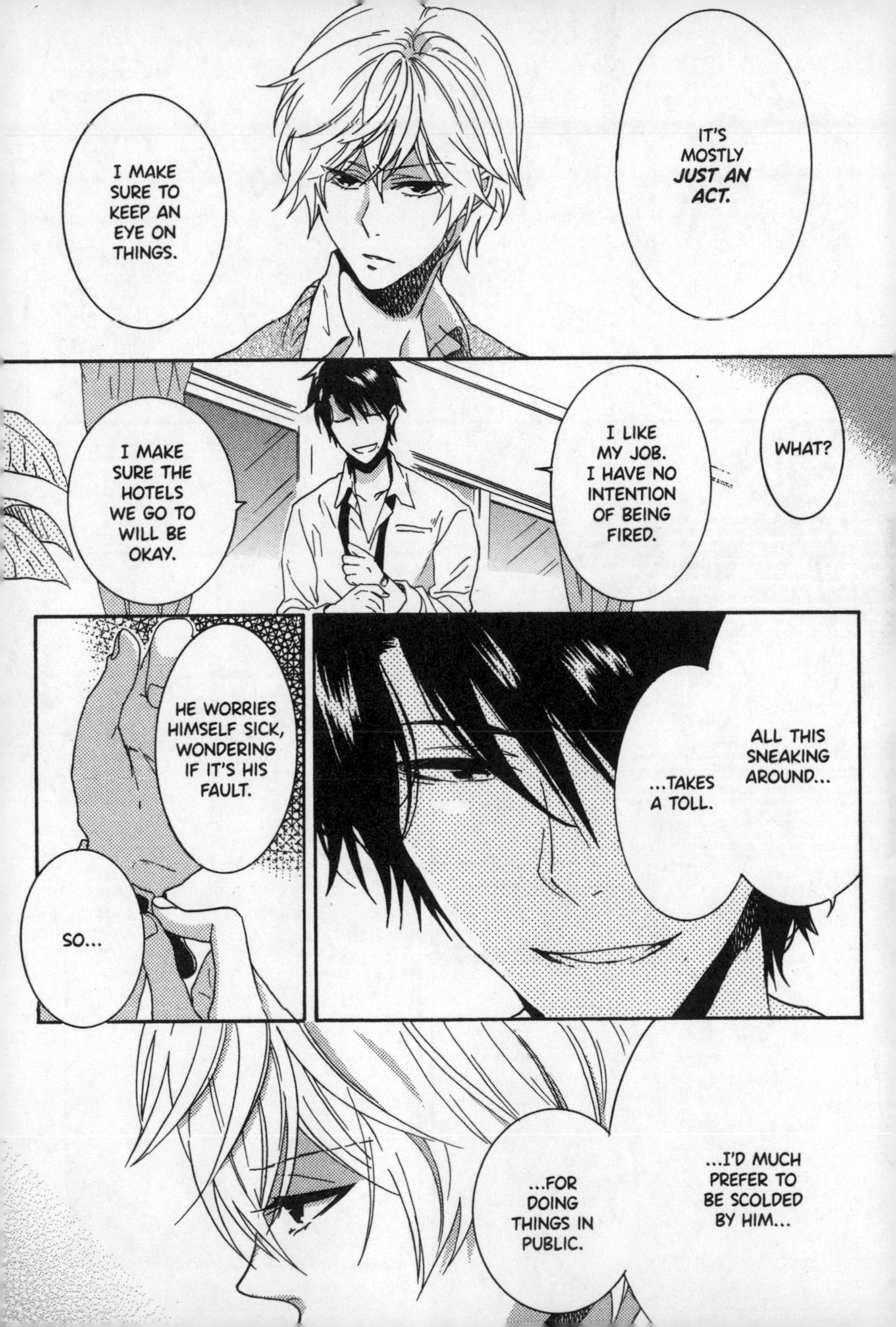
IT'S MOSTLY *JUST AN ACT.*
I MAKE SURE TO KEEP AN EYE ON THINGS.
WHAT?
I LIKE MY JOB. I HAVE NO INTENTION OF BEING FIRED.
I MAKE SURE THE HOTELS WE GO TO WILL BE OKAY.
ALL THIS SNEAKING AROUND...
...TAKES A TOLL.
HE WORRIES HIMSELF SICK, WONDERING IF IT'S HIS FAULT.
SO...
...I'D MUCH PREFER TO BE SCOLDED BY HIM...
...FOR DOING THINGS IN PUBLIC.

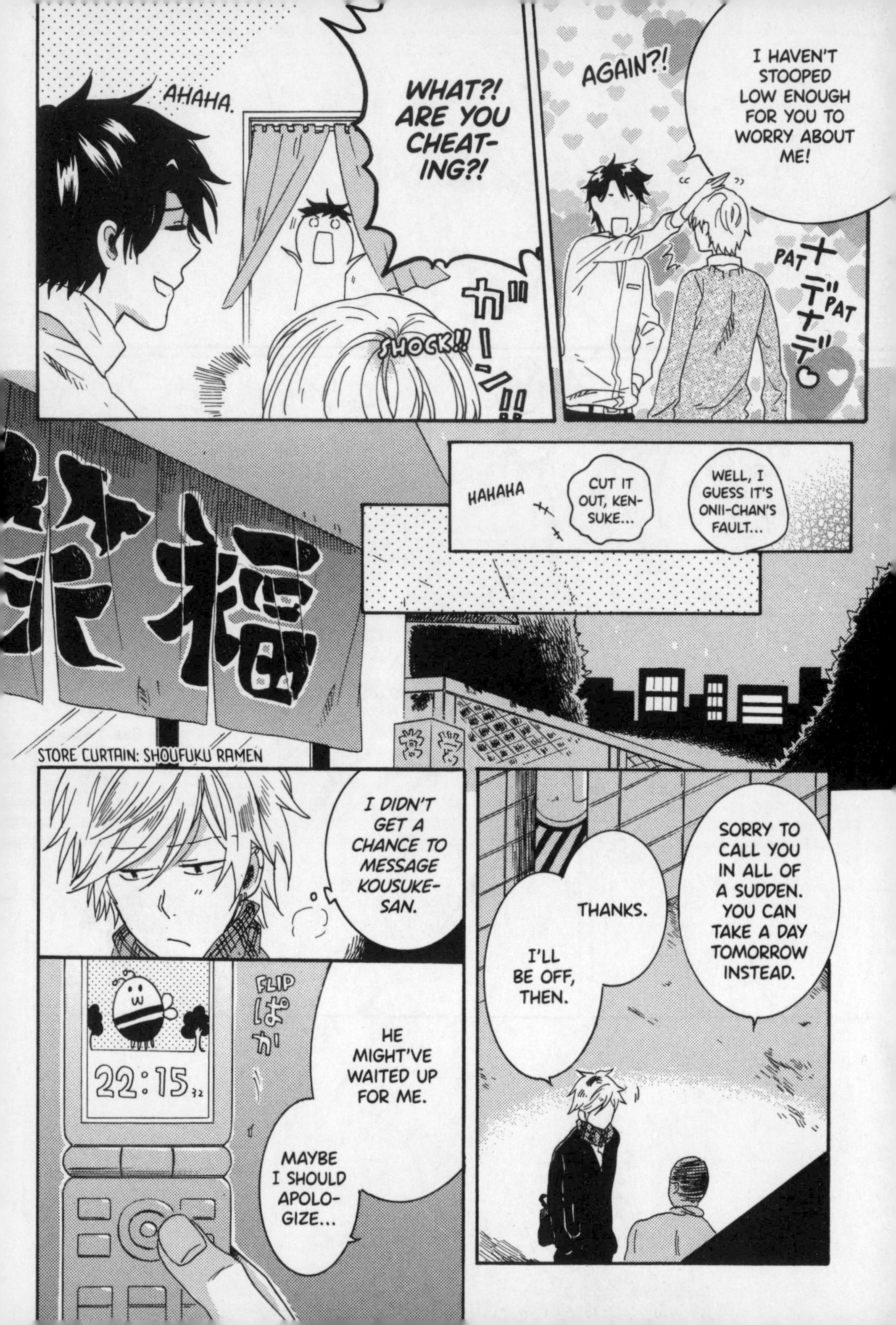
AGAIN?!
I HAVEN'T STOOPED LOW ENOUGH FOR YOU TO WORRY ABOUT ME!
PAT PAT
WHAT?! ARE YOU CHEAT-ING?!
AHAHA.
SHOCK!!
WELL, I GUESS IT'S ONII-CHAN'S FAULT...
CUT IT OUT, KEN-SUKE...
HAHAHA
STORE CURTAIN: SHOUFUKU RAMEN
SORRY TO CALL YOU IN ALL OF A SUDDEN. YOU CAN TAKE A DAY TOMORROW INSTEAD.
THANKS.
I'LL BE OFF, THEN.
I DIDN'T GET A CHANCE TO MESSAGE KOUSUKE-SAN.
FLIP
22:15
HE MIGHT'VE WAITED UP FOR ME.
MAYBE I SHOULD APOLO-GIZE...

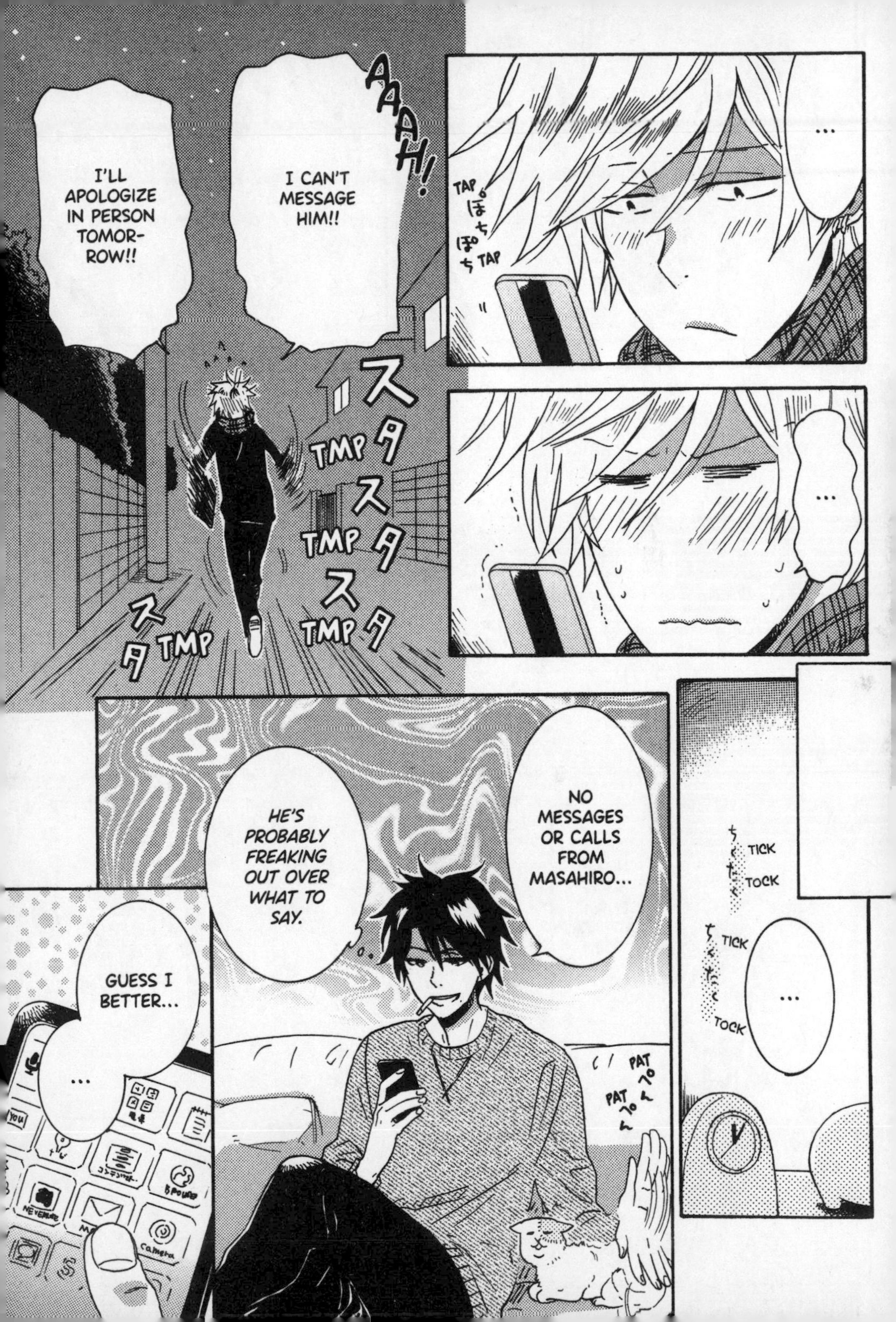
…
TAP ぽち
ぽち TAP
…
AAAH!
I CAN'T MESSAGE HIM!!
I'LL APOLOGIZE IN PERSON TOMORROW!!
スタ TMP
スタ TMP
スタ TMP
スタ TMP
TICK TOCK
TICK TOCK
…
NO MESSAGES OR CALLS FROM MASAHIRO…
HE'S PROBABLY FREAKING OUT OVER WHAT TO SAY.
PAT ぺん
PAT ぺん
GUESS I BETTER…
…

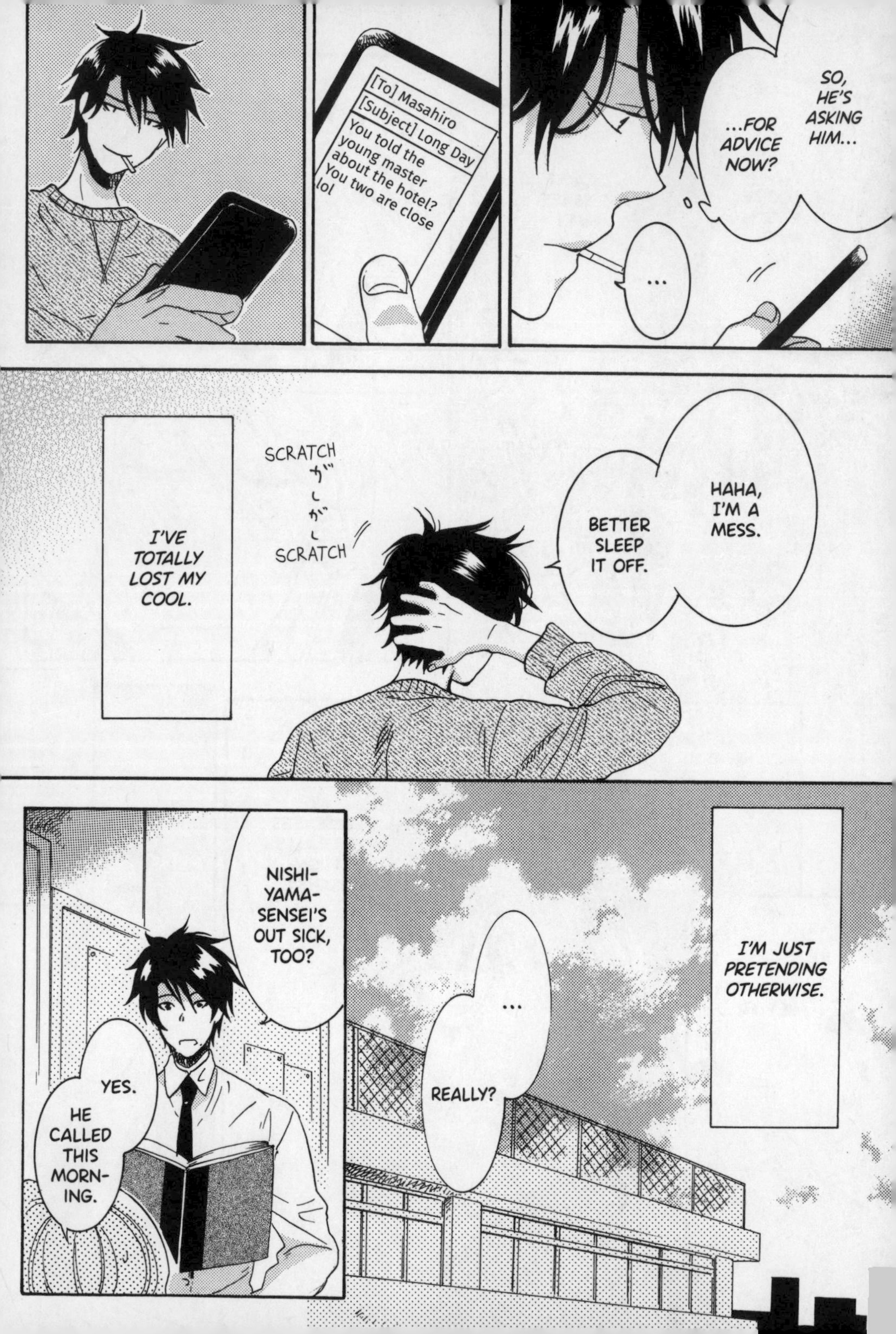
SO, HE'S ASKING HIM...
...FOR ADVICE NOW?
...
[To] Masahiro
[Subject] Long Day
You told the young master about the hotel? You two are close lol
HAHA, I'M A MESS.
BETTER SLEEP IT OFF.
SCRATCH がしがし SCRATCH
I'VE TOTALLY LOST MY COOL.
I'M JUST PRETENDING OTHERWISE.
NISHI-YAMA-SENSEI'S OUT SICK, TOO?
YES. HE CALLED THIS MORN-ING.
... REALLY?

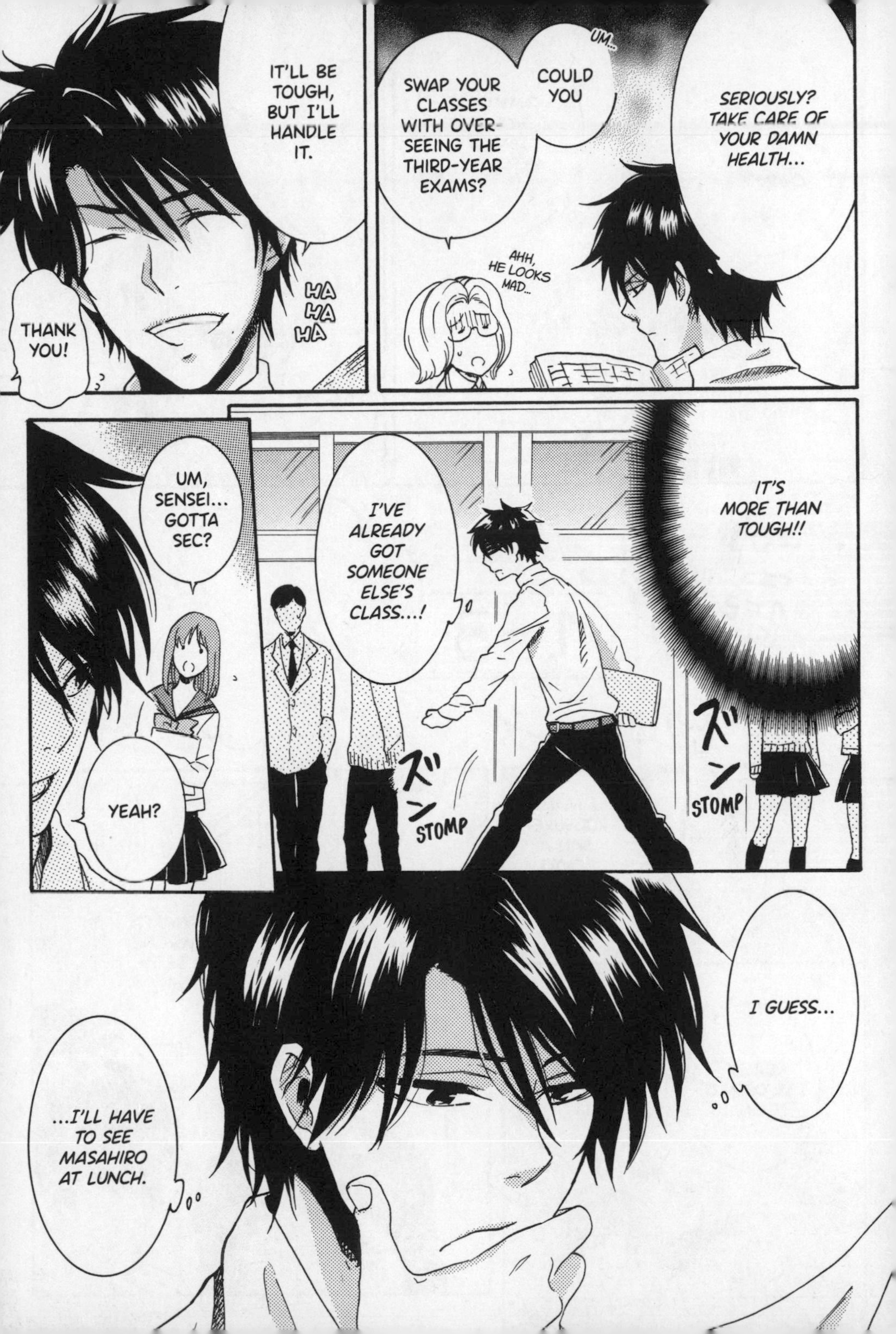
SERIOUSLY? TAKE CARE OF YOUR DAMN HEALTH...
UM...
COULD YOU
SWAP YOUR CLASSES WITH OVER-SEEING THE THIRD-YEAR EXAMS?
AHH, HE LOOKS MAD...
IT'LL BE TOUGH, BUT I'LL HANDLE IT.
HA HA HA
THANK YOU!
IT'S MORE THAN TOUGH!!
ズン
STOMP
I'VE ALREADY GOT SOMEONE ELSE'S CLASS...!
ズン
STOMP
UM, SENSEI... GOTTA SEC?
YEAH?
I GUESS...
...I'LL HAVE TO SEE MASAHIRO AT LUNCH.

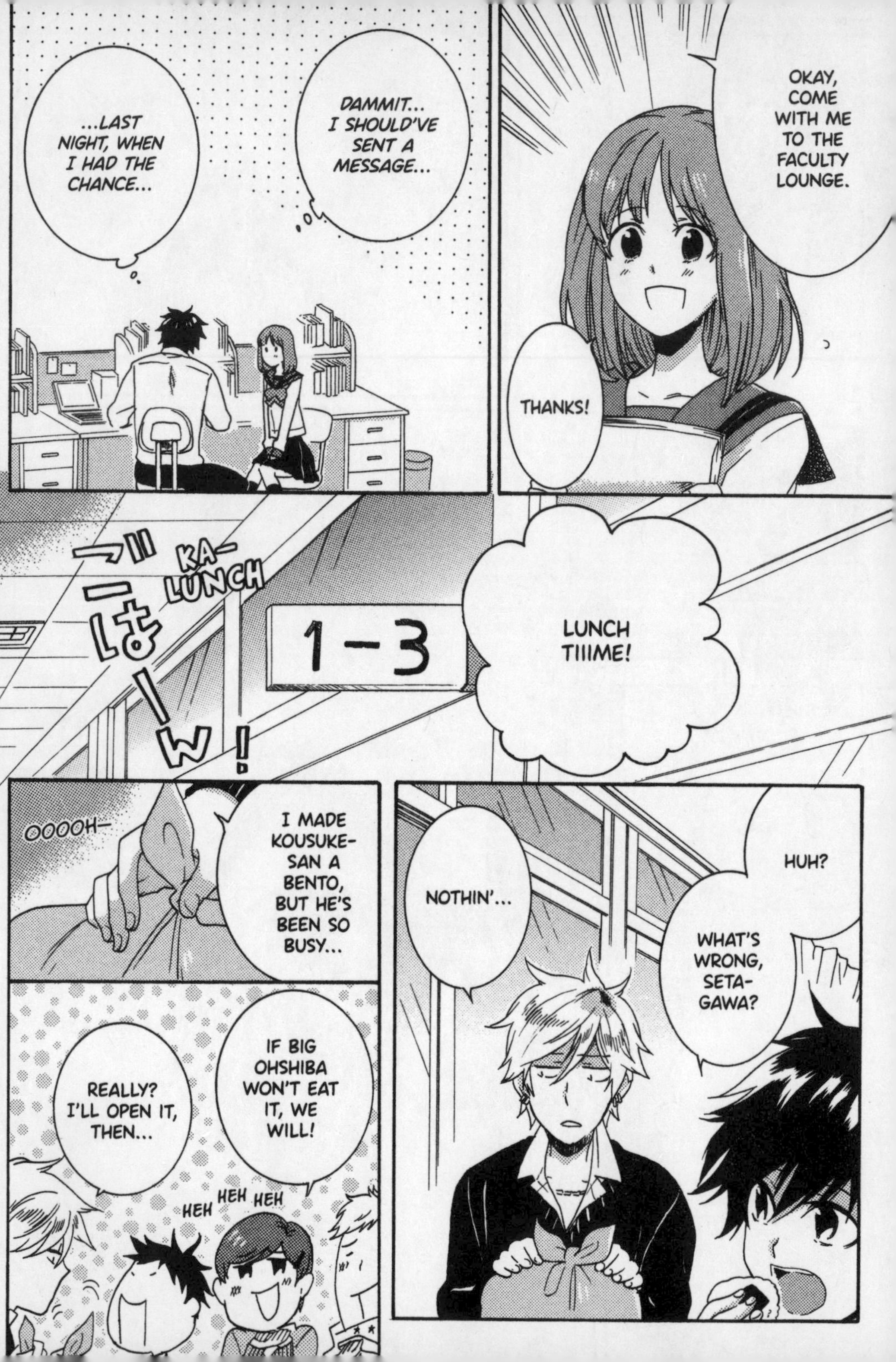
OKAY, COME WITH ME TO THE FACULTY LOUNGE.
THANKS!
DAMMIT... I SHOULD'VE SENT A MESSAGE...
...LAST NIGHT, WHEN I HAD THE CHANCE...
LUNCH TIIIME!
1-3
KA-LUNCH
HUH?
WHAT'S WRONG, SETA-GAWA?
NOTHIN'...
I MADE KOUSUKE-SAN A BENTO, BUT HE'S BEEN SO BUSY...
OOOOH-
IF BIG OHSHIBA WON'T EAT IT, WE WILL!
REALLY? I'LL OPEN IT, THEN...
HEH HEH HEH

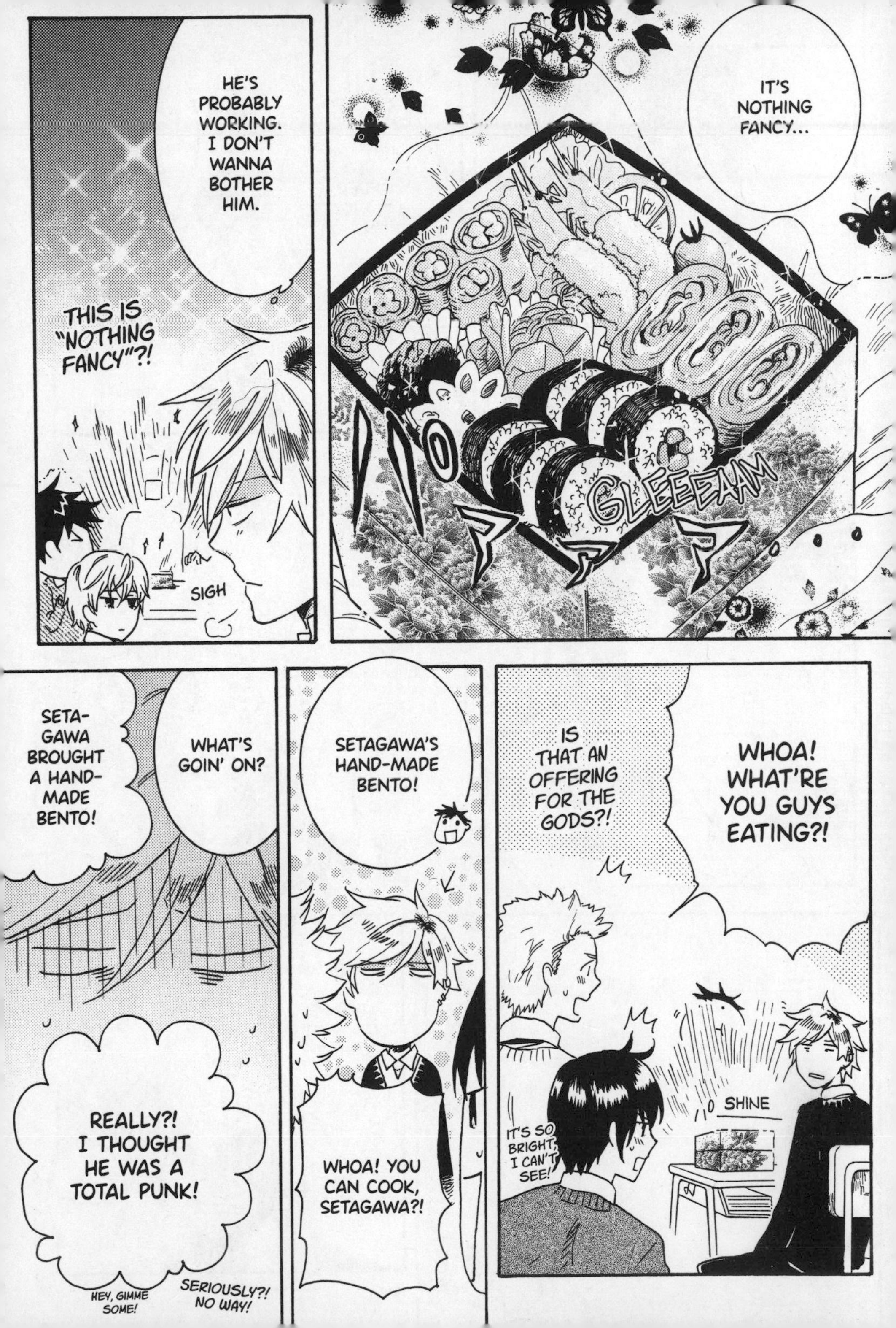
IT'S NOTHING FANCY...
GLEEEAAM
HE'S PROBABLY WORKING. I DON'T WANNA BOTHER HIM.
THIS IS "NOTHING FANCY"?!
SIGH
WHOA! WHAT'RE YOU GUYS EATING?!
IS THAT AN OFFERING FOR THE GODS?!
SHINE
IT'S SO BRIGHT, I CAN'T SEE!
SETAGAWA'S HAND-MADE BENTO!
WHOA! YOU CAN COOK, SETAGAWA?!
WHAT'S GOIN' ON?
SETAGAWA BROUGHT A HAND-MADE BENTO!
REALLY?! I THOUGHT HE WAS A TOTAL PUNK!
SERIOUSLY?! NO WAY!
HEY, GIMME SOME!

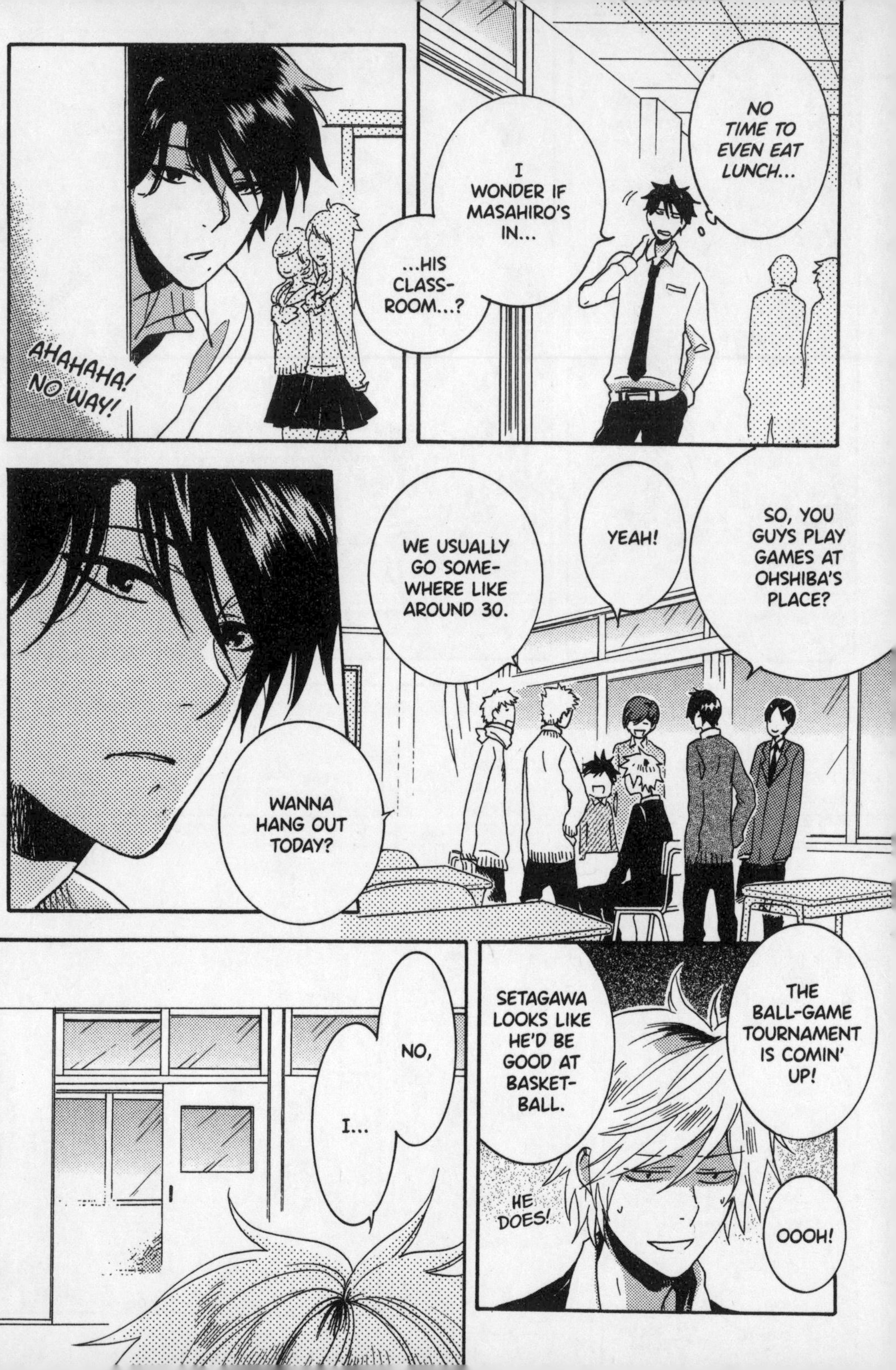
NO TIME TO EVEN EAT LUNCH...
I WONDER IF MASAHIRO'S IN...
...HIS CLASS-ROOM...?
AHAHAHA! NO WAY!
SO, YOU GUYS PLAY GAMES AT OHSHIBA'S PLACE?
YEAH!
WE USUALLY GO SOME-WHERE LIKE AROUND 30.
WANNA HANG OUT TODAY?
THE BALL-GAME TOURNAMENT IS COMIN' UP!
SETAGAWA LOOKS LIKE HE'D BE GOOD AT BASKET-BALL.
HE DOES!
OOOH!
NO,
I...

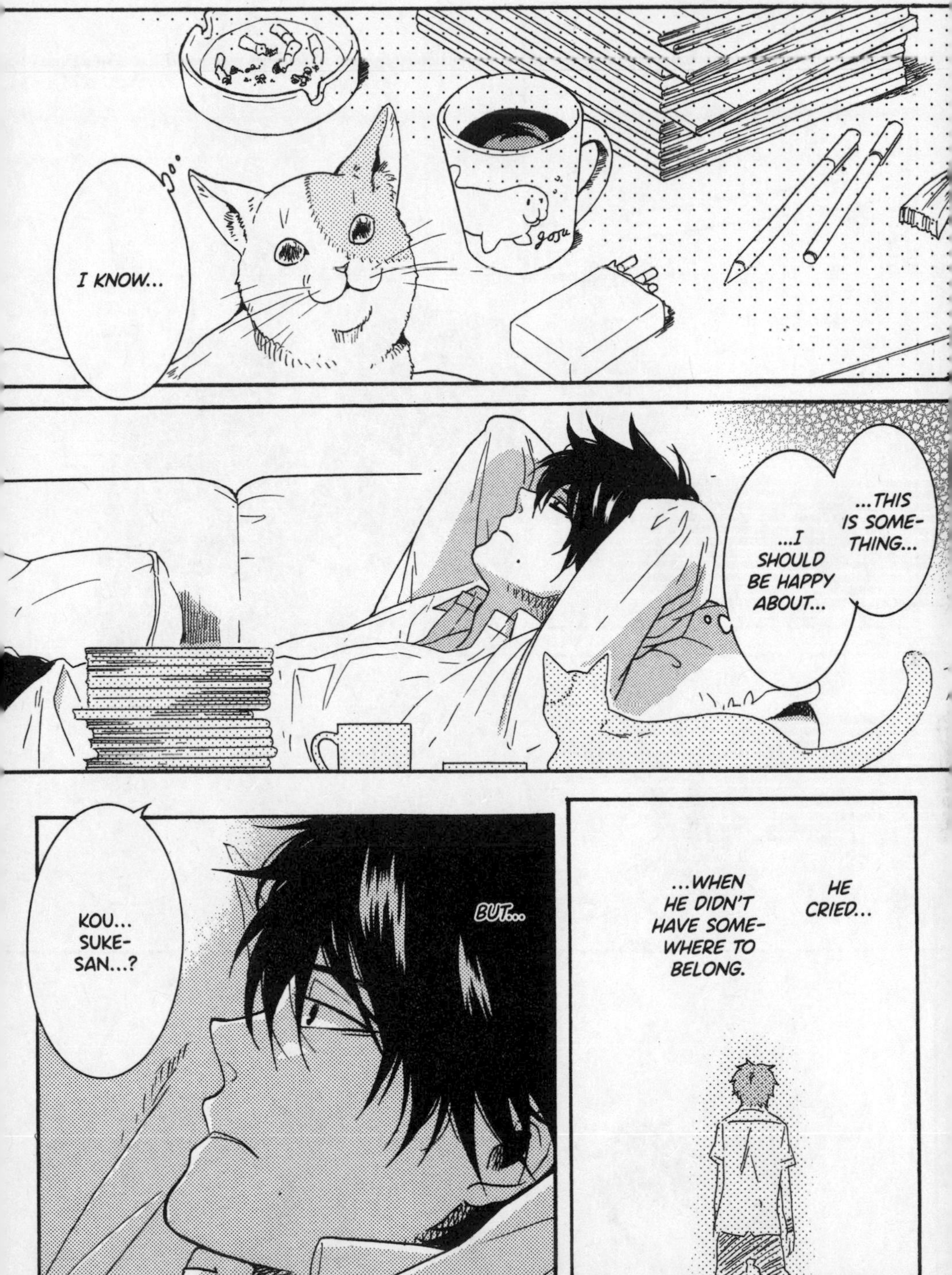
I KNOW...
...THIS IS SOME-THING...
...I SHOULD BE HAPPY ABOUT...
HE CRIED...
...WHEN HE DIDN'T HAVE SOME-WHERE TO BELONG.
BUT...
KOU... SUKE-SAN...?

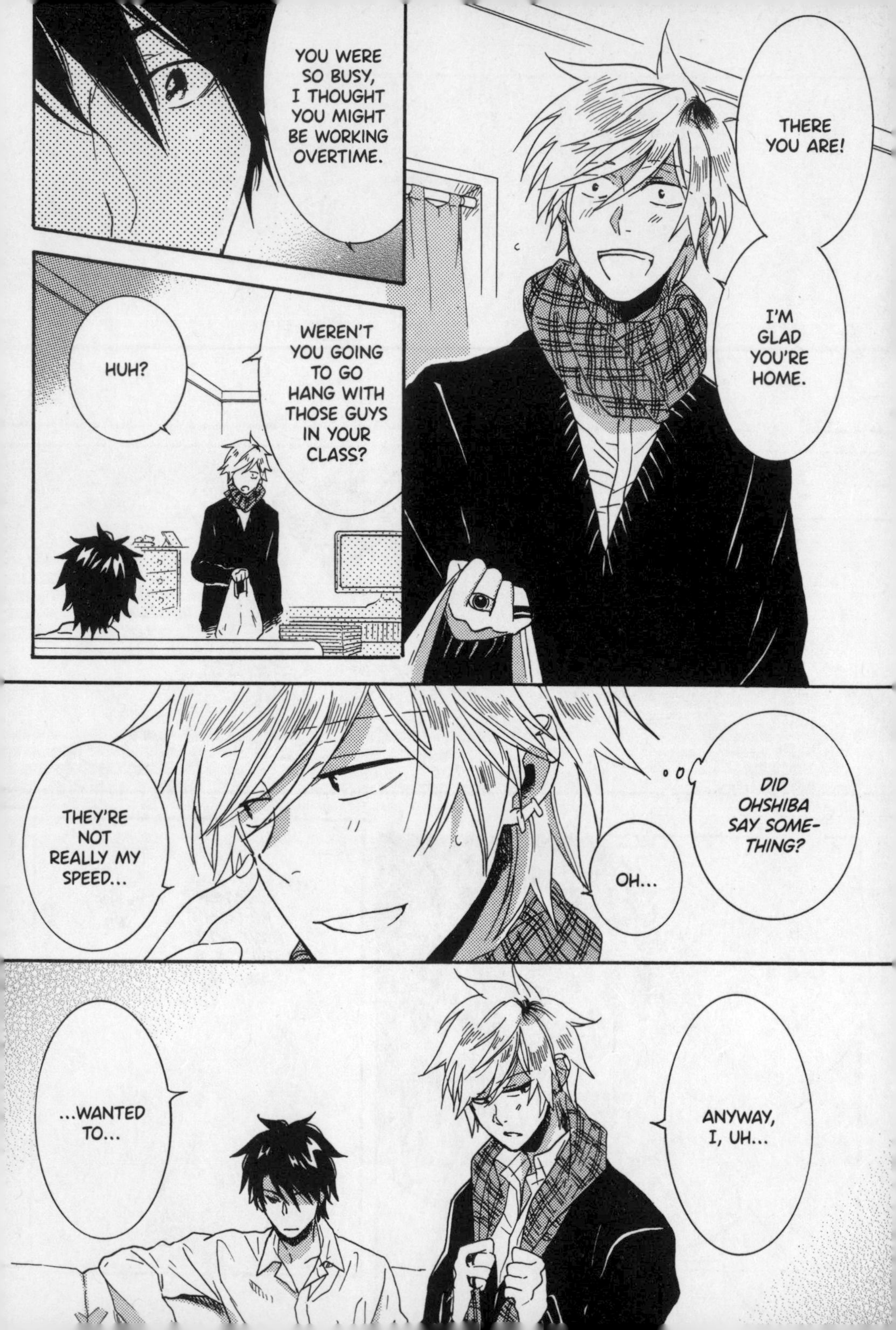
THERE YOU ARE!
I'M GLAD YOU'RE HOME.
YOU WERE SO BUSY, I THOUGHT YOU MIGHT BE WORKING OVERTIME.
WEREN'T YOU GOING TO GO HANG WITH THOSE GUYS IN YOUR CLASS?
HUH?
DID OHSHIBA SAY SOME-THING?
OH...
THEY'RE NOT REALLY MY SPEED...
ANYWAY, I, UH...
...WANTED TO...

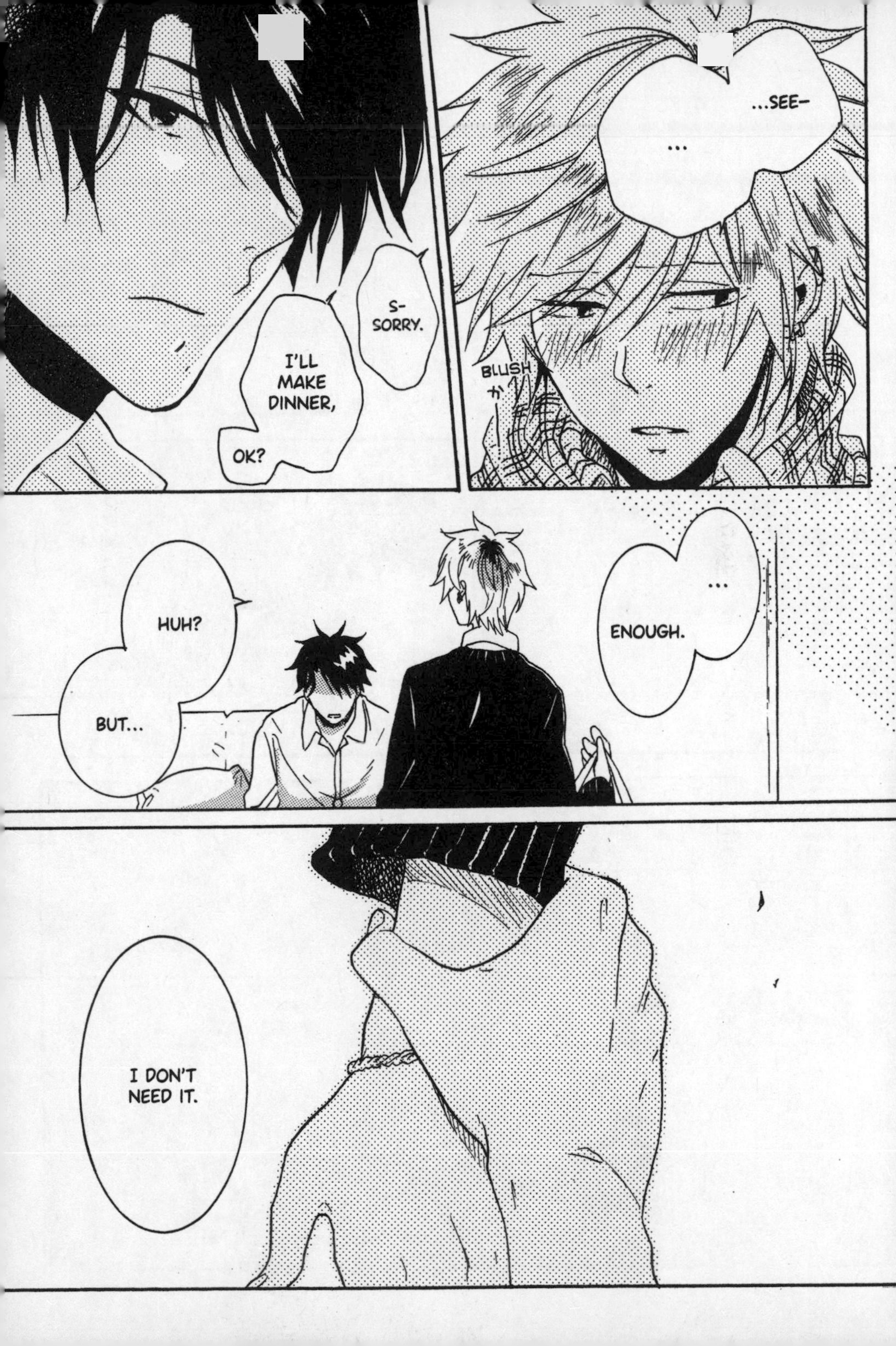
...SEE-
...
BLUSH
か
S-SORRY.
I'LL MAKE DINNER, OK?
... ENOUGH.
HUH? BUT...
I DON'T NEED IT.

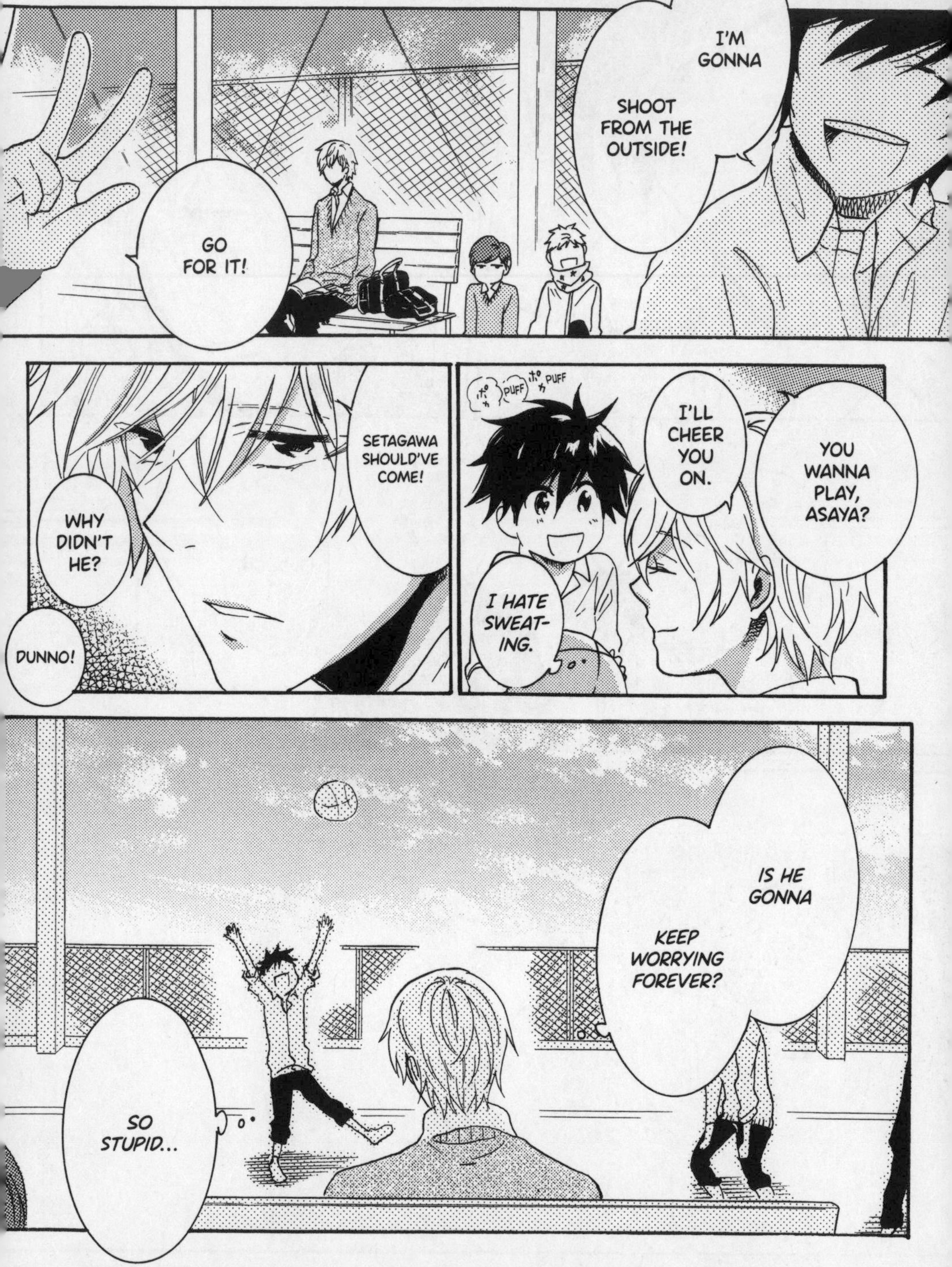
I'M GONNA
SHOOT FROM THE OUTSIDE!
GO FOR IT!
PUFF PUFF
YOU WANNA PLAY, ASAYA?
I'LL CHEER YOU ON.
I HATE SWEAT-ING.
SETAGAWA SHOULD'VE COME!
WHY DIDN'T HE?
DUNNO!
IS HE GONNA
KEEP WORRYING FOREVER?
SO STUPID...

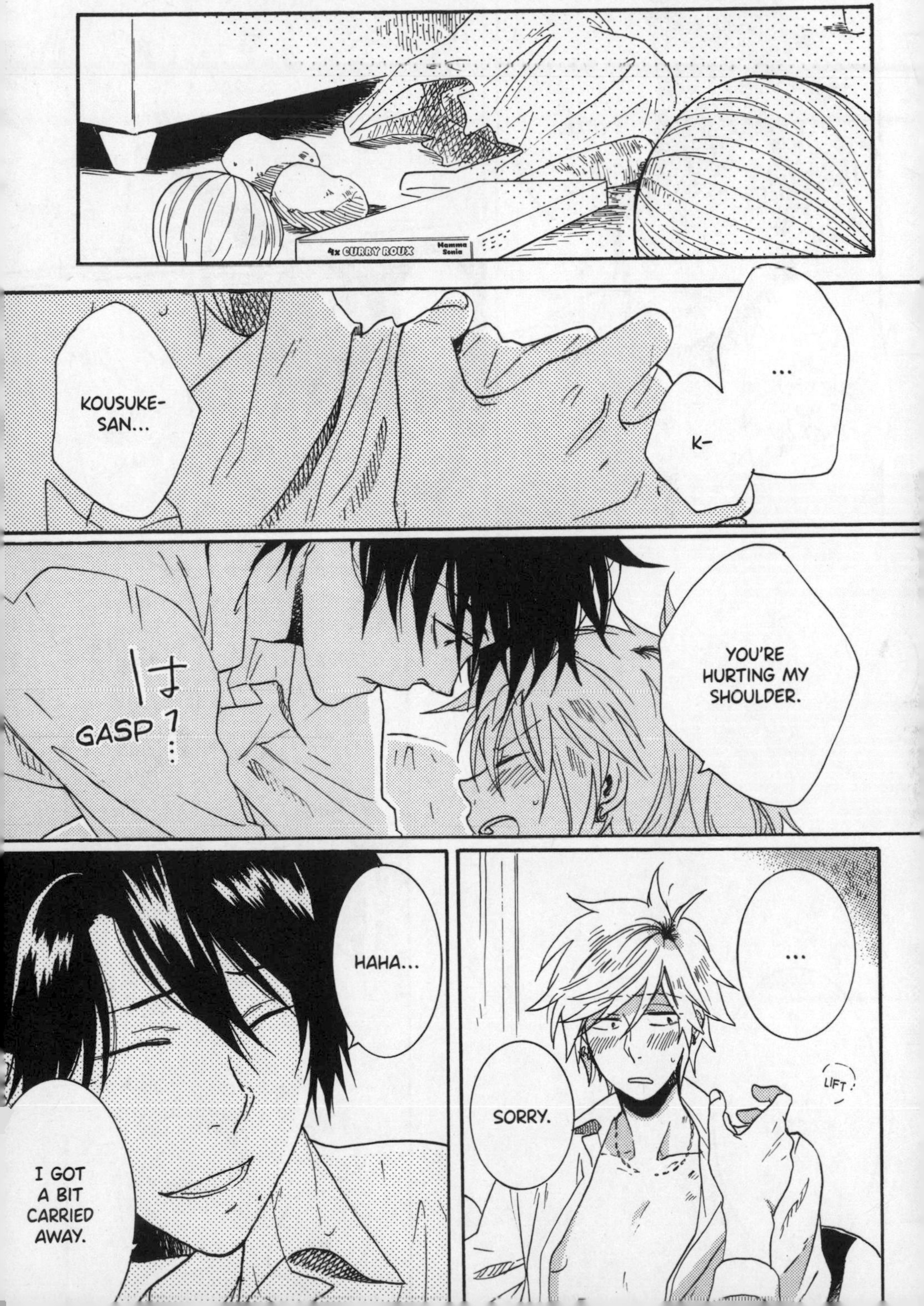
CURRY ROUX
Mamma Sonia
... K-
KOUSUKE-SAN...
YOU'RE HURTING MY SHOULDER.
は
GASP
...
LIFT
SORRY.
HAHA...
I GOT A BIT CARRIED AWAY.

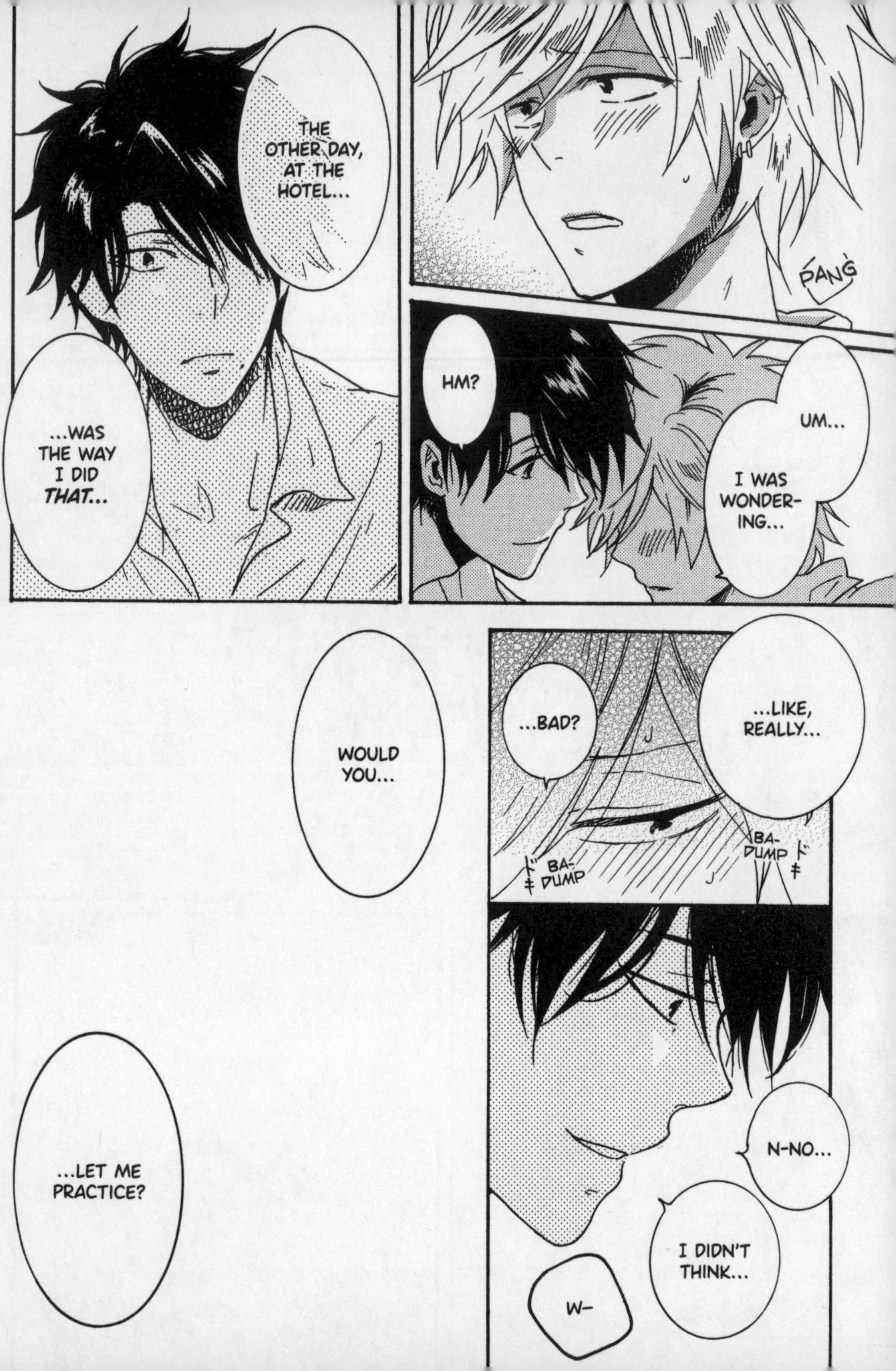
PANG
UM...
I WAS WONDER-ING...
HM?
THE OTHER DAY, AT THE HOTEL...
...WAS THE WAY I DID THAT...
...LIKE, REALLY...
...BAD?
BA-DUMP
ドキ
BA-DUMP
ドキ
N-NO...
I DIDN'T THINK...
W-
WOULD YOU...
...LET ME PRACTICE?

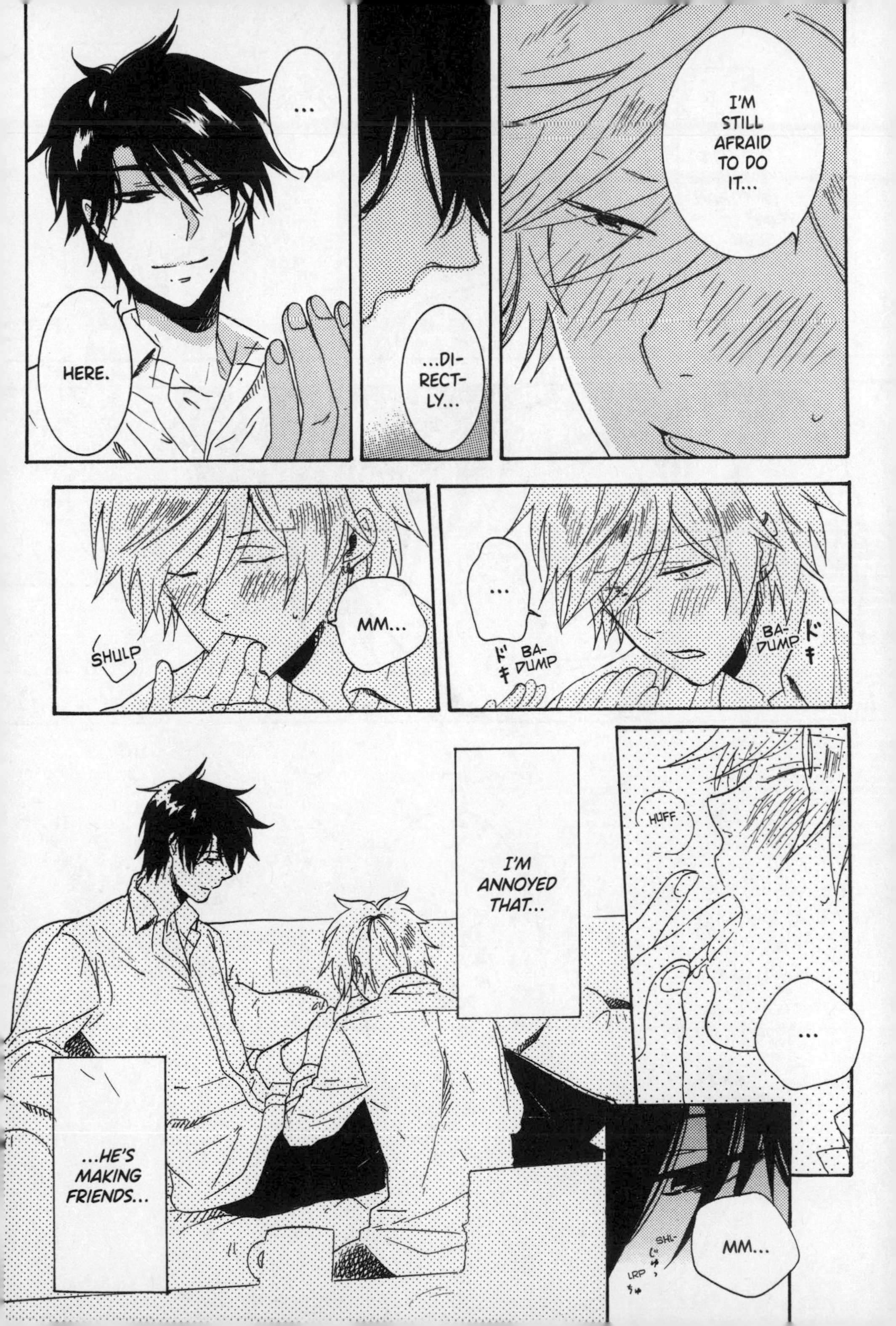
I'M STILL AFRAID TO DO IT...
...DI-RECT-LY...
...
HERE.
...
BA-DUMP ドキ
ドキ BA-DUMP
MM...
SHULP
HUFF.
...
MM...
SHL- じゅ
LRP ちゅ
I'M ANNOYED THAT...
...HE'S MAKING FRIENDS...

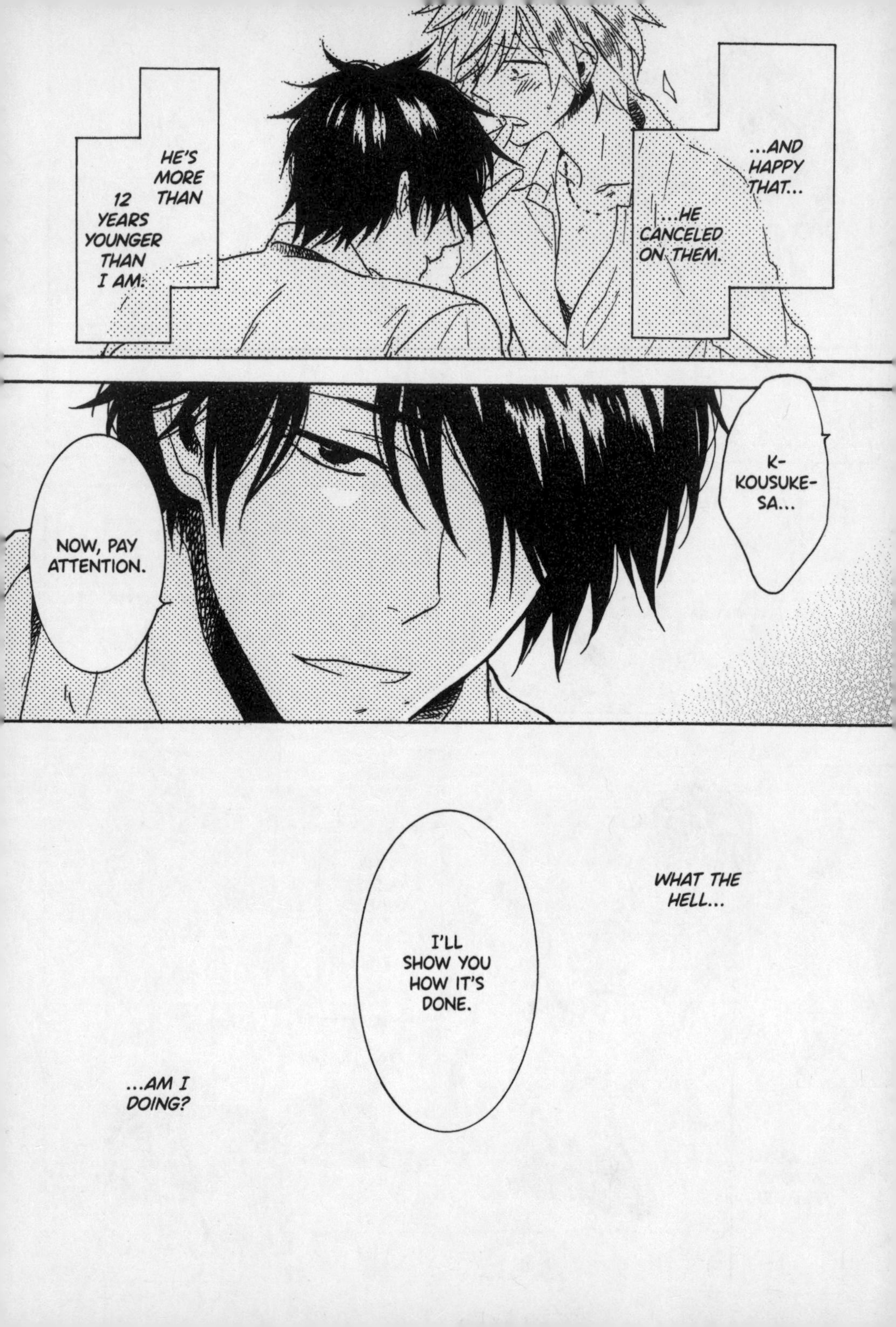
...AND HAPPY THAT...
...HE CANCELED ON THEM.
HE'S MORE THAN 12 YEARS YOUNGER THAN I AM.
K-KOUSUKE-SA...
NOW, PAY ATTENTION.
WHAT THE HELL...
I'LL SHOW YOU HOW IT'S DONE.
...AM I DOING?

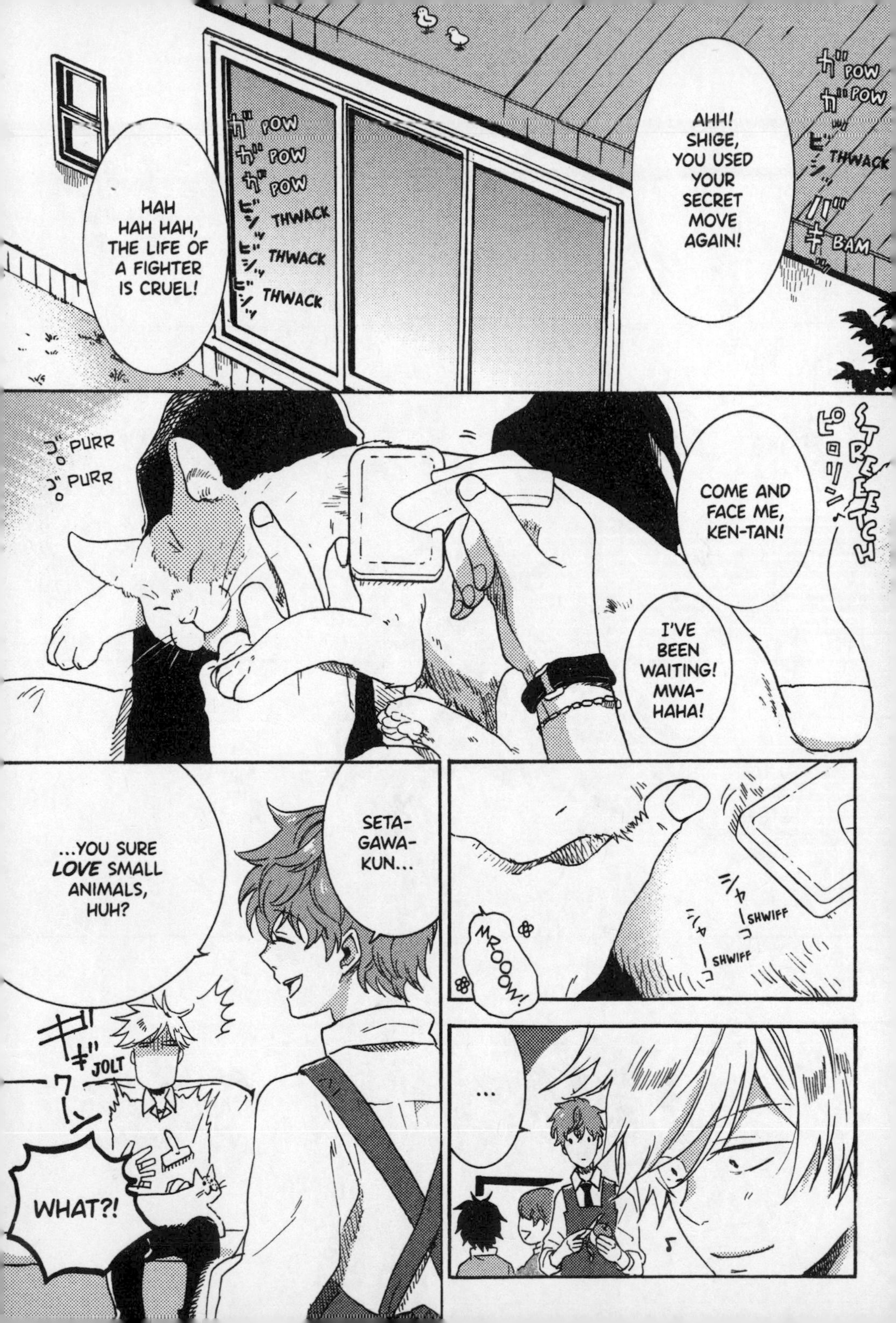

POW
POW
THWACK
BAM
AHH! SHIGE, YOU USED YOUR SECRET MOVE AGAIN!
POW
POW
POW
THWACK
THWACK
THWACK
HAH HAH HAH, THE LIFE OF A FIGHTER IS CRUEL!
STREEETCH
COME AND FACE ME, KEN-TAN!
I'VE BEEN WAITING! MWA-HAHA!
PURR
PURR
SHWIFF
SHWIFF
MROOOW!
...
SETA-GAWA-KUN...
...YOU SURE LOVE SMALL ANIMALS, HUH?
JOLT
WHAT?!

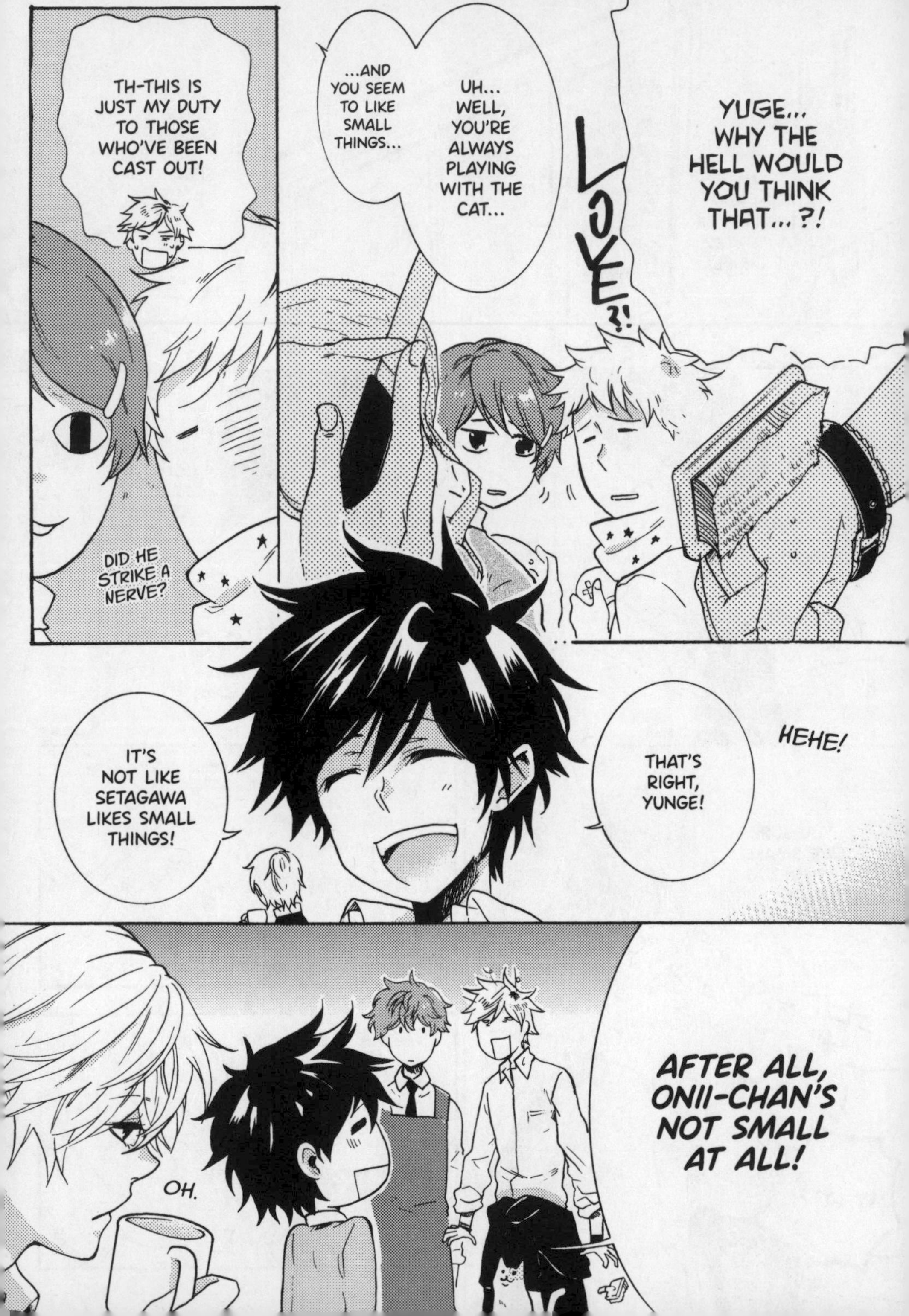
YUGE... WHY THE HELL WOULD YOU THINK THAT...?!
LOVE?!
UH... WELL, YOU'RE ALWAYS PLAYING WITH THE CAT...
...AND YOU SEEM TO LIKE SMALL THINGS...
TH-THIS IS JUST MY DUTY TO THOSE WHO'VE BEEN CAST OUT!
DID HE STRIKE A NERVE?
HEHE!
THAT'S RIGHT, YUNGE!
IT'S NOT LIKE SETAGAWA LIKES SMALL THINGS!
AFTER ALL, ONII-CHAN'S NOT SMALL AT ALL!
OH.

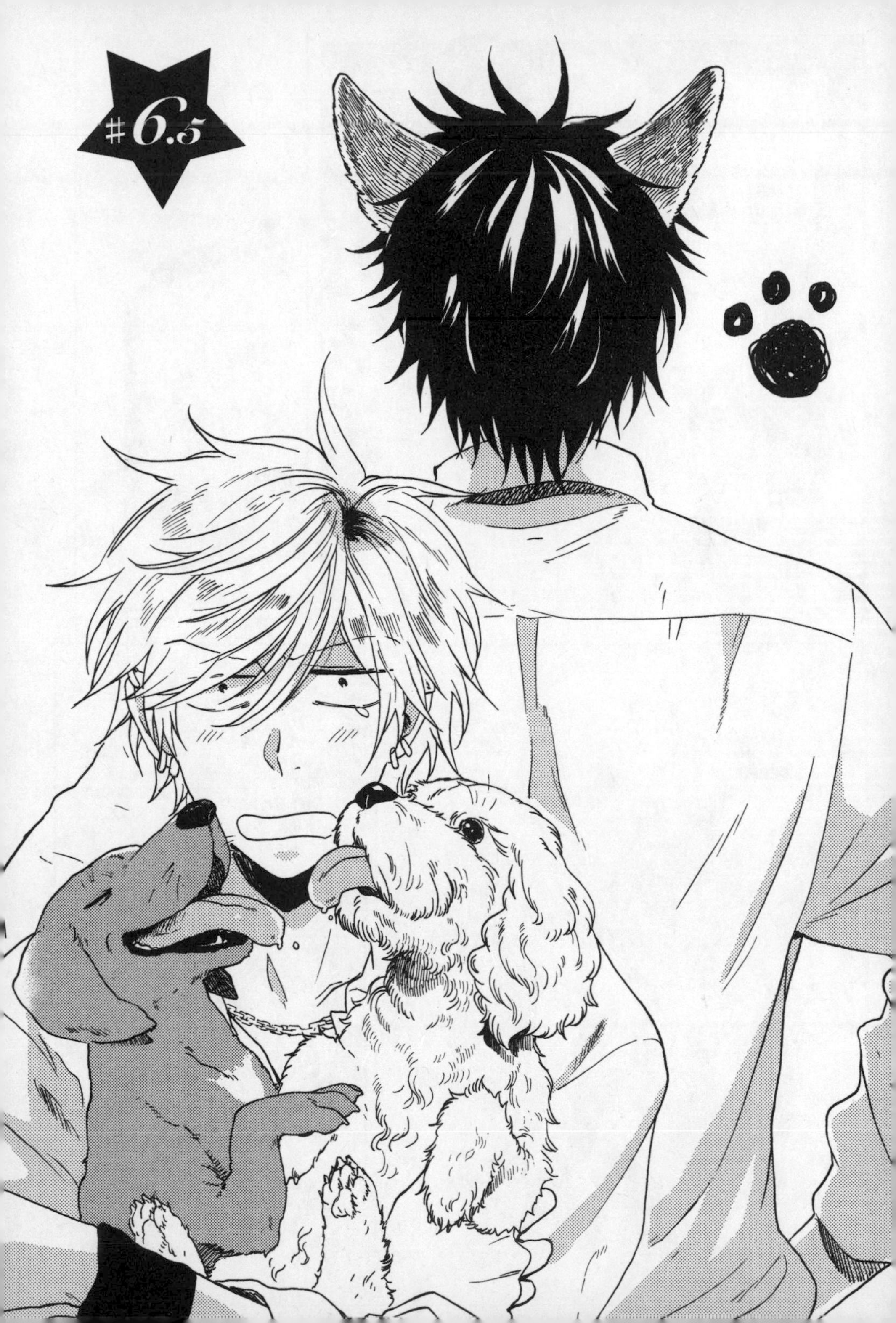
#6.5

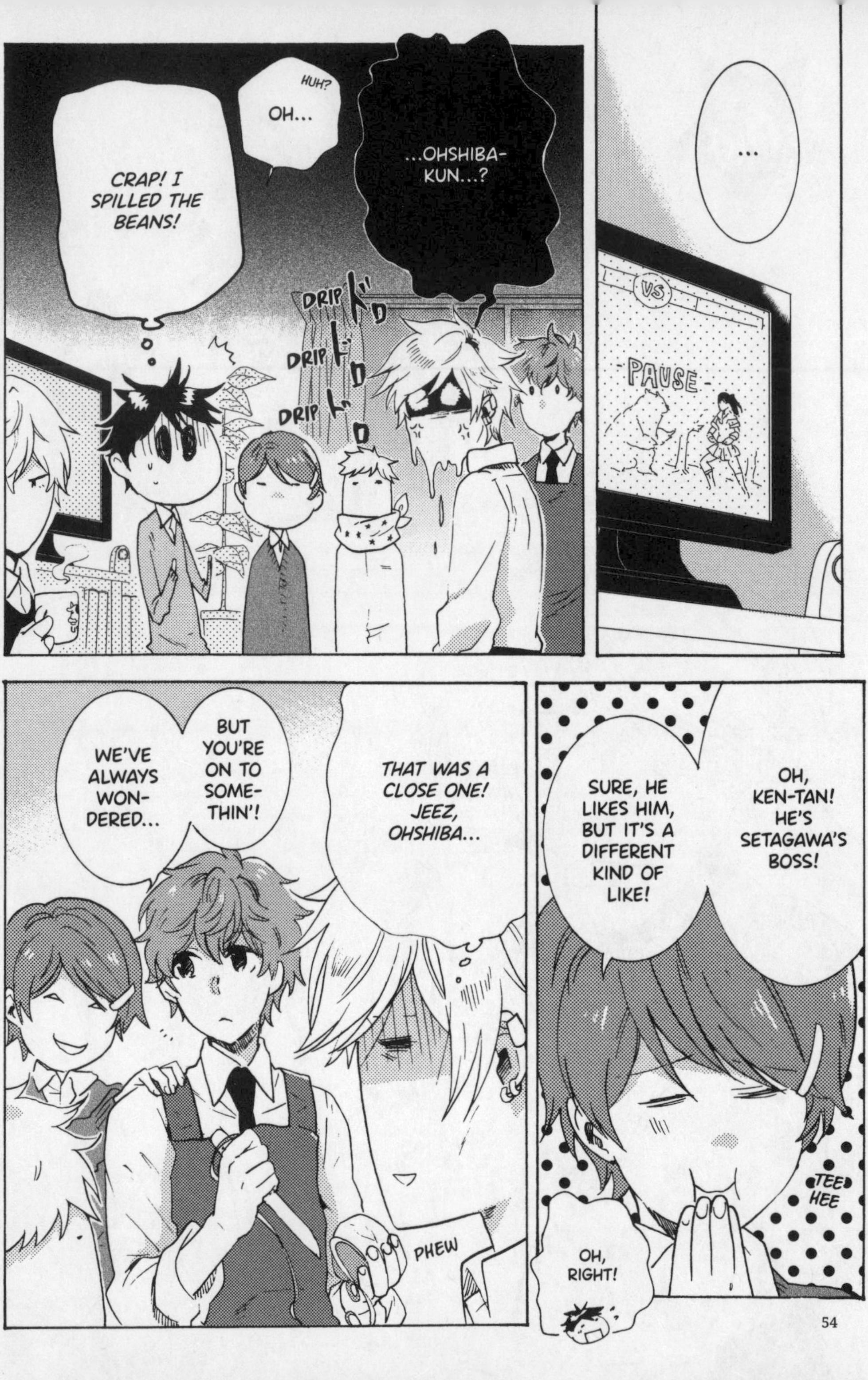
...
...OHSHIBA-KUN...?
HUH?
OH...
CRAP! I SPILLED THE BEANS!
DRIP DRIP DRIP
PAUSE
VS
OH, KEN-TAN! HE'S SETAGAWA'S BOSS!
SURE, HE LIKES HIM, BUT IT'S A DIFFERENT KIND OF LIKE!
TEE HEE
OH, RIGHT!
THAT WAS A CLOSE ONE! JEEZ, OHSHIBA...
BUT YOU'RE ON TO SOMETHIN'!
WE'VE ALWAYS WONDERED...
PHEW

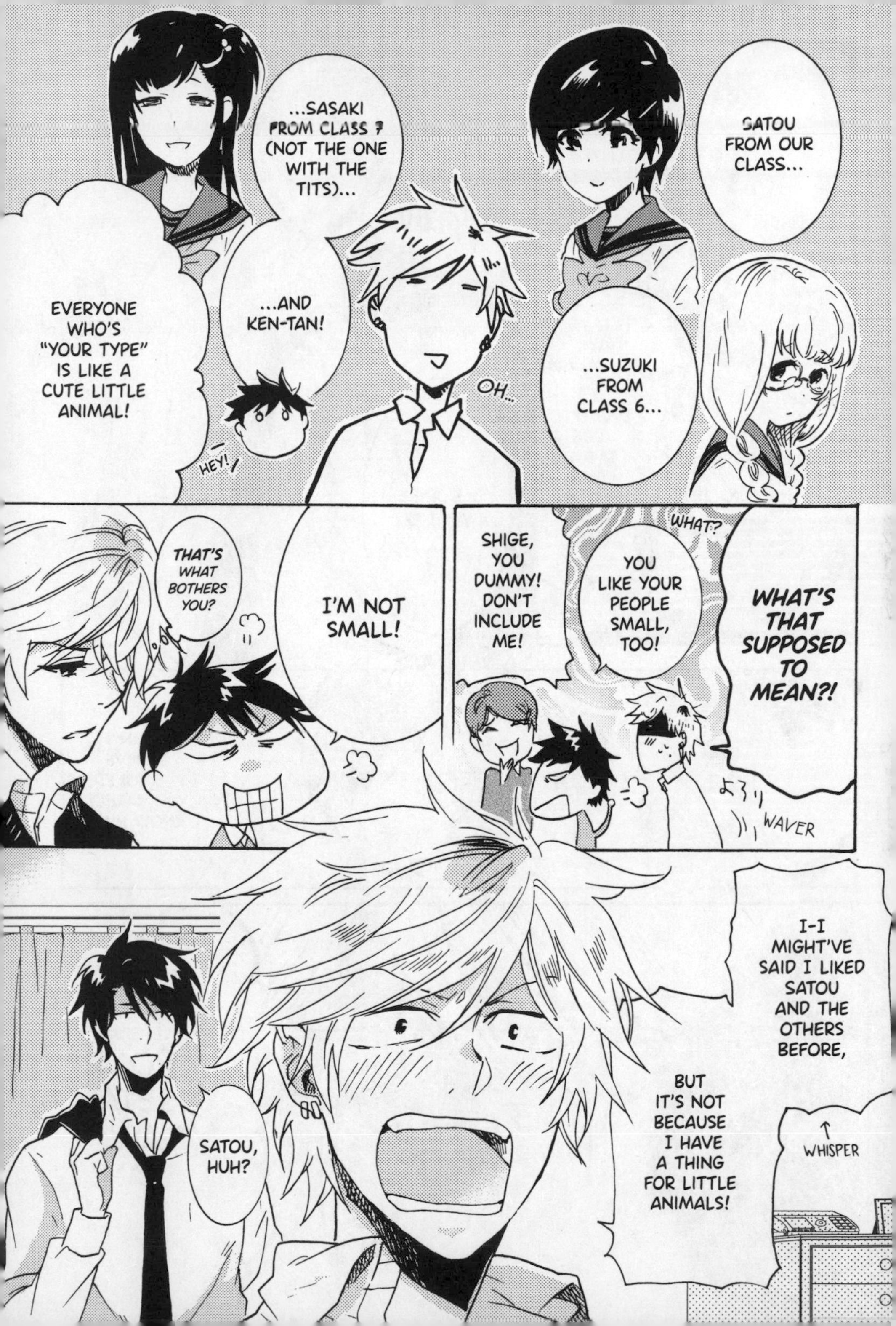
SATOU FROM OUR CLASS...
...SASAKI FROM CLASS 7 (NOT THE ONE WITH THE TITS)...
...SUZUKI FROM CLASS 6...
OH...
...AND KEN-TAN!
EVERYONE WHO'S "YOUR TYPE" IS LIKE A CUTE LITTLE ANIMAL!
HEY!
WHAT'S THAT SUPPOSED TO MEAN?!
WHAT?
YOU LIKE YOUR PEOPLE SMALL, TOO!
SHIGE, YOU DUMMY! DON'T INCLUDE ME!
よろり
WAVER
I'M NOT SMALL!
THAT'S WHAT BOTHERS YOU?
I-I MIGHT'VE SAID I LIKED SATOU AND THE OTHERS BEFORE,
WHISPER
BUT IT'S NOT BECAUSE I HAVE A THING FOR LITTLE ANIMALS!
SATOU, HUH?

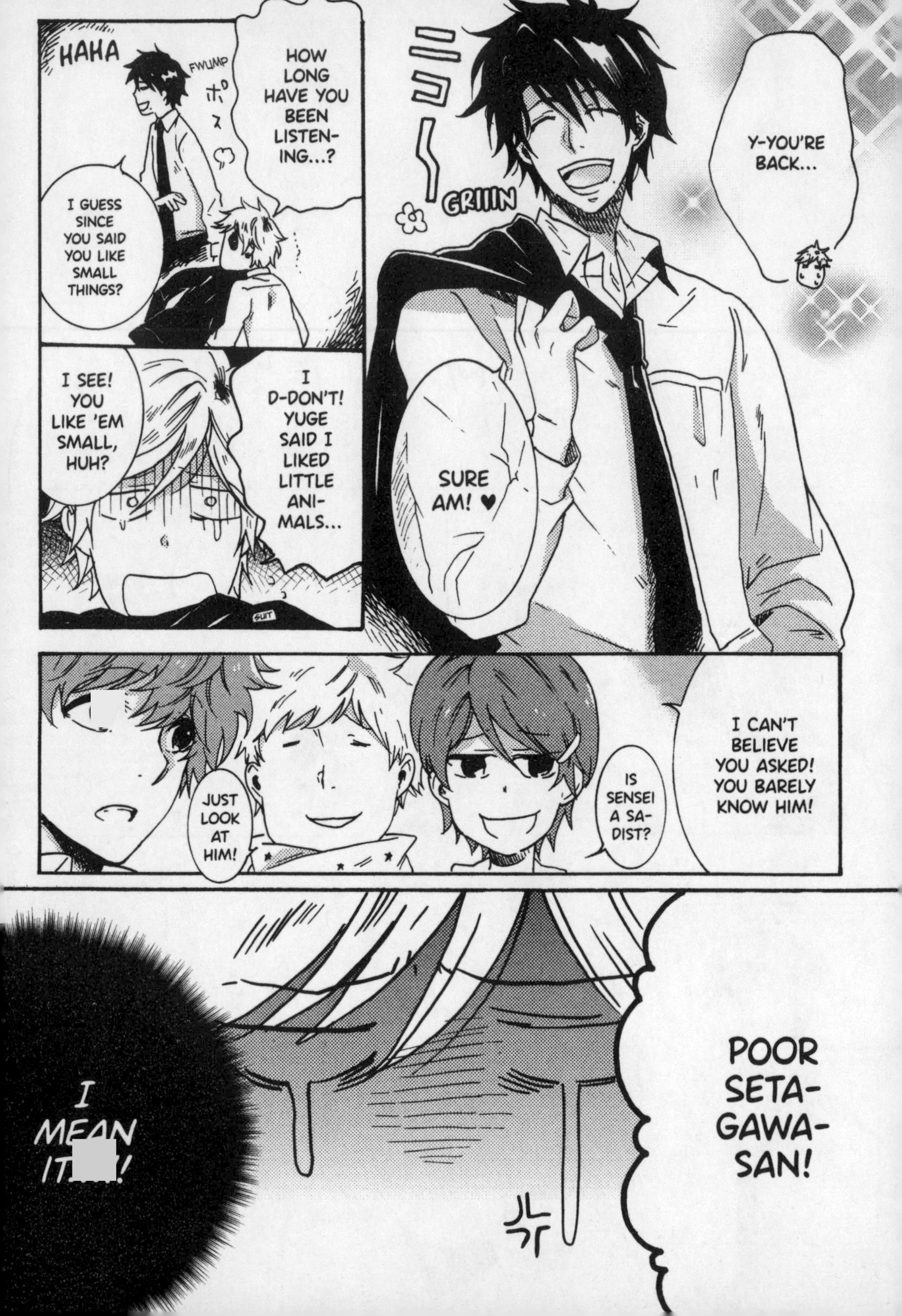
Y-YOU'RE BACK...
ニコ〜
GRIIIN
SURE AM! ♥
HOW LONG HAVE YOU BEEN LISTENING...?
HAHA
FWUMP
ポス
I GUESS SINCE YOU SAID YOU LIKE SMALL THINGS?
I D-DON'T! YUGE SAID I LIKED LITTLE ANIMALS...
I SEE! YOU LIKE 'EM SMALL, HUH?
SUIT
I CAN'T BELIEVE YOU ASKED! YOU BARELY KNOW HIM!
IS SENSEI A SADIST?
JUST LOOK AT HIM!
POOR SETAGAWA-SAN!
I MEAN IT!

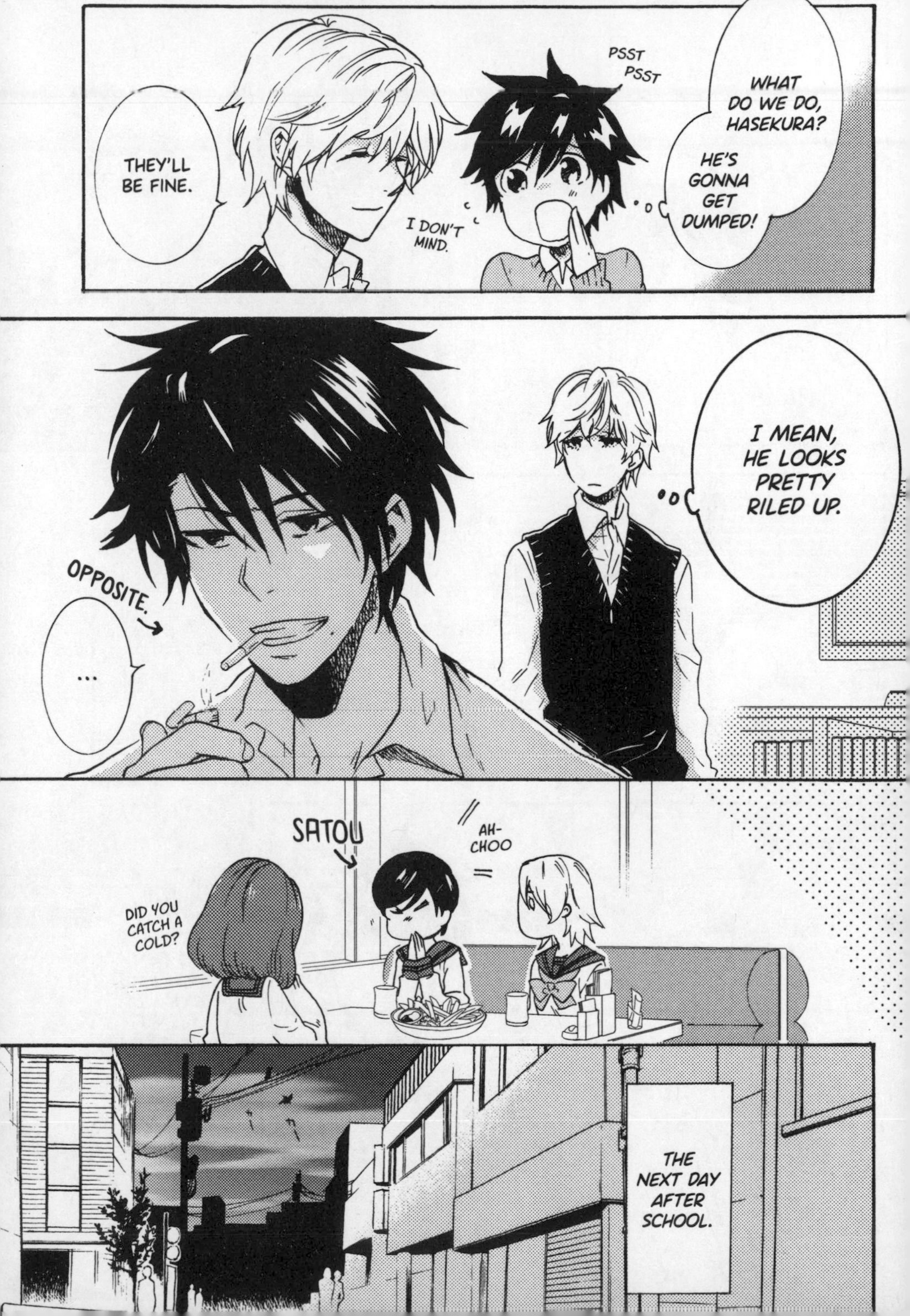
PSST PSST
WHAT DO WE DO, HASEKURA?
HE'S GONNA GET DUMPED!
I DON'T MIND.
THEY'LL BE FINE.
I MEAN, HE LOOKS PRETTY RILED UP.
OPPOSITE.
...
AH-CHOO
SATOU
DID YOU CATCH A COLD?
THE NEXT DAY AFTER SCHOOL.

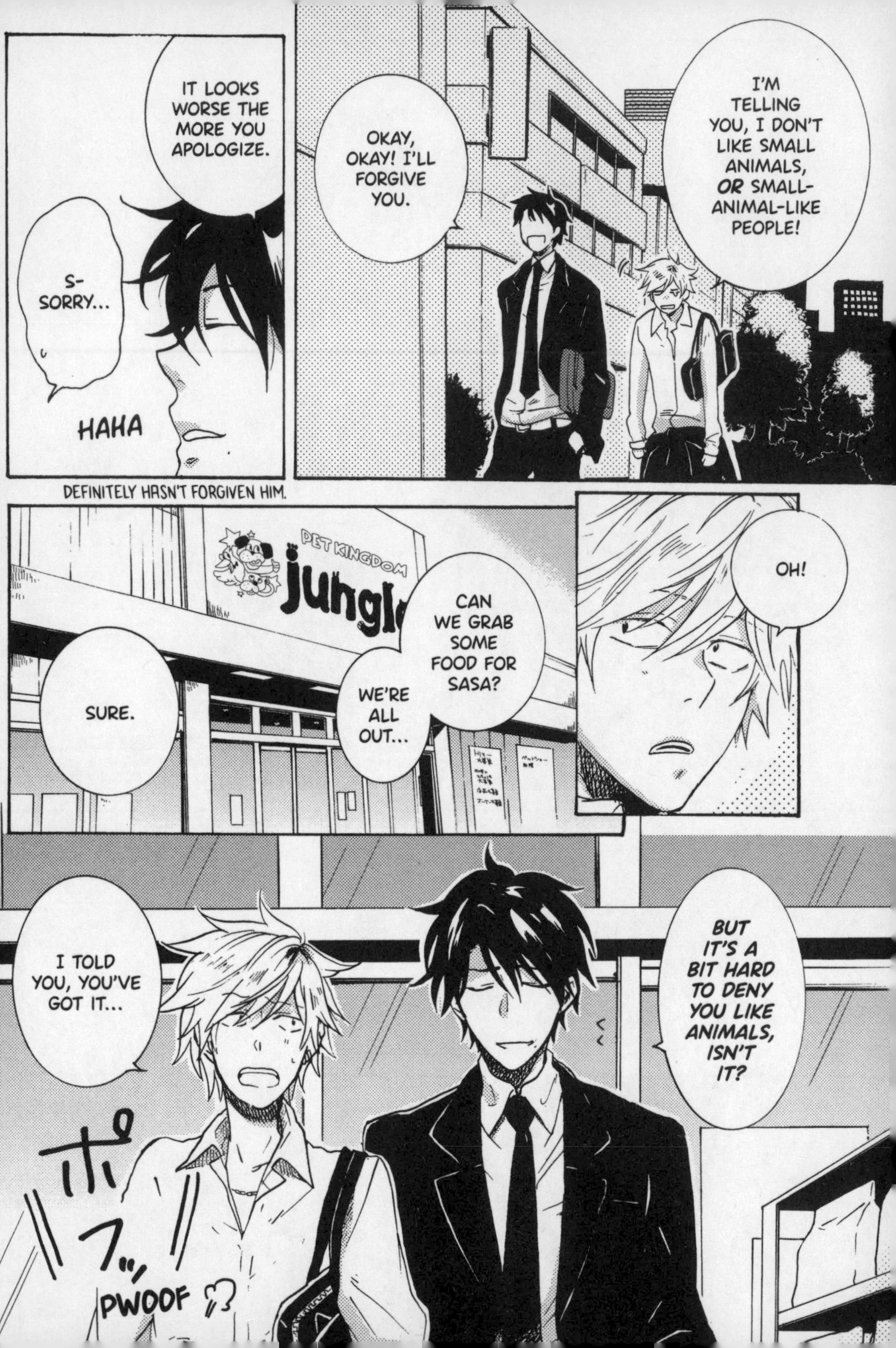
I'M TELLING YOU, I DON'T LIKE SMALL ANIMALS, OR SMALL-ANIMAL-LIKE PEOPLE!
OKAY, OKAY! I'LL FORGIVE YOU.
IT LOOKS WORSE THE MORE YOU APOLOGIZE.
S-SORRY...
HAHA
DEFINITELY HASN'T FORGIVEN HIM.
OH!
PET KINGDOM
jungle
CAN WE GRAB SOME FOOD FOR SASA?
WE'RE ALL OUT...
SURE.
BUT IT'S A BIT HARD TO DENY YOU LIKE ANIMALS, ISN'T IT?
I TOLD YOU, YOU'VE GOT IT...
ポフッ
PWOOF

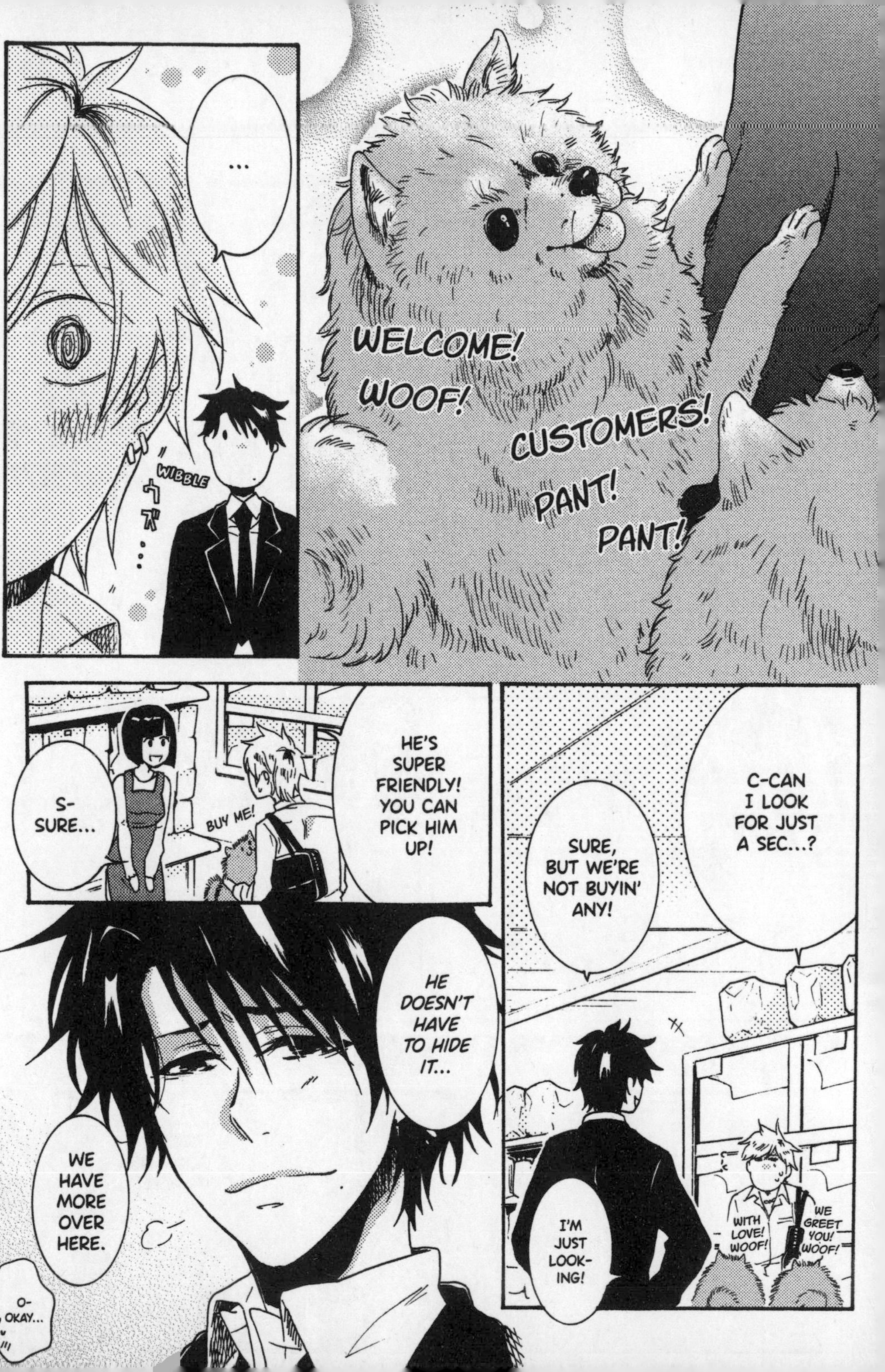
WELCOME!
WOOF!
CUSTOMERS!
PANT!
PANT!
...
WIBBLE
ウズ...
C-CAN I LOOK FOR JUST A SEC...?
SURE, BUT WE'RE NOT BUYIN' ANY!
WE GREET YOU! WOOF!
WITH LOVE! WOOF!
I'M JUST LOOK-ING!
HE'S SUPER FRIENDLY! YOU CAN PICK HIM UP!
BUY ME!
S-SURE...
HE DOESN'T HAVE TO HIDE IT...
WE HAVE MORE OVER HERE.
O-OKAY...

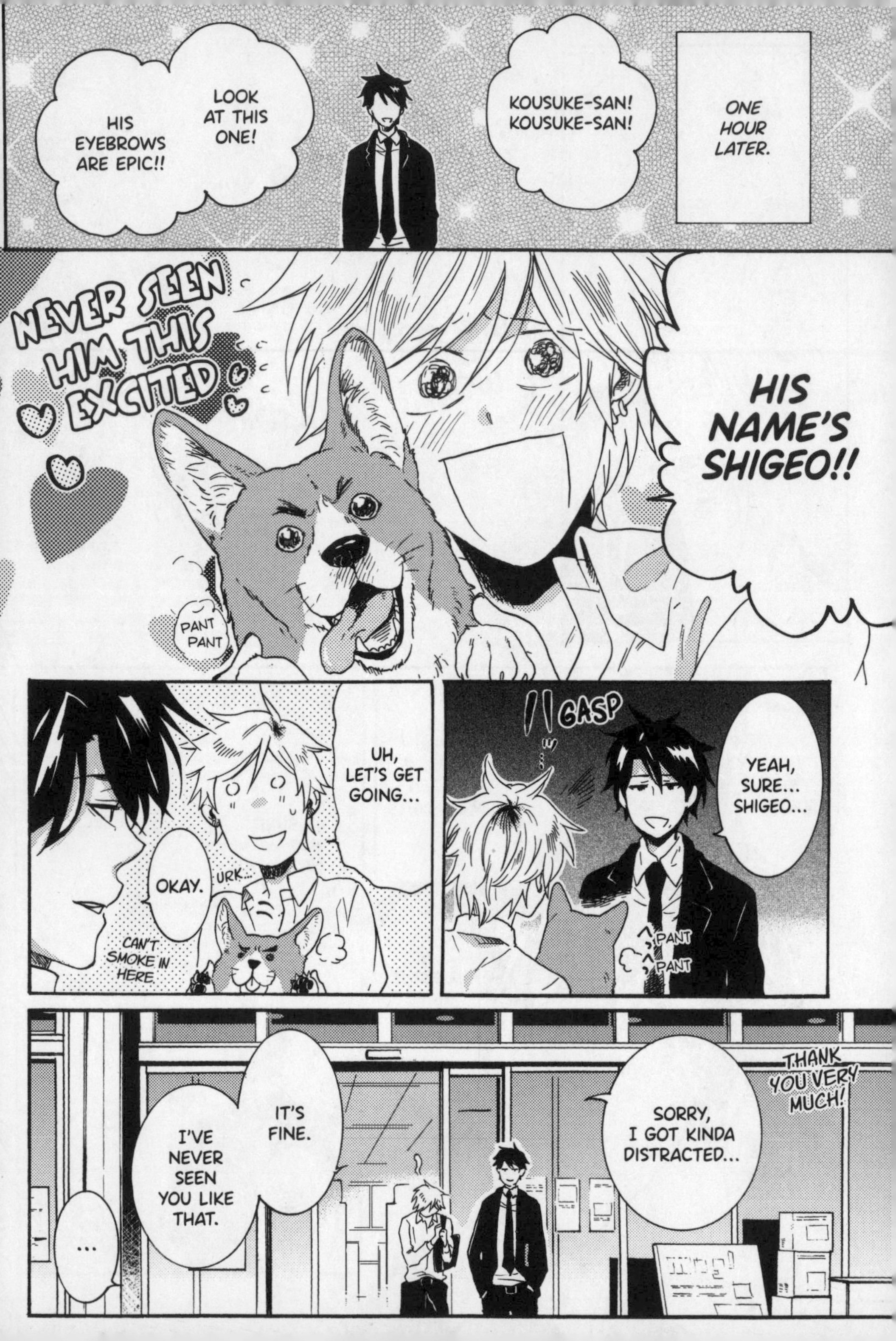
ONE HOUR LATER.
KOUSUKE-SAN! KOUSUKE-SAN!
LOOK AT THIS ONE!
HIS EYEBROWS ARE EPIC!!
HIS NAME'S SHIGEO!!
NEVER SEEN HIM THIS EXCITED
PANT PANT
GASP
YEAH, SURE... SHIGEO...
PANT
PANT
UH, LET'S GET GOING...
URK...
OKAY.
CAN'T SMOKE IN HERE.
THANK YOU VERY MUCH!
SORRY, I GOT KINDA DISTRACTED...
IT'S FINE.
I'VE NEVER SEEN YOU LIKE THAT.
...

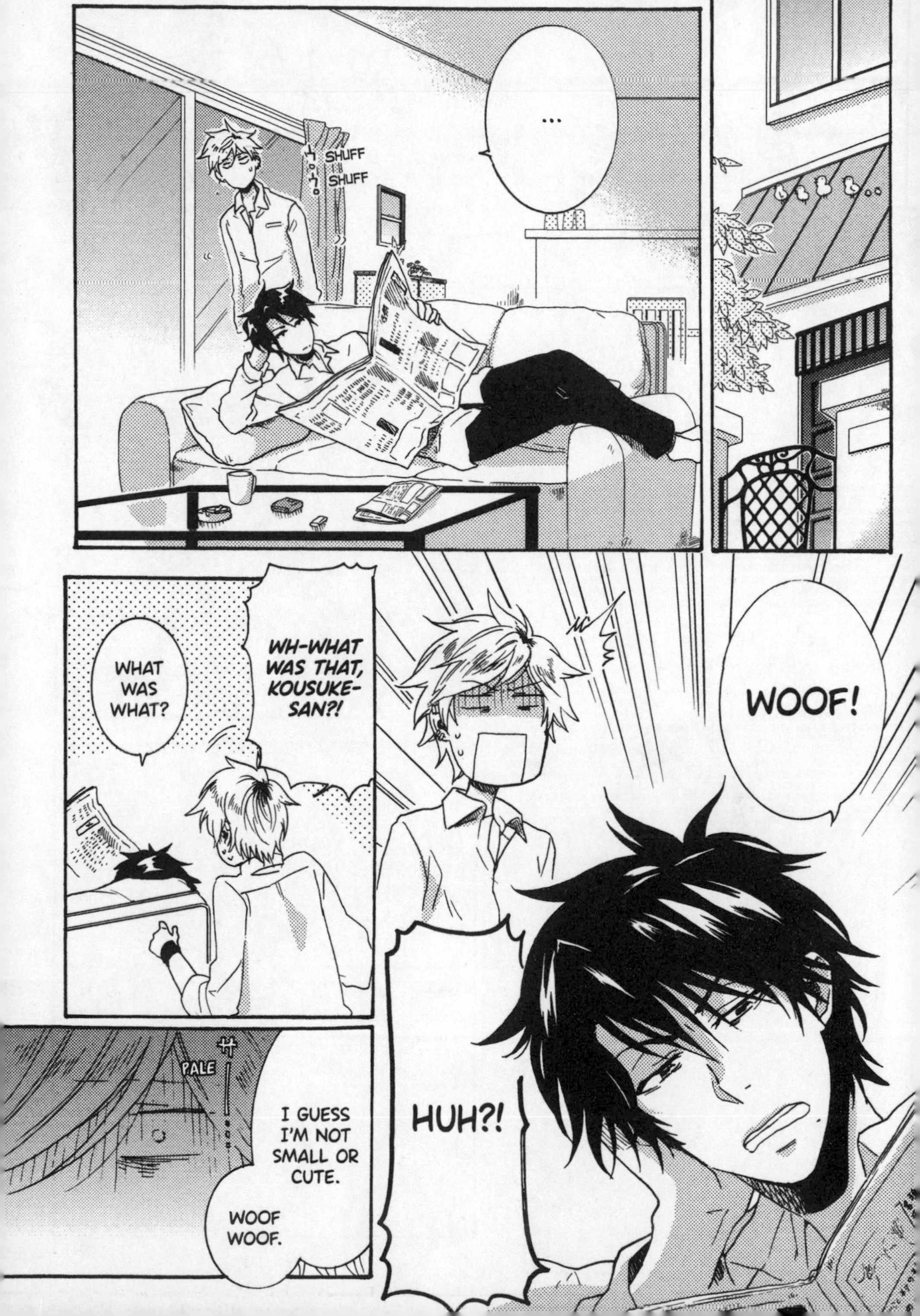
...
SHUFF
SHUFF
WOOF!
HUH?!
WH-WHAT WAS THAT, KOUSUKE-SAN?!
WHAT WAS WHAT?
PALE
I GUESS I'M NOT SMALL OR CUTE.
WOOF WOOF.

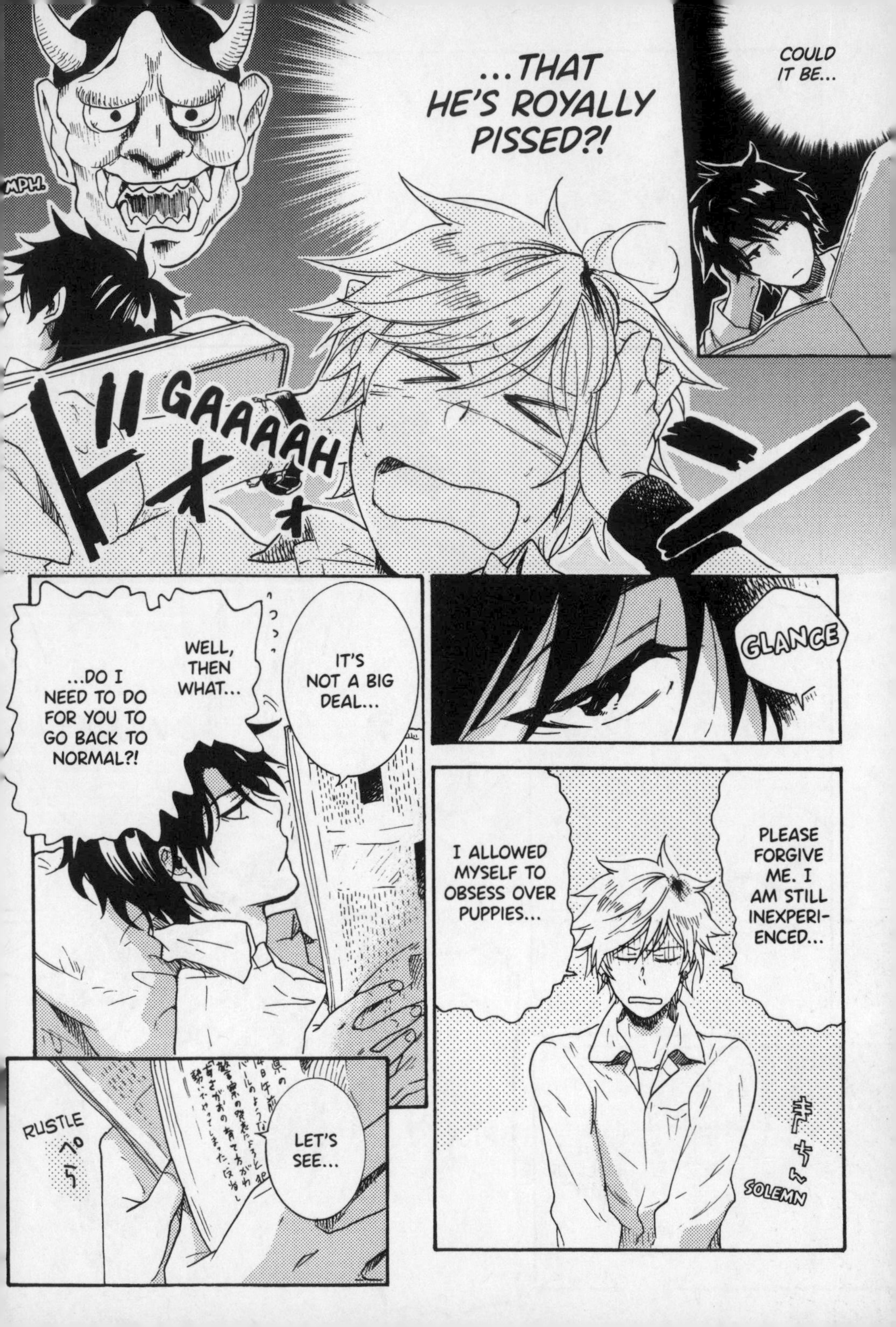
COULD IT BE...
...THAT HE'S ROYALLY PISSED?!
MPH.
GAAAAAH
GLANCE
IT'S NOT A BIG DEAL...
WELL, THEN WHAT...
...DO I NEED TO DO FOR YOU TO GO BACK TO NORMAL?!
PLEASE FORGIVE ME. I AM STILL INEXPERI-ENCED...
I ALLOWED MYSELF TO OBSESS OVER PUPPIES...
SOLEMN
LET'S SEE...
RUSTLE

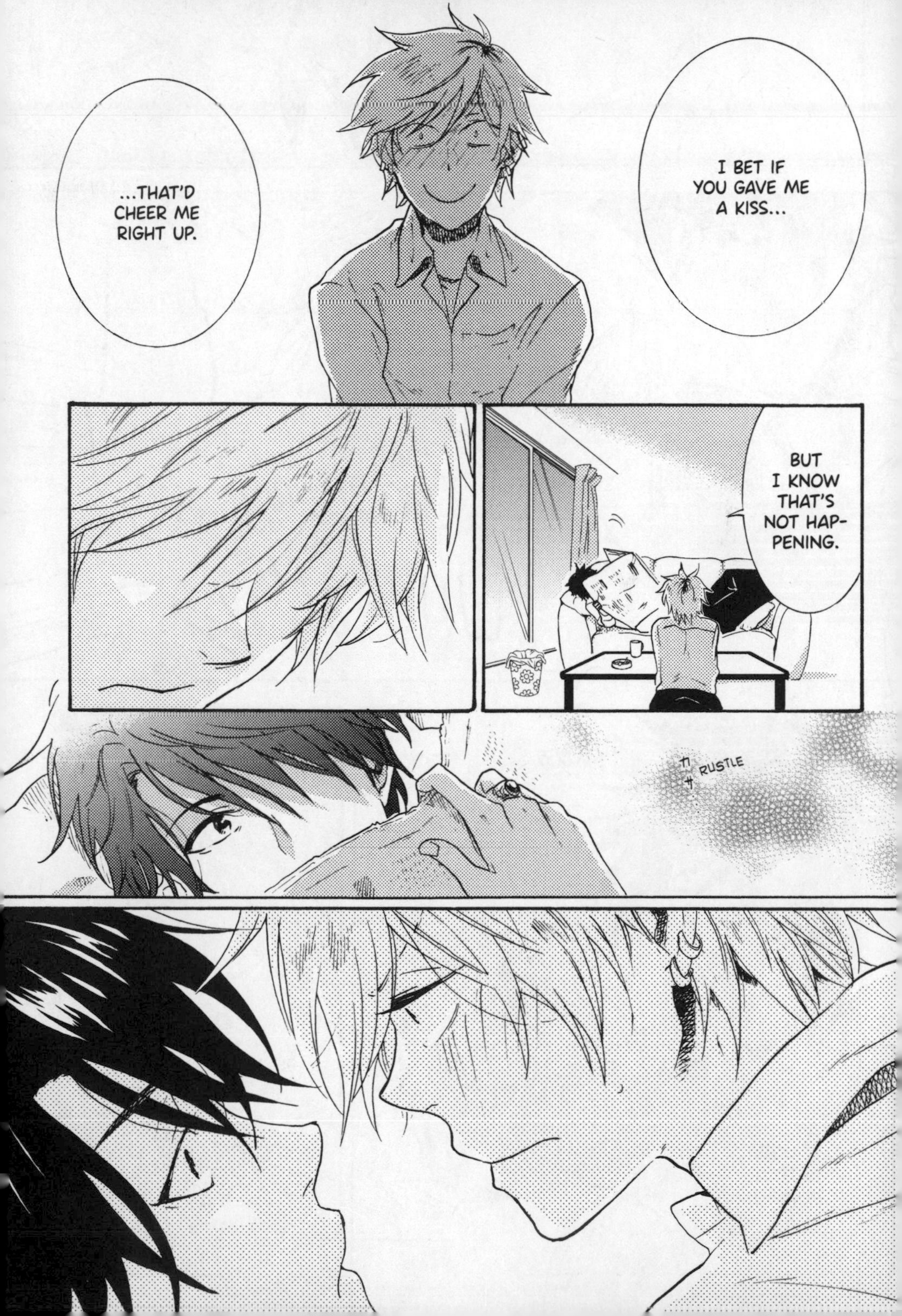
I BET IF YOU GAVE ME A KISS...
...THAT'D CHEER ME RIGHT UP.
BUT I KNOW THAT'S NOT HAP-PENING.
RUSTLE

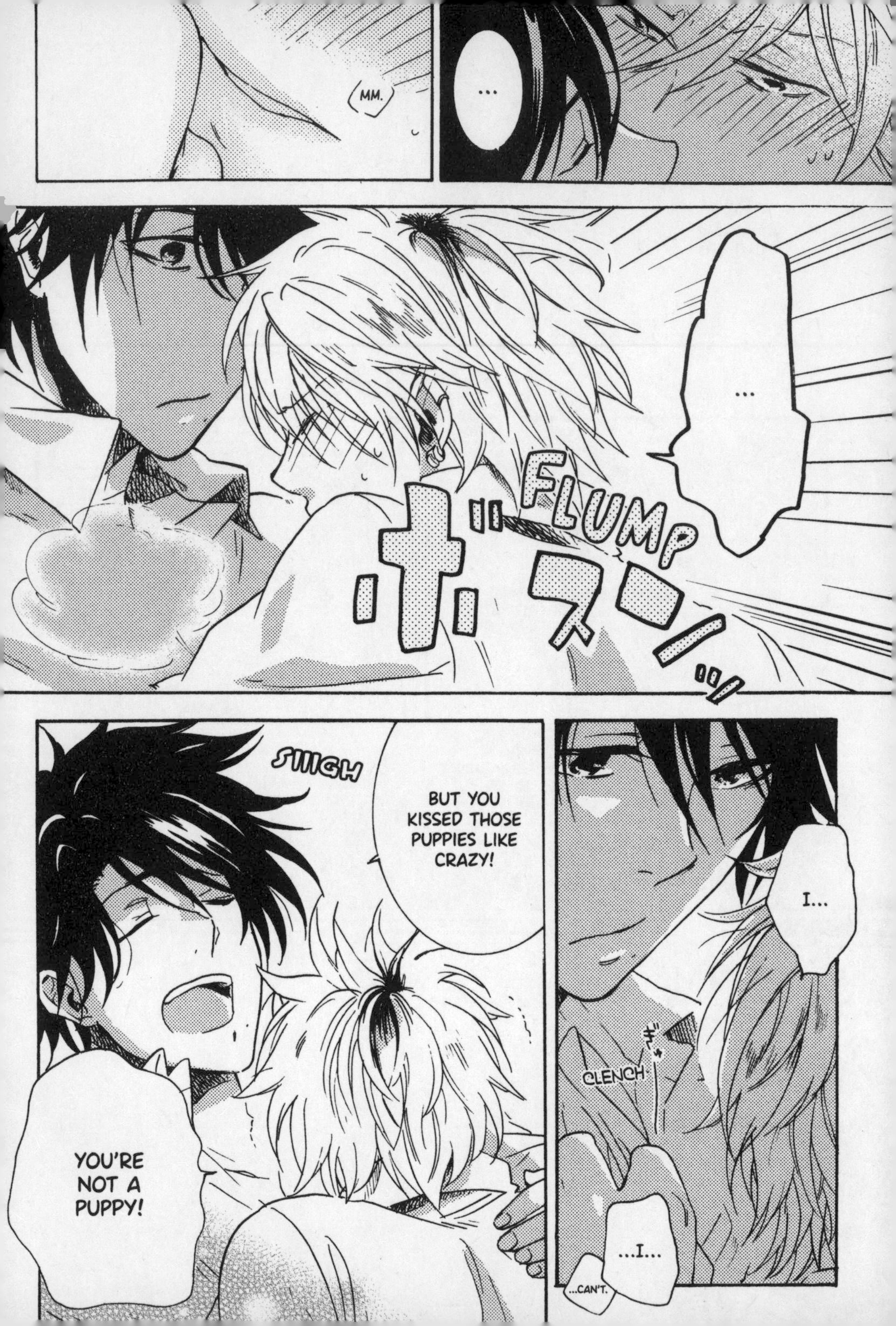
...
MM.
...
FLUMP
ボスン
I...
CLENCH
...I...
...CAN'T.
SIIIGH
BUT YOU KISSED THOSE PUPPIES LIKE CRAZY!
YOU'RE NOT A PUPPY!

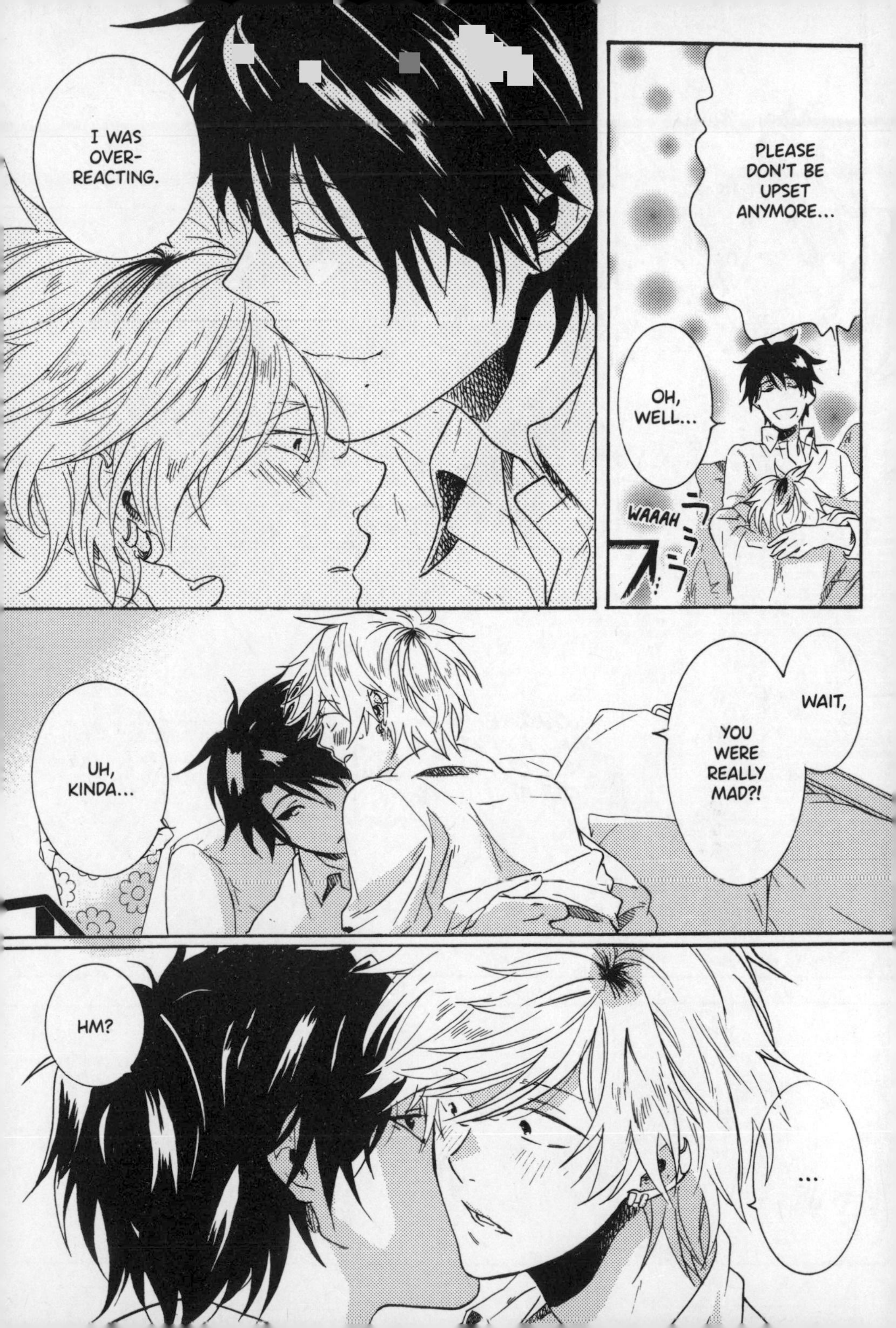
PLEASE DON'T BE UPSET ANYMORE...
OH, WELL...
WAAAH
I WAS OVER-REACTING.
WAIT, YOU WERE REALLY MAD?!
UH, KINDA...
HM?
...

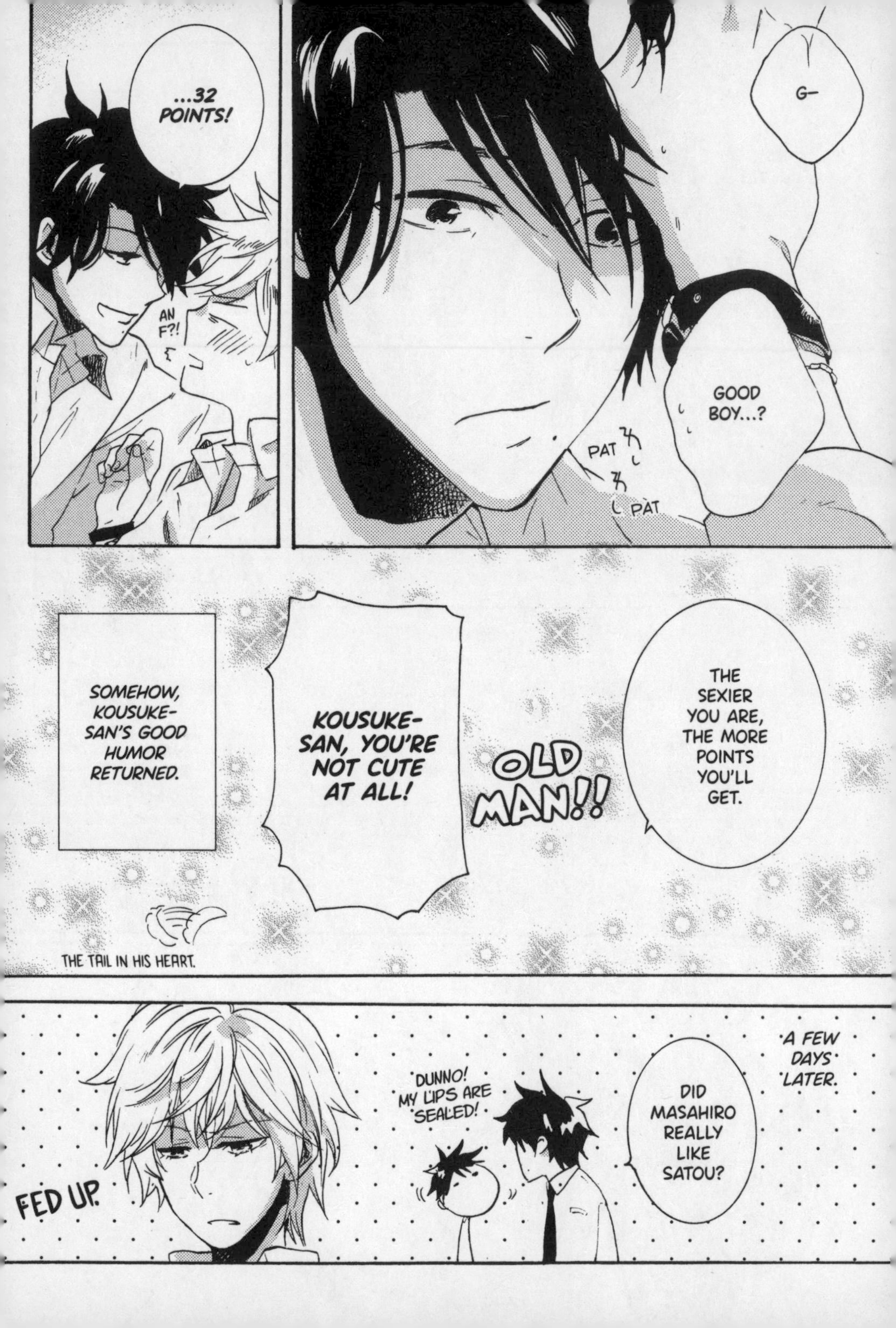
G—
GOOD BOY...?
PAT
PAT
...32 POINTS!
AN F?!
THE SEXIER YOU ARE, THE MORE POINTS YOU'LL GET.
OLD MAN!!
KOUSUKE-SAN, YOU'RE NOT CUTE AT ALL!
SOMEHOW, KOUSUKE-SAN'S GOOD HUMOR RETURNED.
THE TAIL IN HIS HEART.
A FEW DAYS LATER.
DID MASAHIRO REALLY LIKE SATOU?
DUNNO! MY LIPS ARE SEALED!
FED UP.

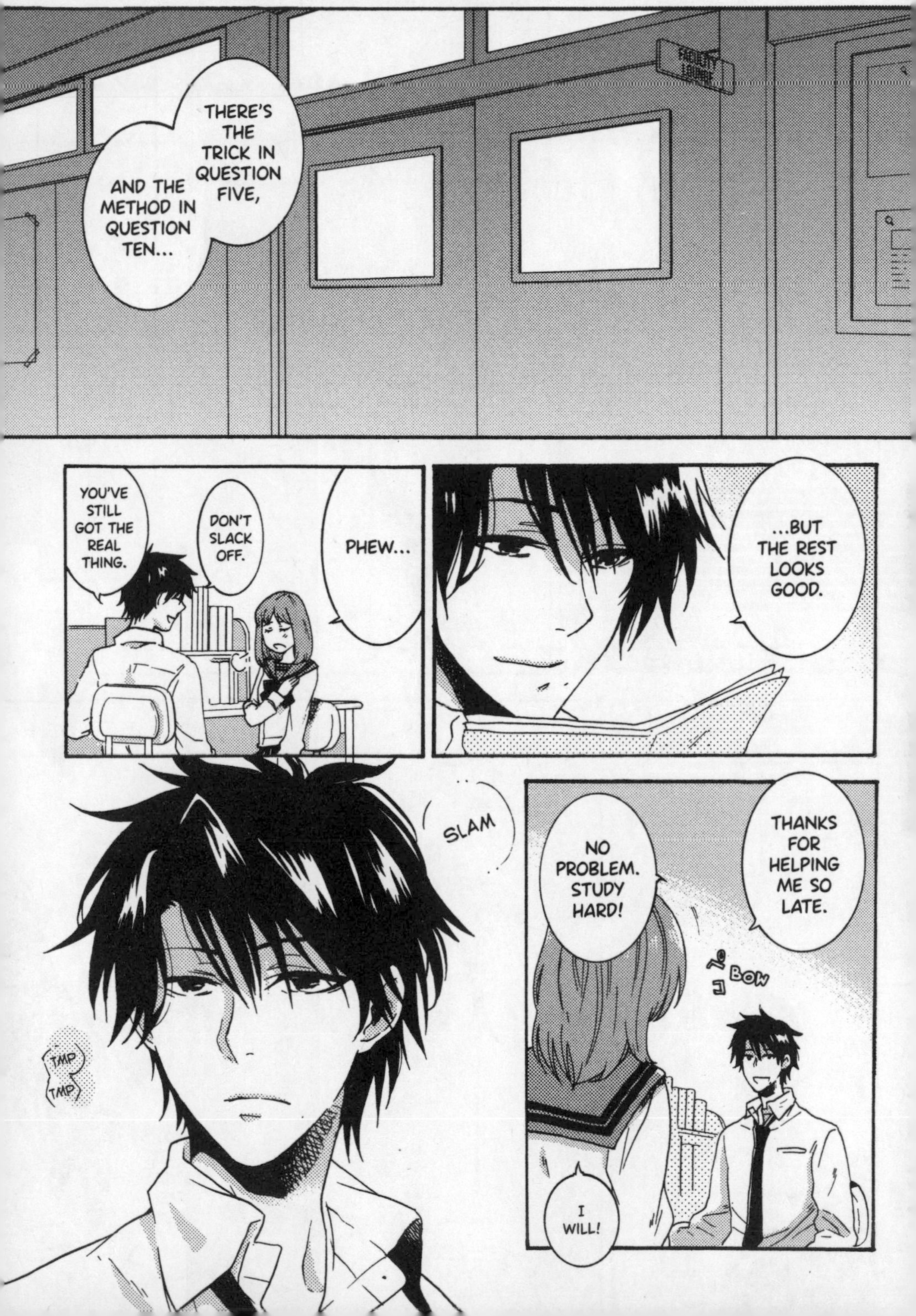
FACULTY LOUNGE
THERE'S THE TRICK IN QUESTION FIVE,
AND THE METHOD IN QUESTION TEN...
...BUT THE REST LOOKS GOOD.
PHEW...
DON'T SLACK OFF.
YOU'VE STILL GOT THE REAL THING.
THANKS FOR HELPING ME SO LATE.
BOW
NO PROBLEM. STUDY HARD!
I WILL!
SLAM
TMP
TMP

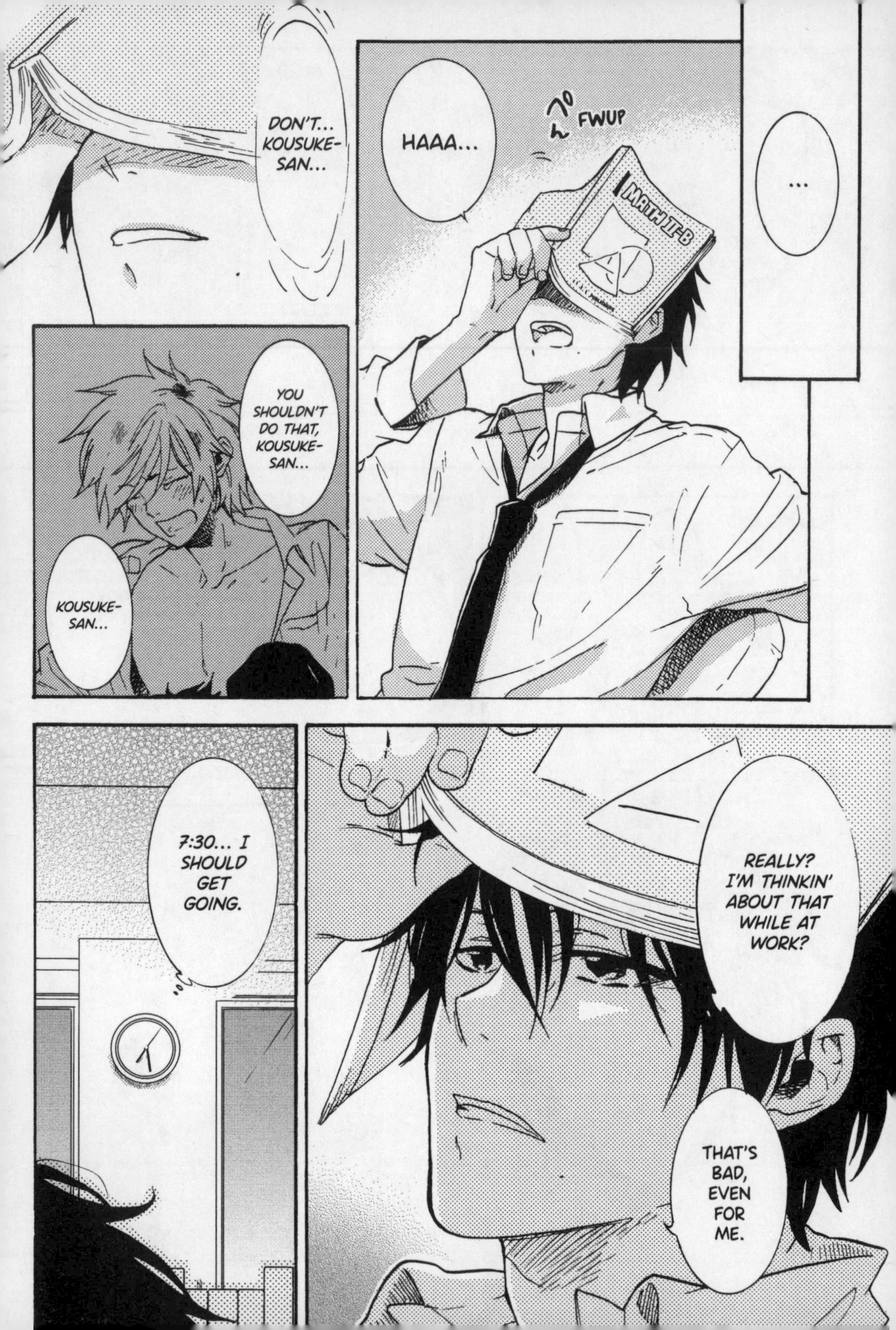
...
HAAA...
FWUP
MATH II-B
DON'T... KOUSUKE-SAN...
YOU SHOULDN'T DO THAT, KOUSUKE-SAN...
KOUSUKE-SAN...
REALLY? I'M THINKIN' ABOUT THAT WHILE AT WORK?
THAT'S BAD, EVEN FOR ME.
7:30... I SHOULD GET GOING.

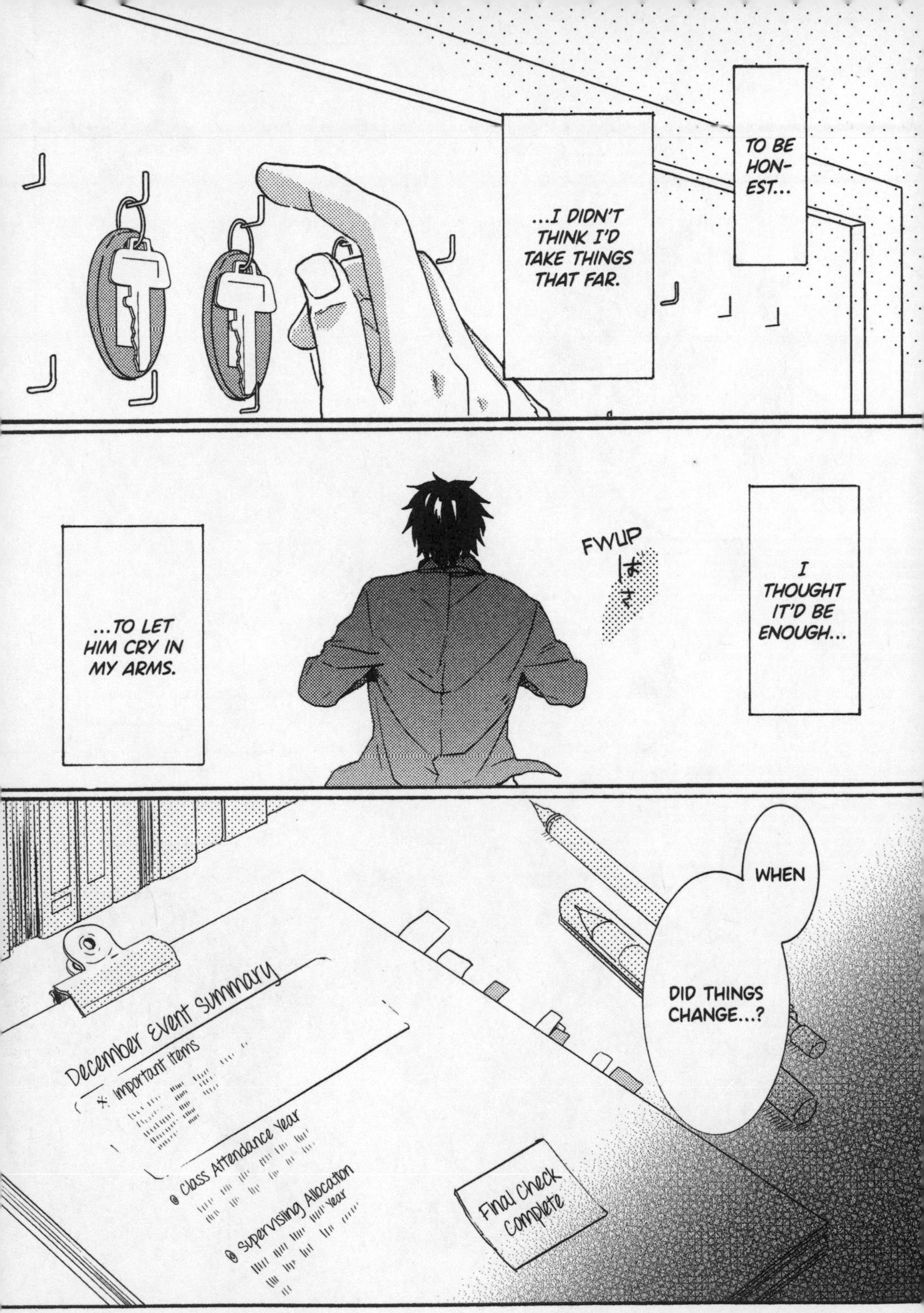
TO BE HONEST...
...I DIDN'T THINK I'D TAKE THINGS THAT FAR.
I THOUGHT IT'D BE ENOUGH...
FWUP
...TO LET HIM CRY IN MY ARMS.
WHEN
DID THINGS CHANGE...?
Final Check Complete
December Event Summary
Important Items
Class Attendance Year
Supervising Allocation Year

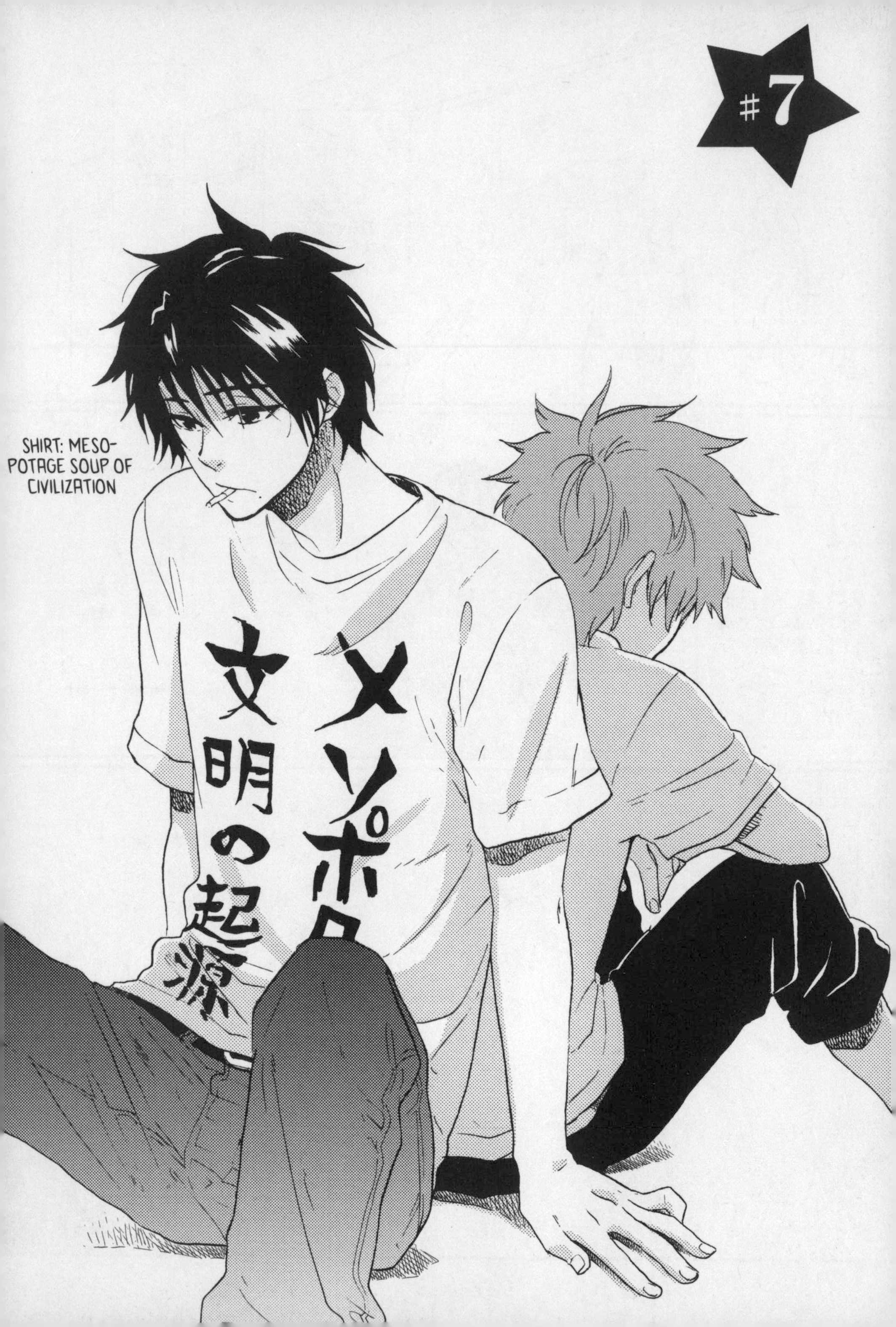
#7
SHIRT: MESO-POTAGE SOUP OF CIVILIZATION
メソポタ
文明の起源

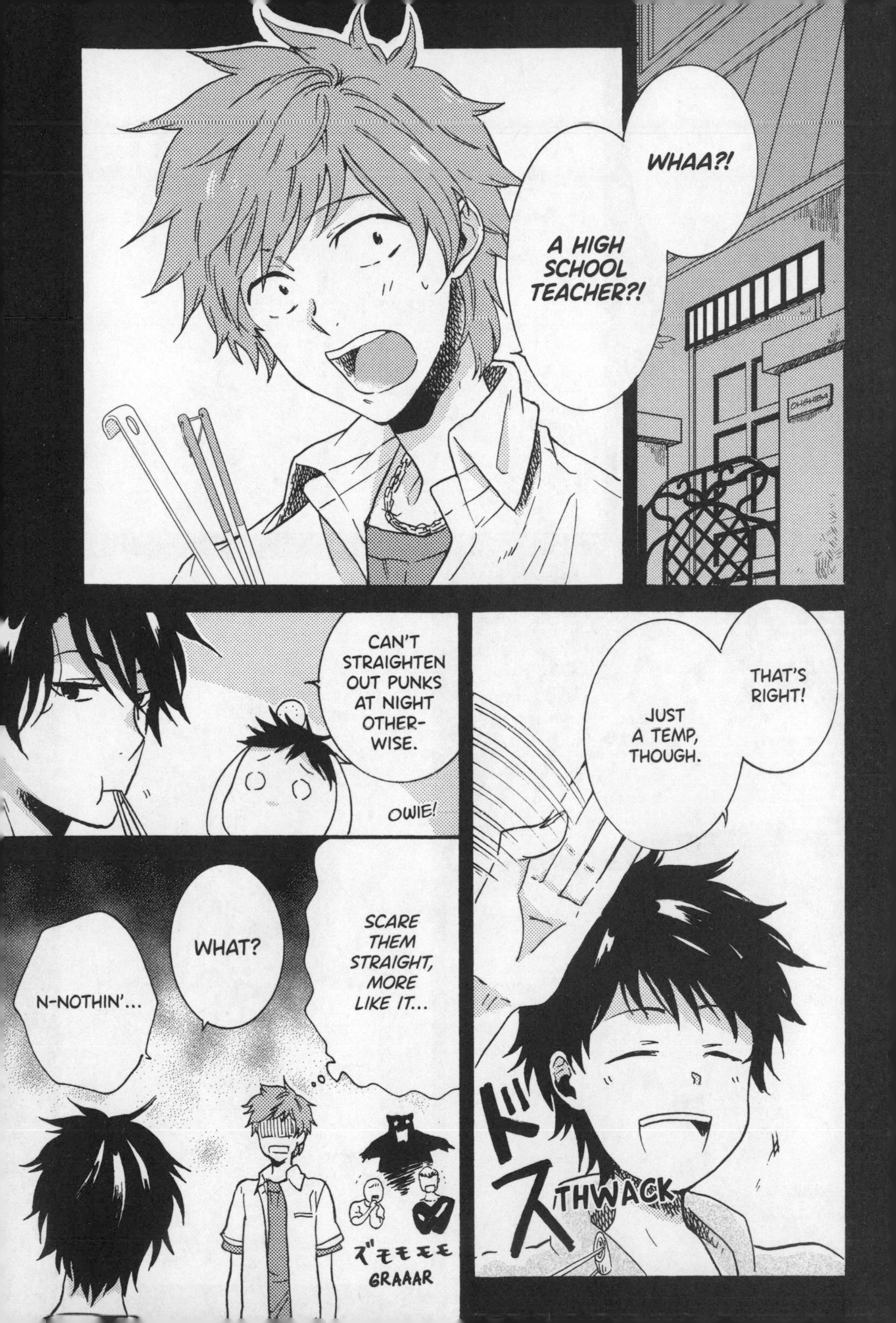
WHAA?!
A HIGH SCHOOL TEACHER?!
THAT'S RIGHT!
JUST A TEMP, THOUGH.
ドス
THWACK
CAN'T STRAIGHTEN OUT PUNKS AT NIGHT OTHER-WISE.
OWIE!
SCARE THEM STRAIGHT, MORE LIKE IT...
WHAT?
N-NOTHIN'...
ズモモモモ
GRAAAR

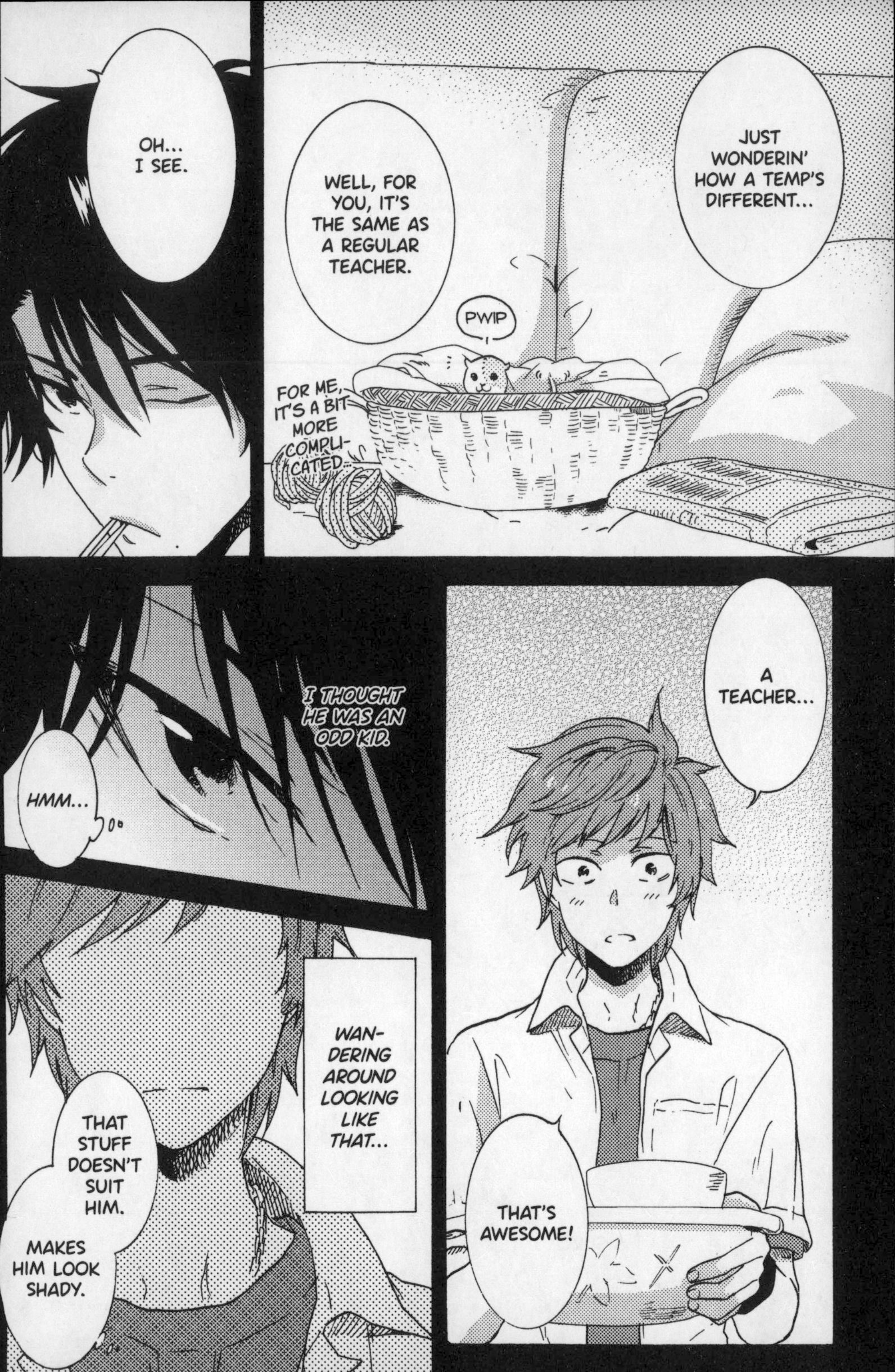
JUST WONDERIN' HOW A TEMP'S DIFFERENT...
WELL, FOR YOU, IT'S THE SAME AS A REGULAR TEACHER.
PWIP
FOR ME, IT'S A BIT MORE COMPLI-CATED...
OH... I SEE.
A TEACHER...
THAT'S AWESOME!
I THOUGHT HE WAS AN ODD KID.
HMM...
WAN-DERING AROUND LOOKING LIKE THAT...
THAT STUFF DOESN'T SUIT HIM.
MAKES HIM LOOK SHADY.

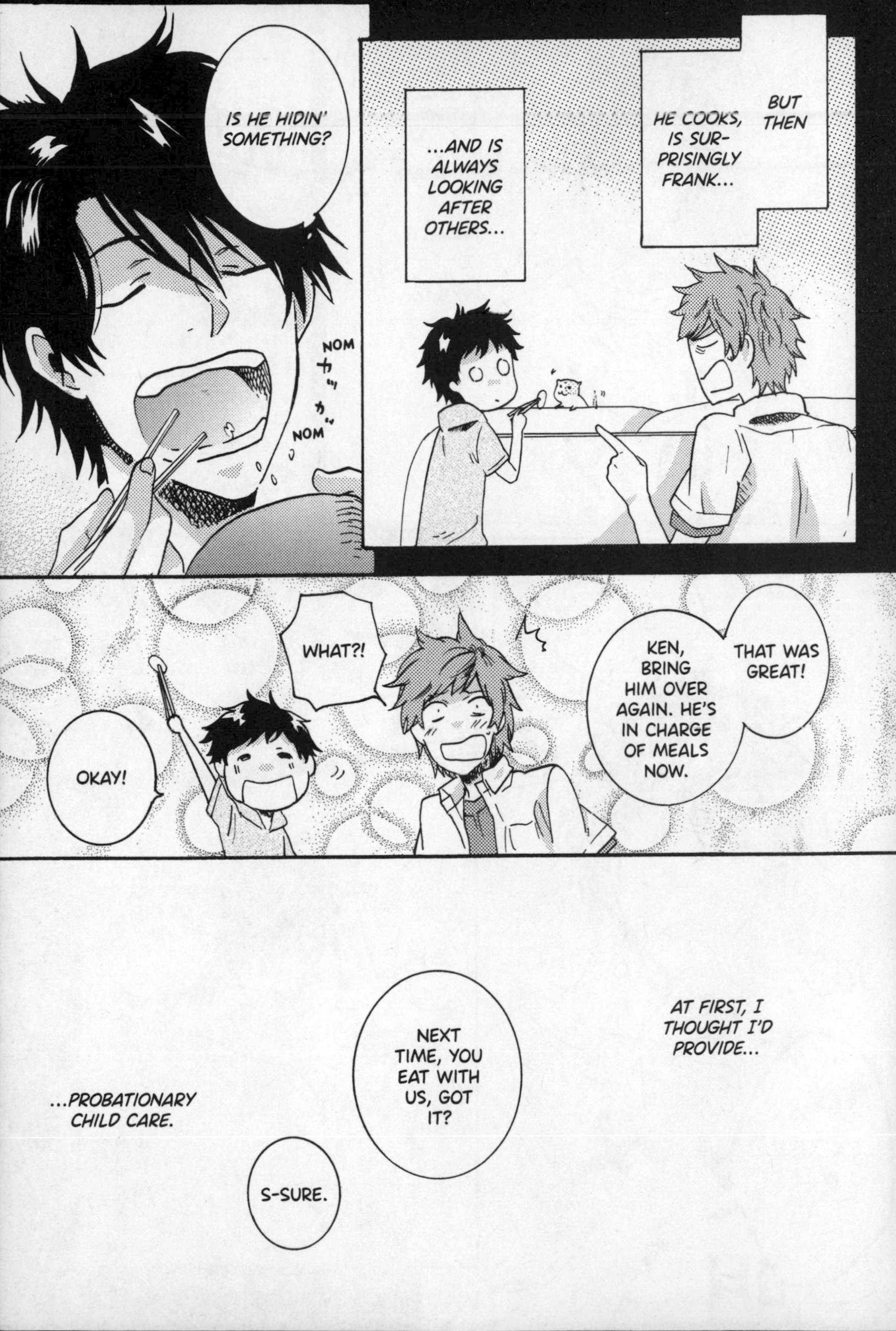
BUT THEN
HE COOKS, IS SUR-PRISINGLY FRANK...
...AND IS ALWAYS LOOKING AFTER OTHERS...
IS HE HIDIN' SOMETHING?
NOM
NOM
THAT WAS GREAT!
KEN, BRING HIM OVER AGAIN. HE'S IN CHARGE OF MEALS NOW.
WHAT?!
OKAY!
AT FIRST, I THOUGHT I'D PROVIDE...
NEXT TIME, YOU EAT WITH US, GOT IT?
S-SURE.
...PROBATIONARY CHILD CARE.

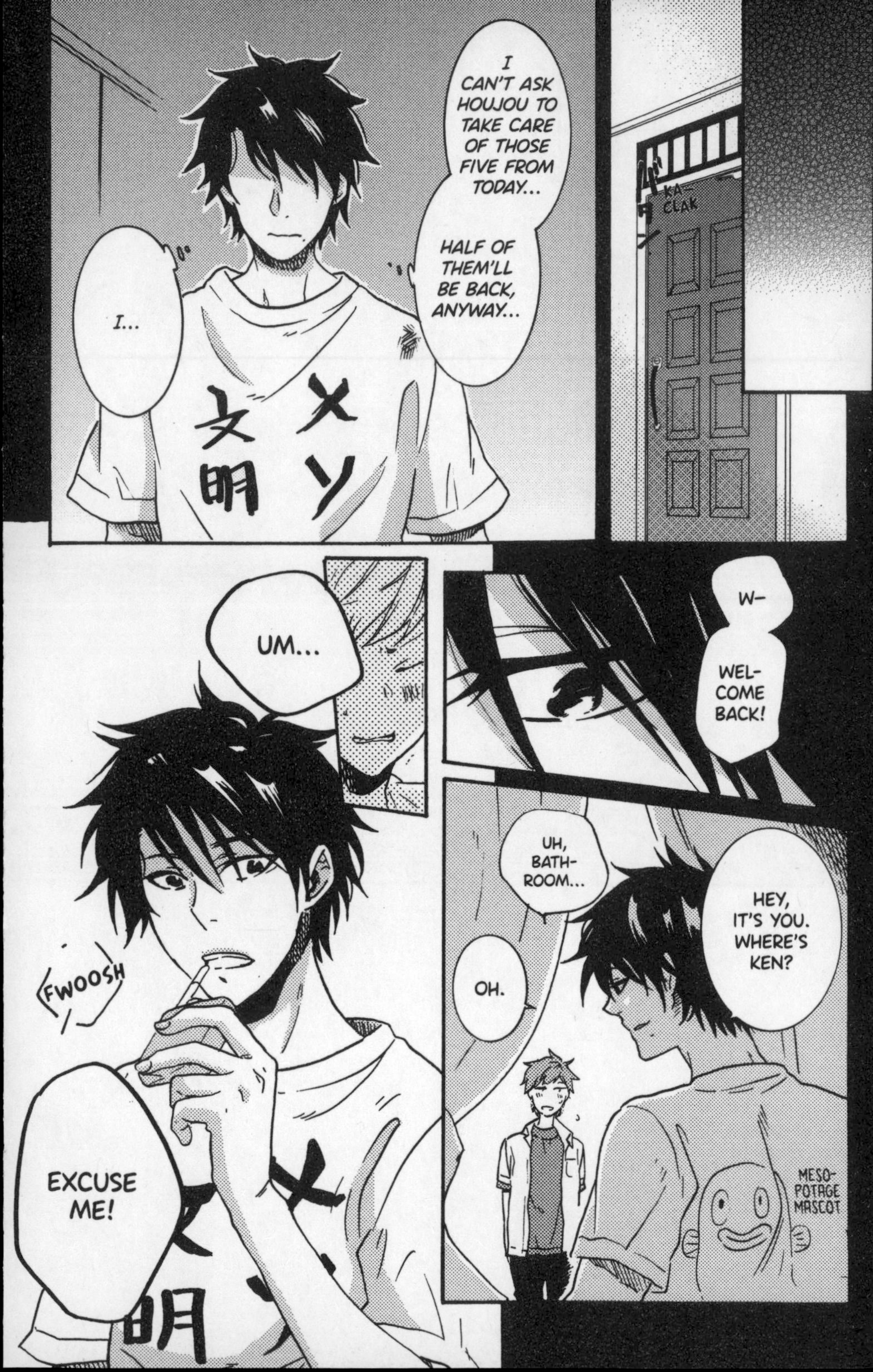
KA-CLAK
I CAN'T ASK HOUJOU TO TAKE CARE OF THOSE FIVE FROM TODAY...
HALF OF THEM'LL BE BACK, ANYWAY...
I...
メソ文明
W- WEL-COME BACK!
HEY, IT'S YOU. WHERE'S KEN?
UH, BATH-ROOM...
OH.
MESO-POTAGE MASCOT
UM...
FWOOSH
EXCUSE ME!

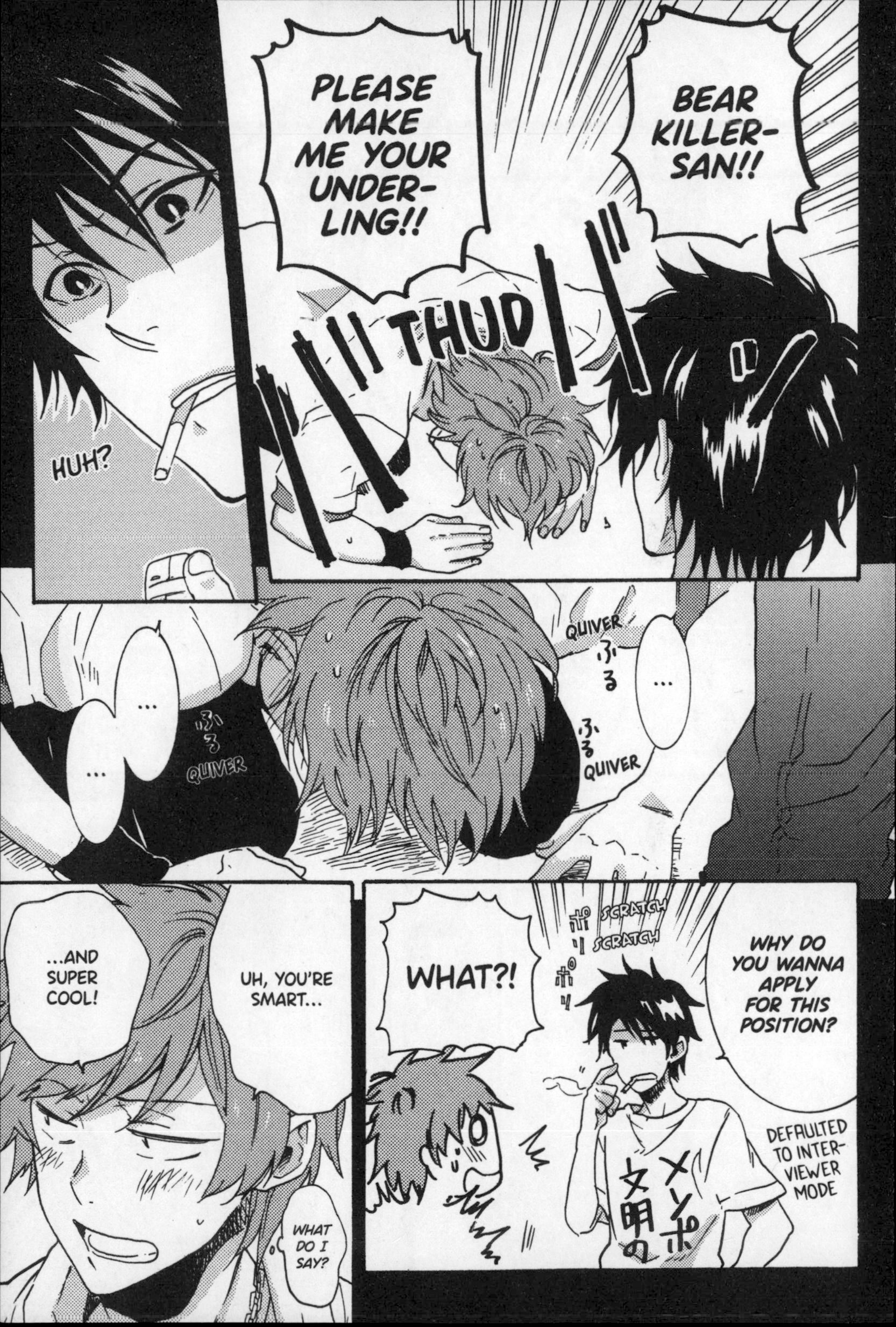

BEAR KILLER-SAN!!
PLEASE MAKE ME YOUR UNDERLING!!
THUD
HUH?
QUIVER
ふる
...
ふる
QUIVER
...
ふる
QUIVER
...
WHY DO YOU WANNA APPLY FOR THIS POSITION?
ポリ SCRATCH
ポリ SCRATCH
WHAT?!
メンポ
文明の
DEFAULTED TO INTERVIEWER MODE
UH, YOU'RE SMART...
...AND SUPER COOL!
WHAT DO I SAY?

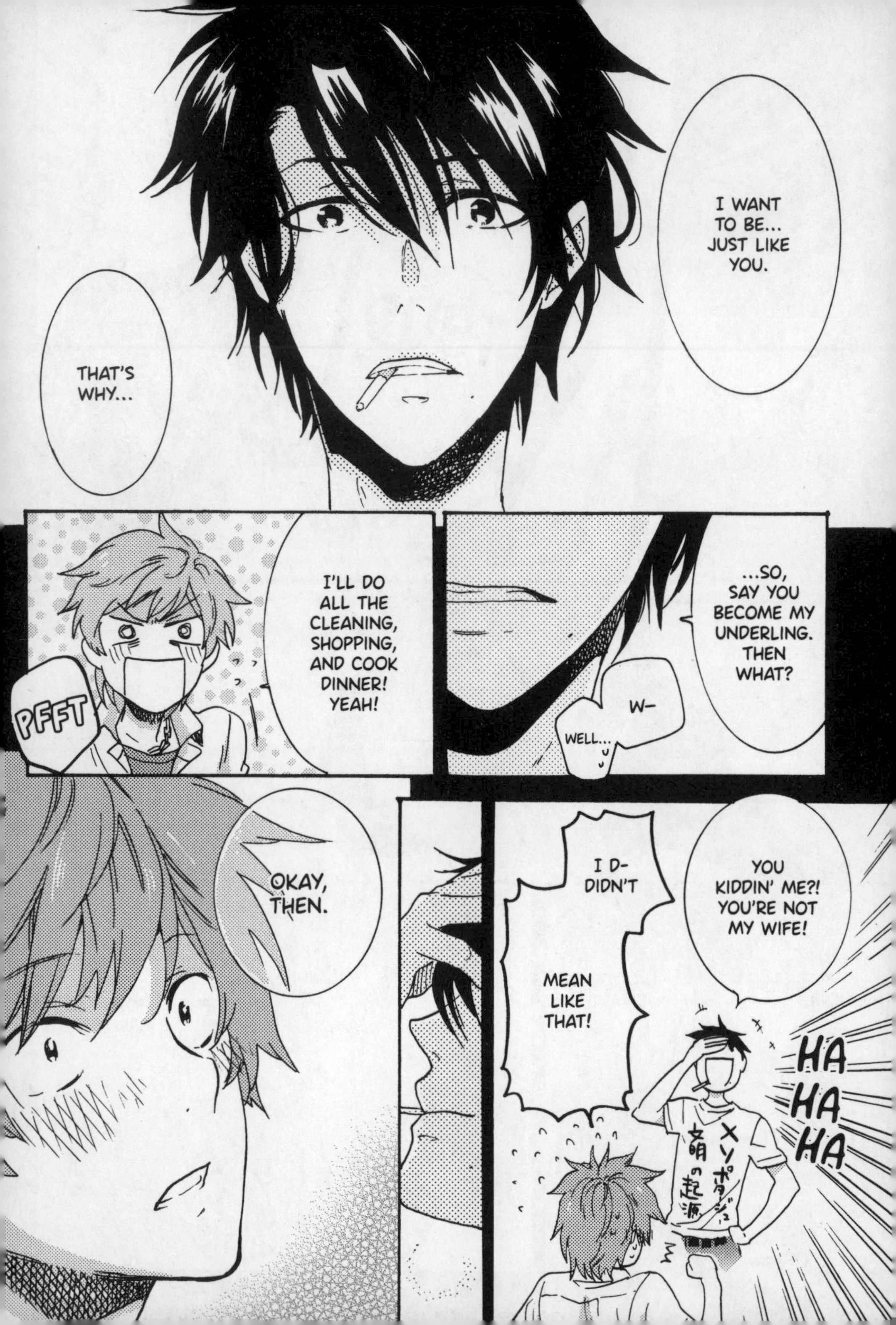
I WANT TO BE... JUST LIKE YOU.
THAT'S WHY...
...SO, SAY YOU BECOME MY UNDERLING. THEN WHAT?
W-
WELL...
I'LL DO ALL THE CLEANING, SHOPPING, AND COOK DINNER! YEAH!
PFFT
YOU KIDDIN' ME?! YOU'RE NOT MY WIFE!
HA HA HA
I D-DIDN'T
MEAN LIKE THAT!
OKAY, THEN.

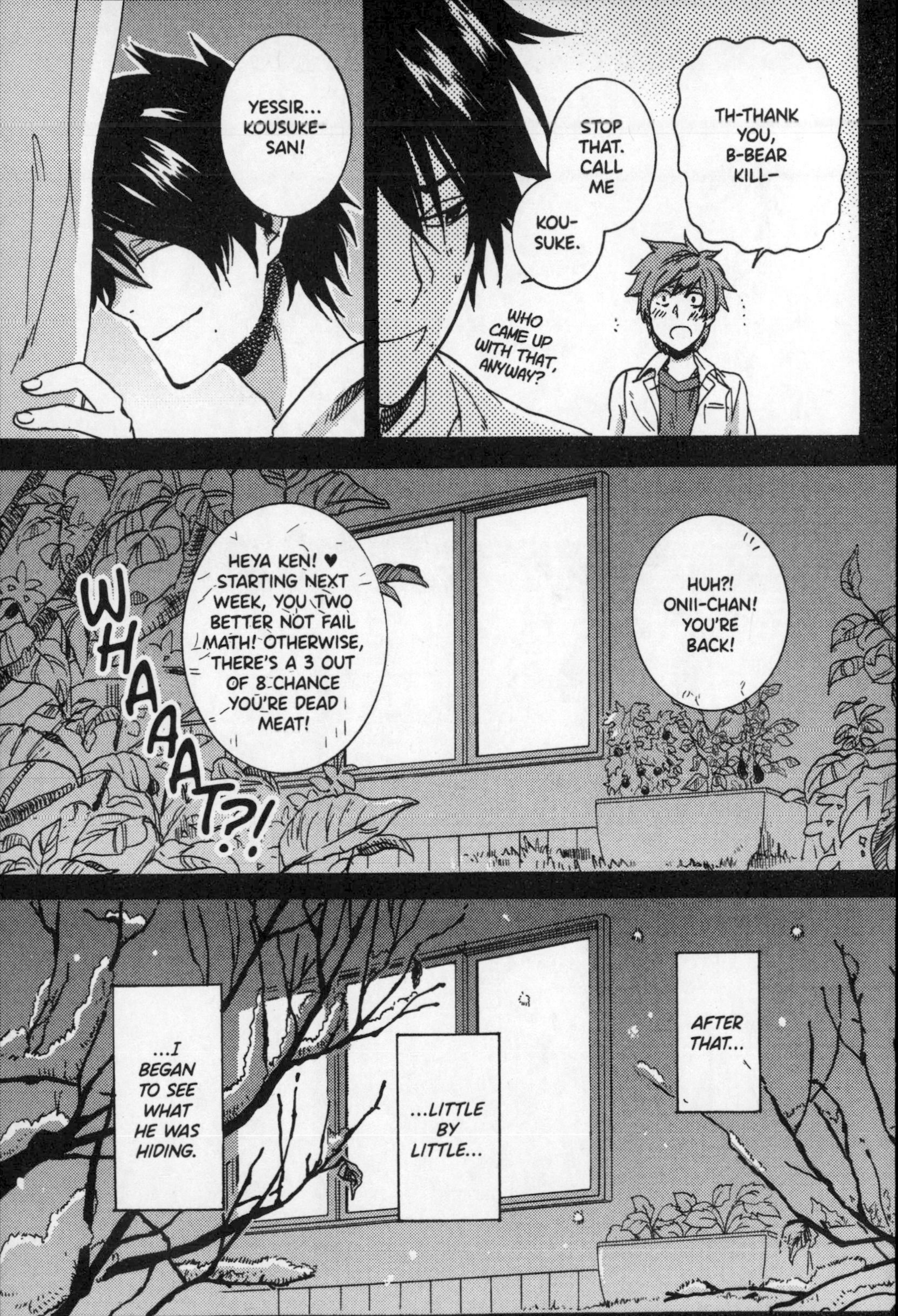
TH-THANK YOU, B-BEAR KILL—
STOP THAT. CALL ME
KOU-SUKE.
WHO CAME UP WITH THAT, ANYWAY?
YESSIR... KOUSUKE-SAN!
HUH?! ONII-CHAN! YOU'RE BACK!
HEYA KEN! ♥ STARTING NEXT WEEK, YOU TWO BETTER NOT FAIL MATH! OTHERWISE, THERE'S A 3 OUT OF 8 CHANCE YOU'RE DEAD MEAT!
WHAAAT?!
AFTER THAT...
...LITTLE BY LITTLE...
...I BEGAN TO SEE WHAT HE WAS HIDING.

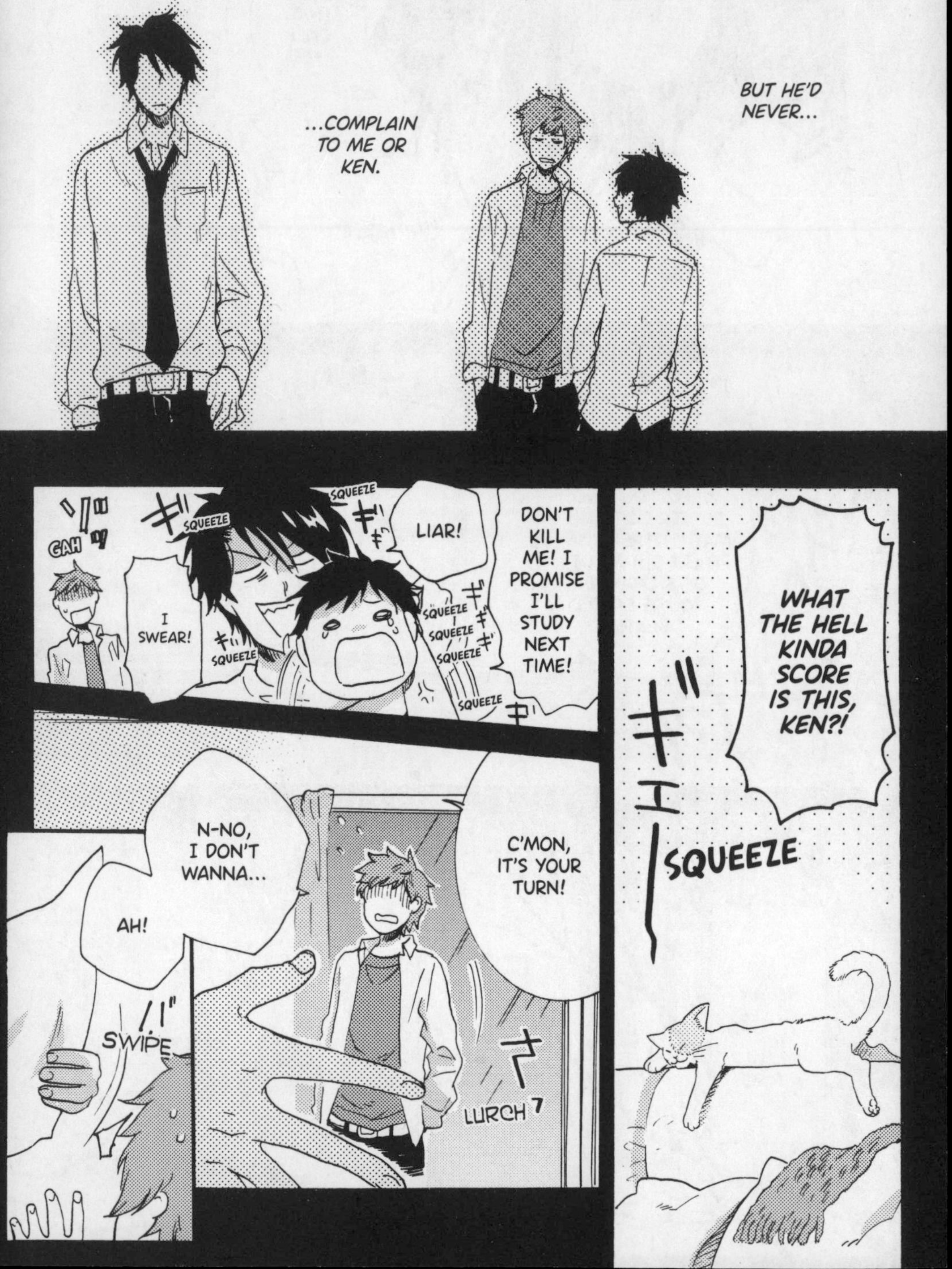
BUT HE'D NEVER...
...COMPLAIN TO ME OR KEN.
WHAT THE HELL KINDA SCORE IS THIS, KEN?!
SQUEEZE
DON'T KILL ME! I PROMISE I'LL STUDY NEXT TIME!
SQUEEZE
SQUEEZE
SQUEEZE
SQUEEZE
LIAR!
SQUEEZE
SQUEEZE
SQUEEZE
I SWEAR!
GAH
C'MON, IT'S YOUR TURN!
LURCH
N-NO, I DON'T WANNA...
AH!
SWIPE

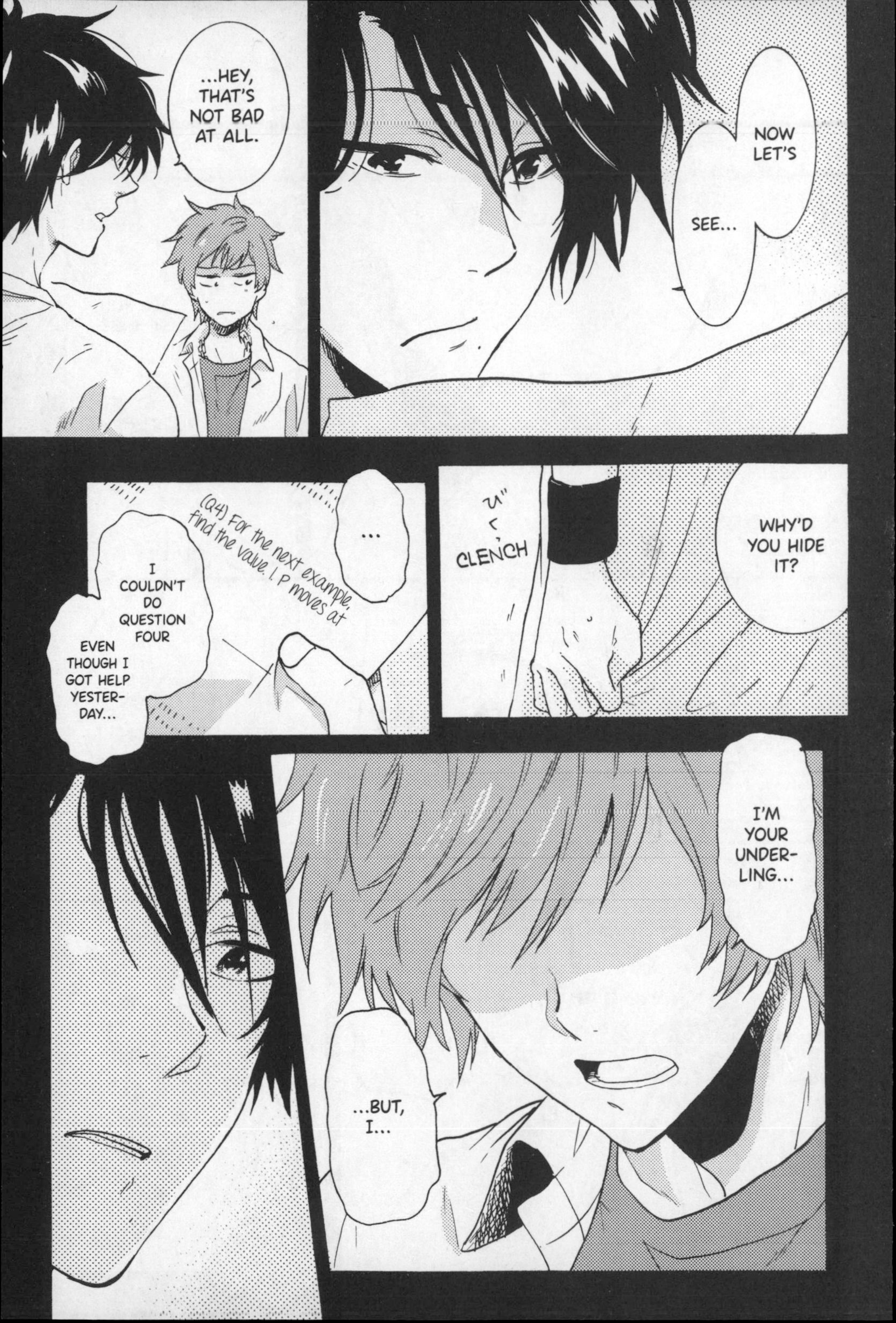
NOW LET'S SEE...
...HEY, THAT'S NOT BAD AT ALL.
WHY'D YOU HIDE IT?
びく
CLENCH
...
(Q4) For the next example, find the value. I, P moves at
I COULDN'T DO QUESTION FOUR
EVEN THOUGH I GOT HELP YESTER-DAY...
I'M YOUR UNDER-LING...
...BUT, I...

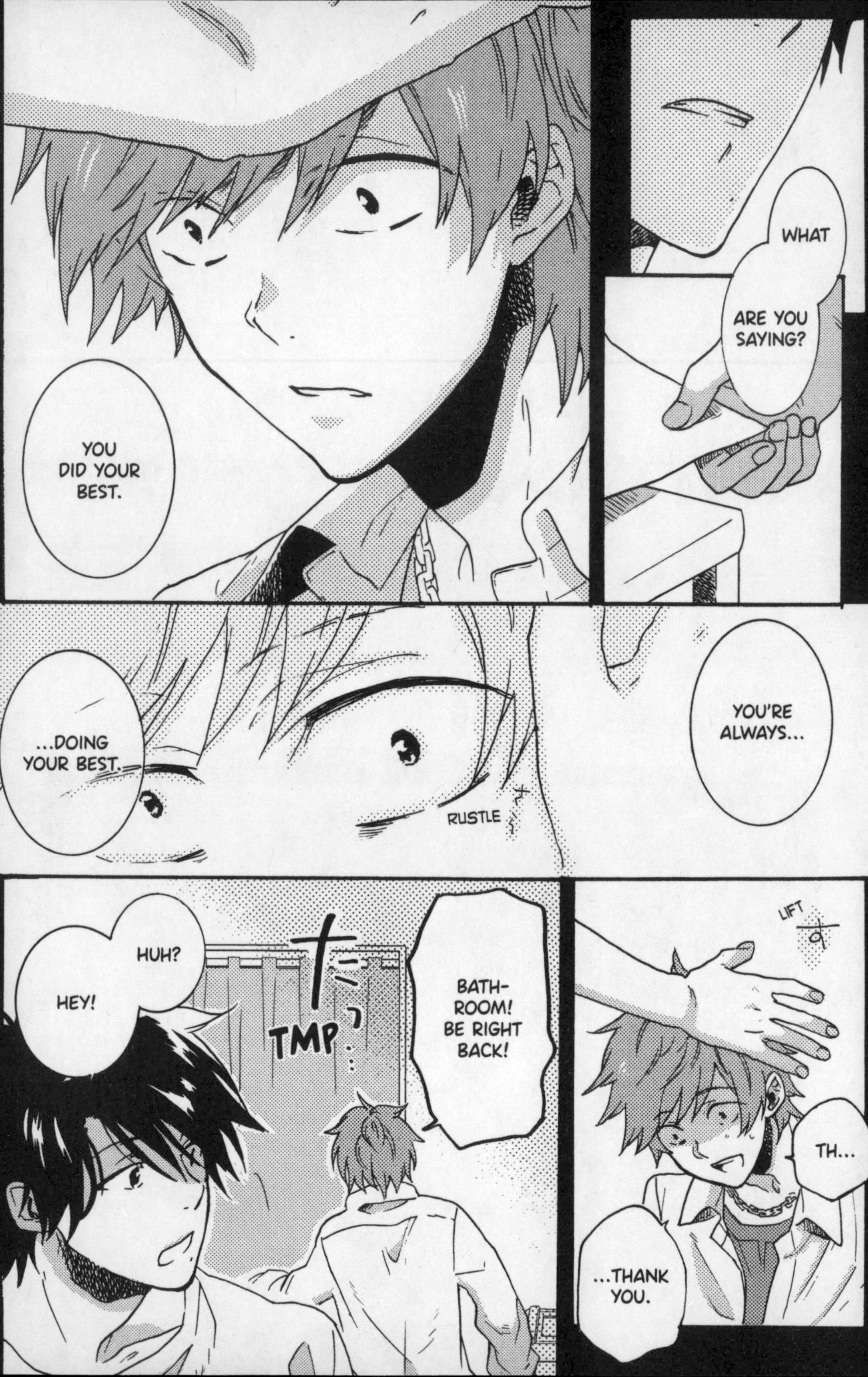
WHAT ARE YOU SAYING?
YOU DID YOUR BEST.
YOU'RE ALWAYS...
RUSTLE
...DOING YOUR BEST.
LIFT
TH...
...THANK YOU.
BATH-ROOM! BE RIGHT BACK!
TMP
HUH?
HEY!

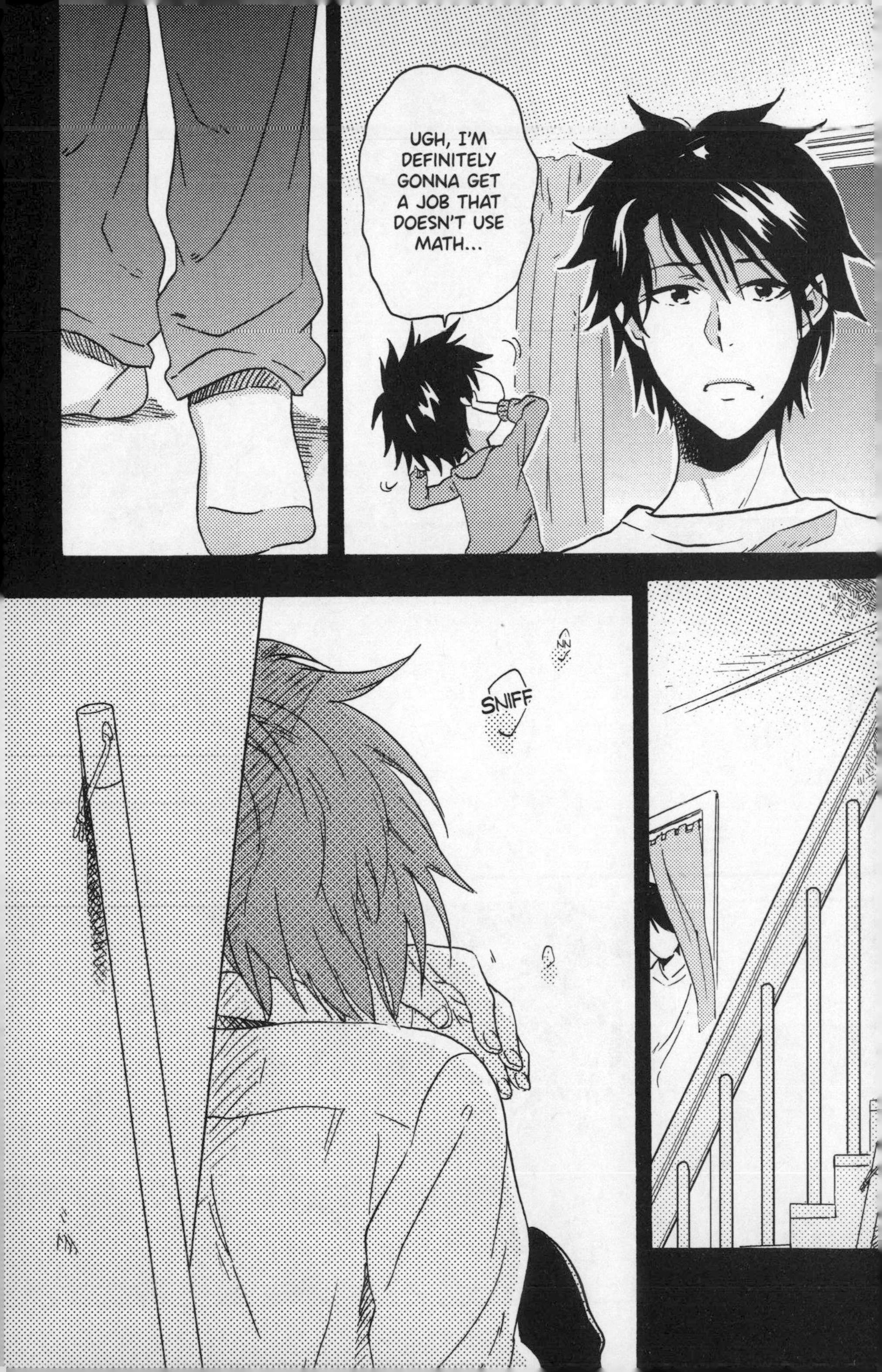
UGH, I'M DEFINITELY GONNA GET A JOB THAT DOESN'T USE MATH...
NN
SNIFF

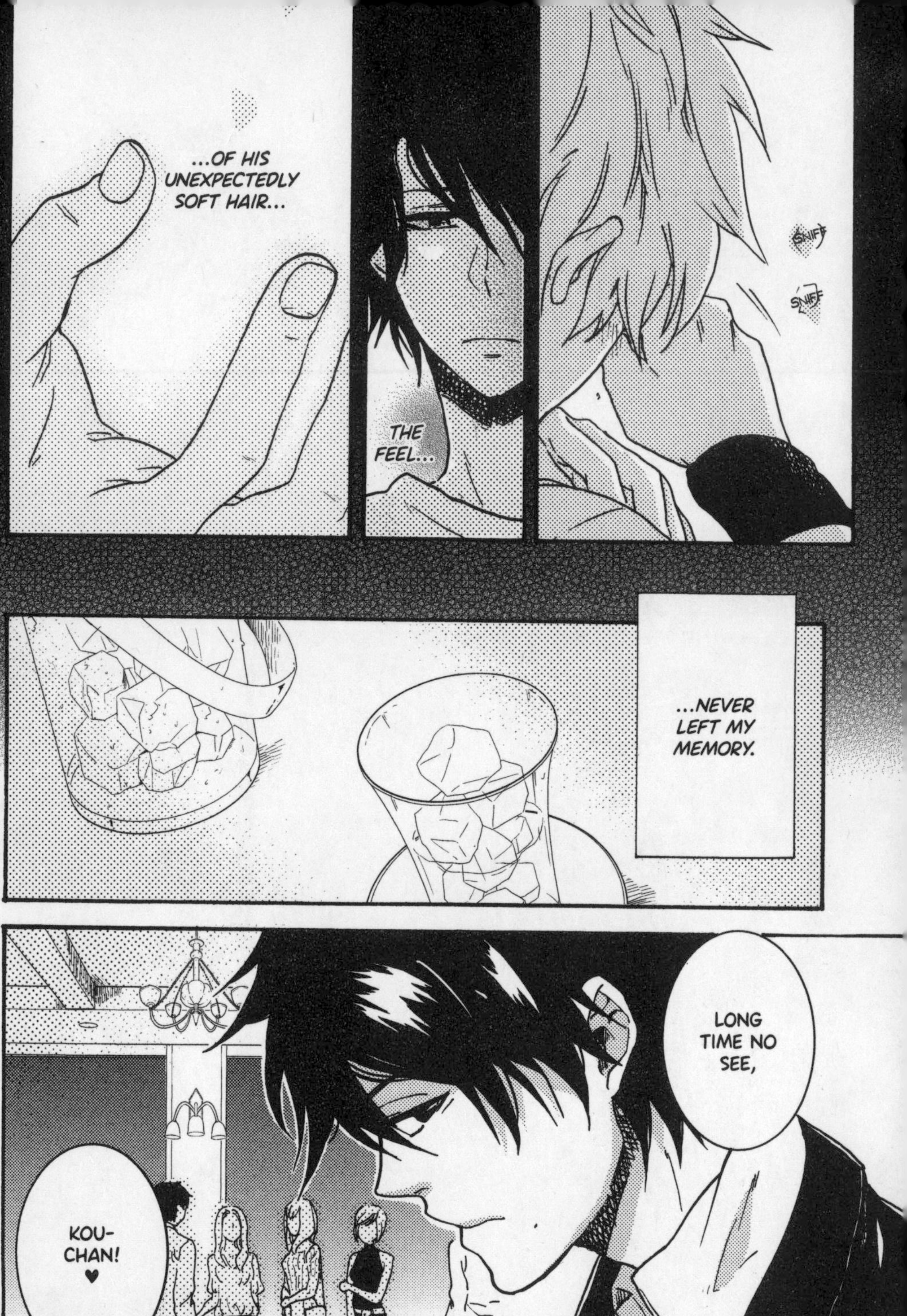
SNIFF
SNIFF
THE FEEL...
...OF HIS UNEXPECTEDLY SOFT HAIR...
...NEVER LEFT MY MEMORY.
LONG TIME NO SEE,
KOU-CHAN! ♥

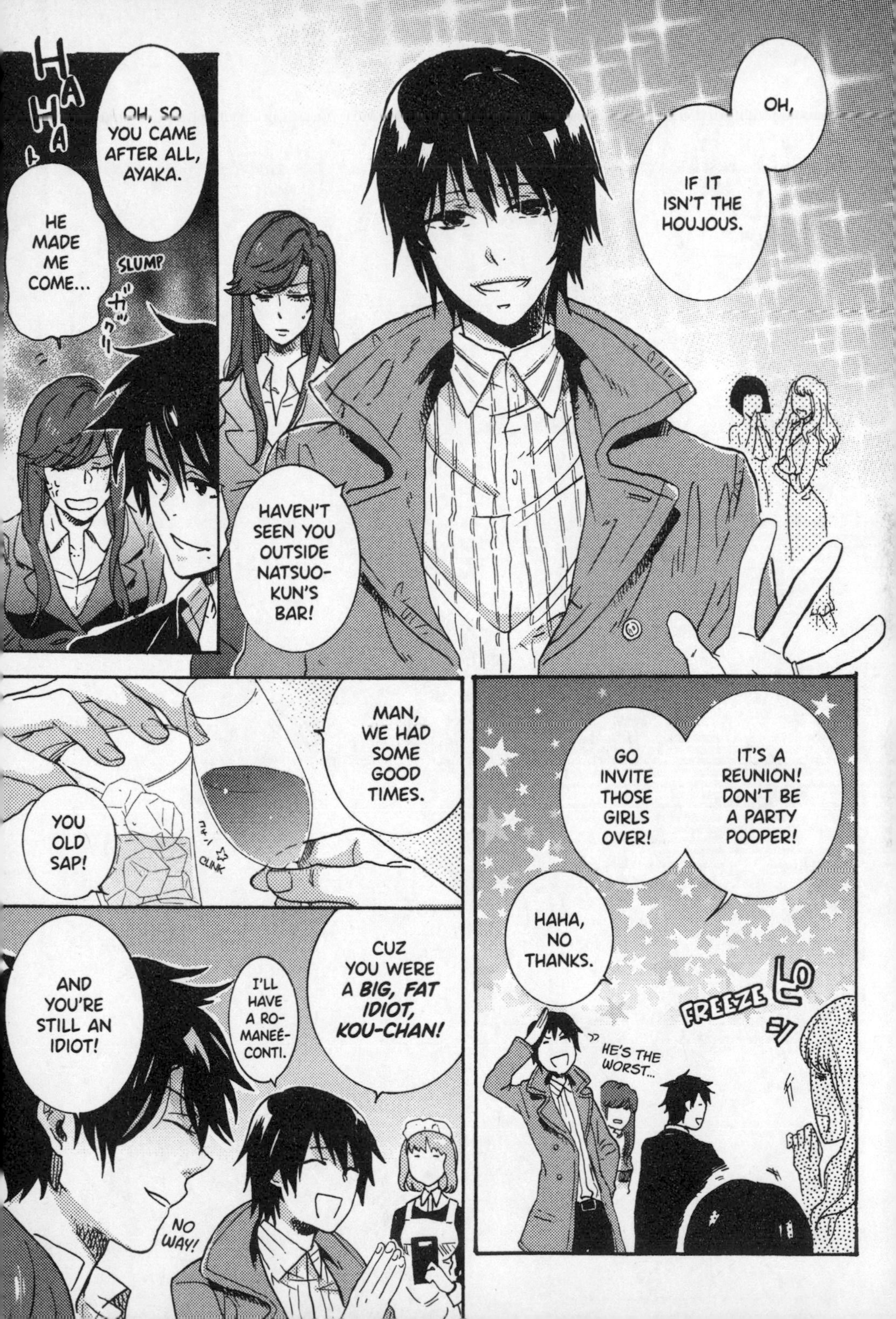
OH, IF IT ISN'T THE HOUJOUS.
HAVEN'T SEEN YOU OUTSIDE NATSUO-KUN'S BAR!
OH, SO YOU CAME AFTER ALL, AYAKA.
HAHAHA
HE MADE ME COME...
SLUMP
IT'S A REUNION! DON'T BE A PARTY POOPER!
GO INVITE THOSE GIRLS OVER!
HAHA, NO THANKS.
FREEZE
HE'S THE WORST...
MAN, WE HAD SOME GOOD TIMES.
CLINK
YOU OLD SAP!
CUZ YOU WERE A BIG, FAT IDIOT, KOU-CHAN!
I'LL HAVE A ROMANEÉ-CONTI.
AND YOU'RE STILL AN IDIOT!
NO WAY!

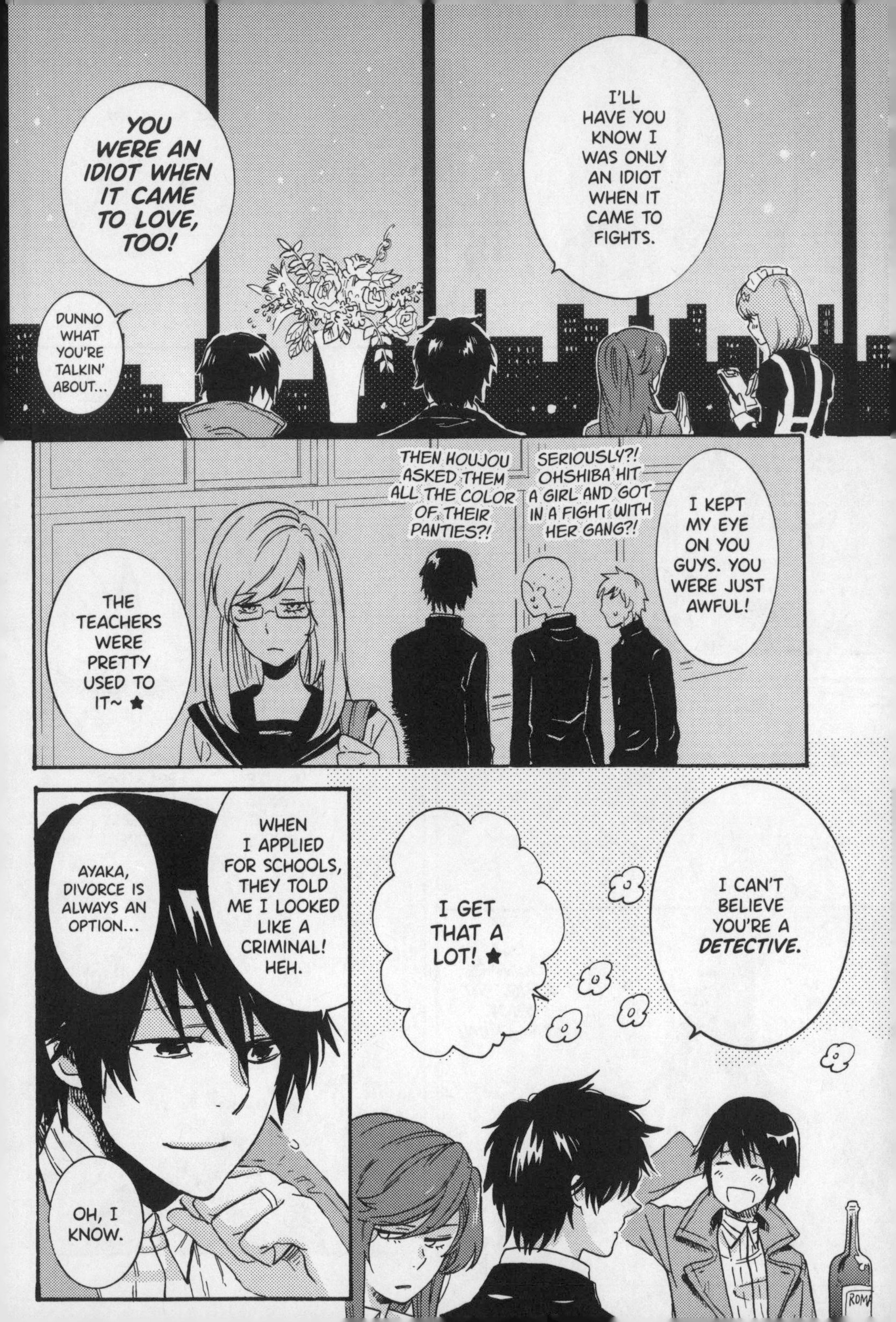
I'LL HAVE YOU KNOW I WAS ONLY AN IDIOT WHEN IT CAME TO FIGHTS.
YOU WERE AN IDIOT WHEN IT CAME TO LOVE, TOO!
DUNNO WHAT YOU'RE TALKIN' ABOUT...
I KEPT MY EYE ON YOU GUYS. YOU WERE JUST AWFUL!
SERIOUSLY?! OHSHIBA HIT A GIRL AND GOT IN A FIGHT WITH HER GANG?!
THEN HOUJOU ASKED THEM ALL THE COLOR OF THEIR PANTIES?!
THE TEACHERS WERE PRETTY USED TO IT~ ★
I CAN'T BELIEVE YOU'RE A DETECTIVE.
I GET THAT A LOT! ★
WHEN I APPLIED FOR SCHOOLS, THEY TOLD ME I LOOKED LIKE A CRIMINAL! HEH.
AYAKA, DIVORCE IS ALWAYS AN OPTION...
OH, I KNOW.

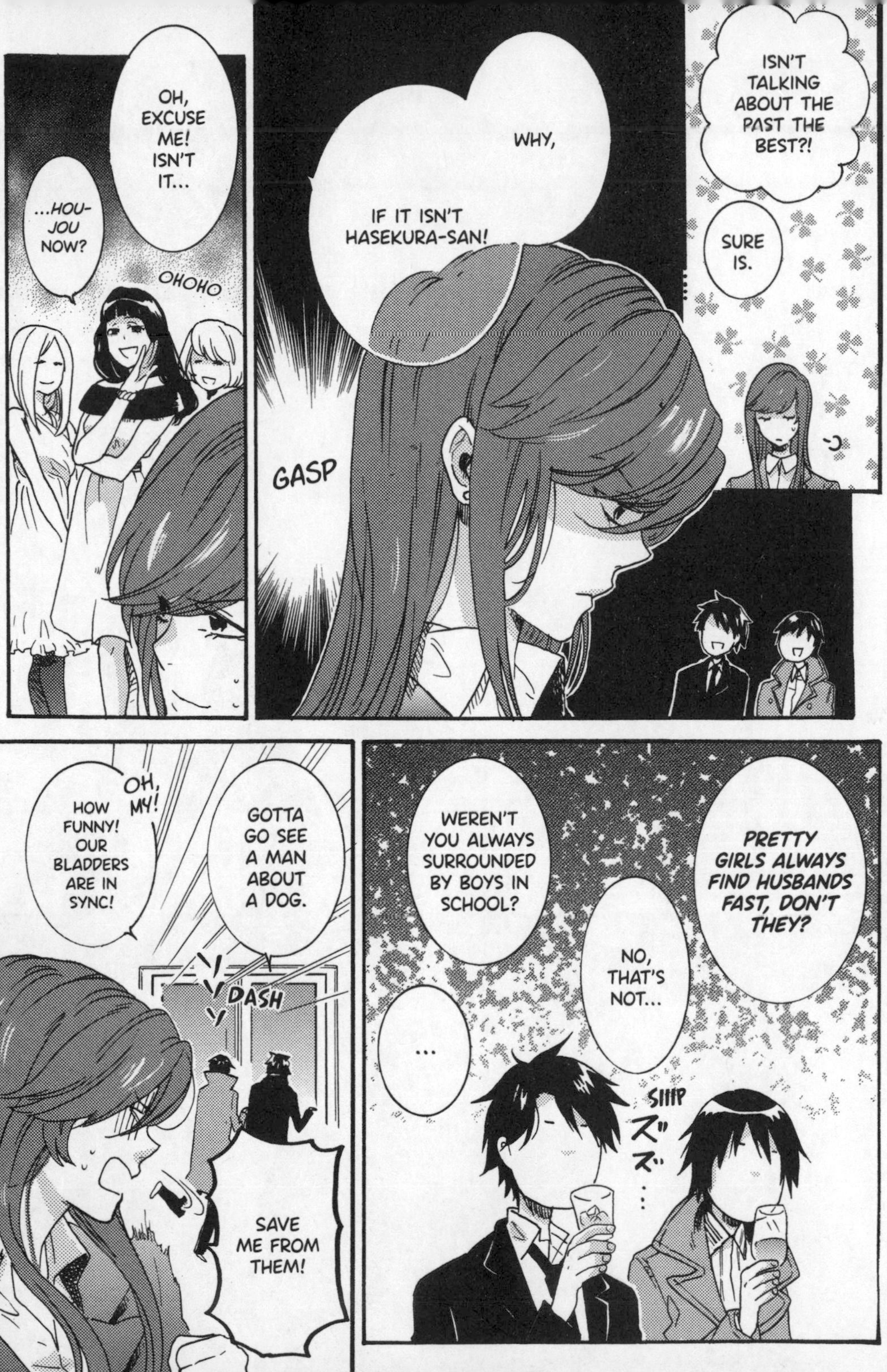
ISN'T TALKING ABOUT THE PAST THE BEST?!
SURE IS.
WHY,
IF IT ISN'T HASEKURA-SAN!
GASP
OH, EXCUSE ME! ISN'T IT...
...HOU-JOU NOW?
OHOHO
PRETTY GIRLS ALWAYS FIND HUSBANDS FAST, DON'T THEY?
WEREN'T YOU ALWAYS SURROUNDED BY BOYS IN SCHOOL?
NO, THAT'S NOT...
...
SIIIP
ズズ…
GOTTA GO SEE A MAN ABOUT A DOG.
OH, MY!
HOW FUNNY! OUR BLADDERS ARE IN SYNC!
DASH
SAVE ME FROM THEM!

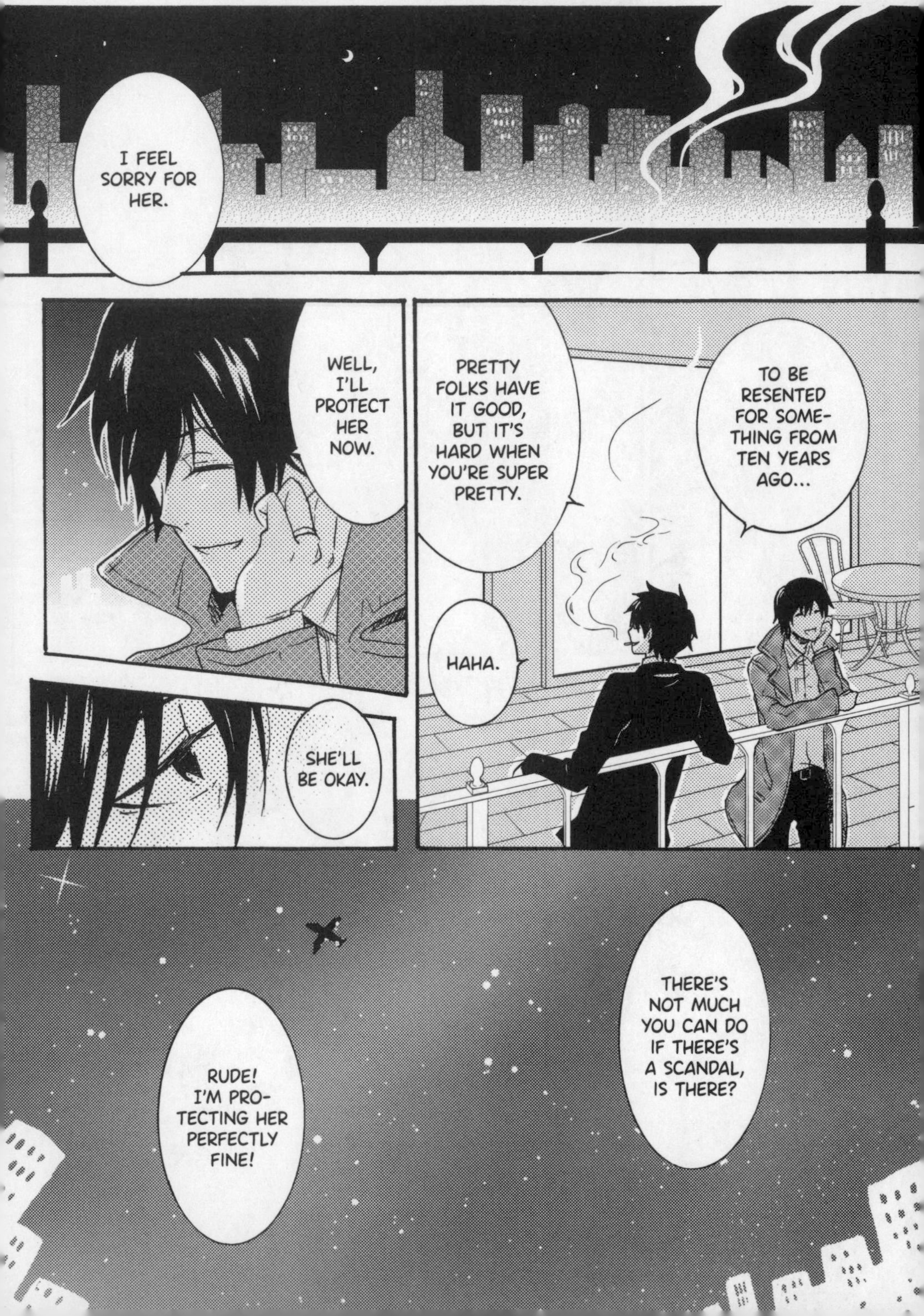
I FEEL SORRY FOR HER.
TO BE RESENTED FOR SOME-THING FROM TEN YEARS AGO...
PRETTY FOLKS HAVE IT GOOD, BUT IT'S HARD WHEN YOU'RE SUPER PRETTY.
HAHA.
WELL, I'LL PROTECT HER NOW.
SHE'LL BE OKAY.
THERE'S NOT MUCH YOU CAN DO IF THERE'S A SCANDAL, IS THERE?
RUDE! I'M PRO-TECTING HER PERFECTLY FINE!

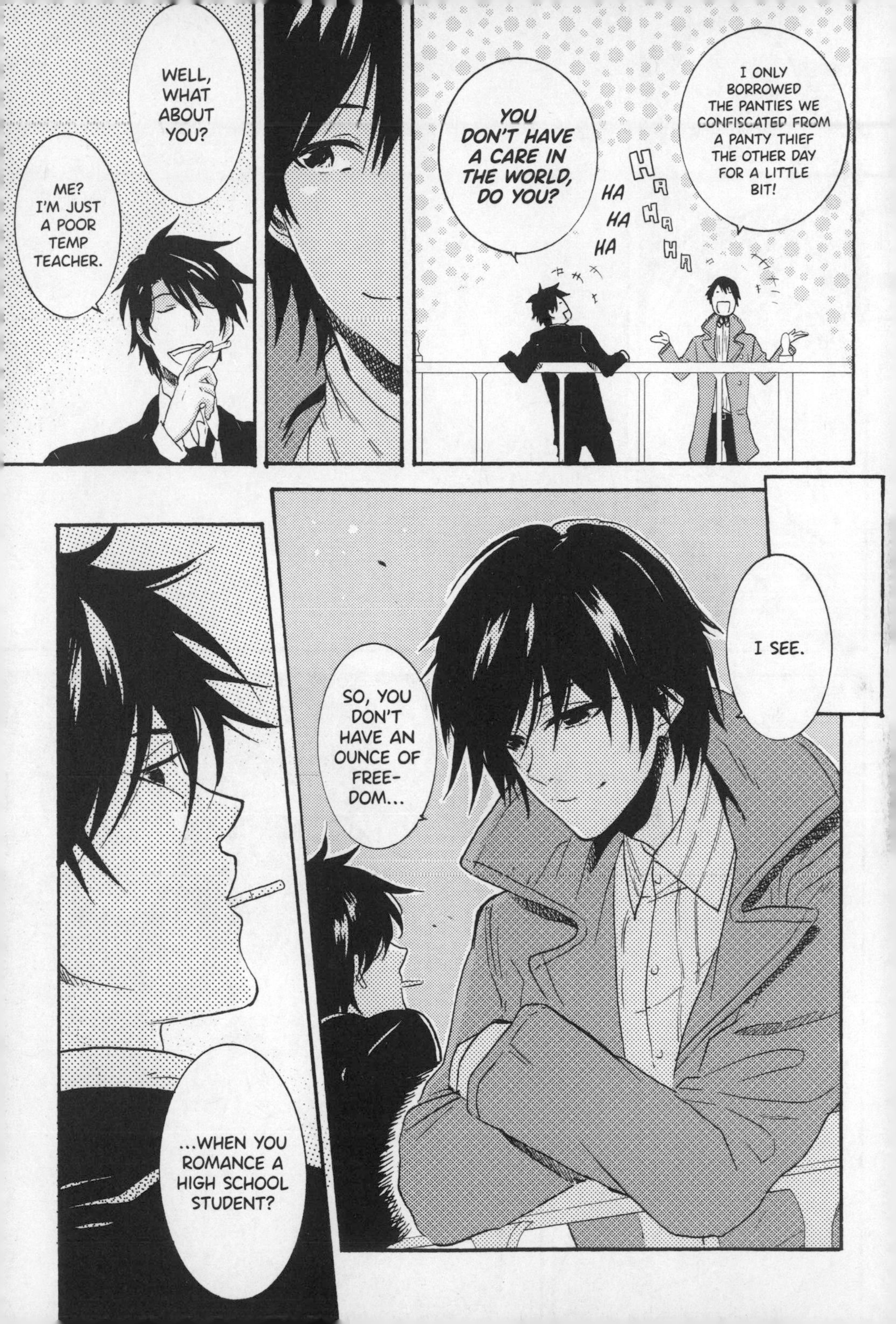
I ONLY BORROWED THE PANTIES WE CONFISCATED FROM A PANTY THIEF THE OTHER DAY FOR A LITTLE BIT!
HA HA HA
HA HA HA
YOU DON'T HAVE A CARE IN THE WORLD, DO YOU?
WELL, WHAT ABOUT YOU?
ME? I'M JUST A POOR TEMP TEACHER.
I SEE.
SO, YOU DON'T HAVE AN OUNCE OF FREE-DOM...
...WHEN YOU ROMANCE A HIGH SCHOOL STUDENT?

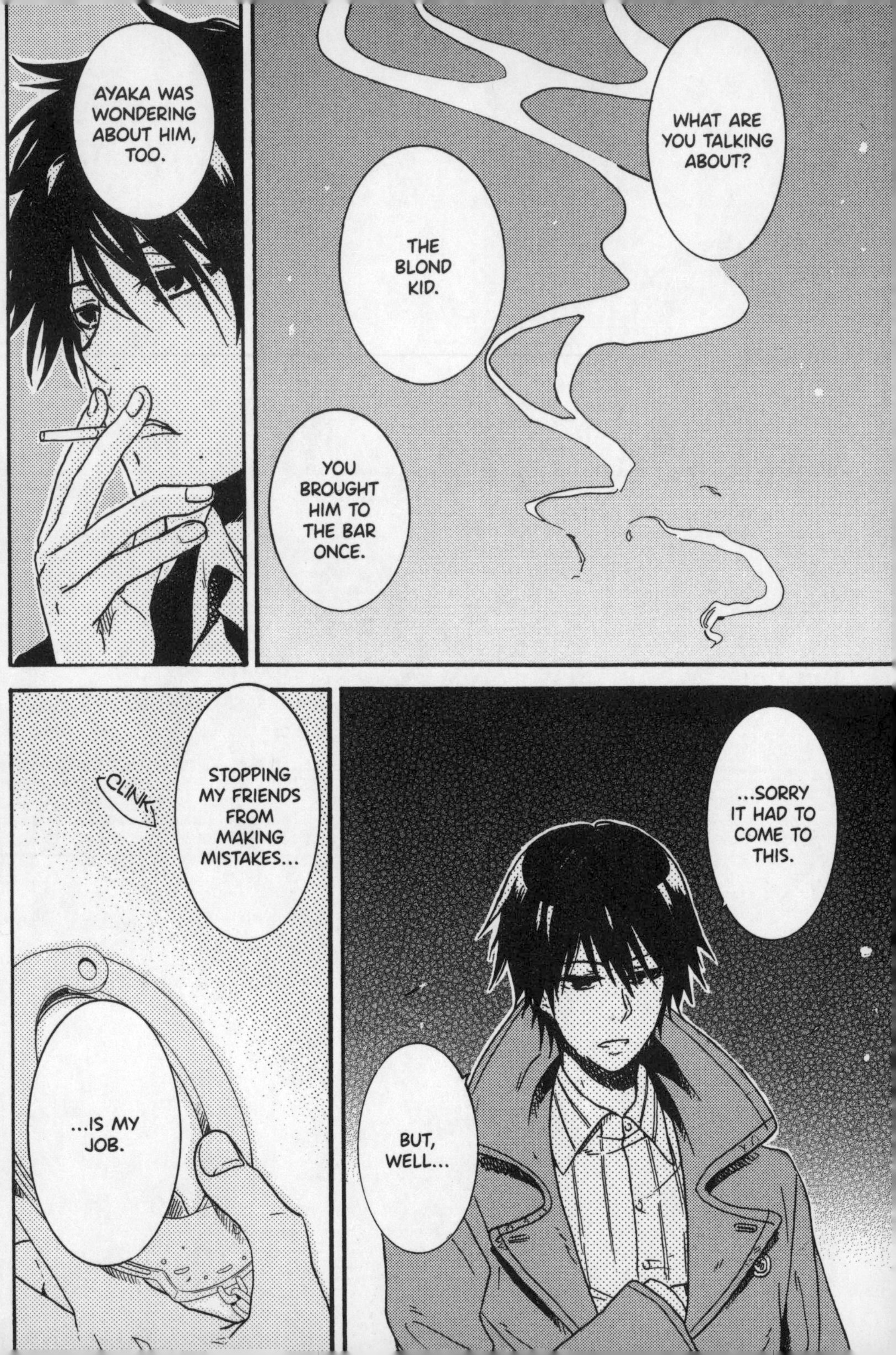
WHAT ARE YOU TALKING ABOUT?
THE BLOND KID.
YOU BROUGHT HIM TO THE BAR ONCE.
AYAKA WAS WONDERING ABOUT HIM, TOO.
...SORRY IT HAD TO COME TO THIS.
BUT, WELL...
STOPPING MY FRIENDS FROM MAKING MISTAKES...
CLINK
...IS MY JOB.

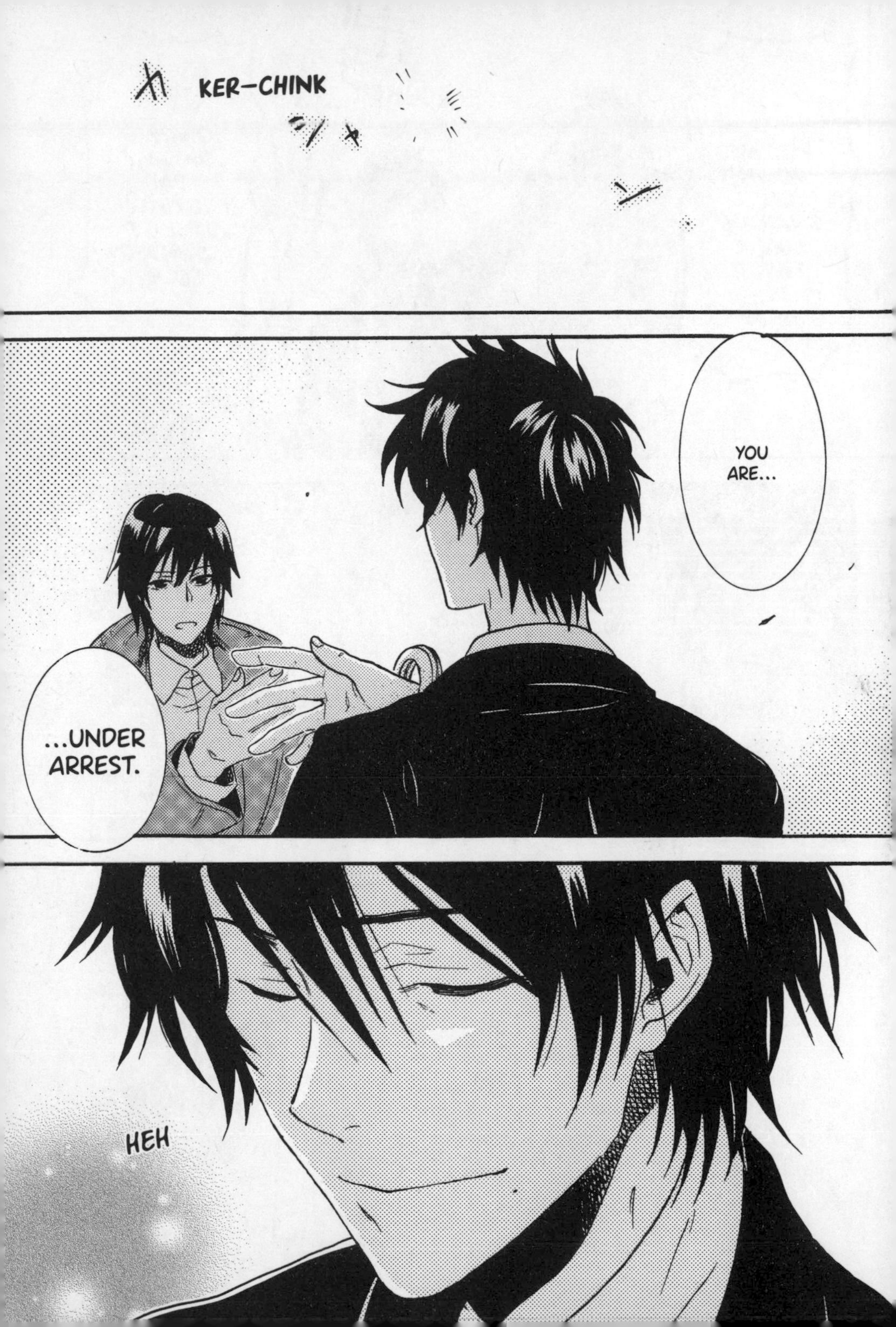
KER-CHINK
YOU ARE...
...UNDER ARREST.
HEH

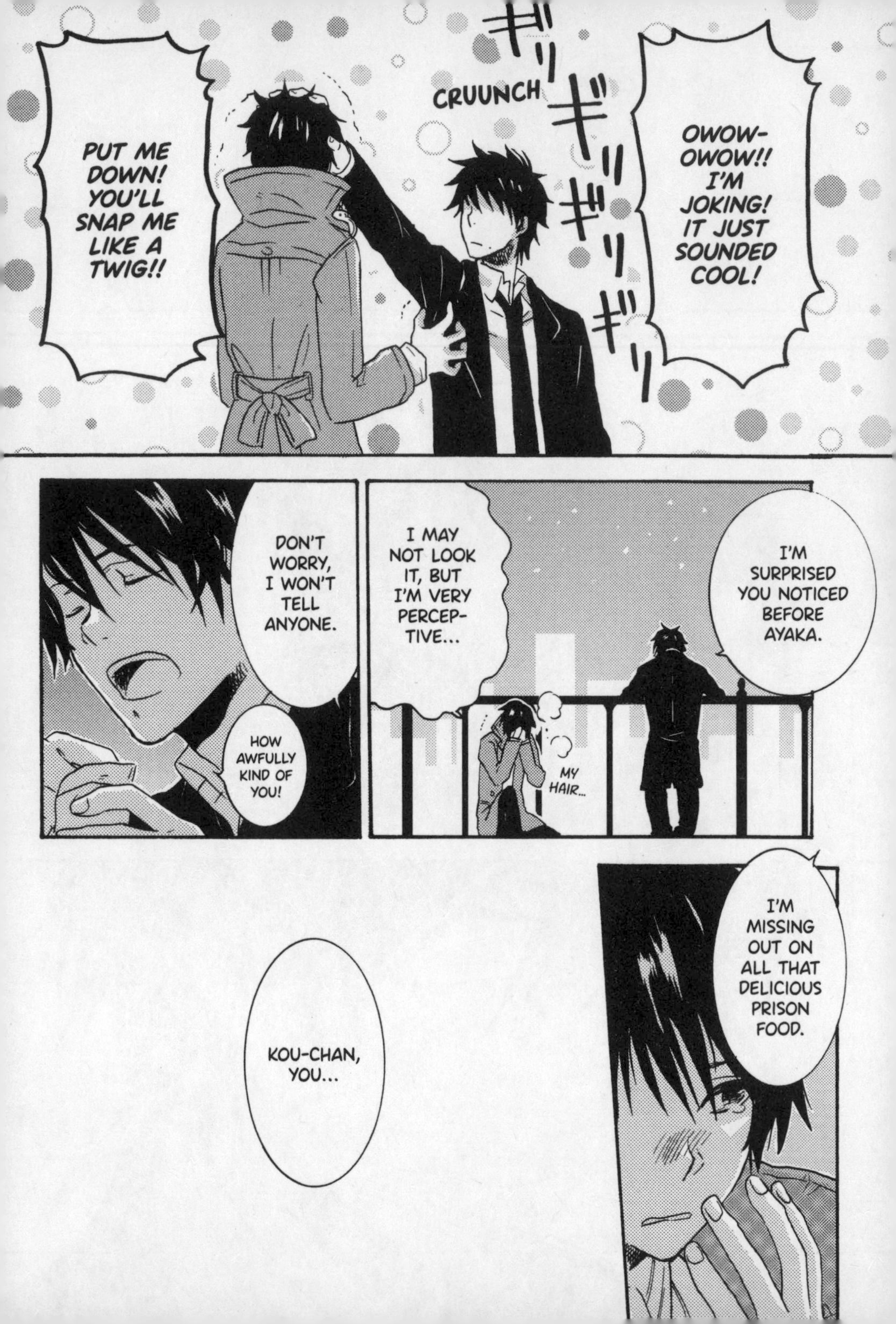
OWOW-OWOW!! I'M JOKING! IT JUST SOUNDED COOL!
CRUUNCH
ギリギリギリギリ
PUT ME DOWN! YOU'LL SNAP ME LIKE A TWIG!!
I'M SURPRISED YOU NOTICED BEFORE AYAKA.
I MAY NOT LOOK IT, BUT I'M VERY PERCEPTIVE...
MY HAIR...
DON'T WORRY, I WON'T TELL ANYONE.
HOW AWFULLY KIND OF YOU!
I'M MISSING OUT ON ALL THAT DELICIOUS PRISON FOOD.
KOU-CHAN, YOU...

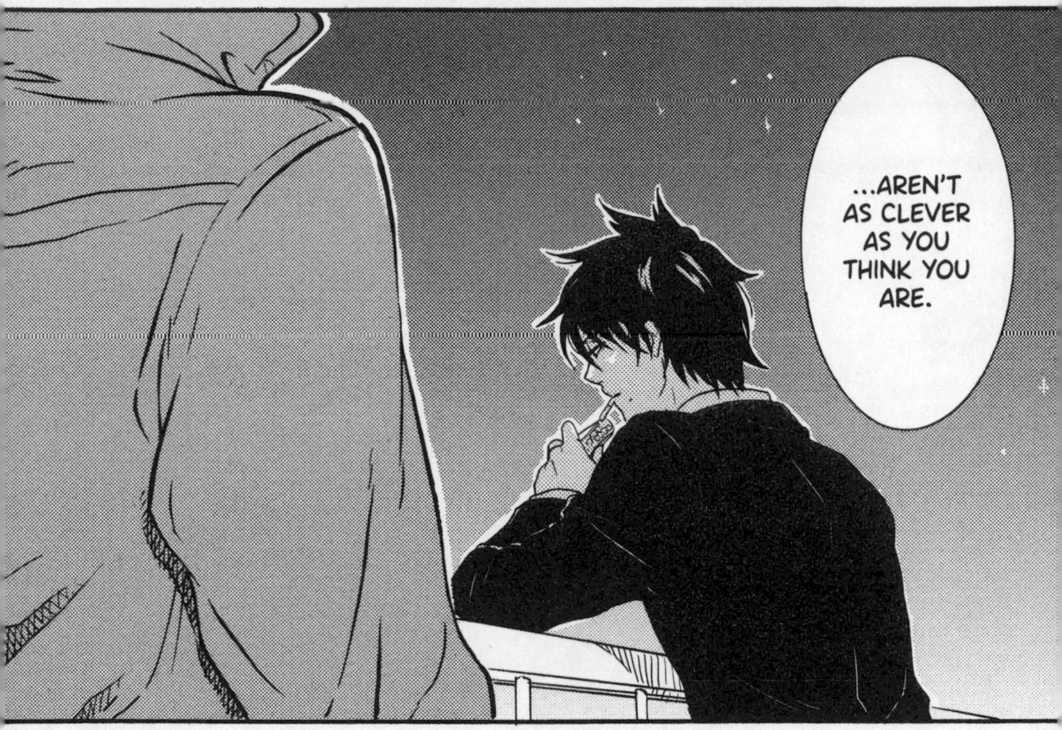
...AREN'T AS CLEVER AS YOU THINK YOU ARE.
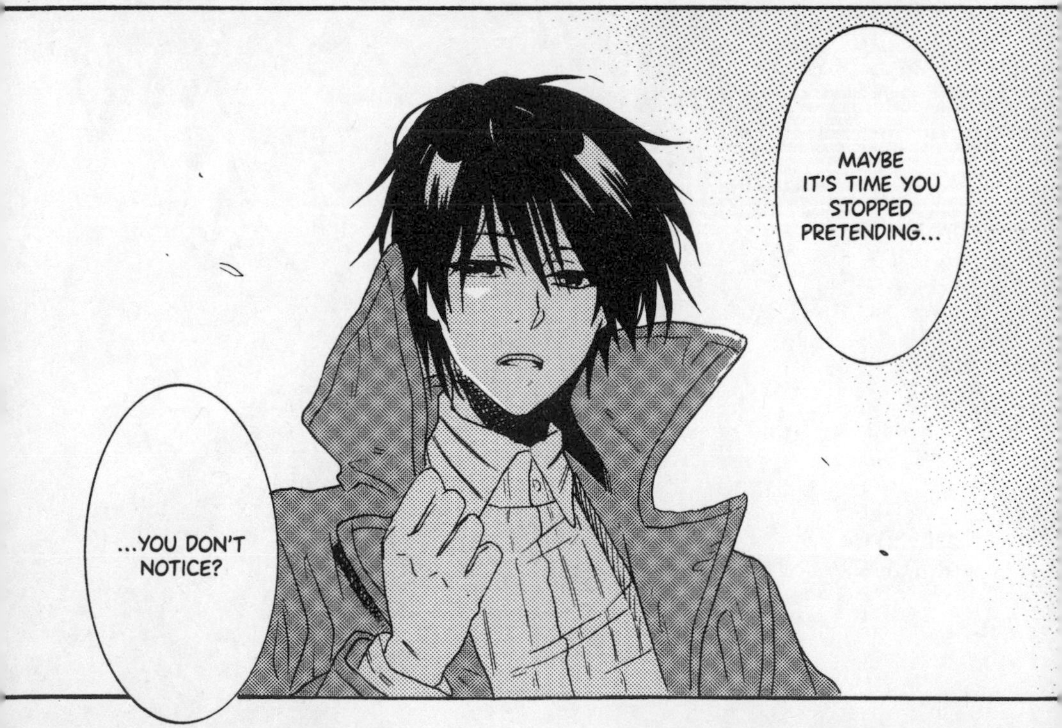
MAYBE IT'S TIME YOU STOPPED PRETENDING...
...YOU DON'T NOTICE?

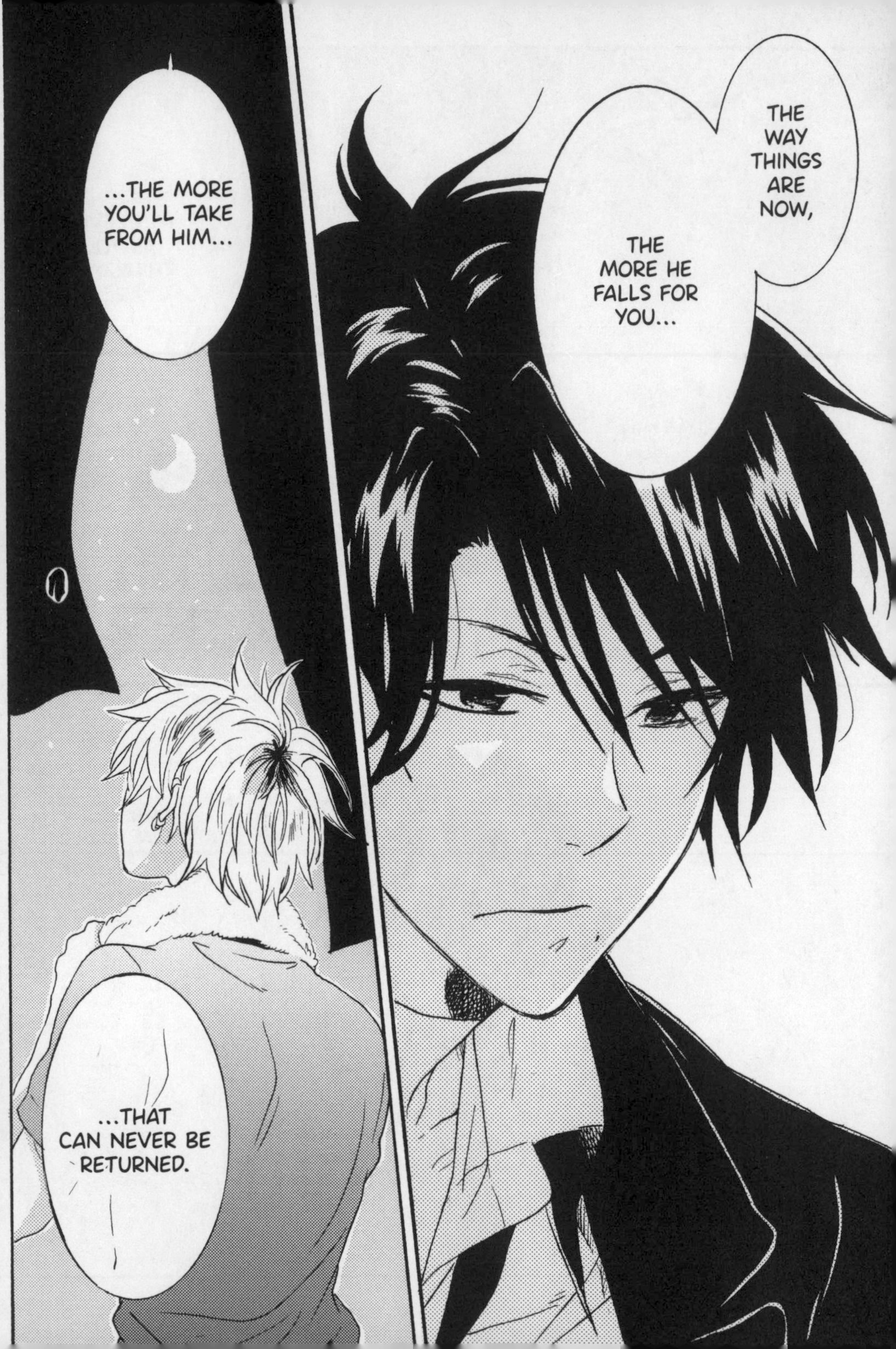
THE WAY THINGS ARE NOW,
THE MORE HE FALLS FOR YOU...
...THE MORE YOU'LL TAKE FROM HIM...
...THAT CAN NEVER BE RETURNED.

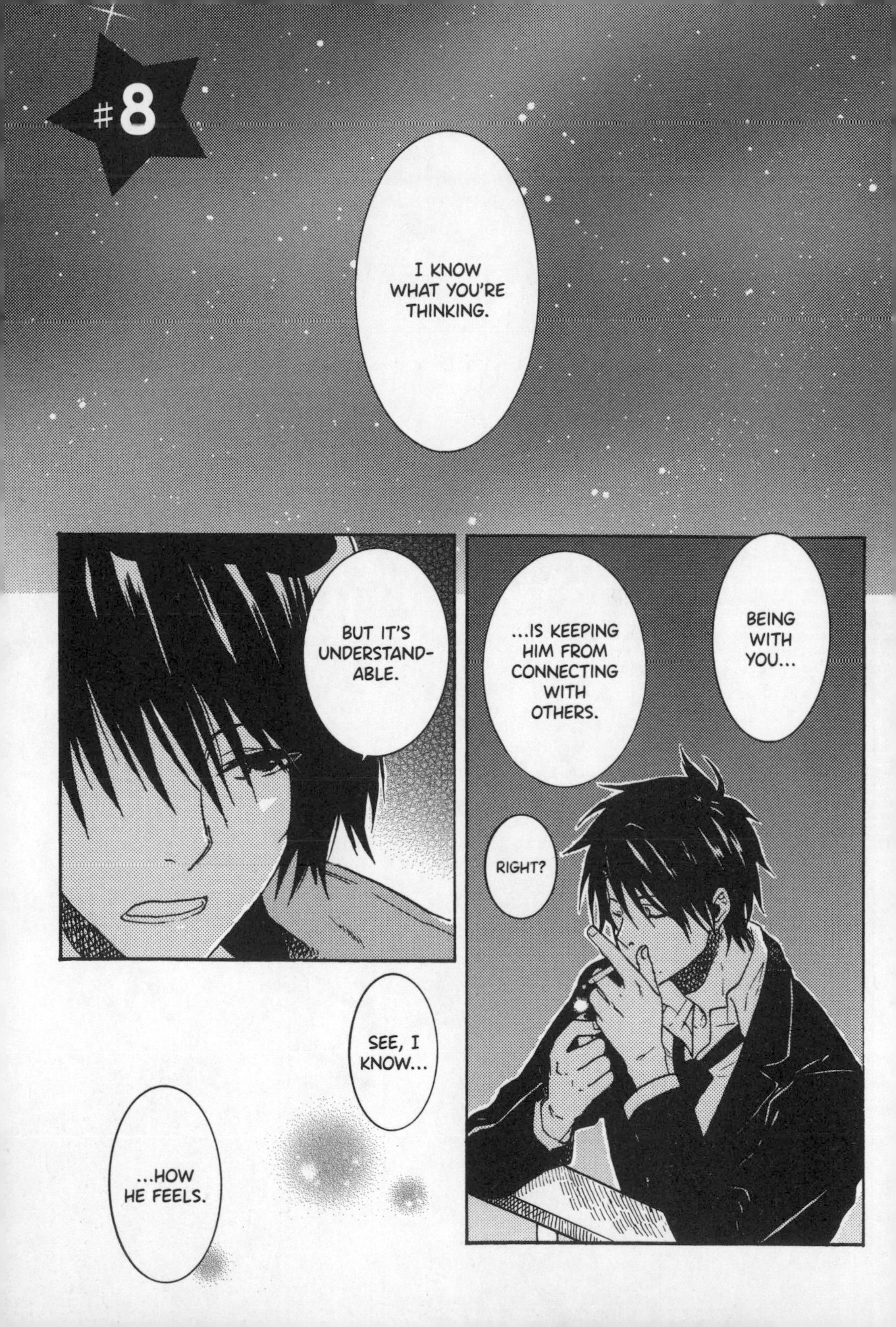
#8
I KNOW WHAT YOU'RE THINKING.
BEING WITH YOU...
...IS KEEPING HIM FROM CONNECTING WITH OTHERS.
RIGHT?
BUT IT'S UNDERSTAND-ABLE.
SEE, I KNOW...
...HOW HE FEELS.

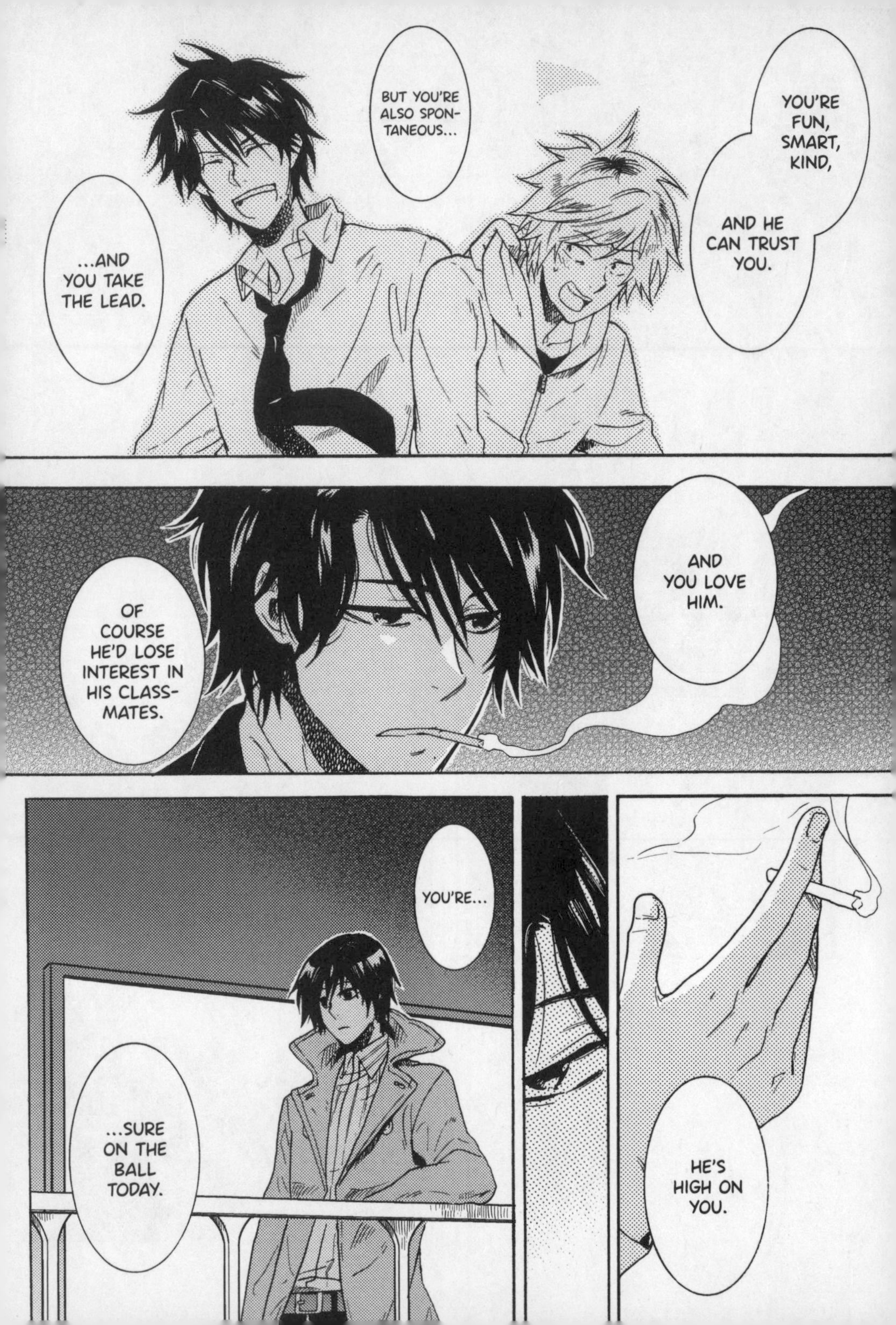
YOU'RE FUN, SMART, KIND, AND HE CAN TRUST YOU.
BUT YOU'RE ALSO SPON-TANEOUS...
...AND YOU TAKE THE LEAD.
AND YOU LOVE HIM.
OF COURSE HE'D LOSE INTEREST IN HIS CLASS-MATES.
HE'S HIGH ON YOU.
YOU'RE...
...SURE ON THE BALL TODAY.

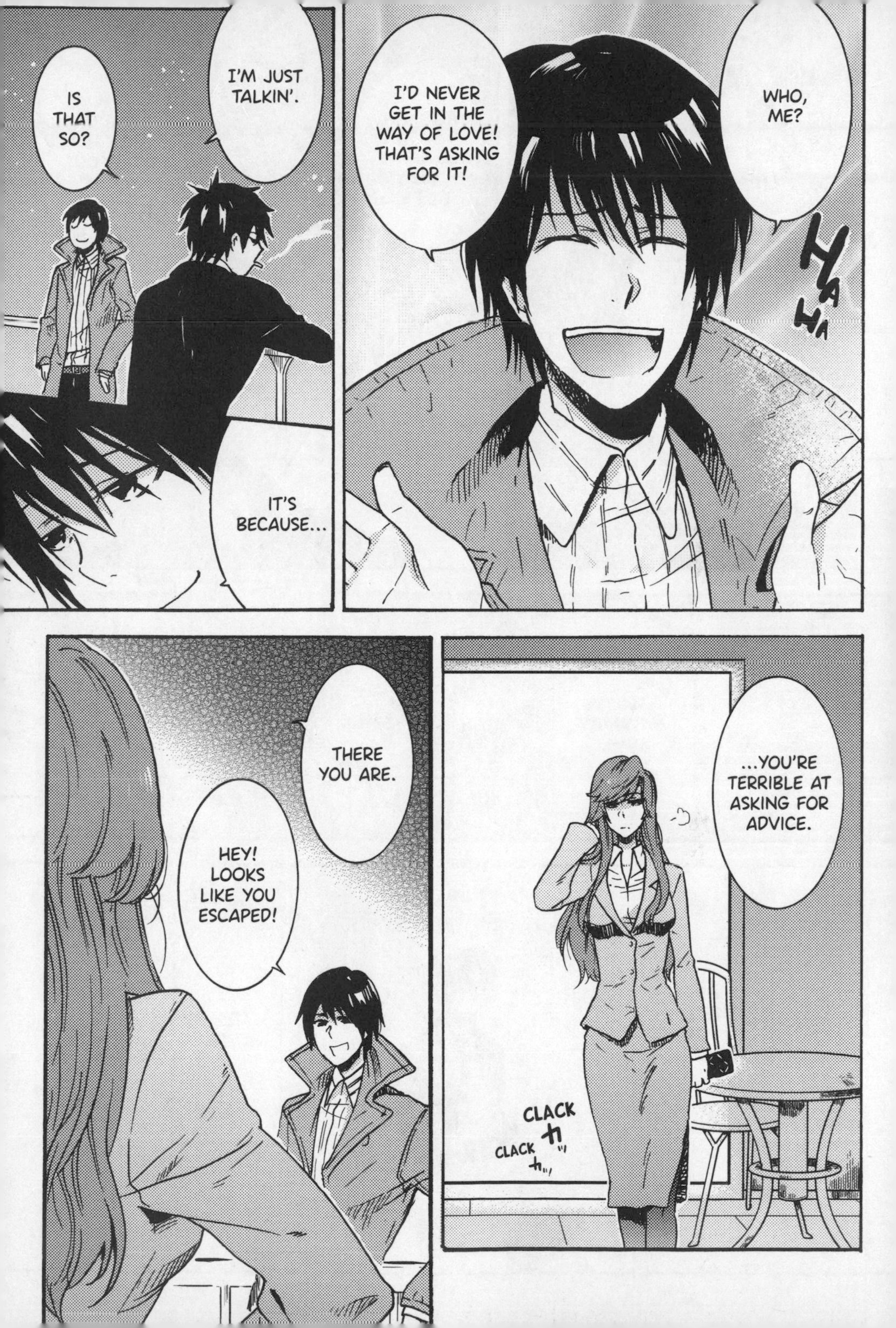
WHO, ME?
HA HA
I'D NEVER GET IN THE WAY OF LOVE! THAT'S ASKING FOR IT!
I'M JUST TALKIN'.
IS THAT SO?
IT'S BECAUSE...
...YOU'RE TERRIBLE AT ASKING FOR ADVICE.
CLACK CLACK
THERE YOU ARE.
HEY! LOOKS LIKE YOU ESCAPED!

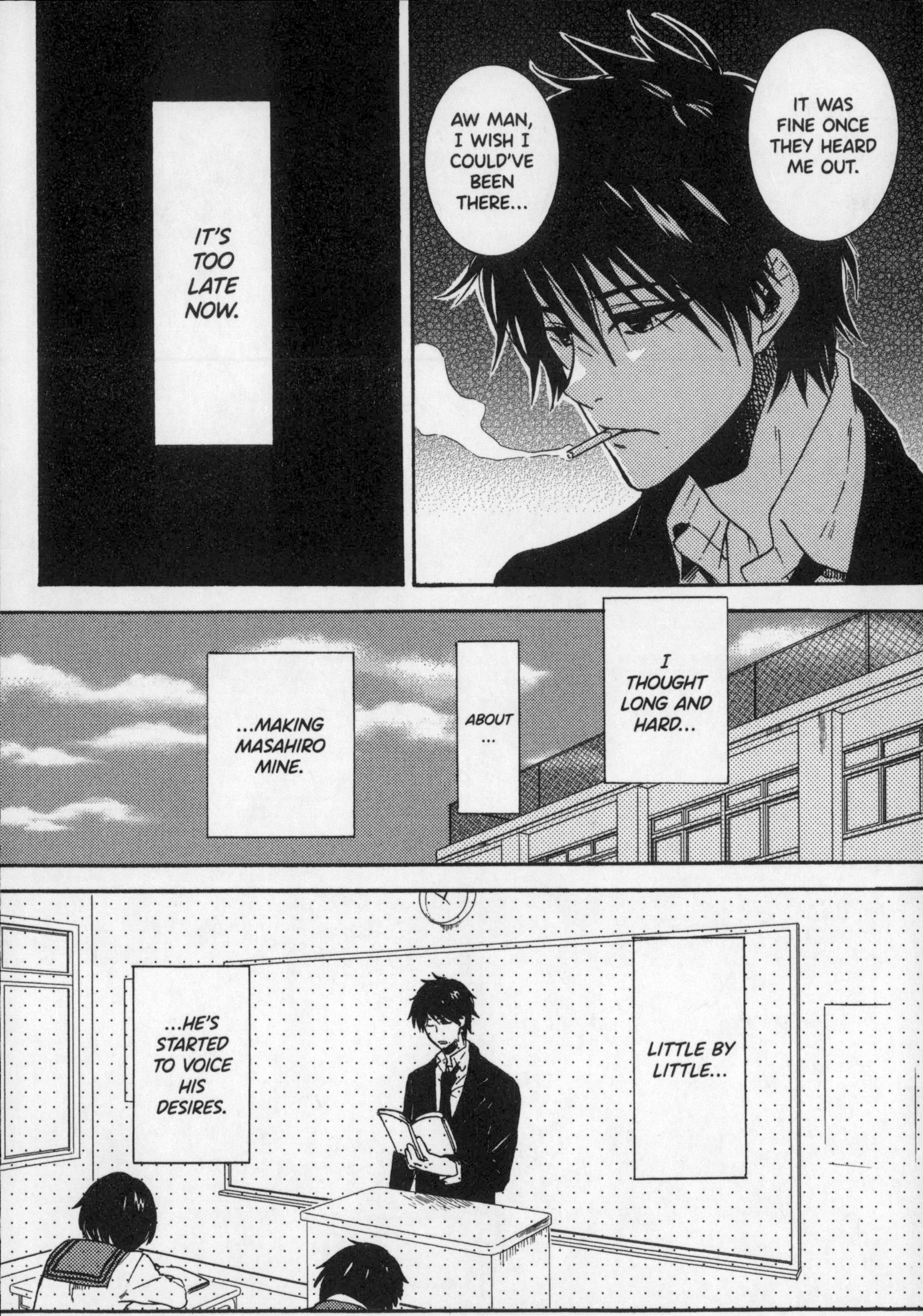
IT WAS FINE ONCE THEY HEARD ME OUT.
AW MAN, I WISH I COULD'VE BEEN THERE...
IT'S TOO LATE NOW.
I THOUGHT LONG AND HARD...
ABOUT...
...MAKING MASAHIRO MINE.
LITTLE BY LITTLE...
...HE'S STARTED TO VOICE HIS DESIRES.

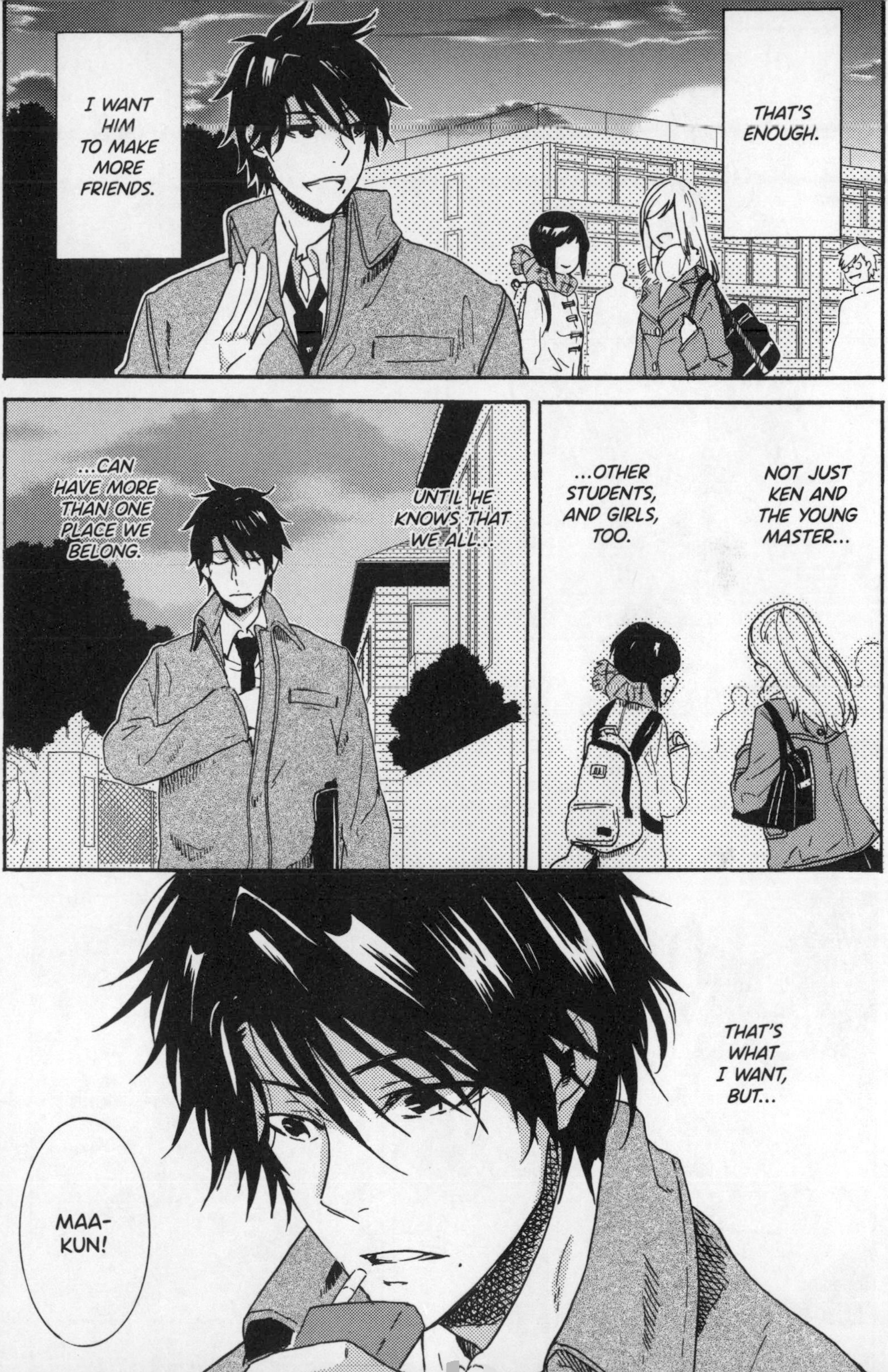
THAT'S ENOUGH.
I WANT HIM TO MAKE MORE FRIENDS.
NOT JUST KEN AND THE YOUNG MASTER...
...OTHER STUDENTS, AND GIRLS, TOO.
UNTIL HE KNOWS THAT WE ALL...
...CAN HAVE MORE THAN ONE PLACE WE BELONG.
THAT'S WHAT I WANT, BUT...
MAA-KUN!

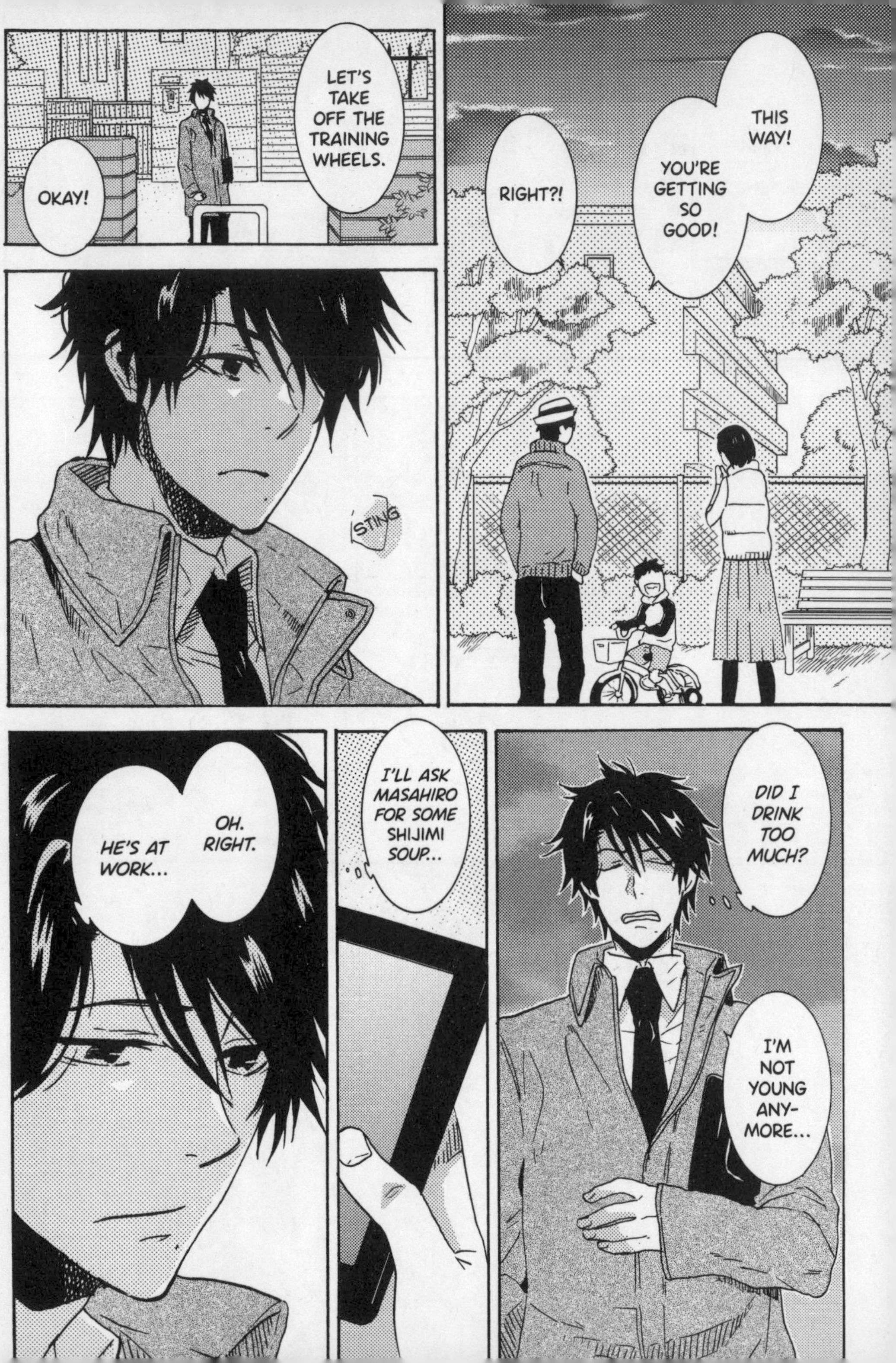
THIS WAY!
YOU'RE GETTING SO GOOD!
RIGHT?!
LET'S TAKE OFF THE TRAINING WHEELS.
OKAY!
STING
DID I DRINK TOO MUCH?
I'M NOT YOUNG ANY-MORE...
I'LL ASK MASAHIRO FOR SOME SHIJIMI SOUP...
OH. RIGHT.
HE'S AT WORK...

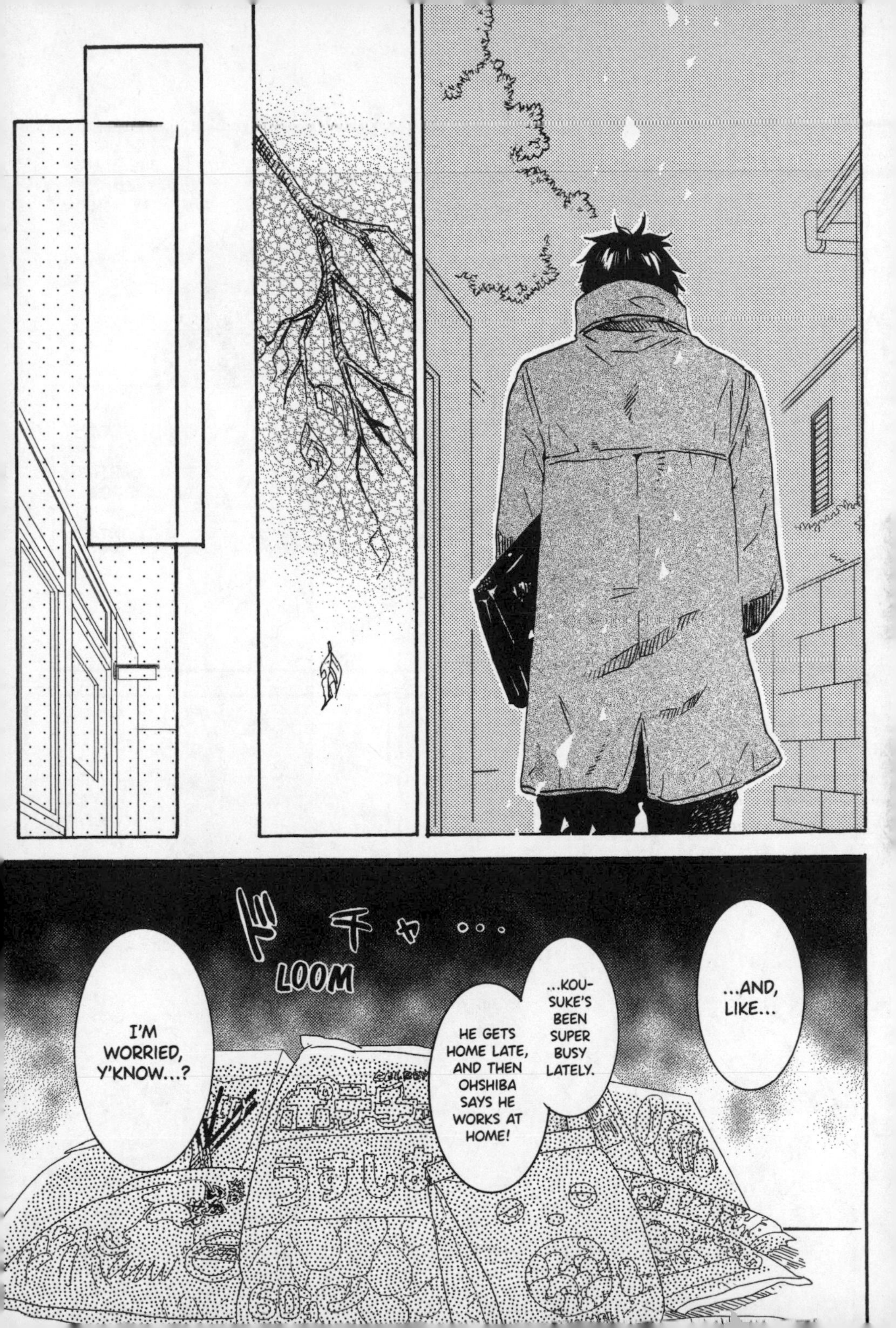
...AND, LIKE...
...KOU-SUKE'S BEEN SUPER BUSY LATELY.
HE GETS HOME LATE, AND THEN OHSHIBA SAYS HE WORKS AT HOME!
LOOM
I'M WORRIED, Y'KNOW...?

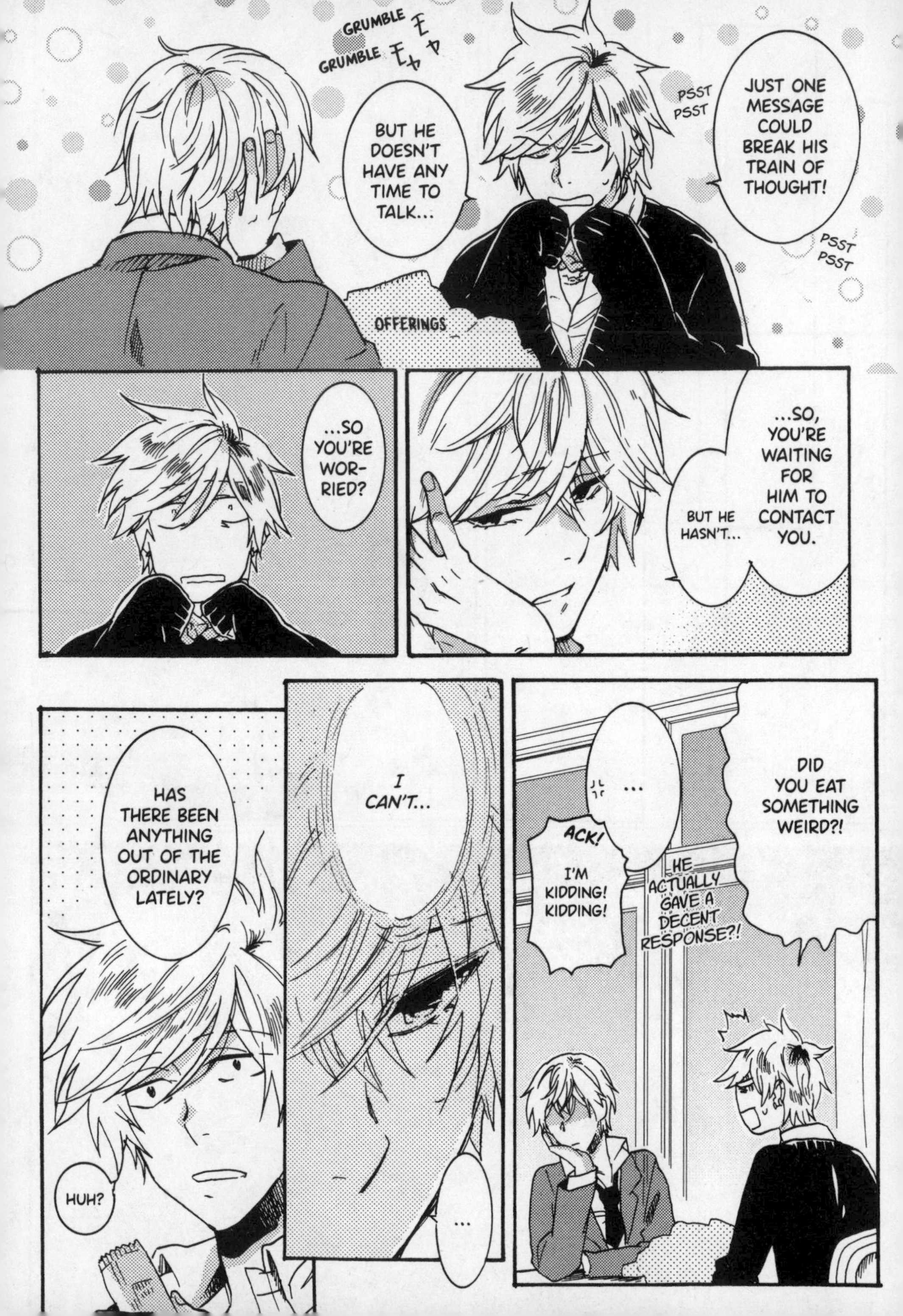
JUST ONE MESSAGE COULD BREAK HIS TRAIN OF THOUGHT!
PSST PSST
PSST PSST
BUT HE DOESN'T HAVE ANY TIME TO TALK...
GRUMBLE GRUMBLE
モヤ モヤ
OFFERINGS
...SO, YOU'RE WAITING FOR HIM TO CONTACT YOU.
BUT HE HASN'T...
...SO YOU'RE WOR-RIED?
DID YOU EAT SOMETHING WEIRD?!
HE ACTUALLY GAVE A DECENT RESPONSE?!
...
ACK!
I'M KIDDING! KIDDING!
I CAN'T...
...
HAS THERE BEEN ANYTHING OUT OF THE ORDINARY LATELY?
HUH?

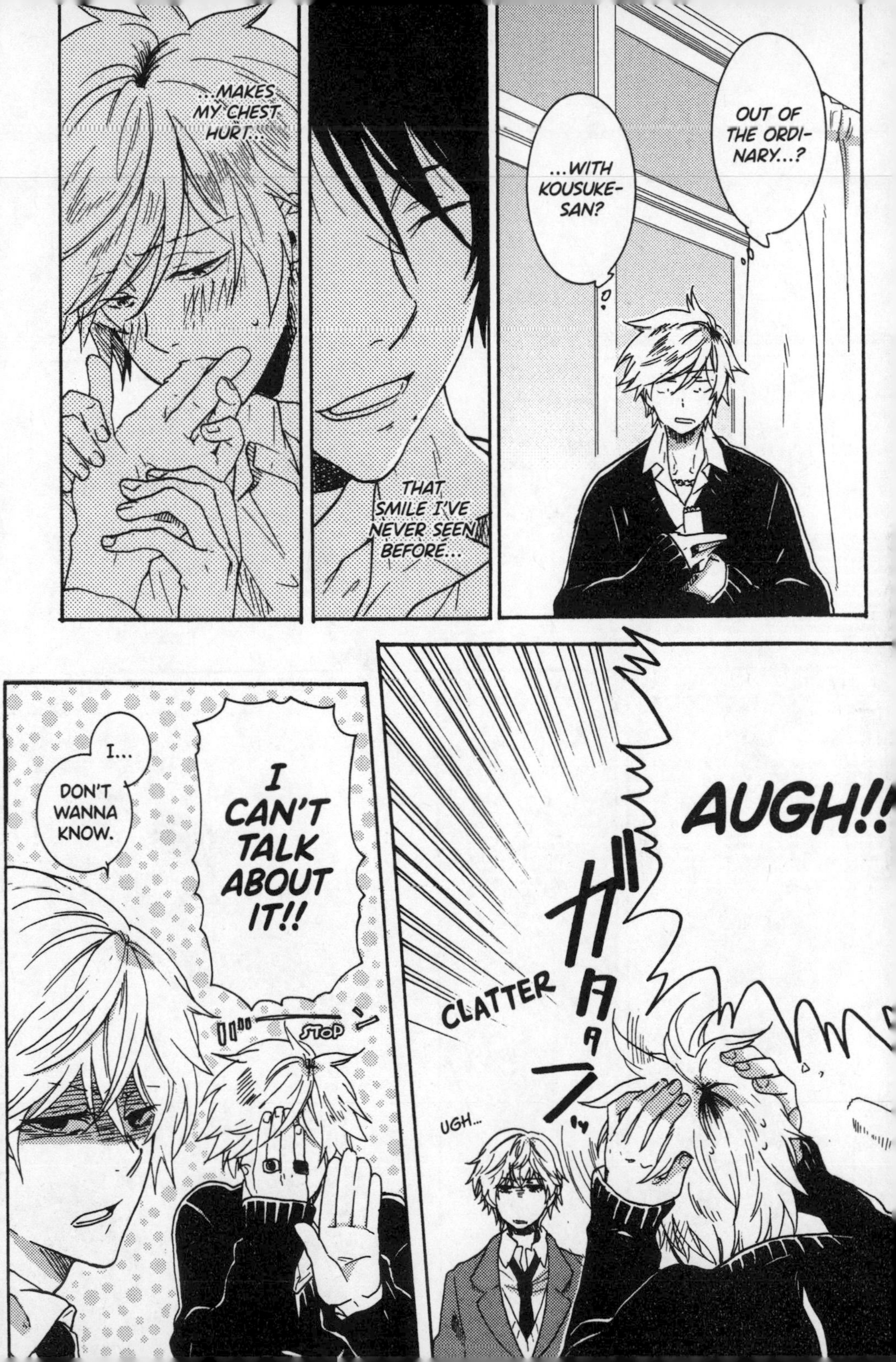
OUT OF THE ORDINARY...?
...WITH KOUSUKE-SAN?
THAT SMILE I'VE NEVER SEEN BEFORE...
...MAKES MY CHEST HURT...
AUGH!!
CLATTER
UGH...
I CAN'T TALK ABOUT IT!!
I... DON'T WANNA KNOW.
STOP

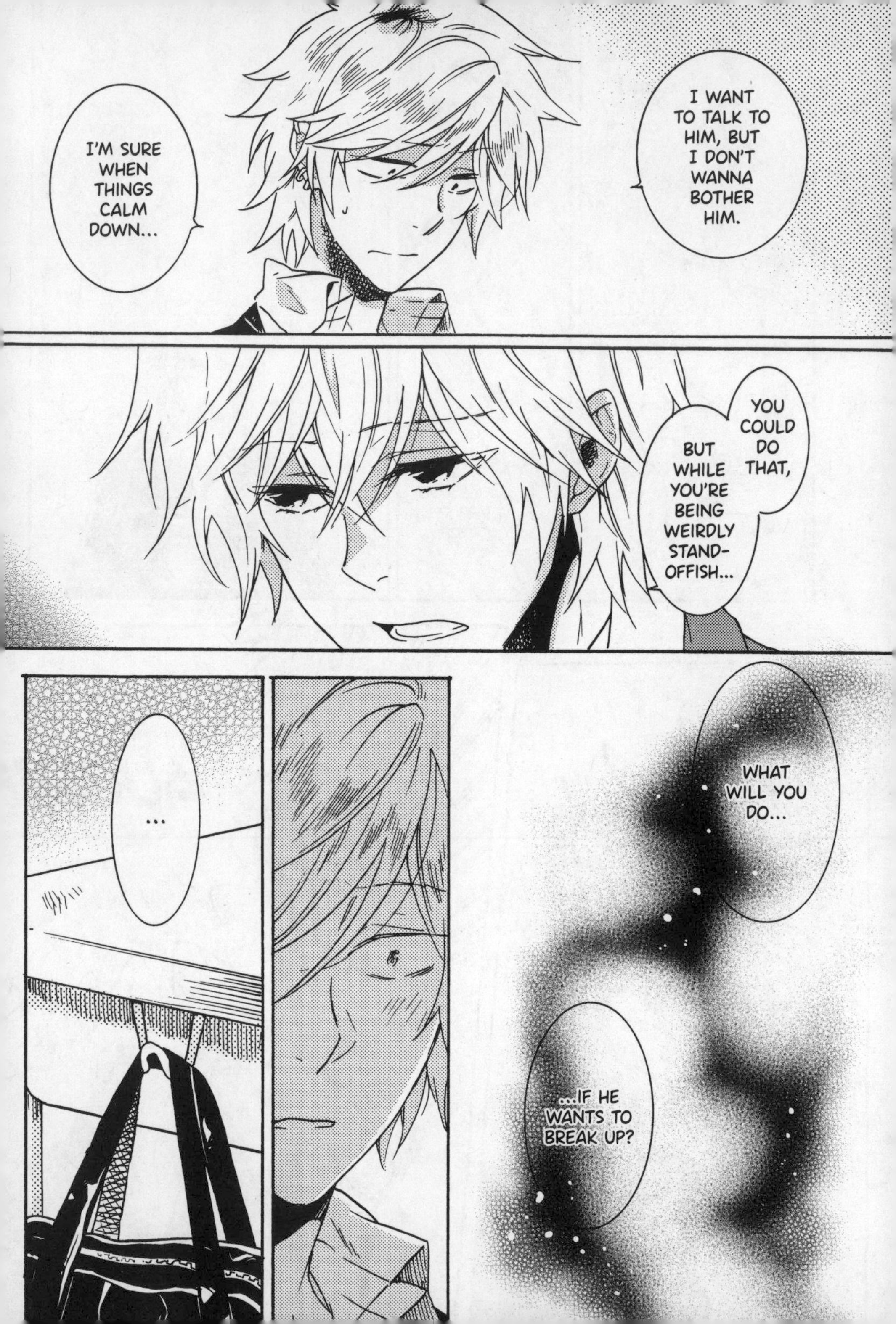
I WANT TO TALK TO HIM, BUT I DON'T WANNA BOTHER HIM.
I'M SURE WHEN THINGS CALM DOWN...
YOU COULD DO THAT,
BUT WHILE YOU'RE BEING WEIRDLY STAND-OFFISH...
WHAT WILL YOU DO...
...IF HE WANTS TO BREAK UP?
...

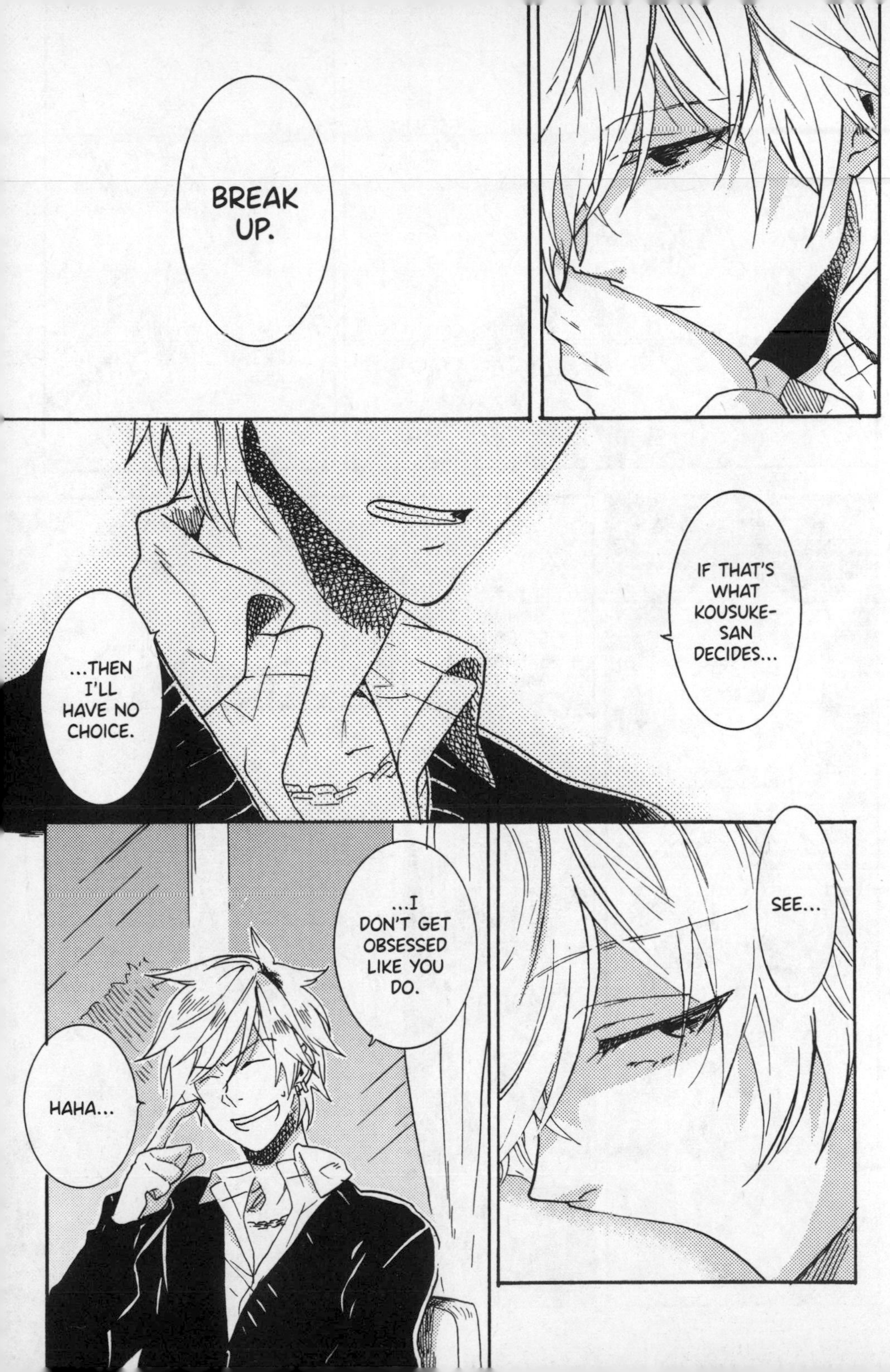
BREAK UP.
IF THAT'S WHAT KOUSUKE-SAN DECIDES...
...THEN I'LL HAVE NO CHOICE.
SEE...
...I DON'T GET OBSESSED LIKE YOU DO.
HAHA...

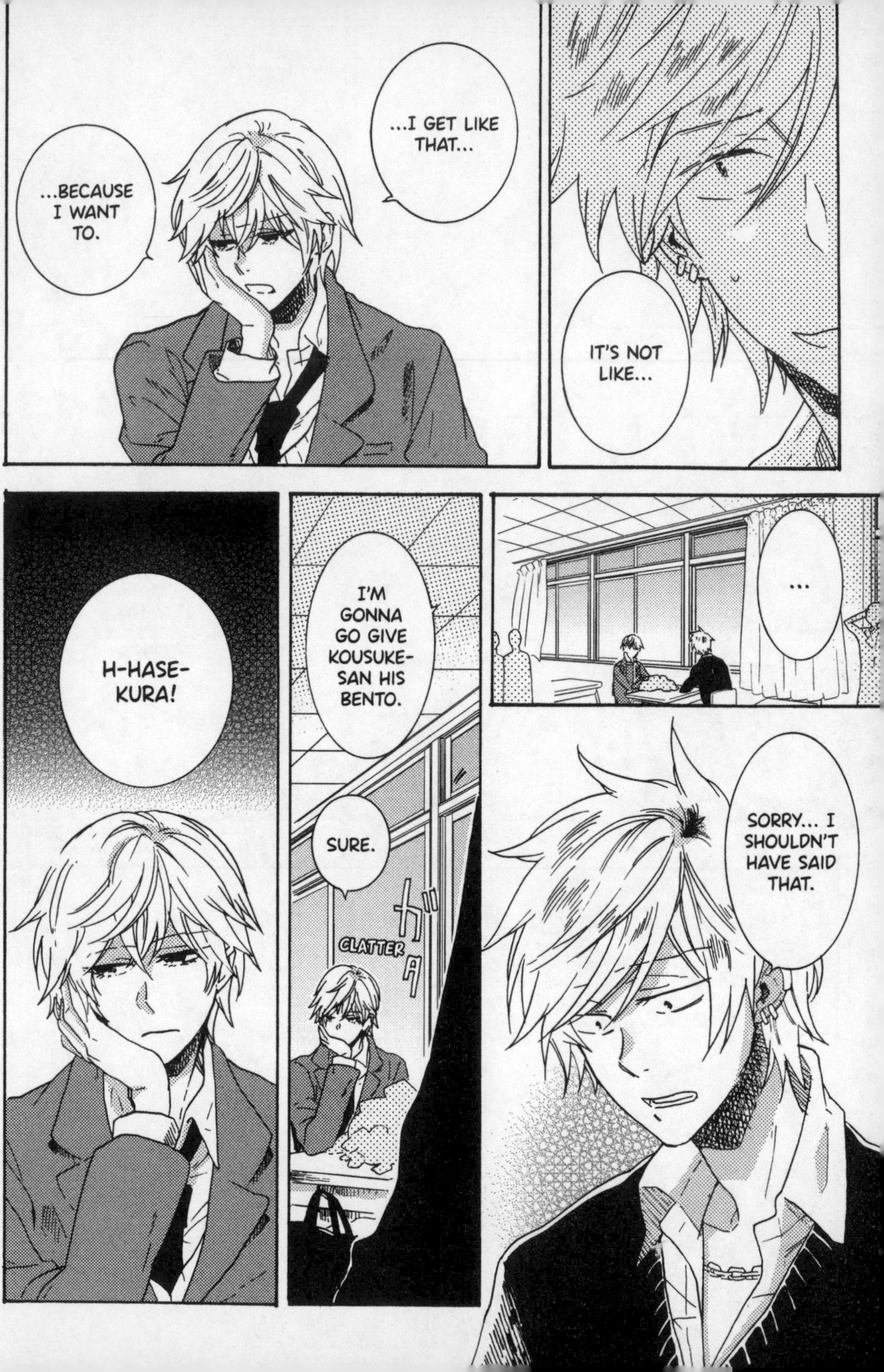
IT'S NOT LIKE...
...I GET LIKE THAT...
...BECAUSE I WANT TO.
...
SORRY... I SHOULDN'T HAVE SAID THAT.
I'M GONNA GO GIVE KOUSUKE-SAN HIS BENTO.
SURE.
CLATTER
H-HASE-KURA!

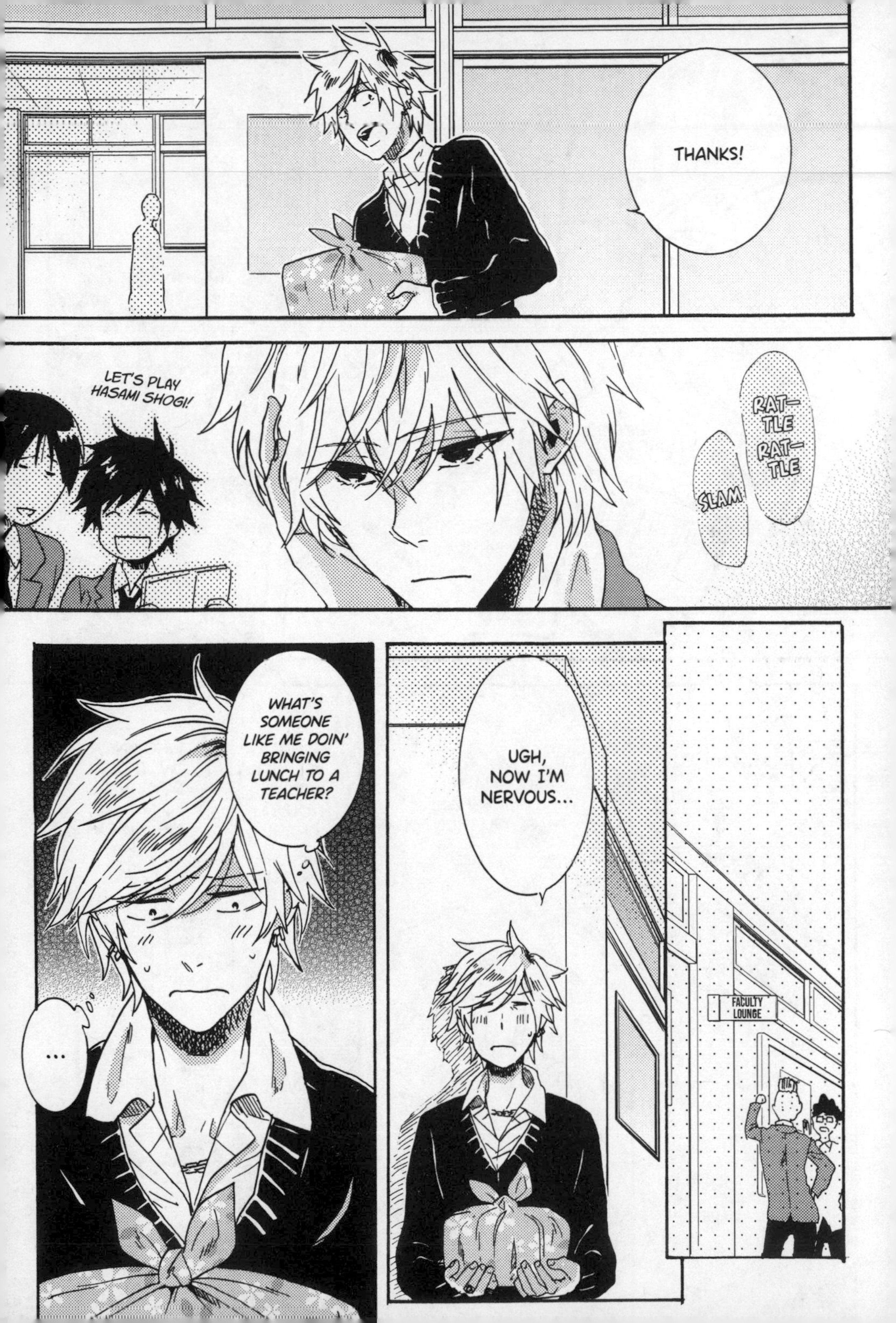
THANKS!
RAT-TLE RAT-TLE
SLAM
LET'S PLAY HASAMI SHOGI!
UGH, NOW I'M NERVOUS...
FACULTY LOUNGE
WHAT'S SOMEONE LIKE ME DOIN' BRINGING LUNCH TO A TEACHER?
...

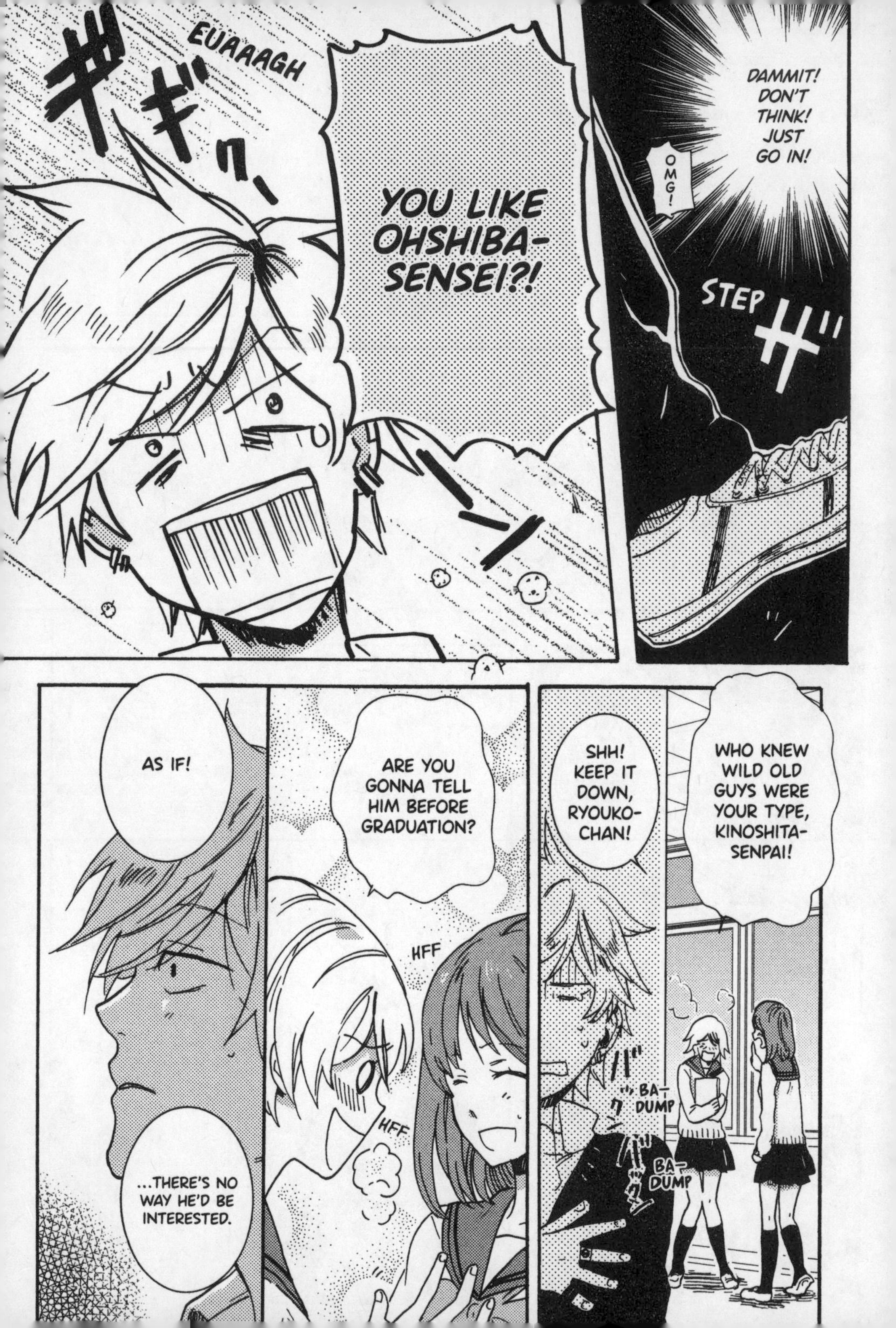
DAMMIT! DON'T THINK! JUST GO IN!
OMG!
STEP
EUAAAGH
YOU LIKE OHSHIBA-SENSEI?!
WHO KNEW WILD OLD GUYS WERE YOUR TYPE, KINOSHITA-SENPAI!
SHH! KEEP IT DOWN, RYOUKO-CHAN!
BA-DUMP
BA-DUMP
ARE YOU GONNA TELL HIM BEFORE GRADUATION?
HFF
HFF
AS IF!
...THERE'S NO WAY HE'D BE INTERESTED.

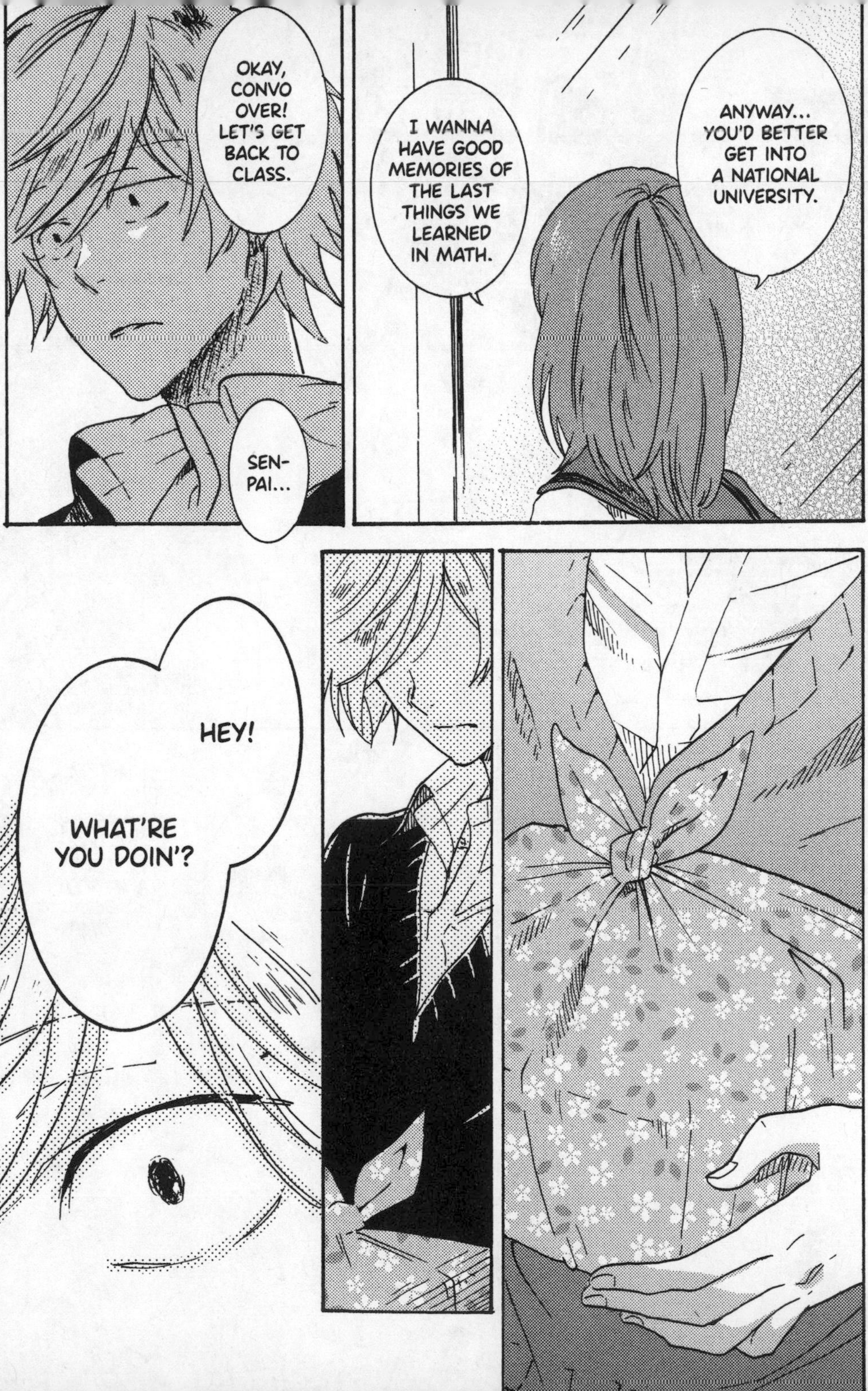
ANYWAY... YOU'D BETTER GET INTO A NATIONAL UNIVERSITY.
I WANNA HAVE GOOD MEMORIES OF THE LAST THINGS WE LEARNED IN MATH.
OKAY, CONVO OVER! LET'S GET BACK TO CLASS.
SEN-PAI...
HEY!
WHAT'RE YOU DOIN'?

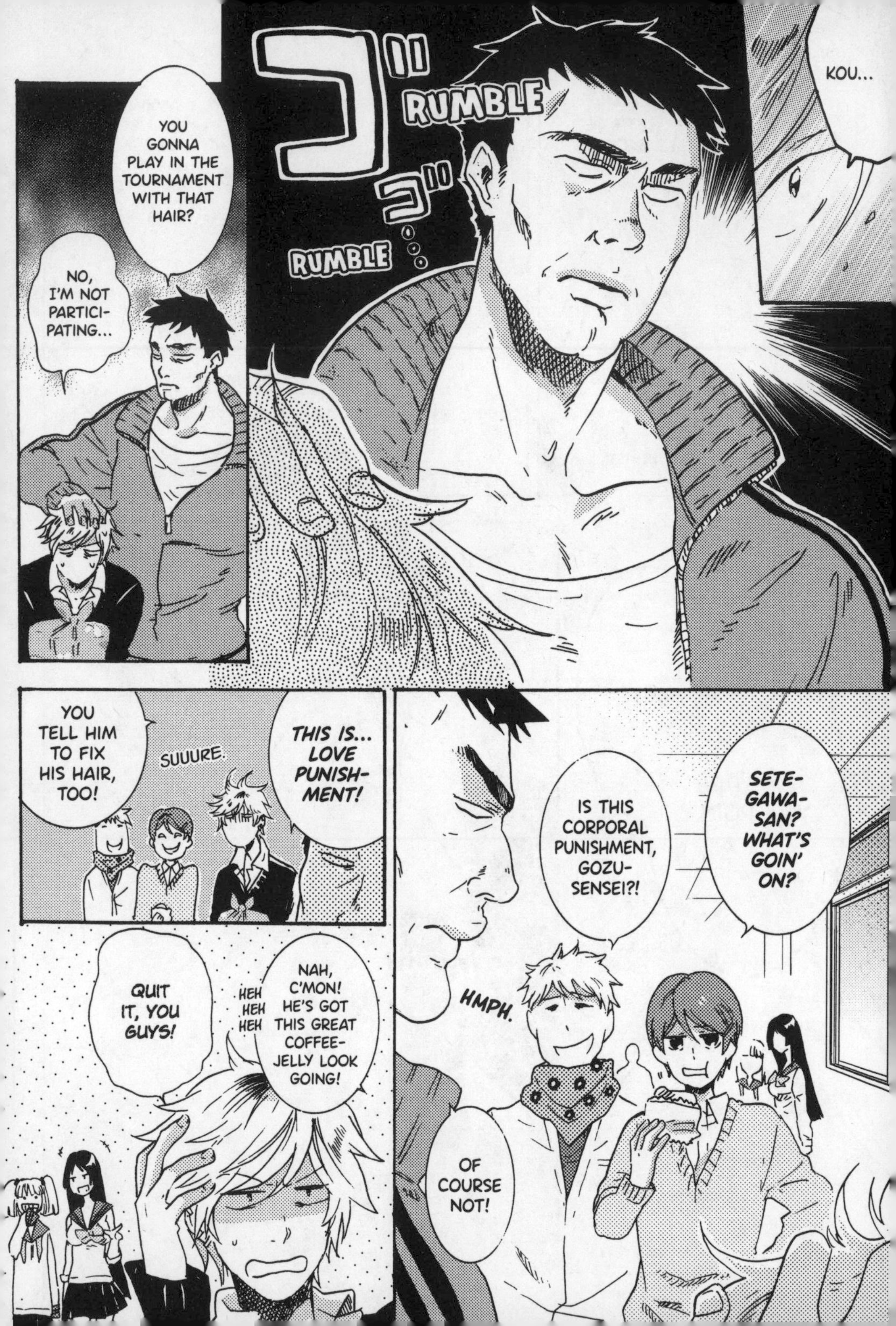
KOU...
RUMBLE
RUMBLE
YOU GONNA PLAY IN THE TOURNAMENT WITH THAT HAIR?
NO, I'M NOT PARTICI-PATING...
SETE-GAWA-SAN? WHAT'S GOIN' ON?
IS THIS CORPORAL PUNISHMENT, GOZU-SENSEI?!
HMPH.
OF COURSE NOT!
THIS IS... LOVE PUNISH-MENT!
SUUURE.
YOU TELL HIM TO FIX HIS HAIR, TOO!
NAH, C'MON! HE'S GOT THIS GREAT COFFEE-JELLY LOOK GOING!
HEH HEH HEH
QUIT IT, YOU GUYS!

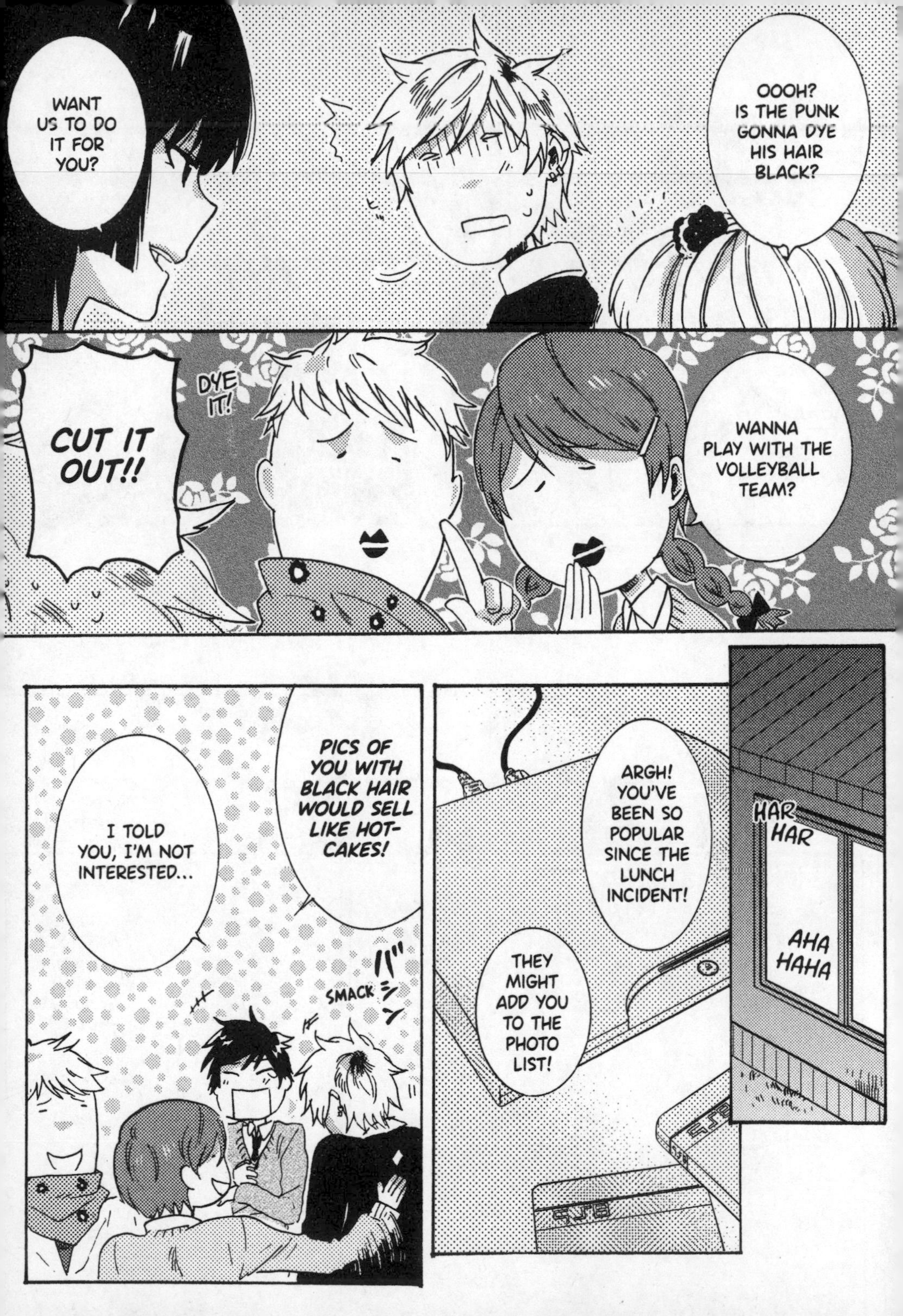
OOOH? IS THE PUNK GONNA DYE HIS HAIR BLACK?
WANT US TO DO IT FOR YOU?
WANNA PLAY WITH THE VOLLEYBALL TEAM?
DYE IT!
CUT IT OUT!!
HAR HAR
AHA HAHA
ARGH! YOU'VE BEEN SO POPULAR SINCE THE LUNCH INCIDENT!
THEY MIGHT ADD YOU TO THE PHOTO LIST!
PICS OF YOU WITH BLACK HAIR WOULD SELL LIKE HOT-CAKES!
I TOLD YOU, I'M NOT INTERESTED...
SMACK

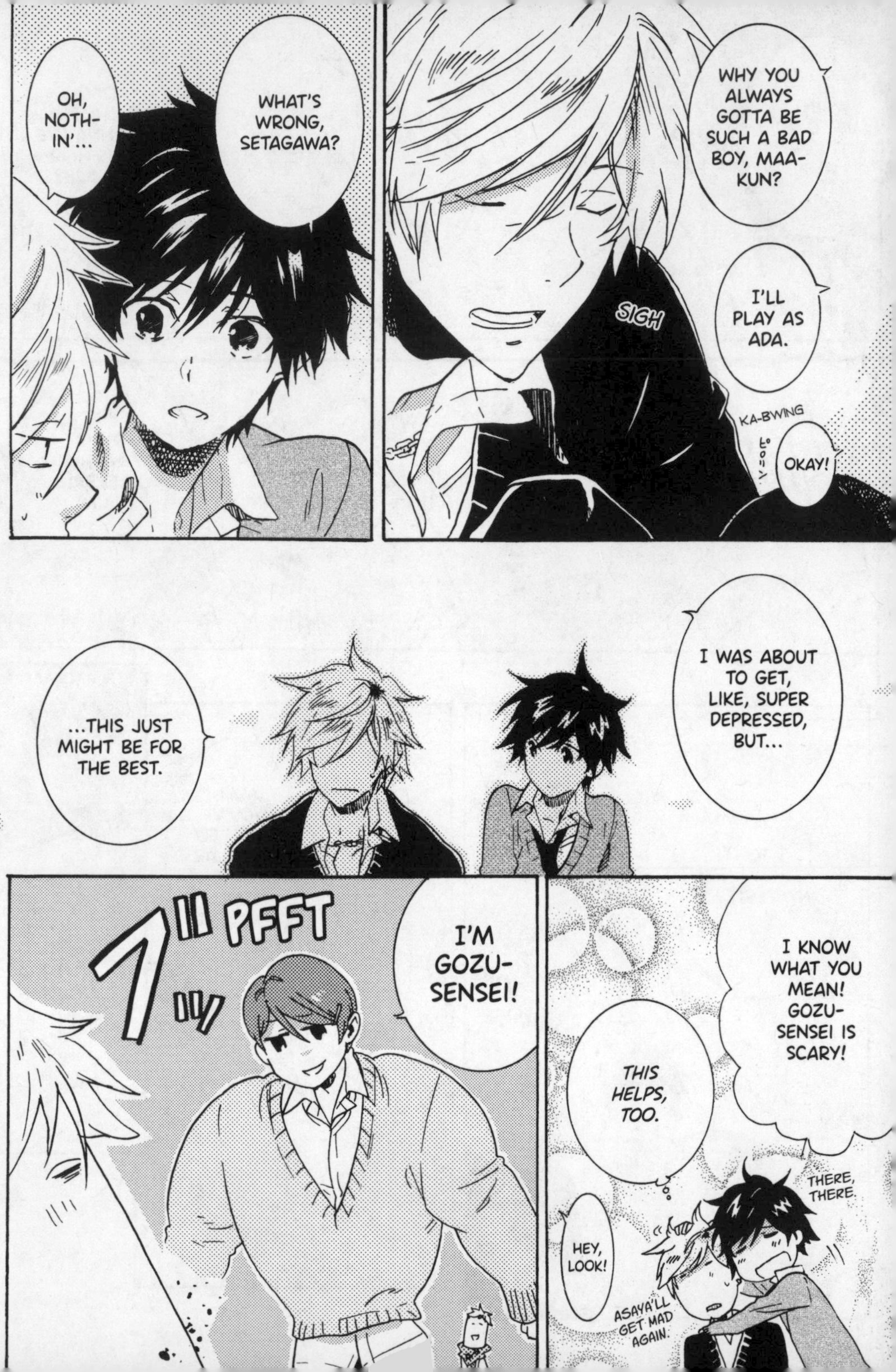
WHY YOU ALWAYS GOTTA BE SUCH A BAD BOY, MAA-KUN?
SIGH
I'LL PLAY AS ADA.
KA-BWING
OKAY!
WHAT'S WRONG, SETAGAWA?
OH, NOTHIN'...
I WAS ABOUT TO GET, LIKE, SUPER DEPRESSED, BUT...
...THIS JUST MIGHT BE FOR THE BEST.
I KNOW WHAT YOU MEAN! GOZU-SENSEI IS SCARY!
THIS HELPS, TOO.
THERE, THERE.
HEY, LOOK!
ASAYA'LL GET MAD AGAIN.
I'M GOZU-SENSEI!
PFFT

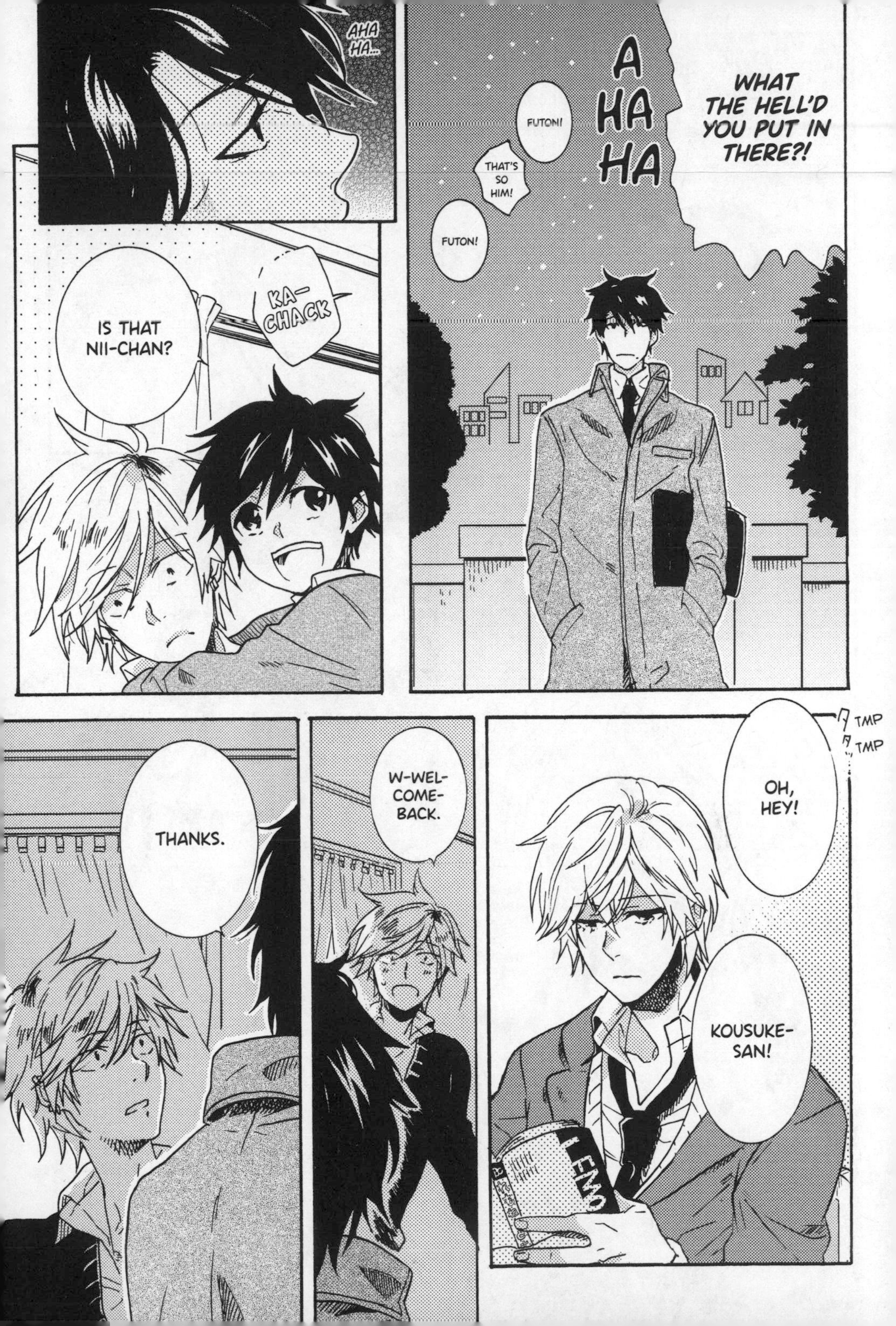
WHAT THE HELL'D YOU PUT IN THERE?!
AHAHAHA
FUTON!
THAT'S SO HIM!
FUTON!
AHAHA...
KA-CHACK
IS THAT NII-CHAN?
TMP
TMP
OH, HEY!
KOUSUKE-SAN!
W-WELCOME-BACK.
THANKS.

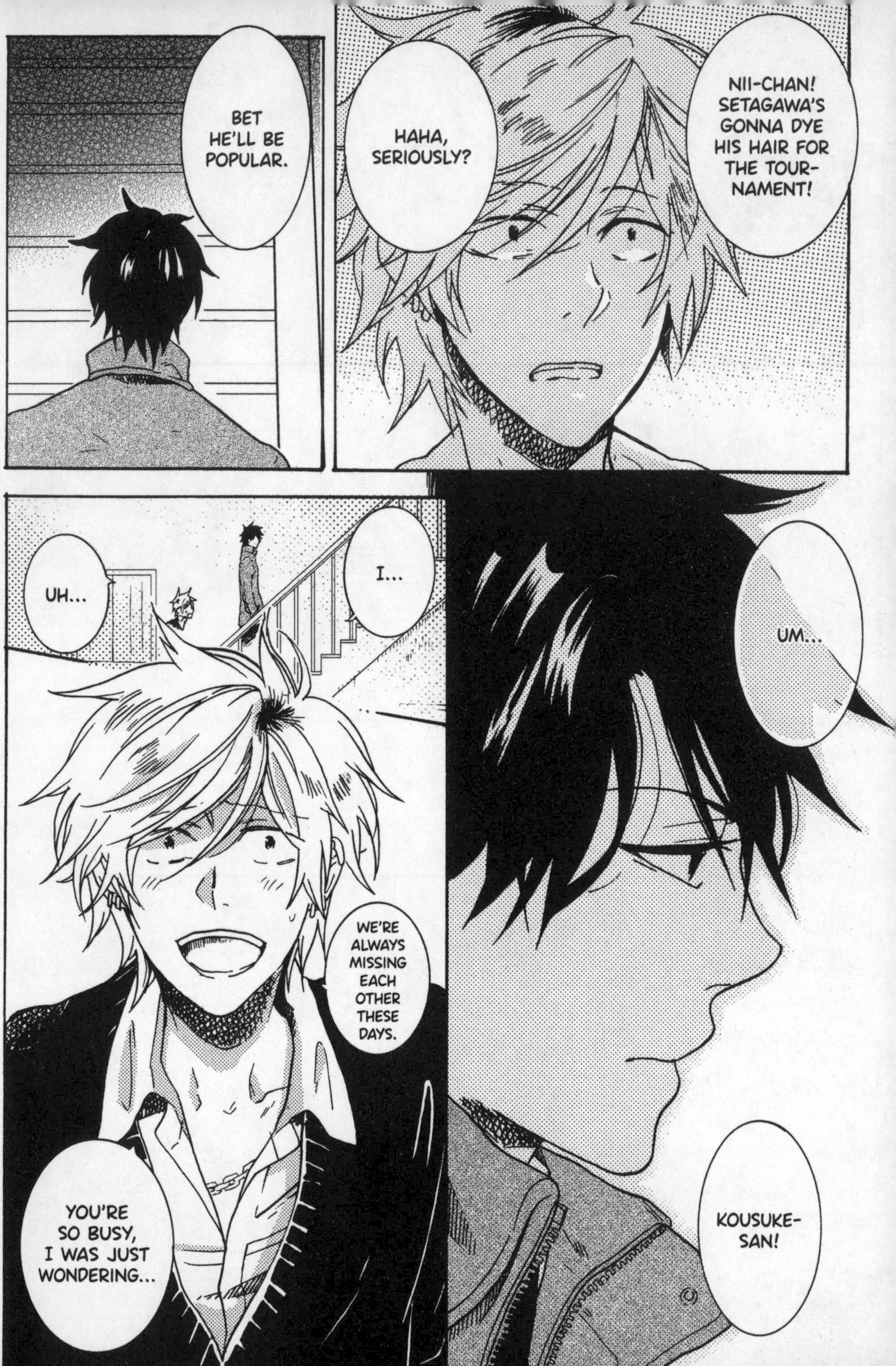
NII-CHAN! SETAGAWA'S GONNA DYE HIS HAIR FOR THE TOURNAMENT!
HAHA, SERIOUSLY?
BET HE'LL BE POPULAR.
UM...
KOUSUKE-SAN!
I...
UH...
WE'RE ALWAYS MISSING EACH OTHER THESE DAYS.
YOU'RE SO BUSY, I WAS JUST WONDERING...

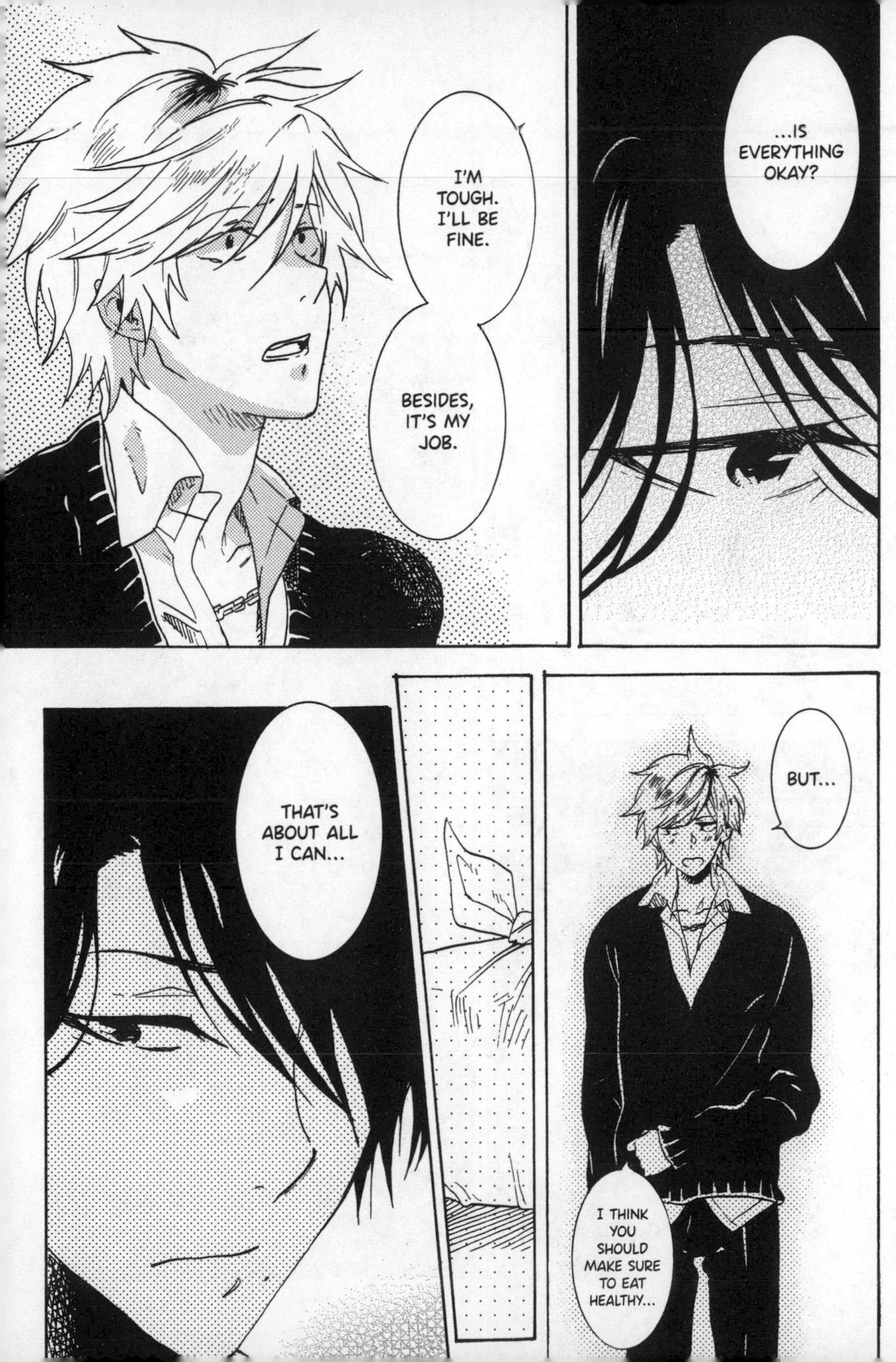
...IS EVERYTHING OKAY?
I'M TOUGH. I'LL BE FINE.
BESIDES, IT'S MY JOB.
BUT...
I THINK YOU SHOULD MAKE SURE TO EAT HEALTHY...
THAT'S ABOUT ALL I CAN...

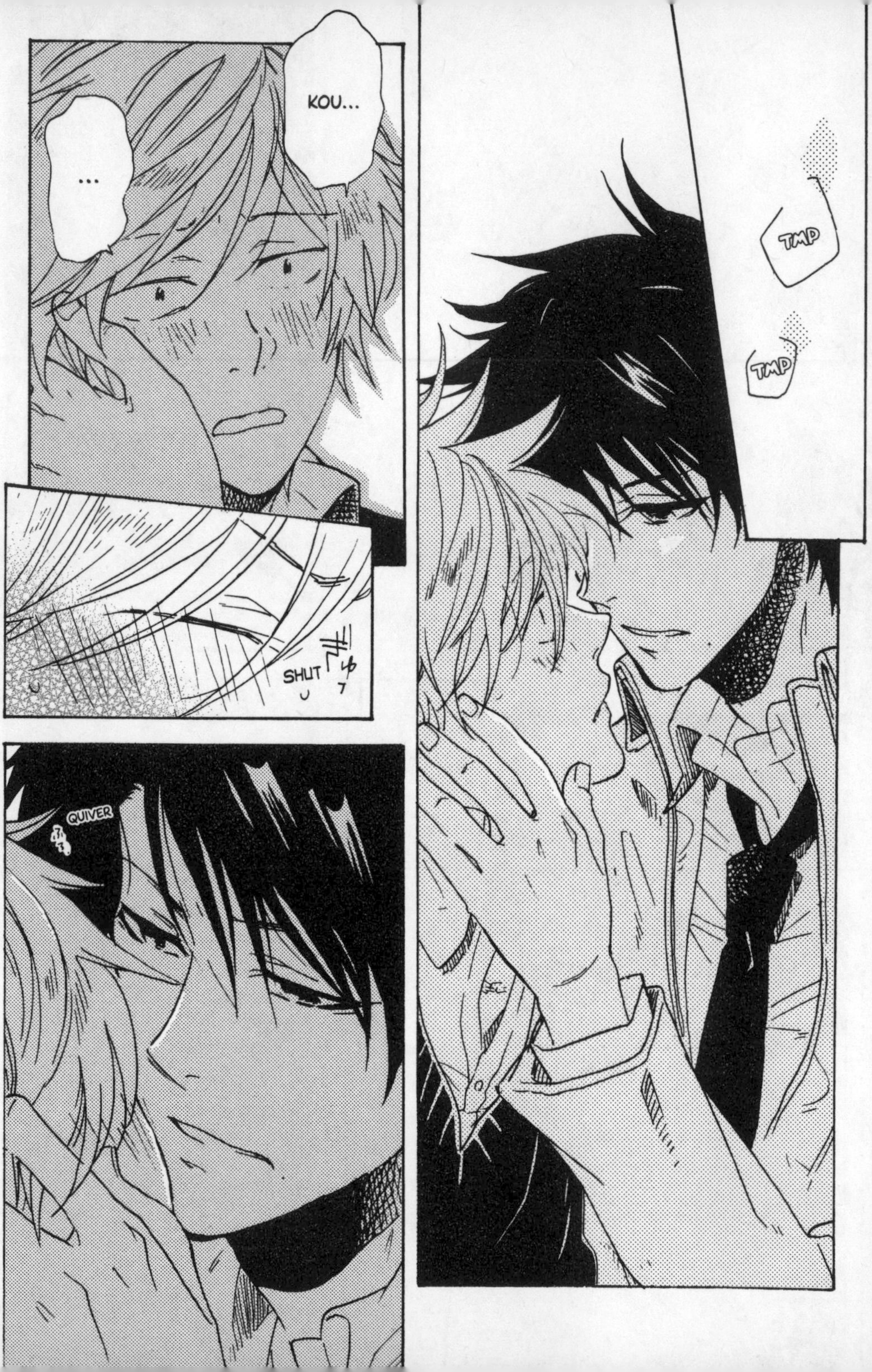
TMP
TMP
KOU...
...
SHUT
QUIVER

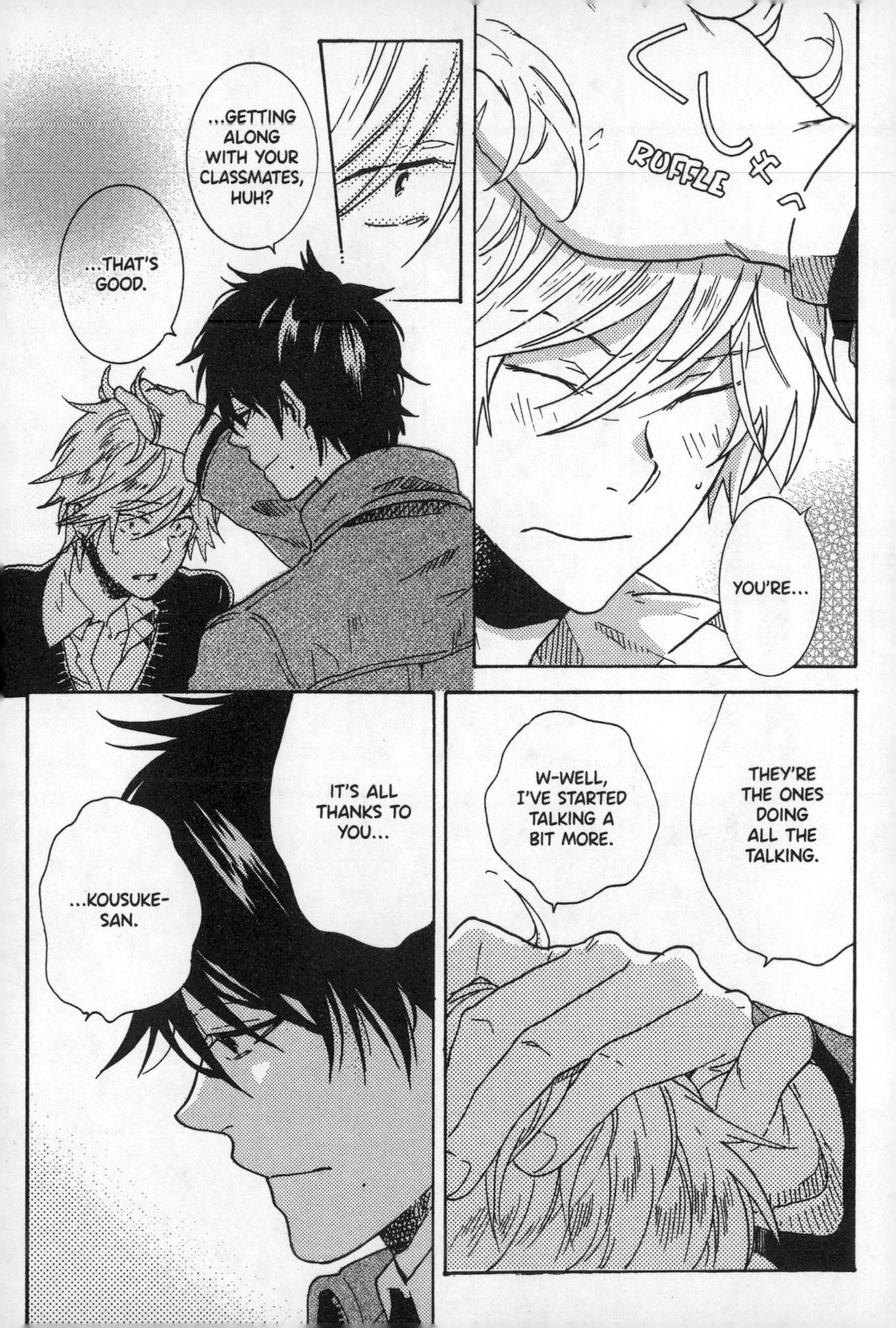
RUFFLE
YOU'RE...
...GETTING ALONG WITH YOUR CLASSMATES, HUH?
...THAT'S GOOD.
THEY'RE THE ONES DOING ALL THE TALKING.
W-WELL, I'VE STARTED TALKING A BIT MORE.
IT'S ALL THANKS TO YOU...
...KOUSUKE-SAN.

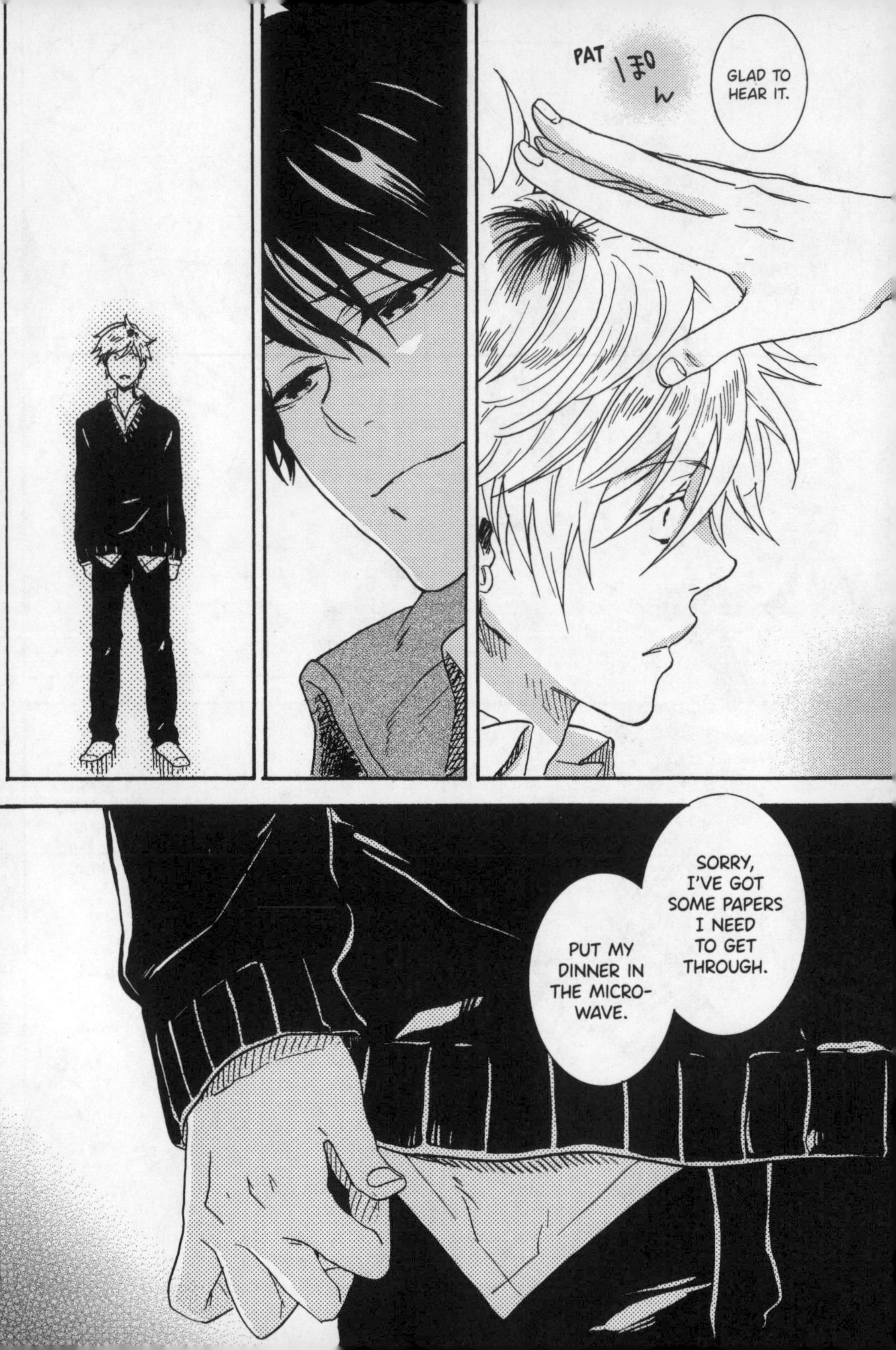
GLAD TO HEAR IT.
PAT
SORRY, I'VE GOT SOME PAPERS I NEED TO GET THROUGH.
PUT MY DINNER IN THE MICRO-WAVE.

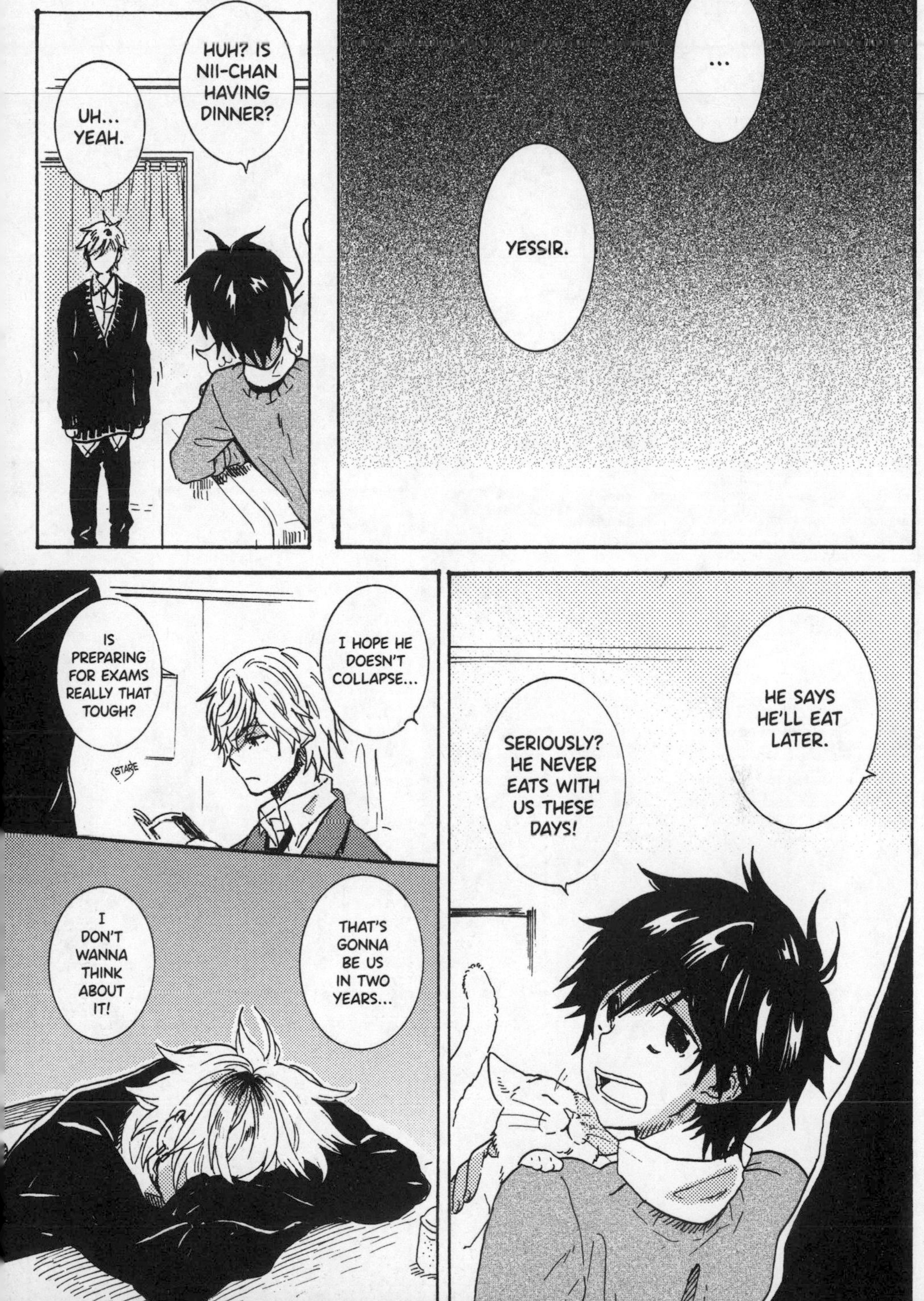
...
YESSIR.
HUH? IS NII-CHAN HAVING DINNER?
UH... YEAH.
HE SAYS HE'LL EAT LATER.
SERIOUSLY? HE NEVER EATS WITH US THESE DAYS!
I HOPE HE DOESN'T COLLAPSE...
IS PREPARING FOR EXAMS REALLY THAT TOUGH?
STARE
THAT'S GONNA BE US IN TWO YEARS...
I DON'T WANNA THINK ABOUT IT!

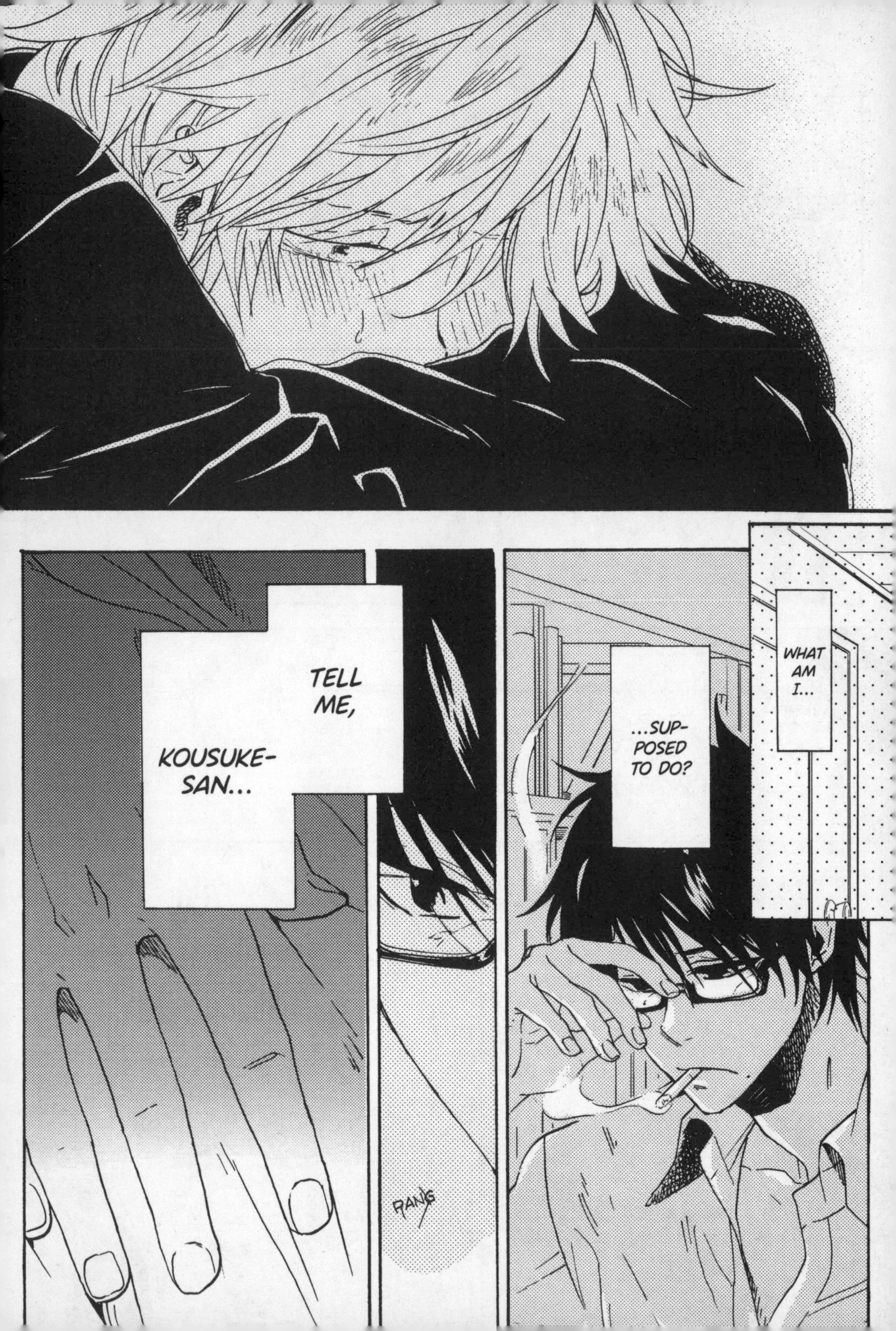
WHAT AM I...
...SUP-POSED TO DO?
RANG
TELL ME,
KOUSUKE-SAN...

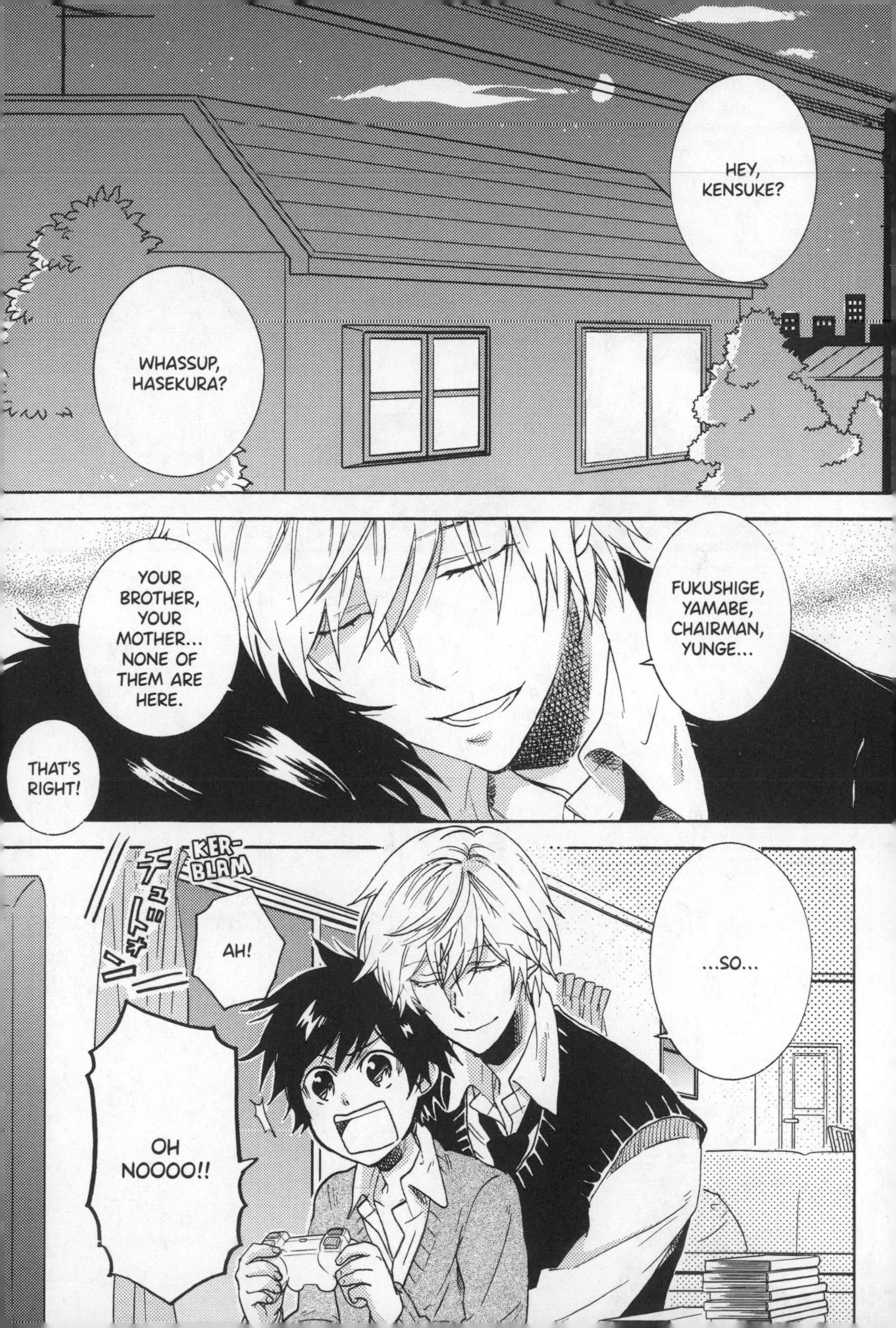
HEY, KENSUKE?
WHASSUP, HASEKURA?
FUKUSHIGE, YAMABE, CHAIRMAN, YUNGE...
YOUR BROTHER, YOUR MOTHER... NONE OF THEM ARE HERE.
THAT'S RIGHT!
...SO...
KER-BLAM
AH!
OH NOOOO!!

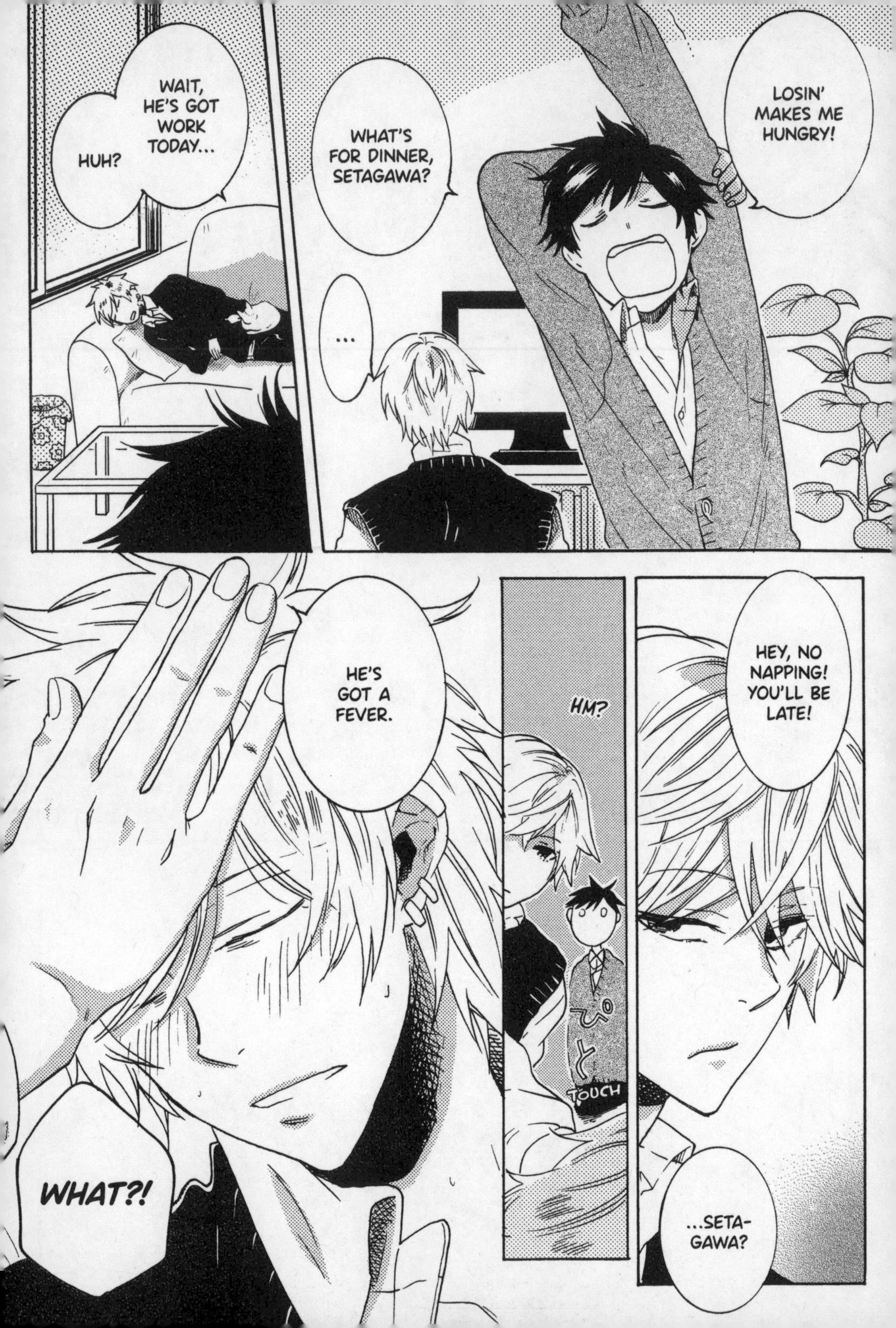
LOSIN' MAKES ME HUNGRY!
WHAT'S FOR DINNER, SETAGAWA?
...
WAIT, HE'S GOT WORK TODAY...
HUH?
HEY, NO NAPPING! YOU'LL BE LATE!
...SETA-GAWA?
HM?
ぴと
TOUCH
HE'S GOT A FEVER.
WHAT?!

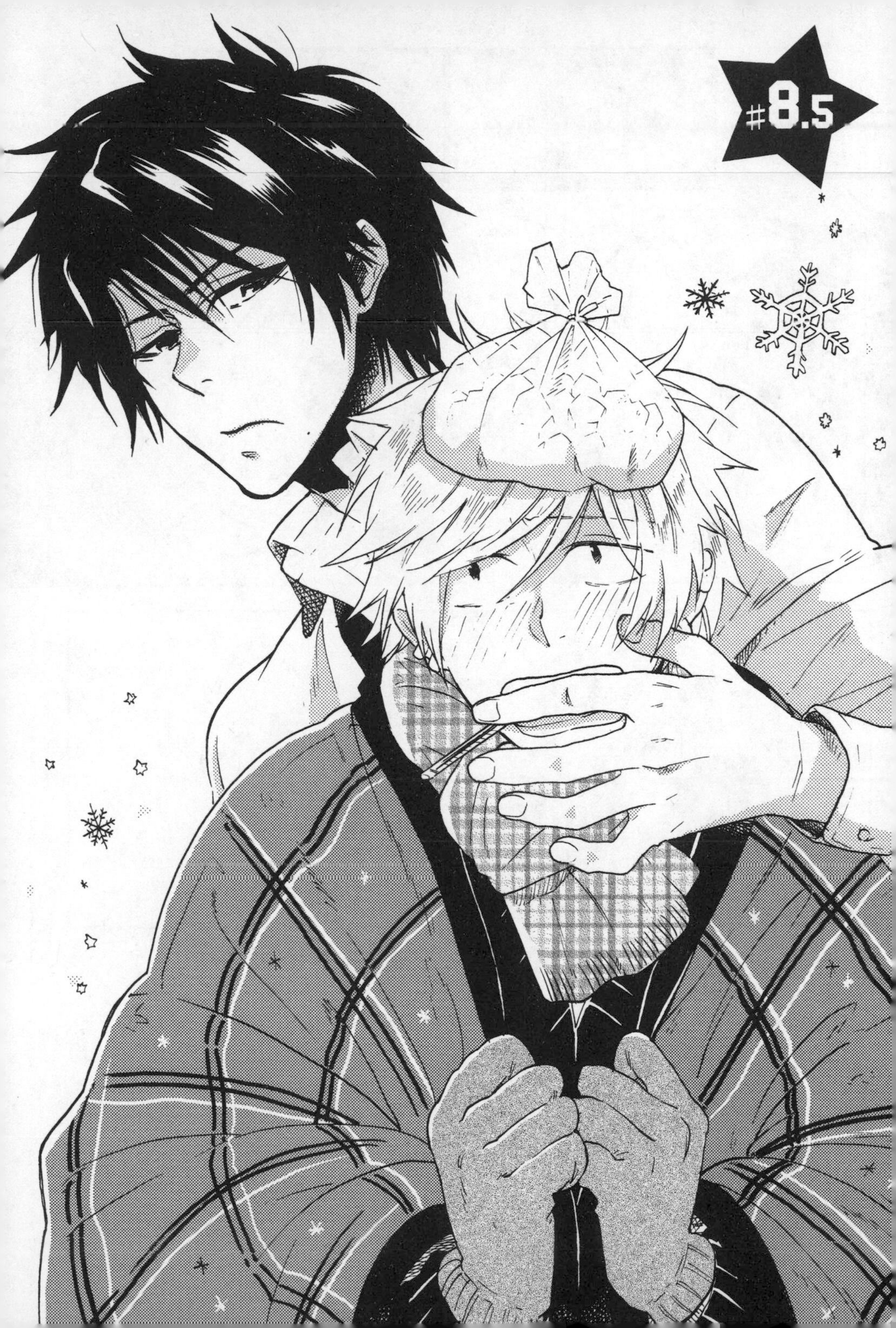
#8.5

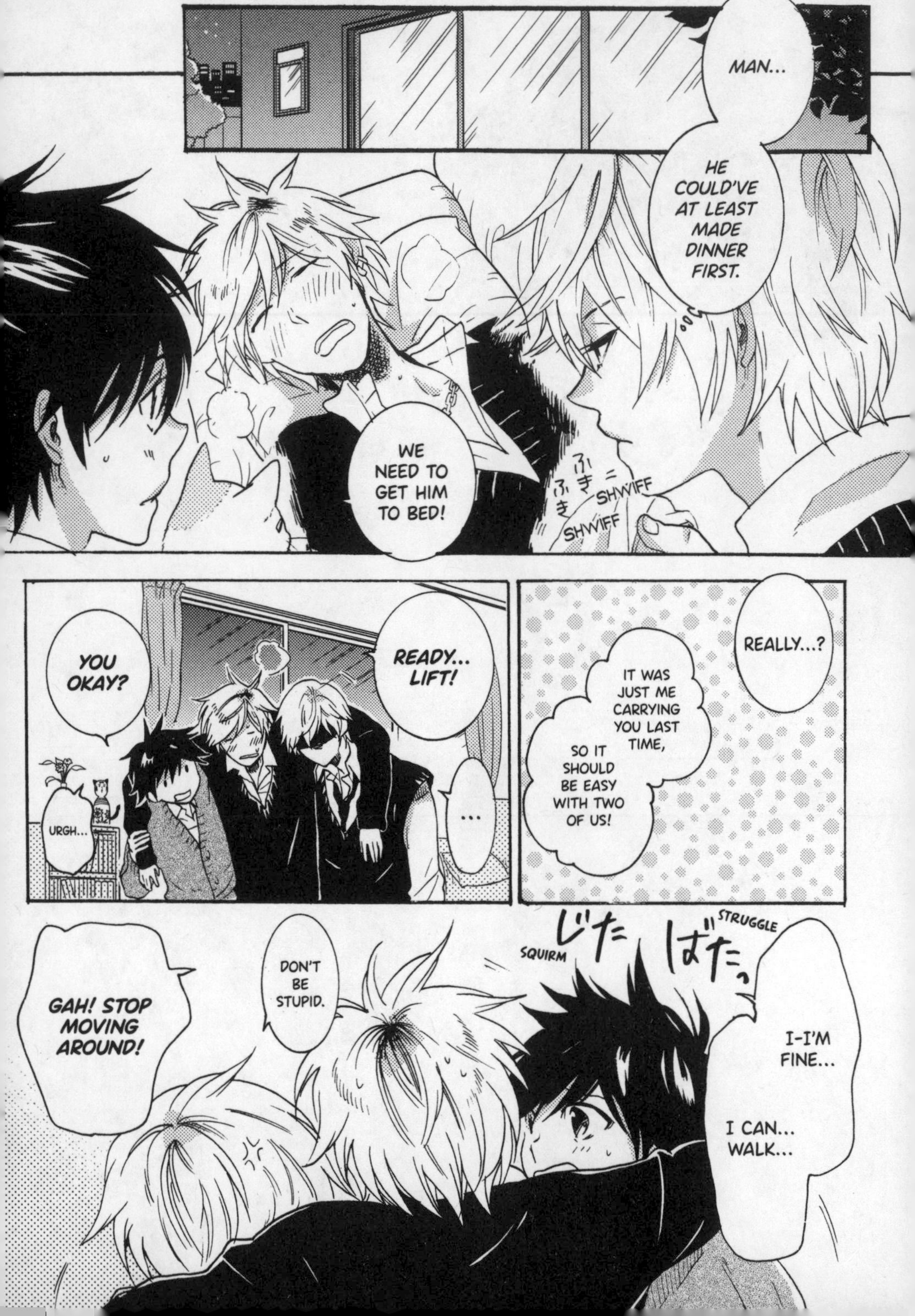
MAN...
HE COULD'VE AT LEAST MADE DINNER FIRST.
ふき ふき
SHWIFF SHWIFF
WE NEED TO GET HIM TO BED!
REALLY...?
IT WAS JUST ME CARRYING YOU LAST TIME,
SO IT SHOULD BE EASY WITH TWO OF US!
READY... LIFT!
...
YOU OKAY?
URGH...
じたばた
STRUGGLE
SQUIRM
I-I'M FINE...
I CAN... WALK...
DON'T BE STUPID.
GAH! STOP MOVING AROUND!

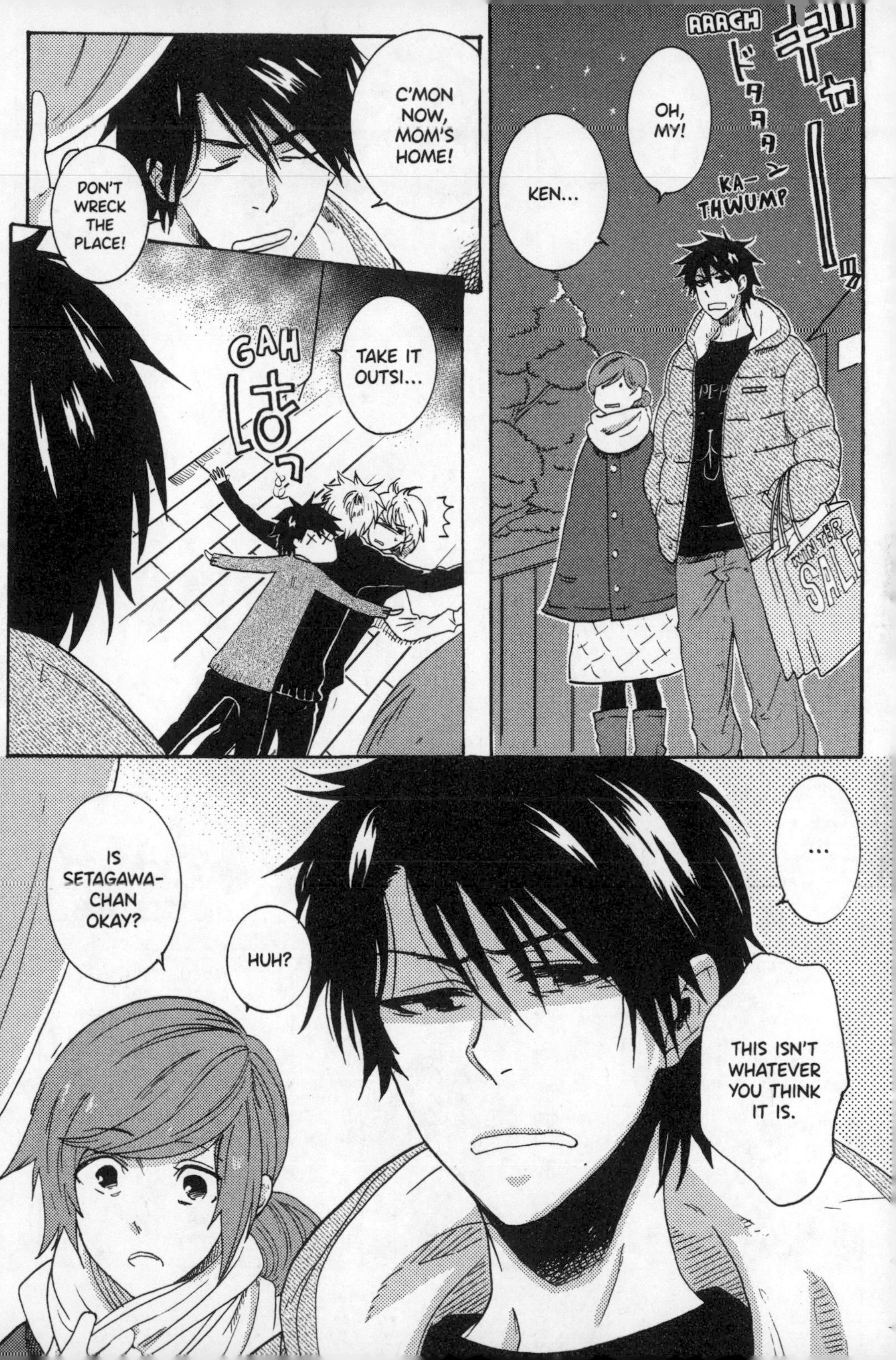
AAAGH
OH, MY!
KA-THWUMP
KEN...
C'MON NOW, MOM'S HOME!
DON'T WRECK THE PLACE!
TAKE IT OUTSI...
GAH
はっ
...
THIS ISN'T WHATEVER YOU THINK IT IS.
IS SETAGAWA-CHAN OKAY?
HUH?

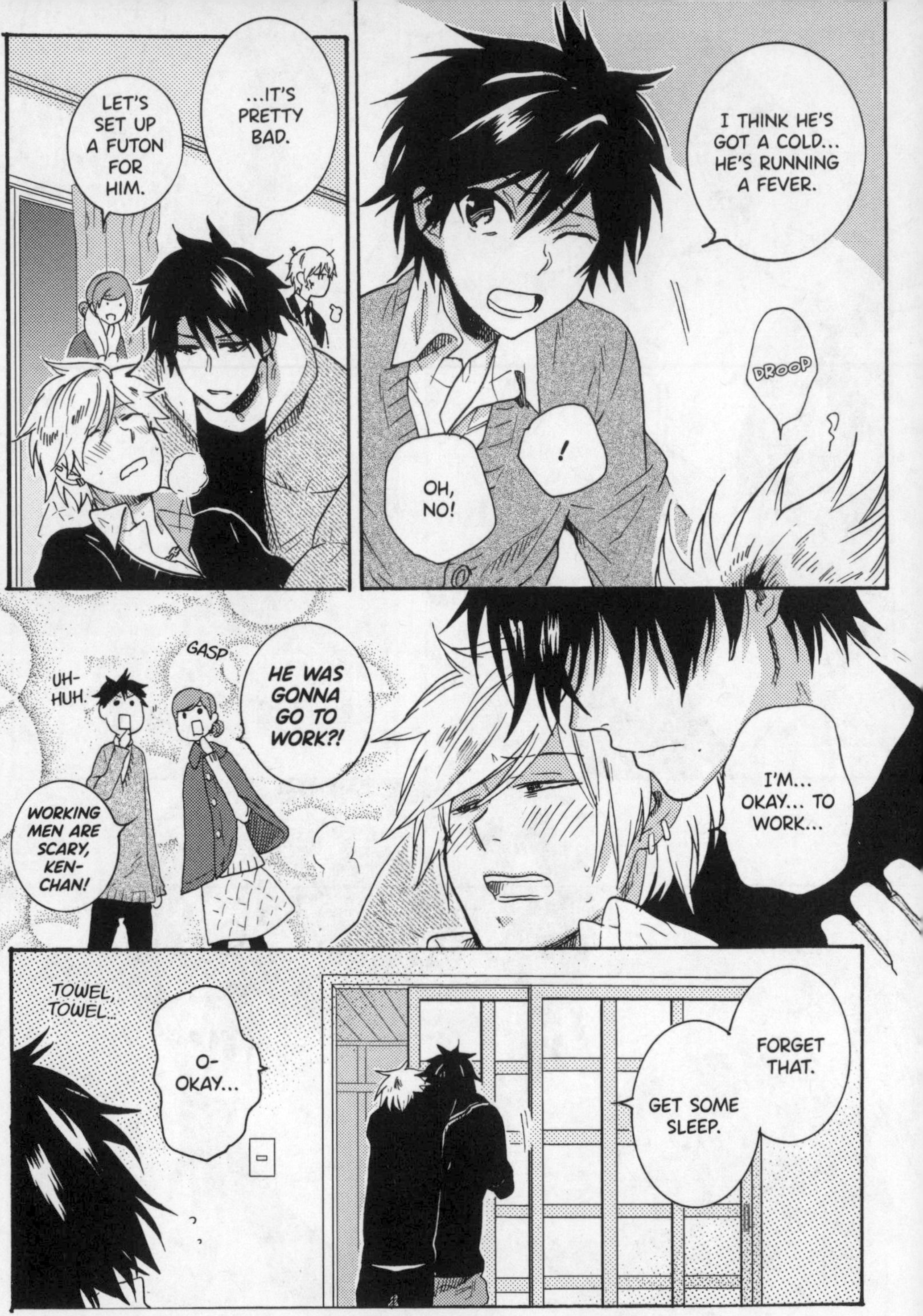
I THINK HE'S GOT A COLD... HE'S RUNNING A FEVER.
DROOP
!
OH, NO!
...IT'S PRETTY BAD.
LET'S SET UP A FUTON FOR HIM.
I'M... OKAY... TO WORK...
HE WAS GONNA GO TO WORK?!
GASP
UH-HUH.
WORKING MEN ARE SCARY, KEN-CHAN!
FORGET THAT.
GET SOME SLEEP.
O-OKAY...
TOWEL, TOWEL...

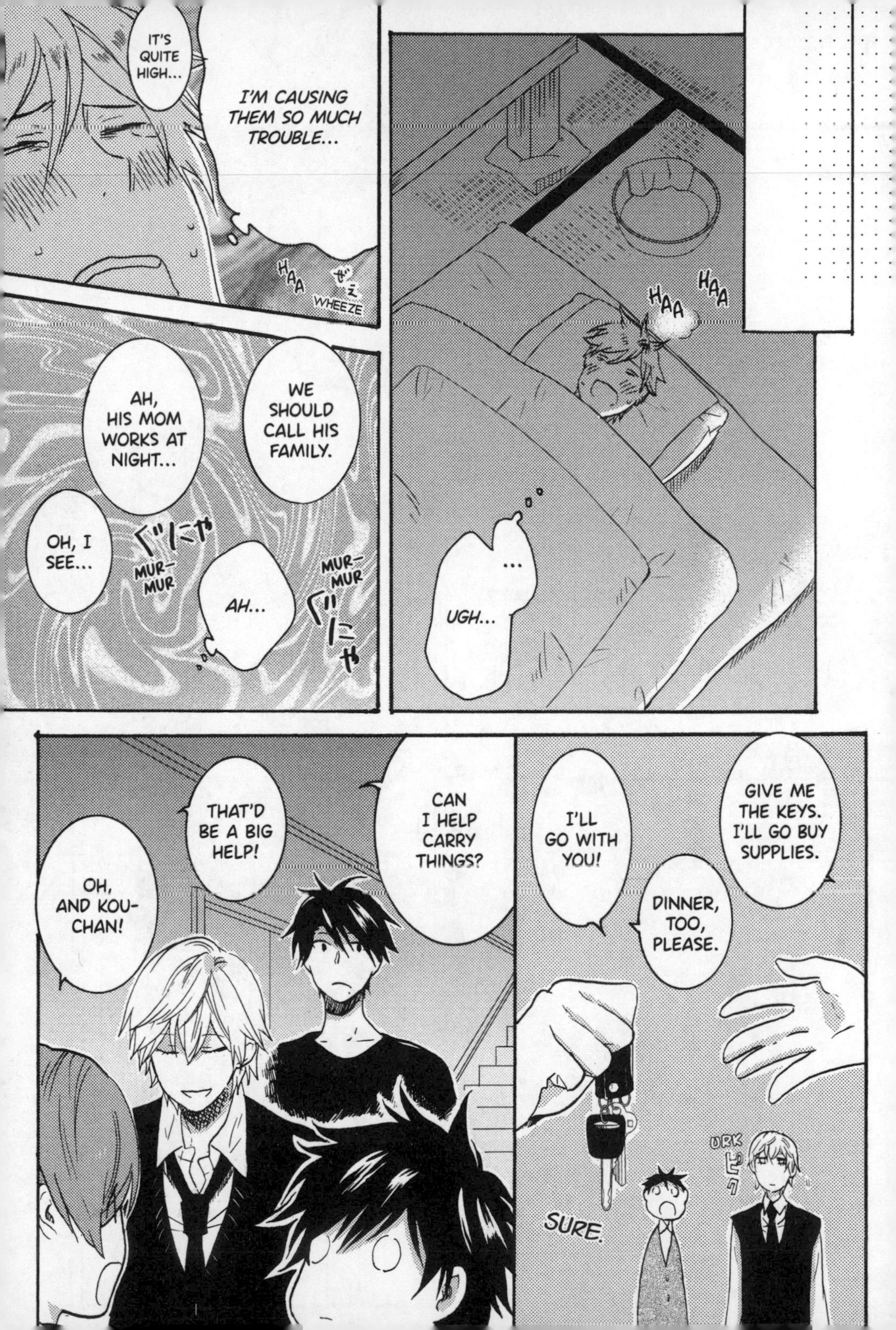
HAA
HAA
...
UGH...
IT'S QUITE HIGH...
I'M CAUSING THEM SO MUCH TROUBLE...
HAA
WHEEZE
WE SHOULD CALL HIS FAMILY.
AH, HIS MOM WORKS AT NIGHT...
OH, I SEE...
MUR-MUR
AH...
MUR-MUR
GIVE ME THE KEYS. I'LL GO BUY SUPPLIES.
I'LL GO WITH YOU!
DINNER, TOO, PLEASE.
URK
SURE.
CAN I HELP CARRY THINGS?
THAT'D BE A BIG HELP!
OH, AND KOU-CHAN!

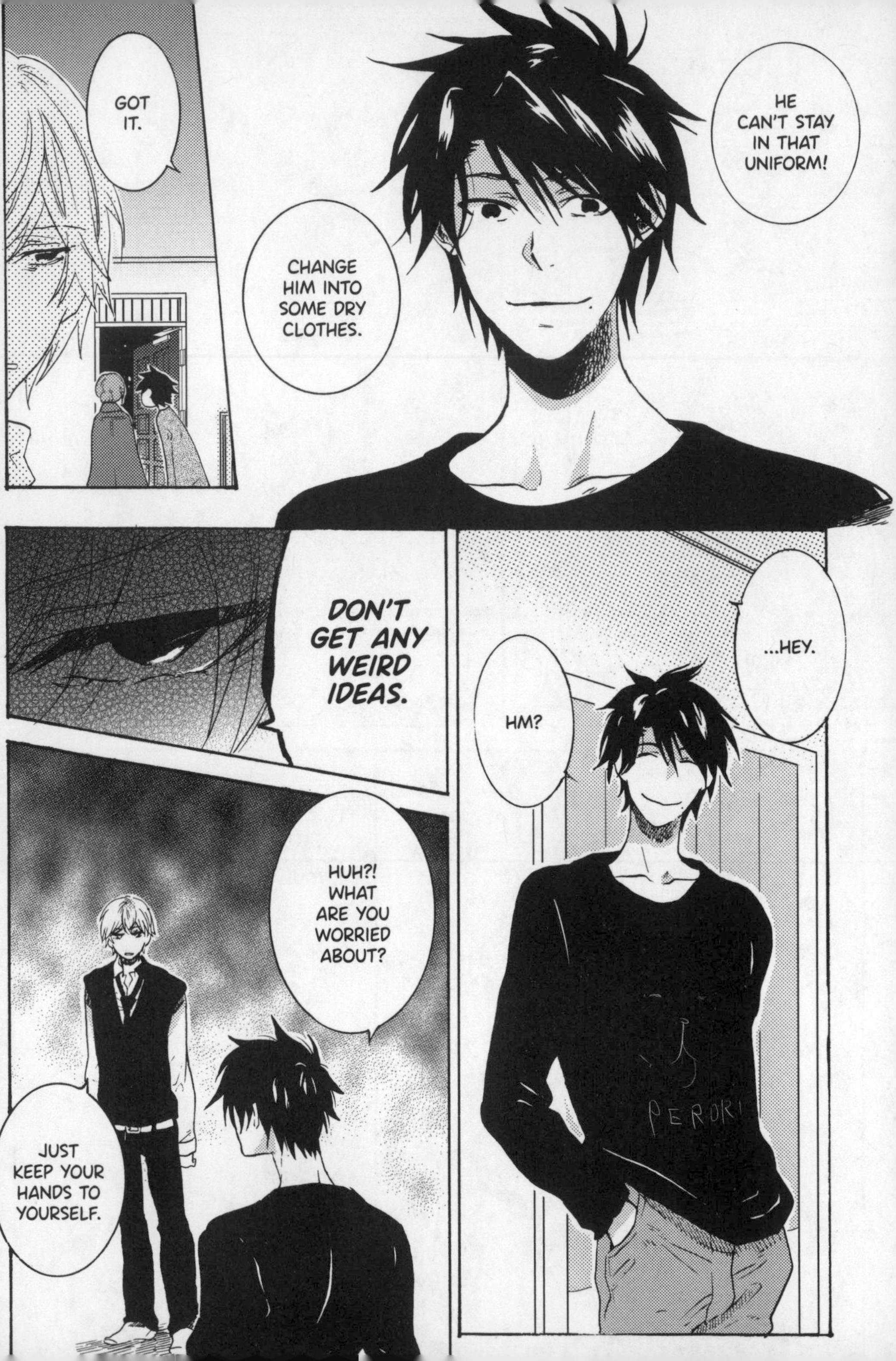
HE CAN'T STAY IN THAT UNIFORM!
CHANGE HIM INTO SOME DRY CLOTHES.
GOT IT.
...HEY.
HM?
PERORI
DON'T GET ANY WEIRD IDEAS.
HUH?! WHAT ARE YOU WORRIED ABOUT?
JUST KEEP YOUR HANDS TO YOURSELF.

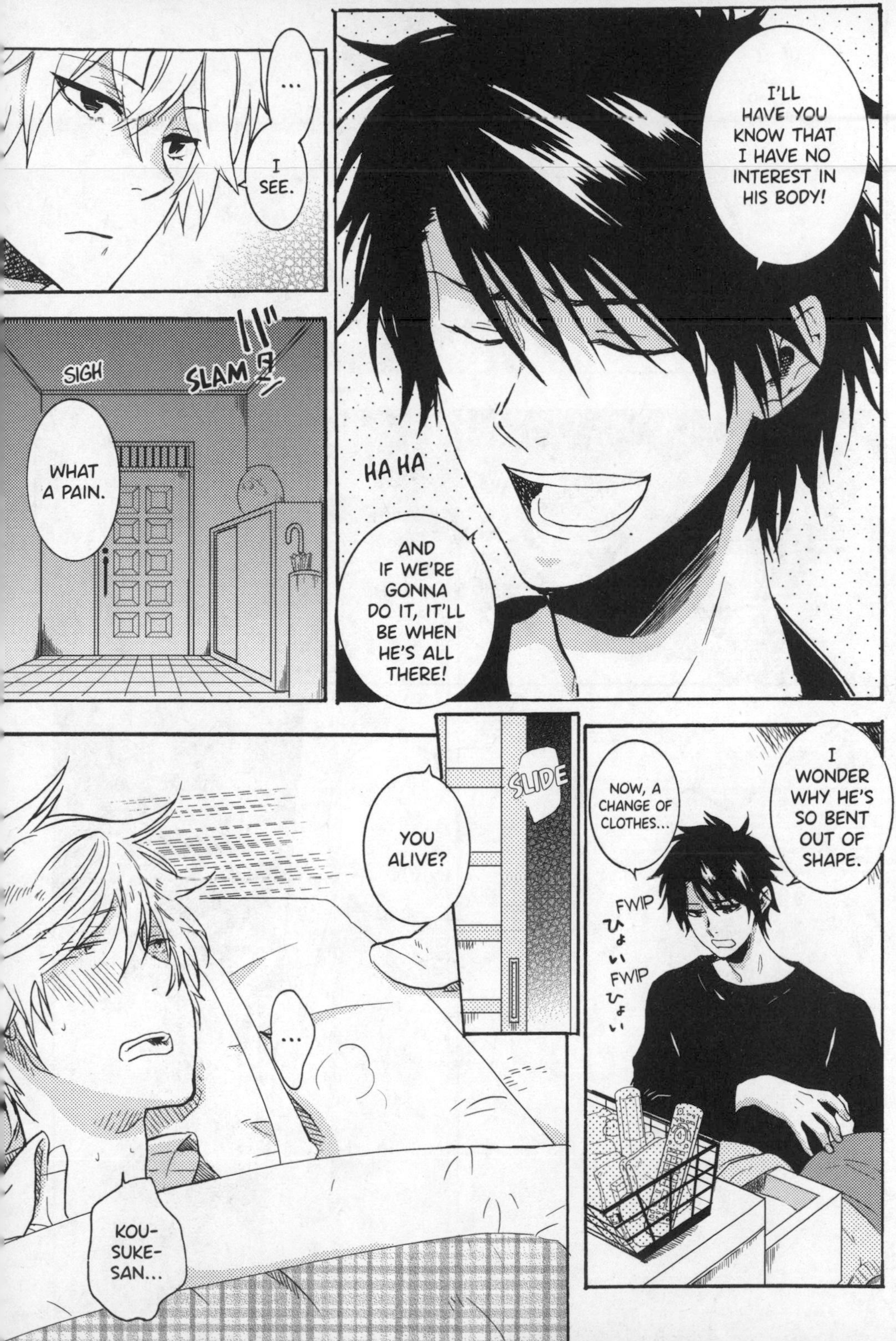
I'LL HAVE YOU KNOW THAT I HAVE NO INTEREST IN HIS BODY!
HA HA
AND IF WE'RE GONNA DO IT, IT'LL BE WHEN HE'S ALL THERE!
...
I SEE.
SIGH
SLAM
WHAT A PAIN.
I WONDER WHY HE'S SO BENT OUT OF SHAPE.
NOW, A CHANGE OF CLOTHES...
FWIP ひょい
FWIP ひょい
SLIDE
YOU ALIVE?
...
KOU-SUKE-SAN...

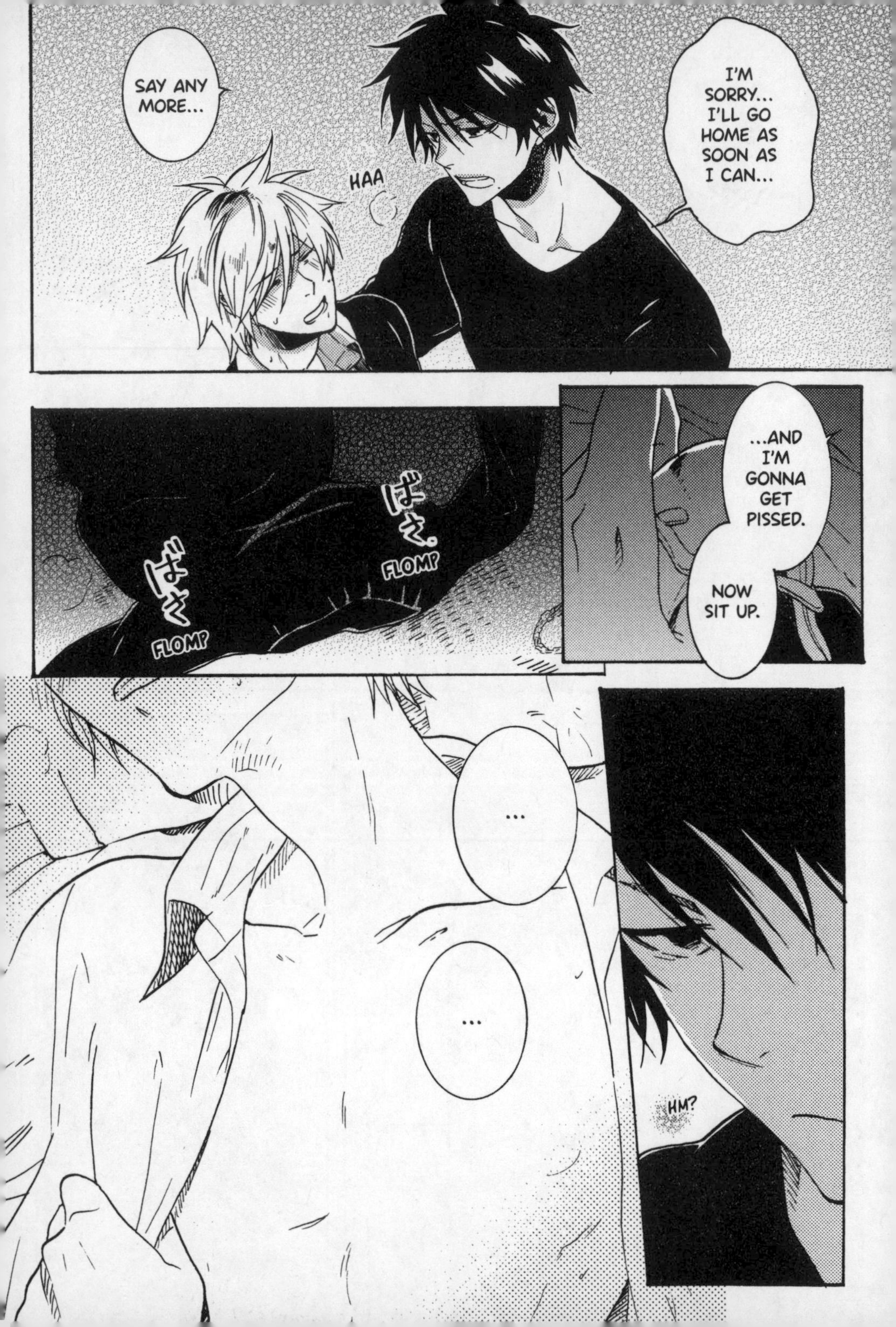
I'M SORRY... I'LL GO HOME AS SOON AS I CAN...
HAA
SAY ANY MORE...
...AND I'M GONNA GET PISSED.
NOW SIT UP.
ばさ。
FLOMP
ばさ
FLOMP
HM?
...
...

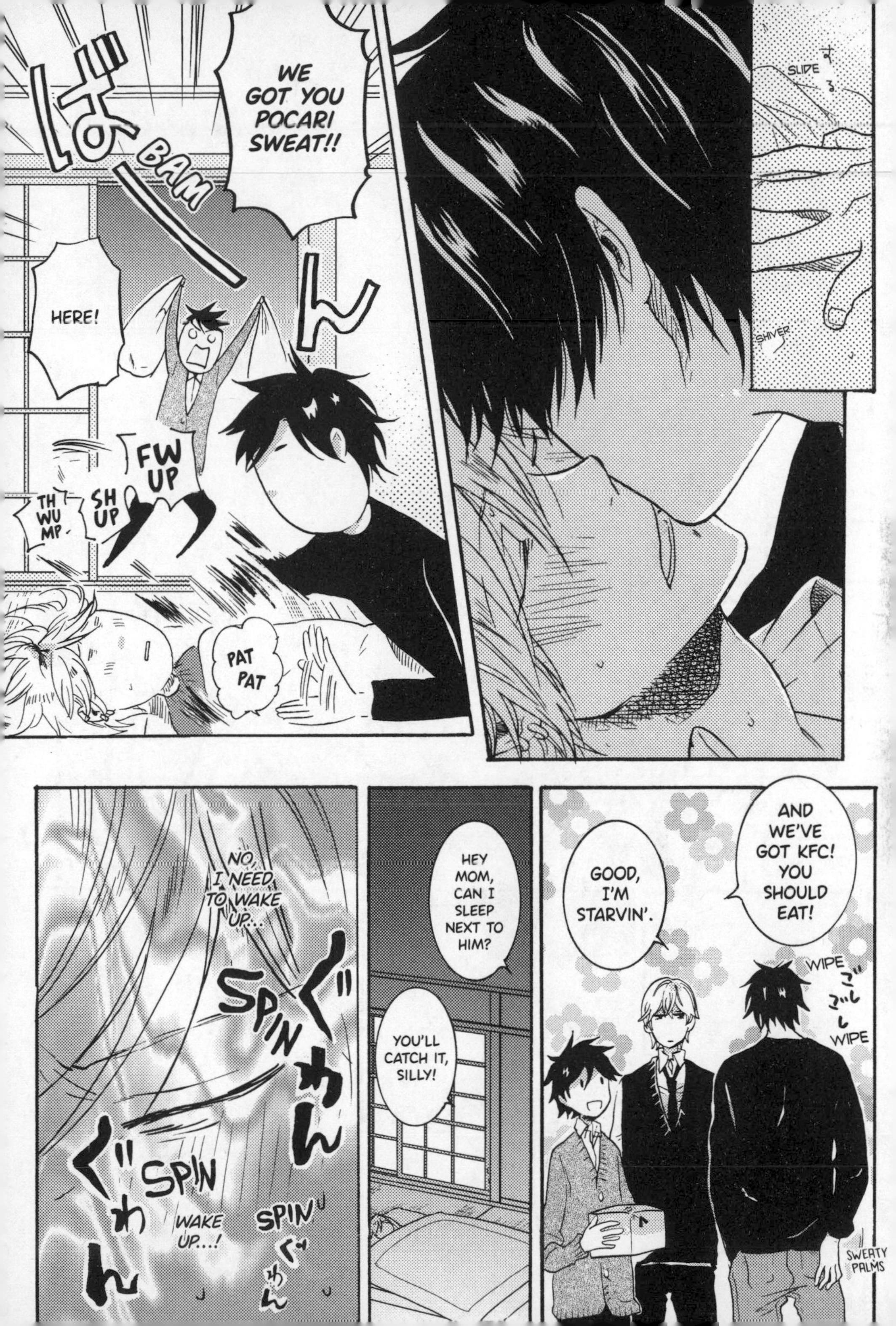
SLIDE
SHIVER
WE GOT YOU POCARI SWEAT!!
BAM
HERE!
FW UP
SH UP
TH WU MP
PAT PAT
AND WE'VE GOT KFC! YOU SHOULD EAT!
GOOD, I'M STARVIN'.
WIPE
WIPE
SWEATY PALMS
HEY MOM, CAN I SLEEP NEXT TO HIM?
YOU'LL CATCH IT, SILLY!
NO, I NEED TO WAKE UP...
SPIN
SPIN
WAKE UP...!
SPIN

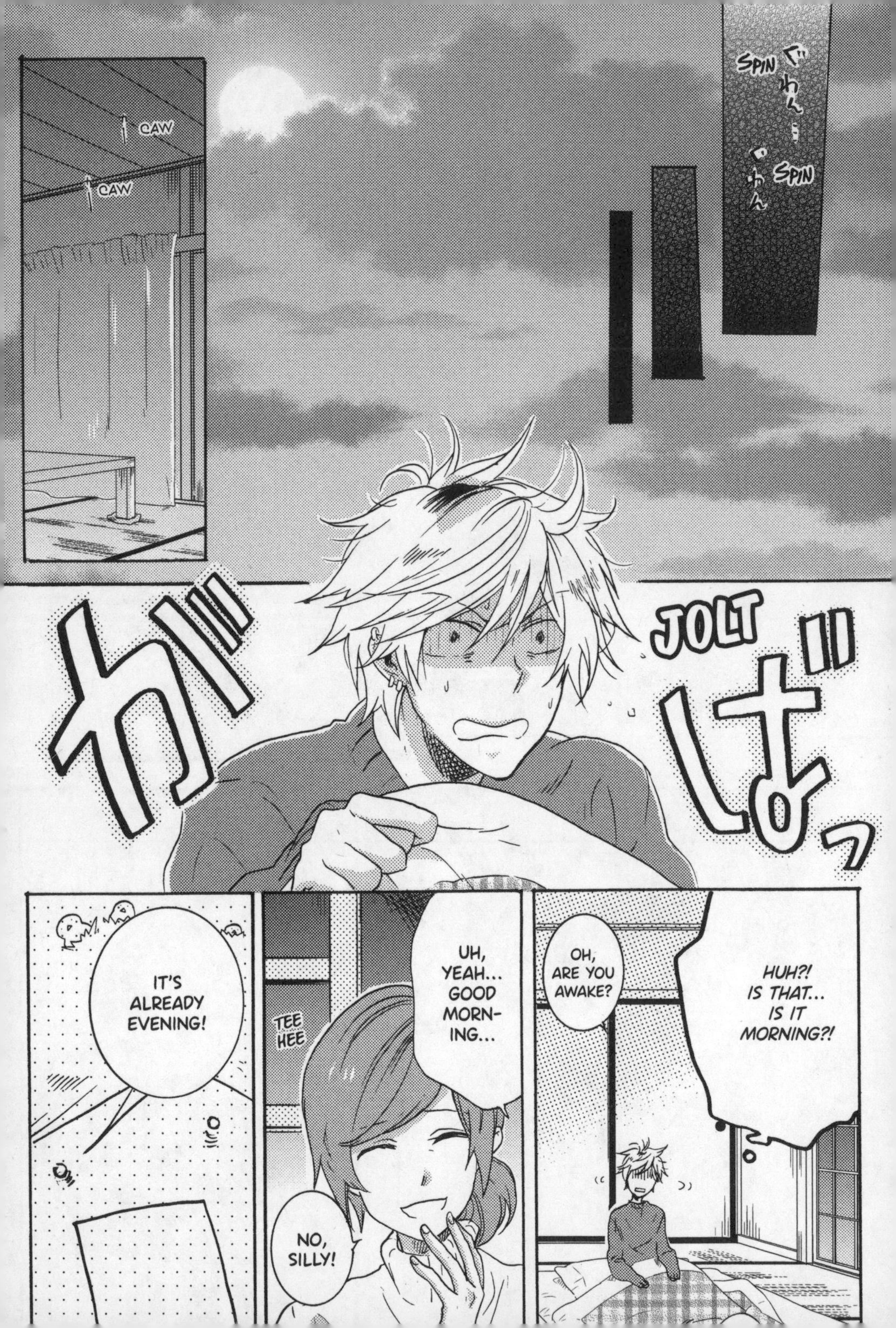
SPIN
ぐわん…ぐわん
SPIN
CAW
CAW
JOLT
ばっ
ガバ
HUH?! IS THAT... IS IT MORNING?!
OH, ARE YOU AWAKE?
UH, YEAH... GOOD MORN-ING...
TEE HEE
NO, SILLY!
IT'S ALREADY EVENING!

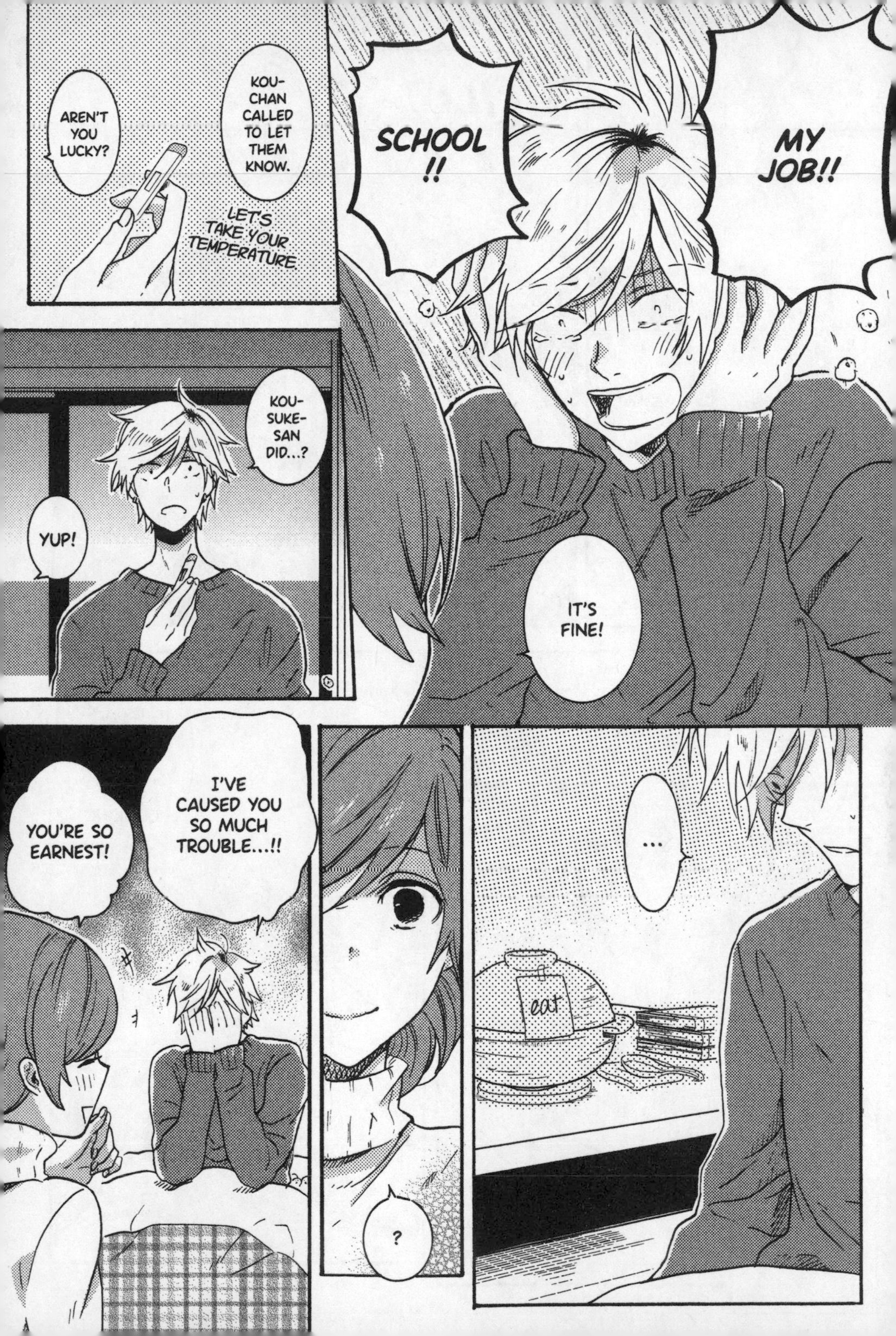
MY JOB!!
SCHOOL !!
IT'S FINE!
KOU-CHAN CALLED TO LET THEM KNOW.
AREN'T YOU LUCKY?
LET'S TAKE YOUR TEMPERATURE.
KOUSUKE-SAN DID...?
YUP!
...
eat
?
I'VE CAUSED YOU SO MUCH TROUBLE...!!
YOU'RE SO EARNEST!

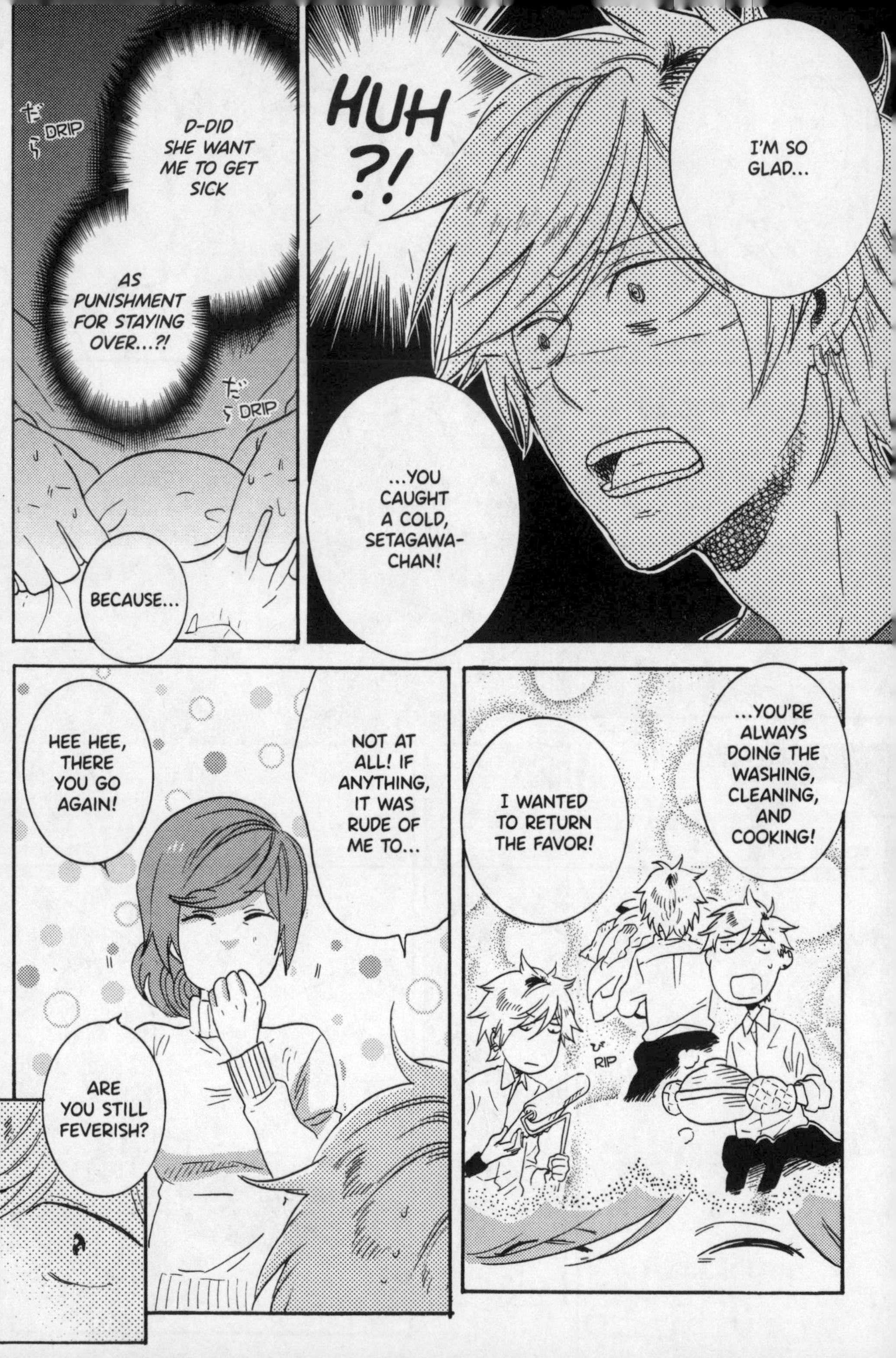
I'M SO GLAD...
...YOU CAUGHT A COLD, SETAGAWA-CHAN!
HUH ?!
D-DID SHE WANT ME TO GET SICK
AS PUNISHMENT FOR STAYING OVER...?!
DRIP
DRIP
BECAUSE...
...YOU'RE ALWAYS DOING THE WASHING, CLEANING, AND COOKING!
I WANTED TO RETURN THE FAVOR!
RIP
NOT AT ALL! IF ANYTHING, IT WAS RUDE OF ME TO...
HEE HEE, THERE YOU GO AGAIN!
ARE YOU STILL FEVERISH?

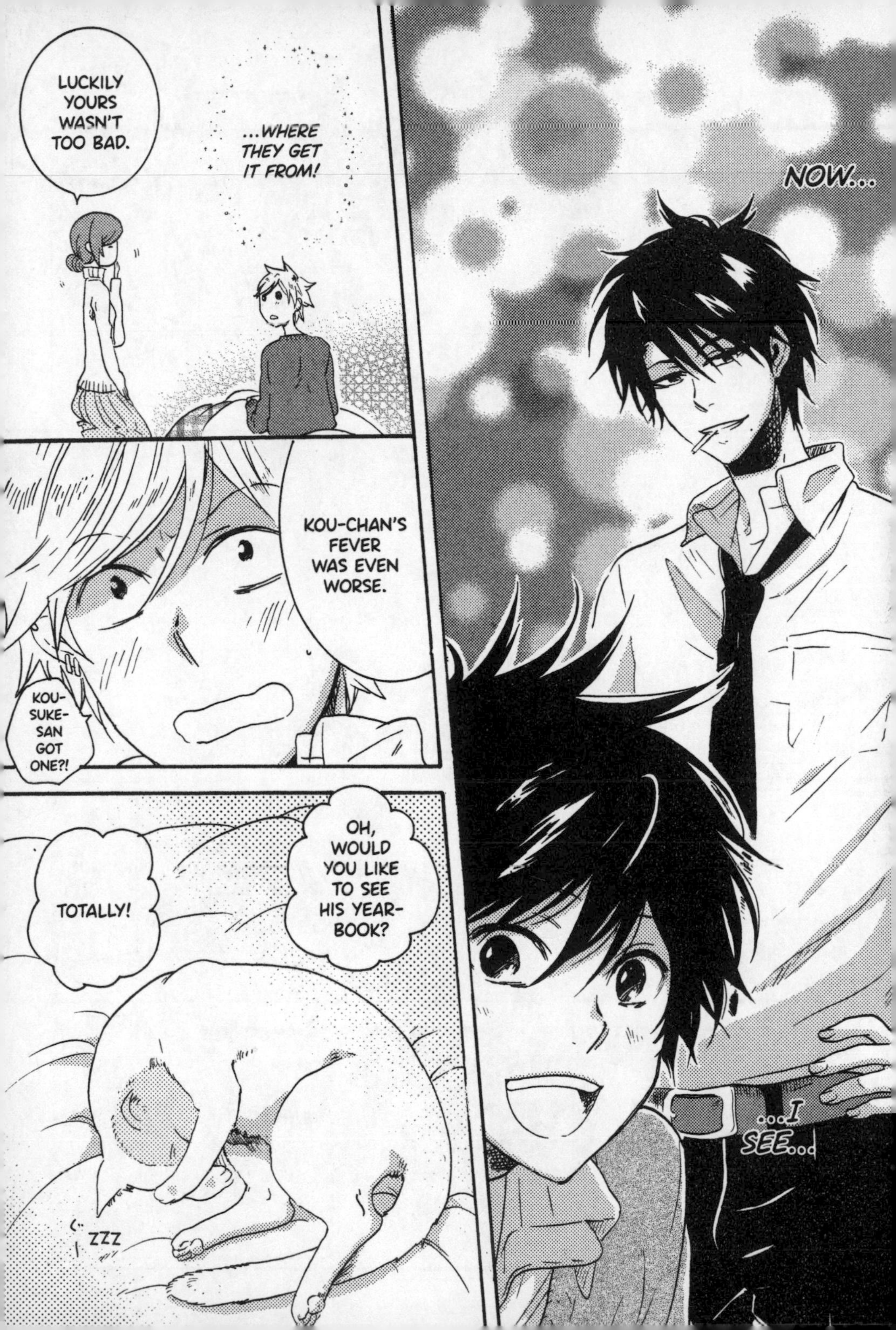
NOW...
...I SEE...
...WHERE THEY GET IT FROM!
LUCKILY YOURS WASN'T TOO BAD.
KOU-CHAN'S FEVER WAS EVEN WORSE.
KOU-SUKE-SAN GOT ONE?!
OH, WOULD YOU LIKE TO SEE HIS YEAR-BOOK?
TOTALLY!
ZZZ

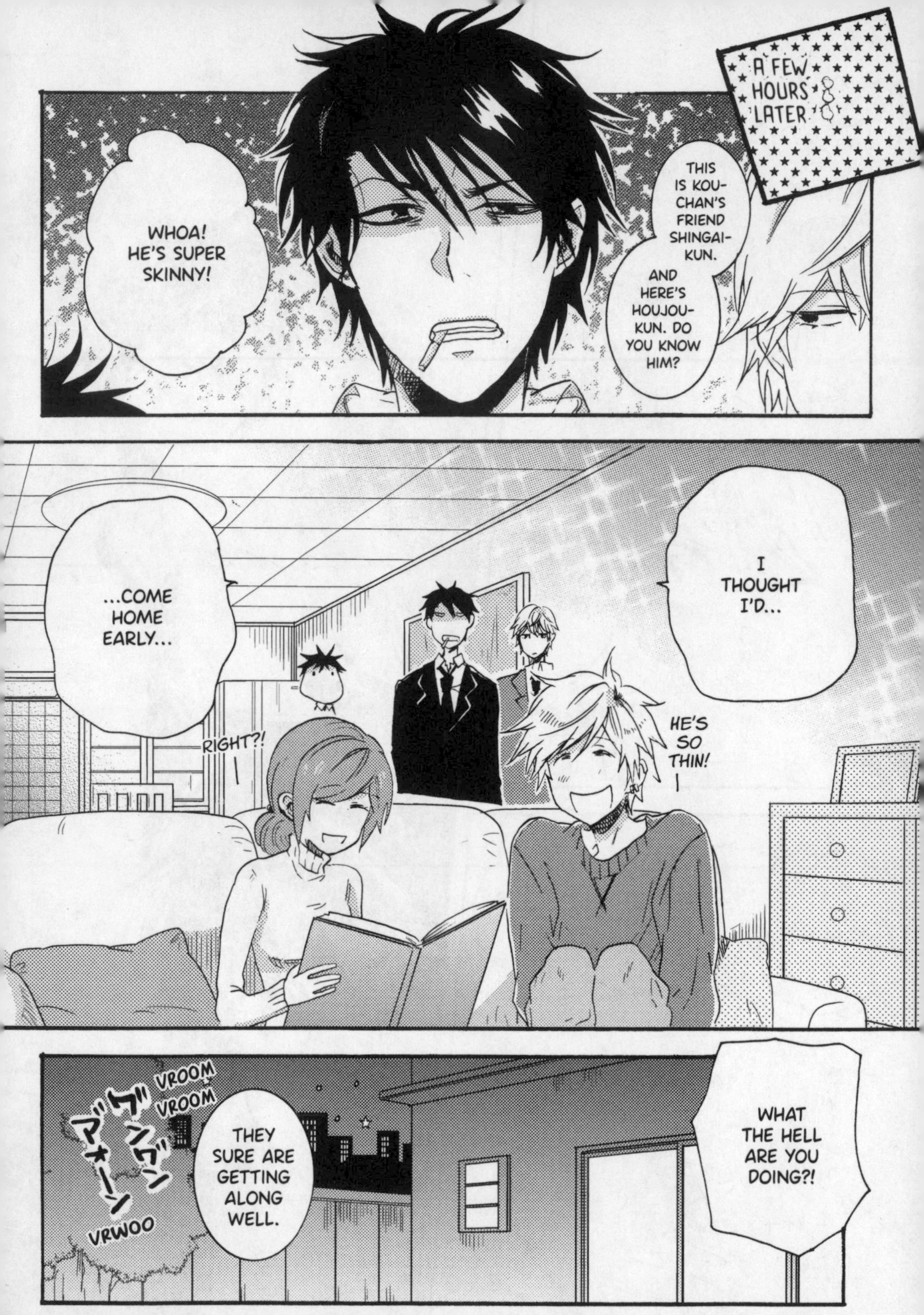
A FEW HOURS LATER
THIS IS KOU-CHAN'S FRIEND SHINGAI-KUN.
AND HERE'S HOUJOU-KUN. DO YOU KNOW HIM?
WHOA! HE'S SUPER SKINNY!
I THOUGHT I'D...
HE'S SO THIN!
RIGHT?!
...COME HOME EARLY...
WHAT THE HELL ARE YOU DOING?!
THEY SURE ARE GETTING ALONG WELL.
VROOM VROOM
VRWOO

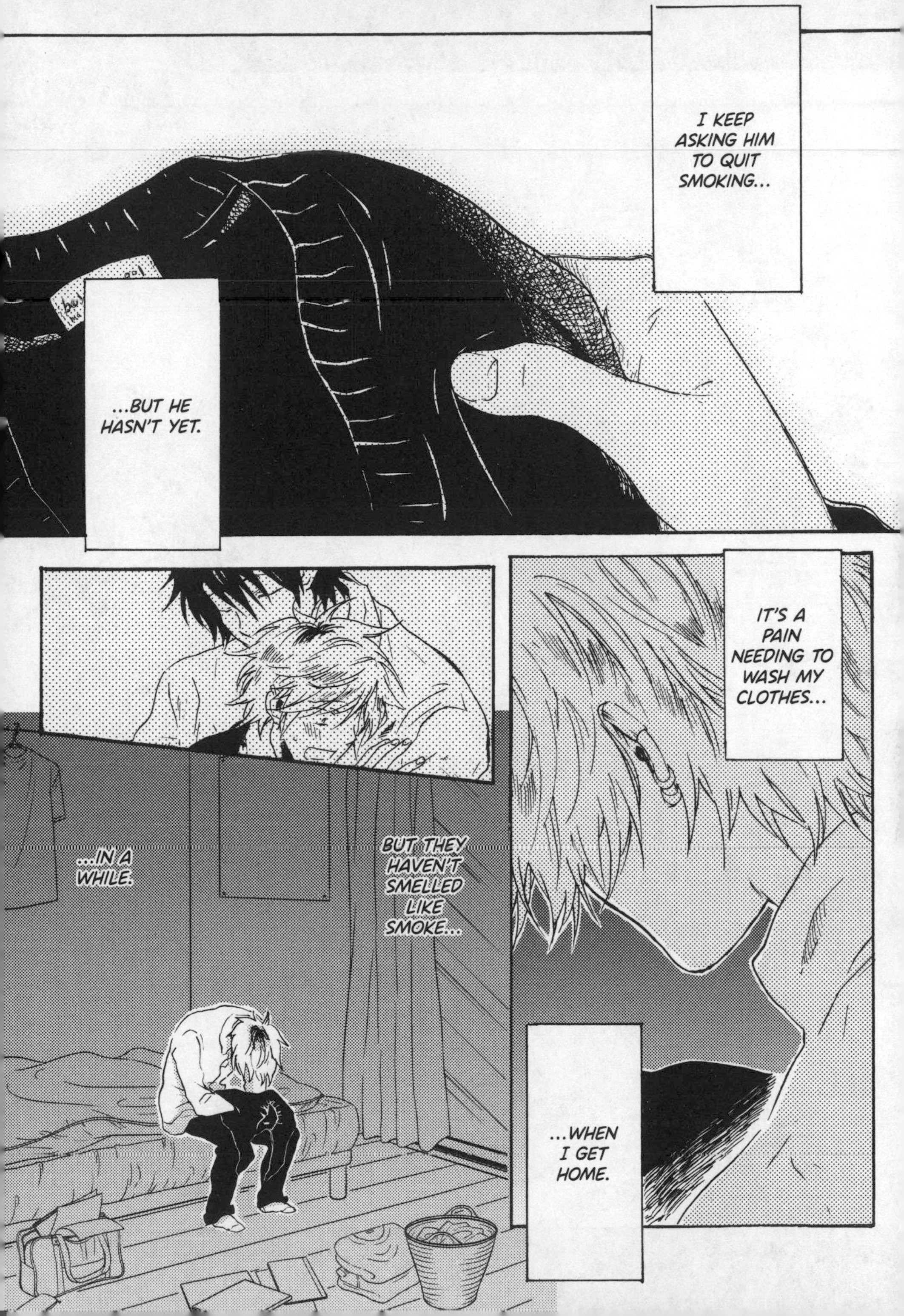
I KEEP ASKING HIM TO QUIT SMOKING...
...BUT HE HASN'T YET.
IT'S A PAIN NEEDING TO WASH MY CLOTHES...
...WHEN I GET HOME.
BUT THEY HAVEN'T SMELLED LIKE SMOKE...
...IN A WHILE.

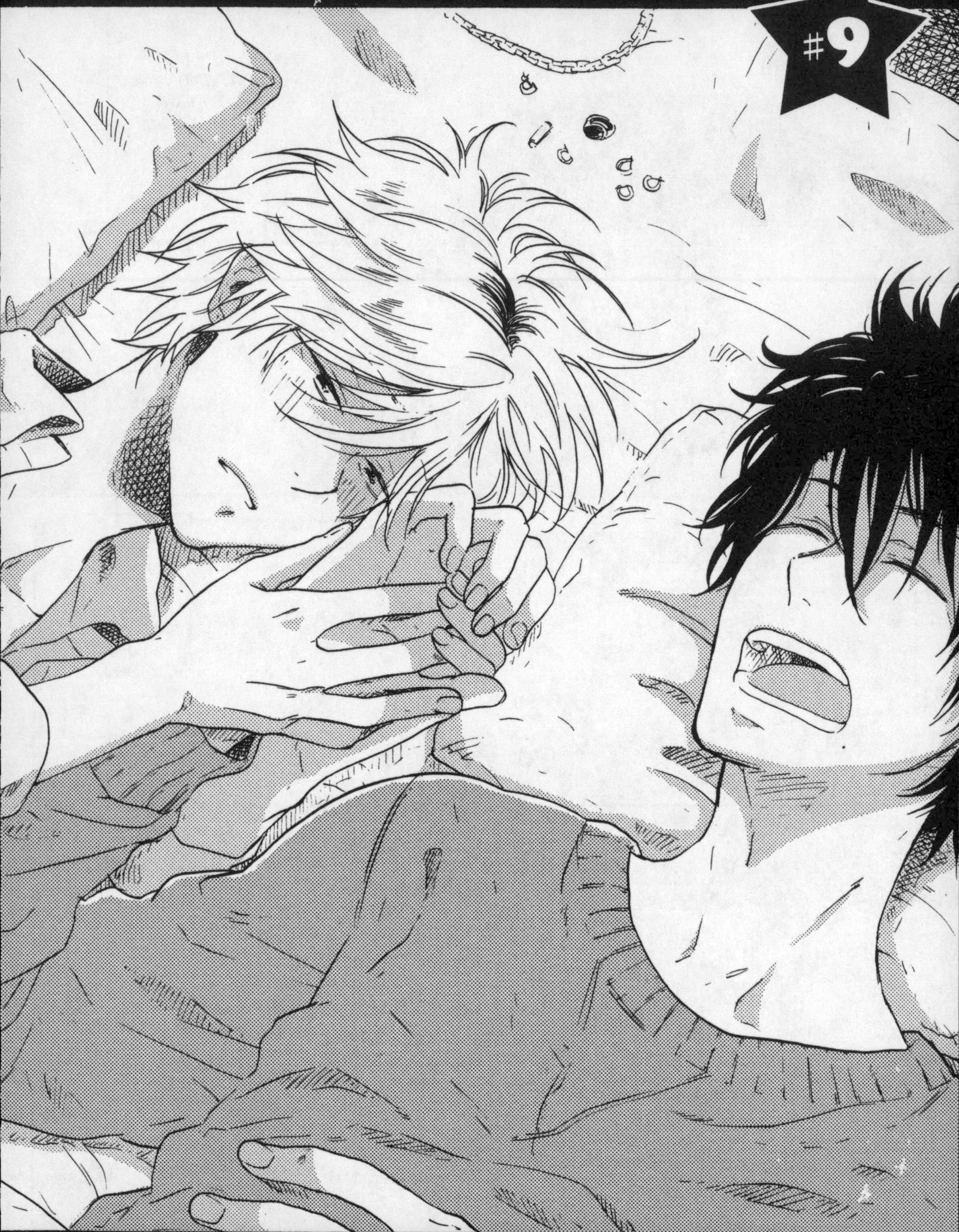
#9

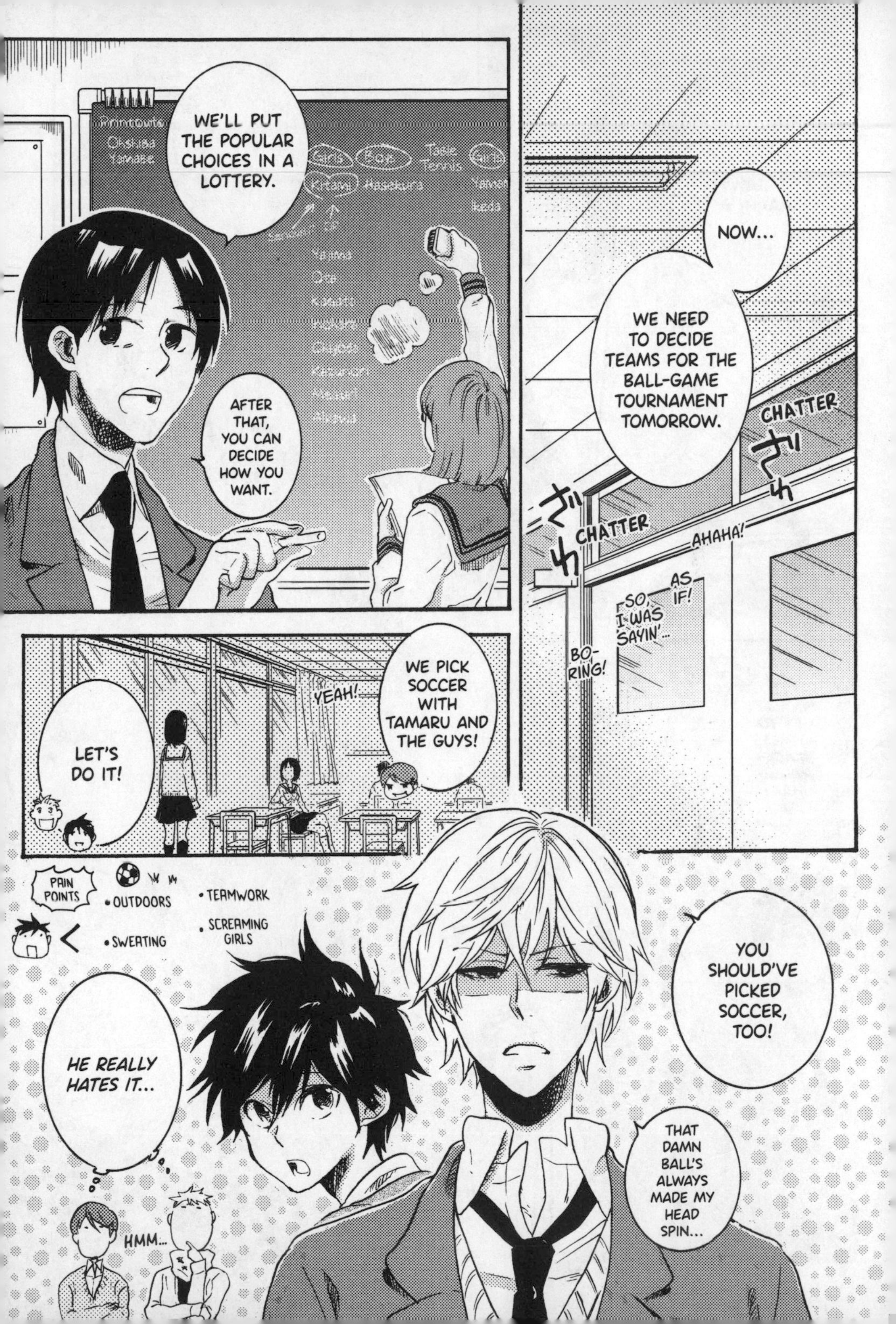
NOW...
WE NEED TO DECIDE TEAMS FOR THE BALL-GAME TOURNAMENT TOMORROW.
CHATTER
ざわ
ざわ
CHATTER
AHAHA!
AS IF!
SO, I WAS SAYIN'...
BO-RING!
WE'LL PUT THE POPULAR CHOICES IN A LOTTERY.
AFTER THAT, YOU CAN DECIDE HOW YOU WANT.
WE PICK SOCCER WITH TAMARU AND THE GUYS!
YEAH!
LET'S DO IT!
YOU SHOULD'VE PICKED SOCCER, TOO!
THAT DAMN BALL'S ALWAYS MADE MY HEAD SPIN...
PAIN POINTS
• OUTDOORS
• TEAMWORK
• SWEATING
• SCREAMING GIRLS
HE REALLY HATES IT...
HMM...

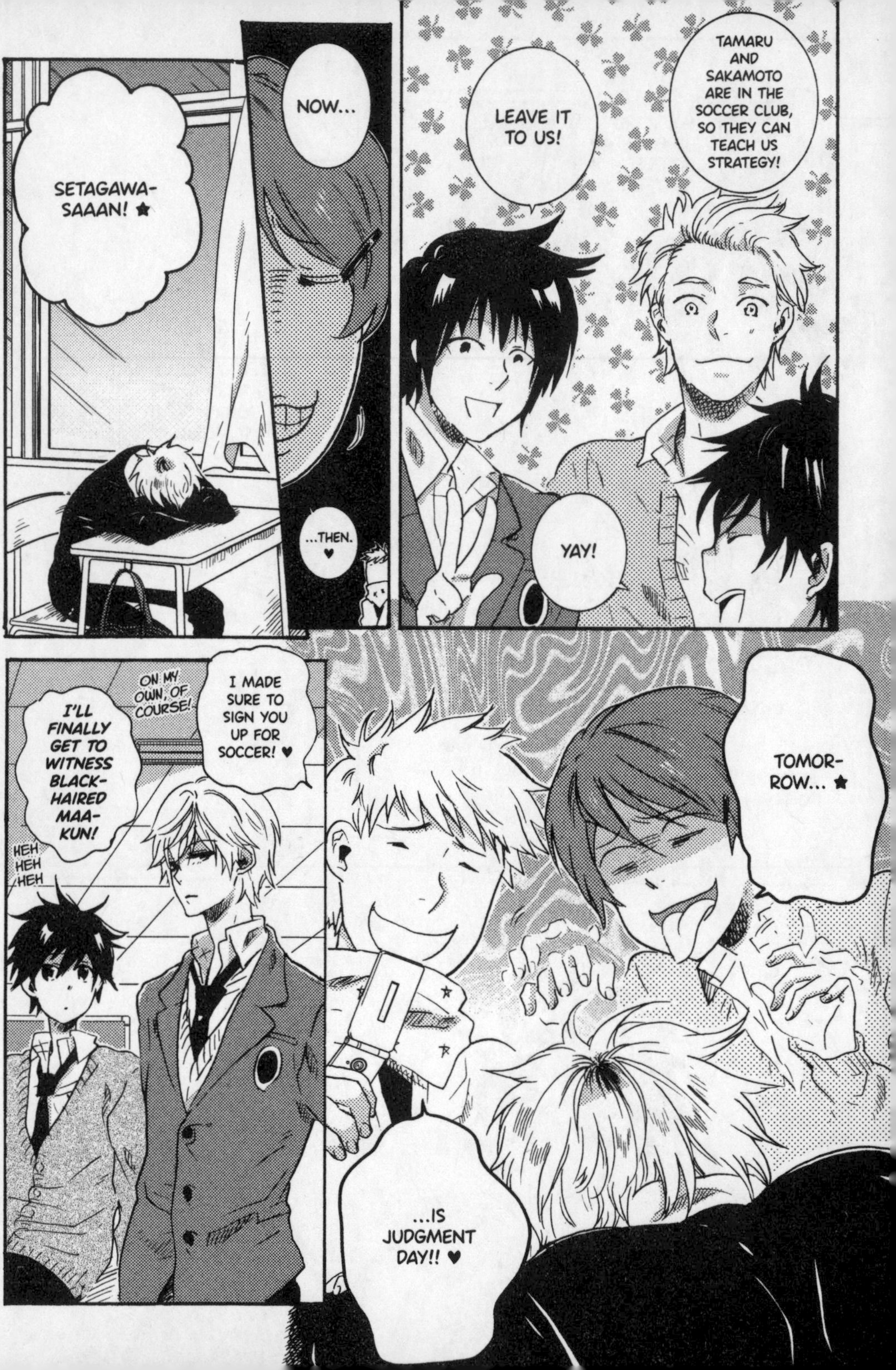
TAMARU AND SAKAMOTO ARE IN THE SOCCER CLUB, SO THEY CAN TEACH US STRATEGY!
LEAVE IT TO US!
YAY!
NOW...
...THEN. ♥
SETAGAWA-SAAAN! ★
TOMOR-ROW... ★
...IS JUDGMENT DAY!! ♥
I MADE SURE TO SIGN YOU UP FOR SOCCER! ♥
ON MY OWN, OF COURSE!
I'LL FINALLY GET TO WITNESS BLACK-HAIRED MAA-KUN!
HEH HEH HEH

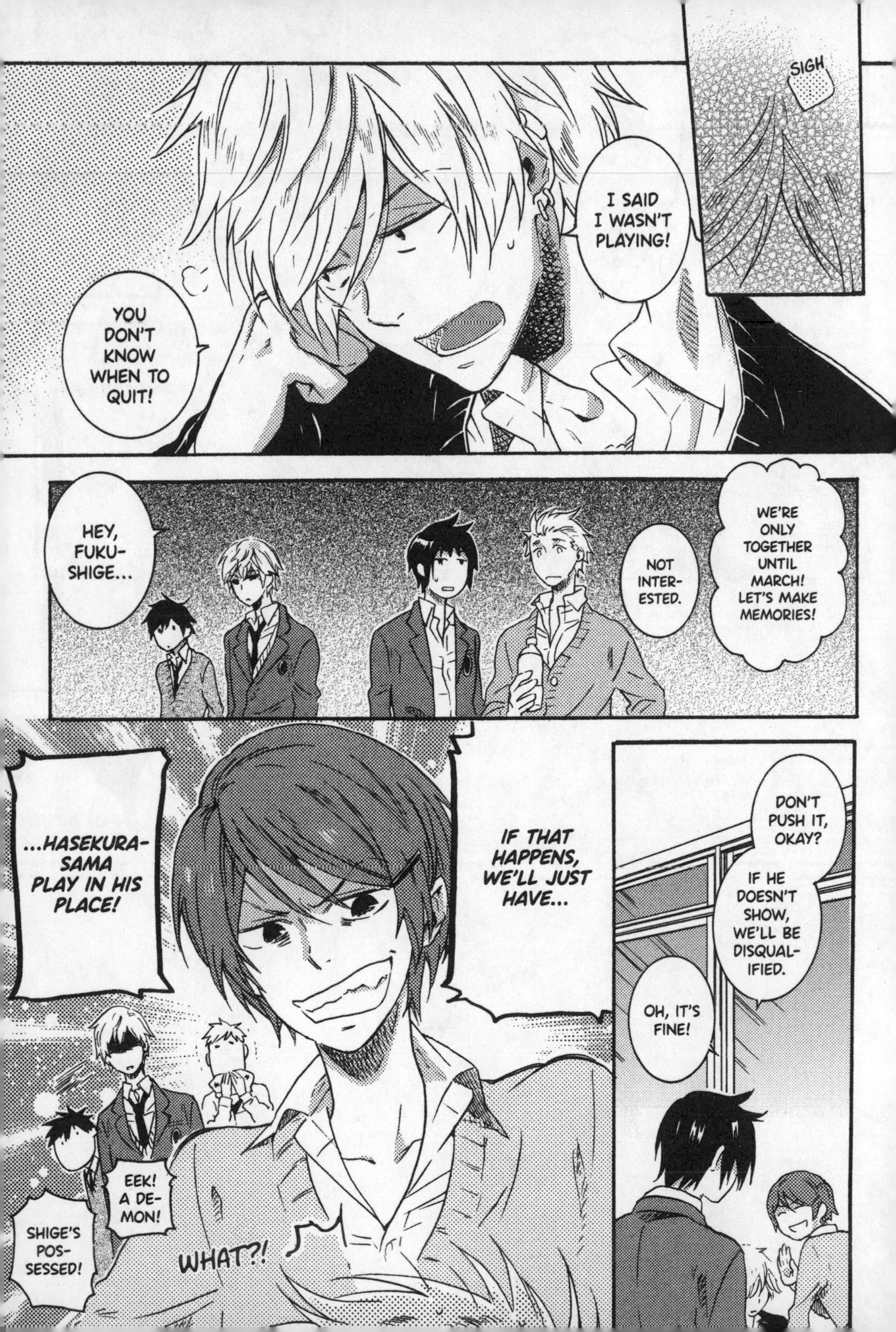
SIGH
I SAID I WASN'T PLAYING!
YOU DON'T KNOW WHEN TO QUIT!
WE'RE ONLY TOGETHER UNTIL MARCH! LET'S MAKE MEMORIES!
NOT INTER-ESTED.
HEY, FUKU-SHIGE...
DON'T PUSH IT, OKAY?
IF HE DOESN'T SHOW, WE'LL BE DISQUAL-IFIED.
OH, IT'S FINE!
IF THAT HAPPENS, WE'LL JUST HAVE...
...HASEKURA-SAMA PLAY IN HIS PLACE!
WHAT?!
EEK! A DE-MON!
SHIGE'S POS-SESSED!

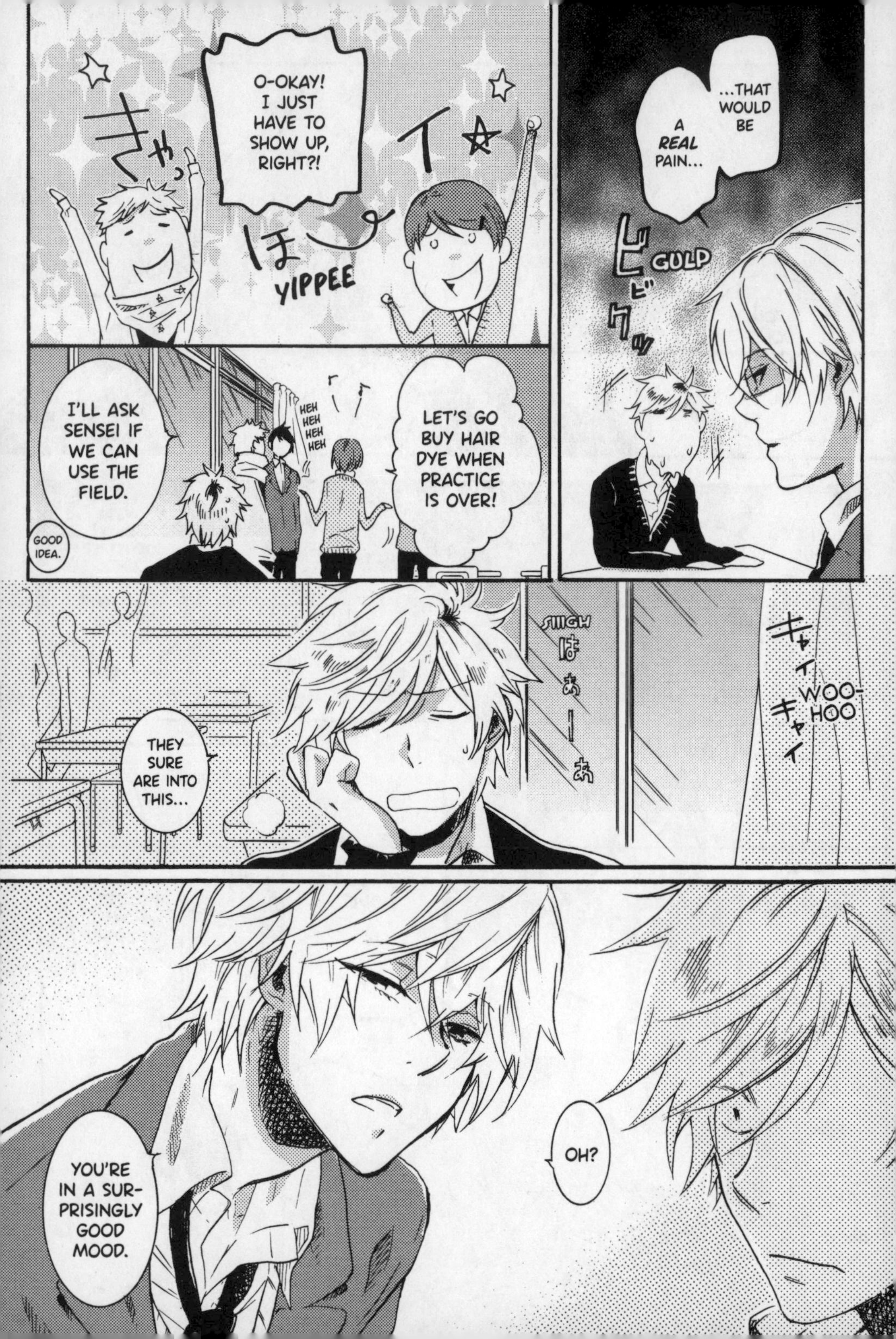
...THAT WOULD BE A REAL PAIN...
GULP
ビビクッ
O-OKAY! I JUST HAVE TO SHOW UP, RIGHT?!
きゃっ
イ☆
ほっ
YIPPEE
LET'S GO BUY HAIR DYE WHEN PRACTICE IS OVER!
HEH HEH HEH HEH
I'LL ASK SENSEI IF WE CAN USE THE FIELD.
GOOD IDEA.
キャイキャイ
WOO-HOO
SIIIGH
はあーーあ
THEY SURE ARE INTO THIS...
OH?
YOU'RE IN A SUR-PRISINGLY GOOD MOOD.

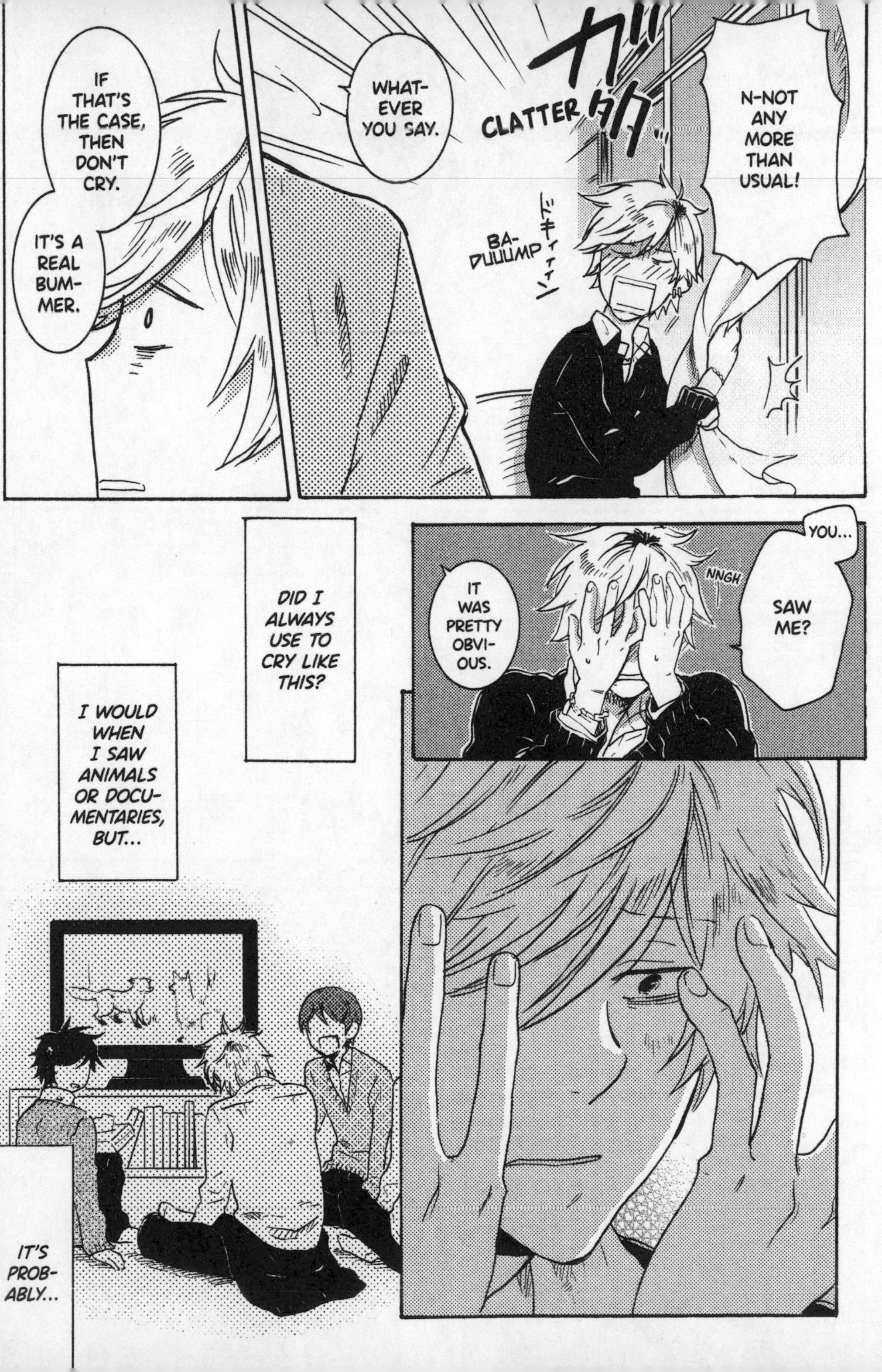

N-NOT ANY MORE THAN USUAL!
CLATTER
BA-DUUUMP
WHAT-EVER YOU SAY.
IF THAT'S THE CASE, THEN DON'T CRY.
IT'S A REAL BUM-MER.
YOU... SAW ME?
NNGH
IT WAS PRETTY OBVI-OUS.
DID I ALWAYS USE TO CRY LIKE THIS?
I WOULD WHEN I SAW ANIMALS OR DOCU-MENTARIES, BUT...
IT'S PROB-ABLY...

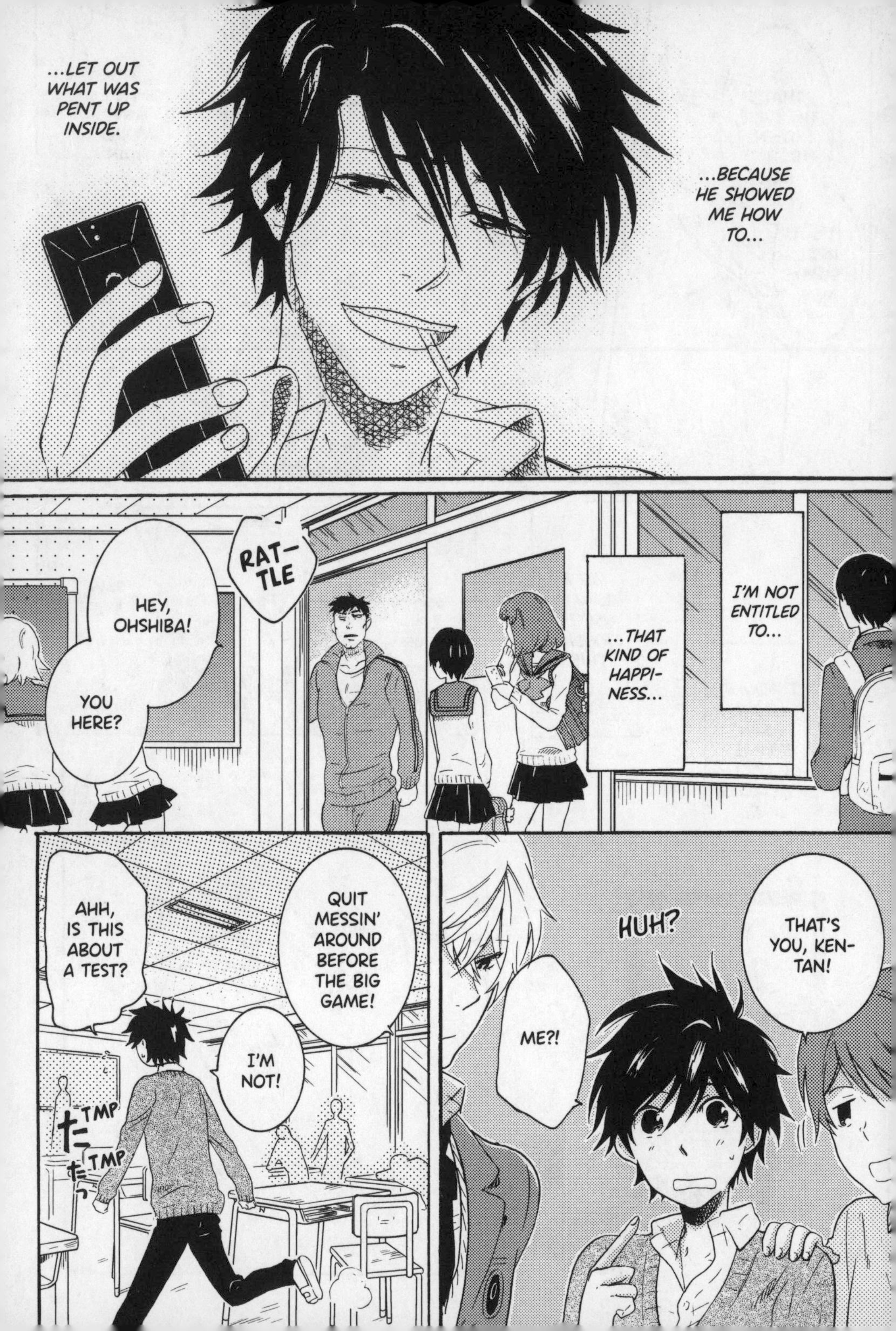

...BECAUSE HE SHOWED ME HOW TO...
...LET OUT WHAT WAS PENT UP INSIDE.
I'M NOT ENTITLED TO...
...THAT KIND OF HAPPINESS...
RAT-TLE
HEY, OHSHIBA!
YOU HERE?
THAT'S YOU, KEN-TAN!
HUH?
ME?!
QUIT MESSIN' AROUND BEFORE THE BIG GAME!
AHH, IS THIS ABOUT A TEST?
I'M NOT!
TMP
TMP

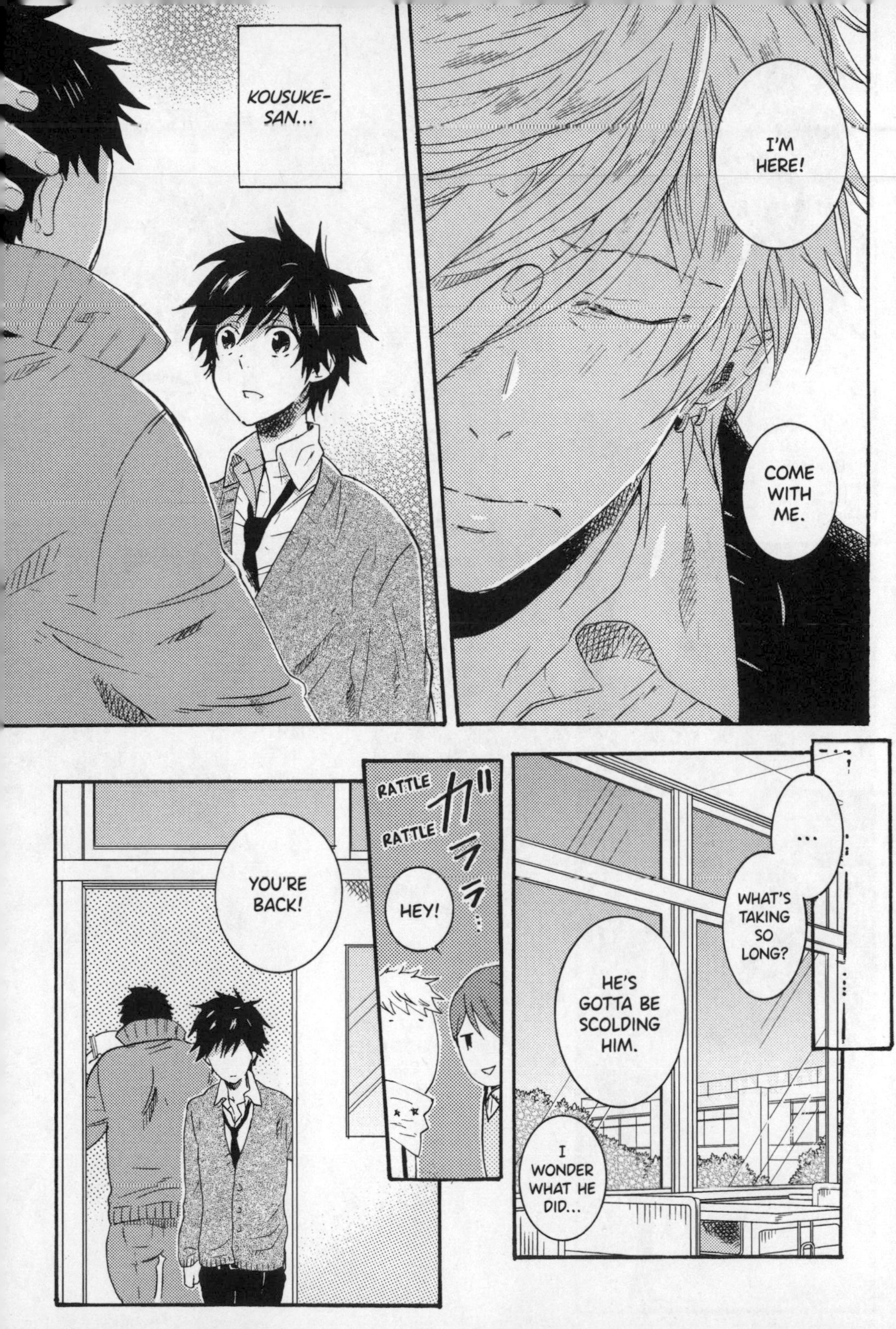
I'M HERE!
COME WITH ME.
KOUSUKE-SAN...
...
WHAT'S TAKING SO LONG?
HE'S GOTTA BE SCOLDING HIM.
I WONDER WHAT HE DID...
RATTLE RATTLE
ガラ…
HEY!
YOU'RE BACK!

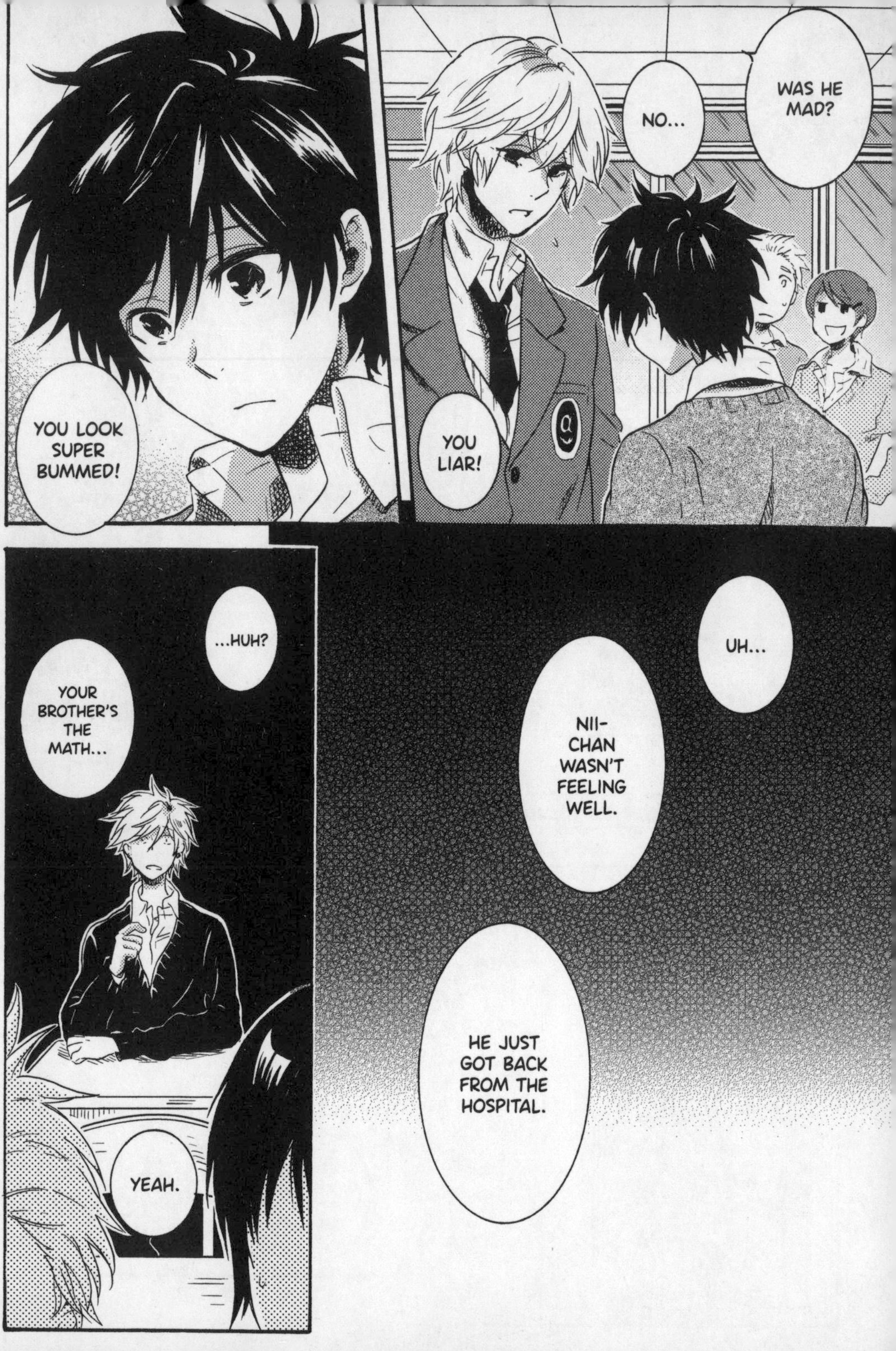
WAS HE MAD?
NO...
YOU LIAR!
YOU LOOK SUPER BUMMED!
UH...
NII-CHAN WASN'T FEELING WELL.
HE JUST GOT BACK FROM THE HOSPITAL.
...HUH?
YOUR BROTHER'S THE MATH...
YEAH.

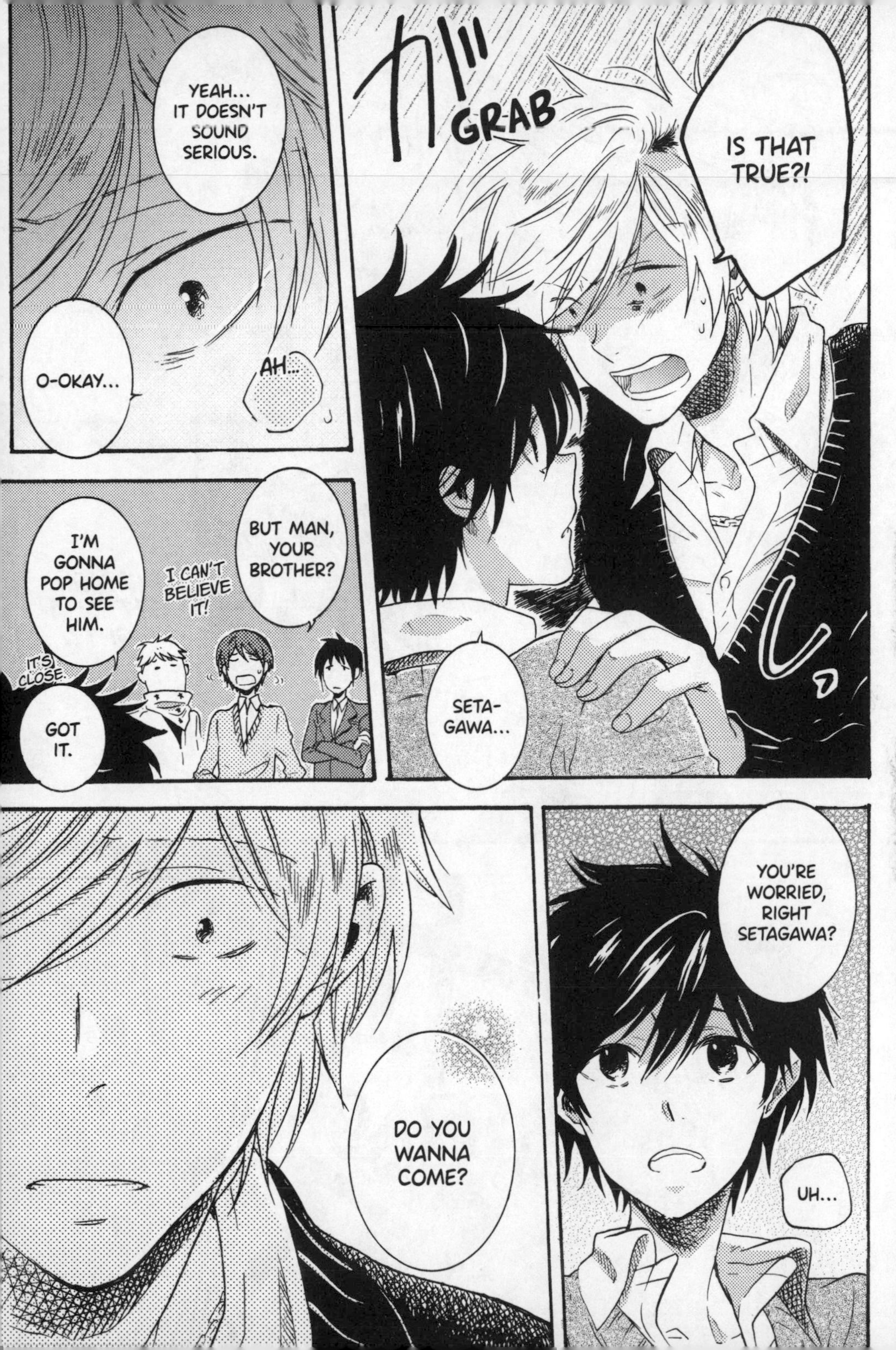
GRAB
IS THAT TRUE?!
SETA-GAWA...
YEAH... IT DOESN'T SOUND SERIOUS.
AH...
O-OKAY...
BUT MAN, YOUR BROTHER?
I CAN'T BELIEVE IT!
I'M GONNA POP HOME TO SEE HIM.
IT'S CLOSE.
GOT IT.
YOU'RE WORRIED, RIGHT SETAGAWA?
UH...
DO YOU WANNA COME?

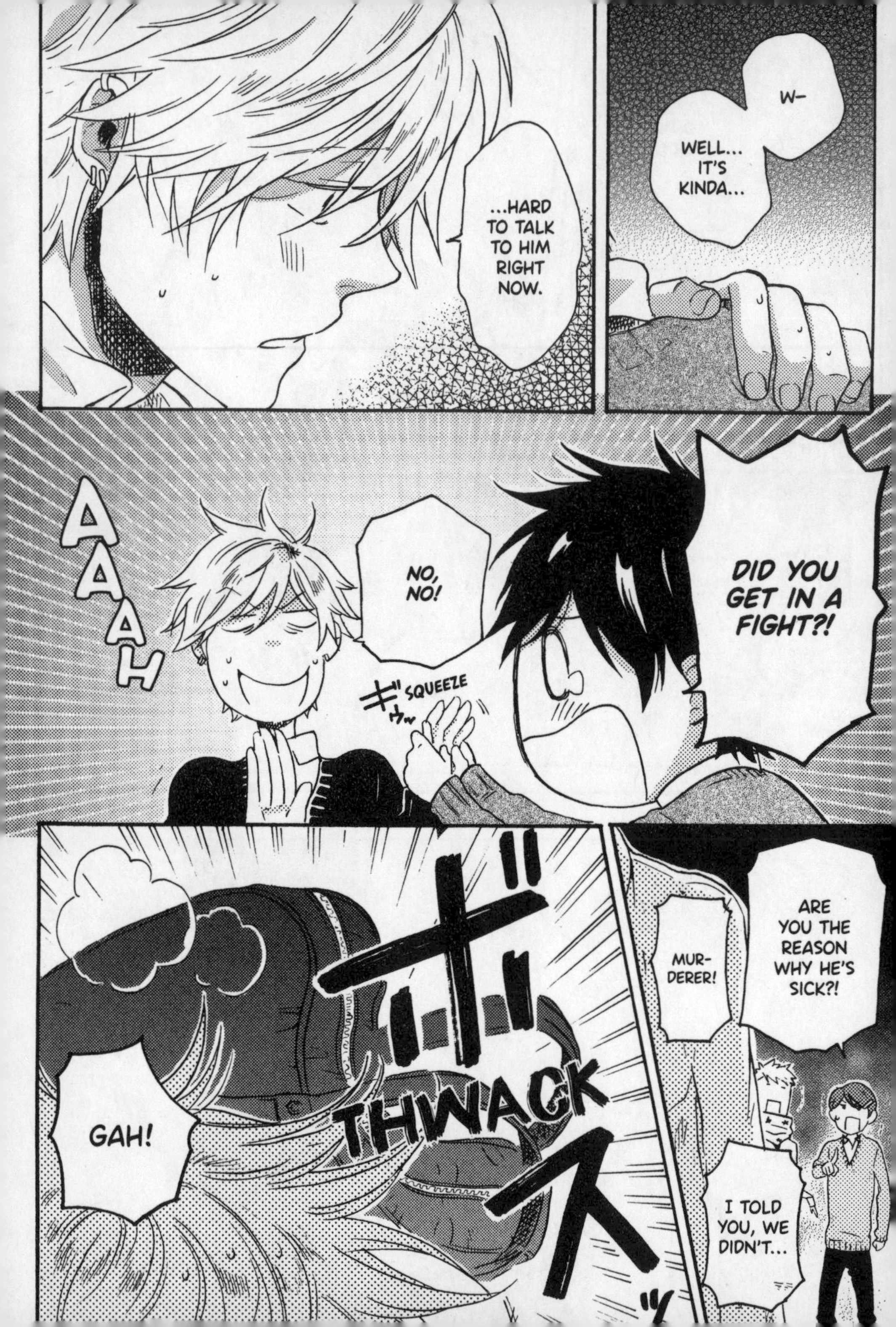
W-
WELL... IT'S KINDA...
...HARD TO TALK TO HIM RIGHT NOW.
DID YOU GET IN A FIGHT?!
SQUEEZE
NO, NO!
AAAH
ARE YOU THE REASON WHY HE'S SICK?!
MUR-DERER!
I TOLD YOU, WE DIDN'T...
THWACK
GAH!

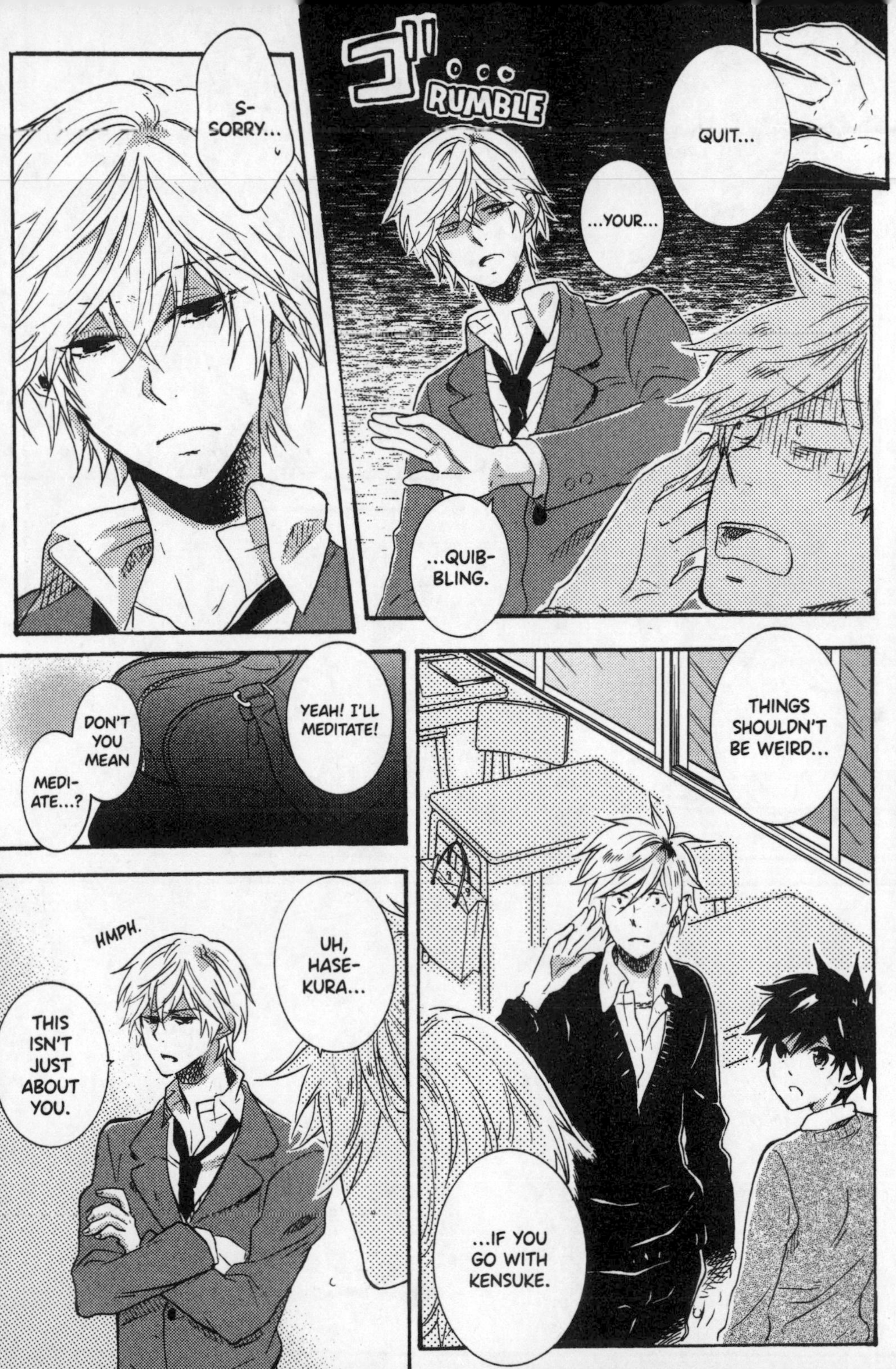
ゴ
RUMBLE
QUIT...
...YOUR...
...QUIB-
BLING.
S-
SORRY...
THINGS
SHOULDN'T
BE WEIRD...
...IF YOU
GO WITH
KENSUKE.
YEAH! I'LL
MEDITATE!
DON'T
YOU
MEAN
MEDI-
ATE...?
UH,
HASE-
KURA...
HMPH.
THIS
ISN'T
JUST
ABOUT
YOU.

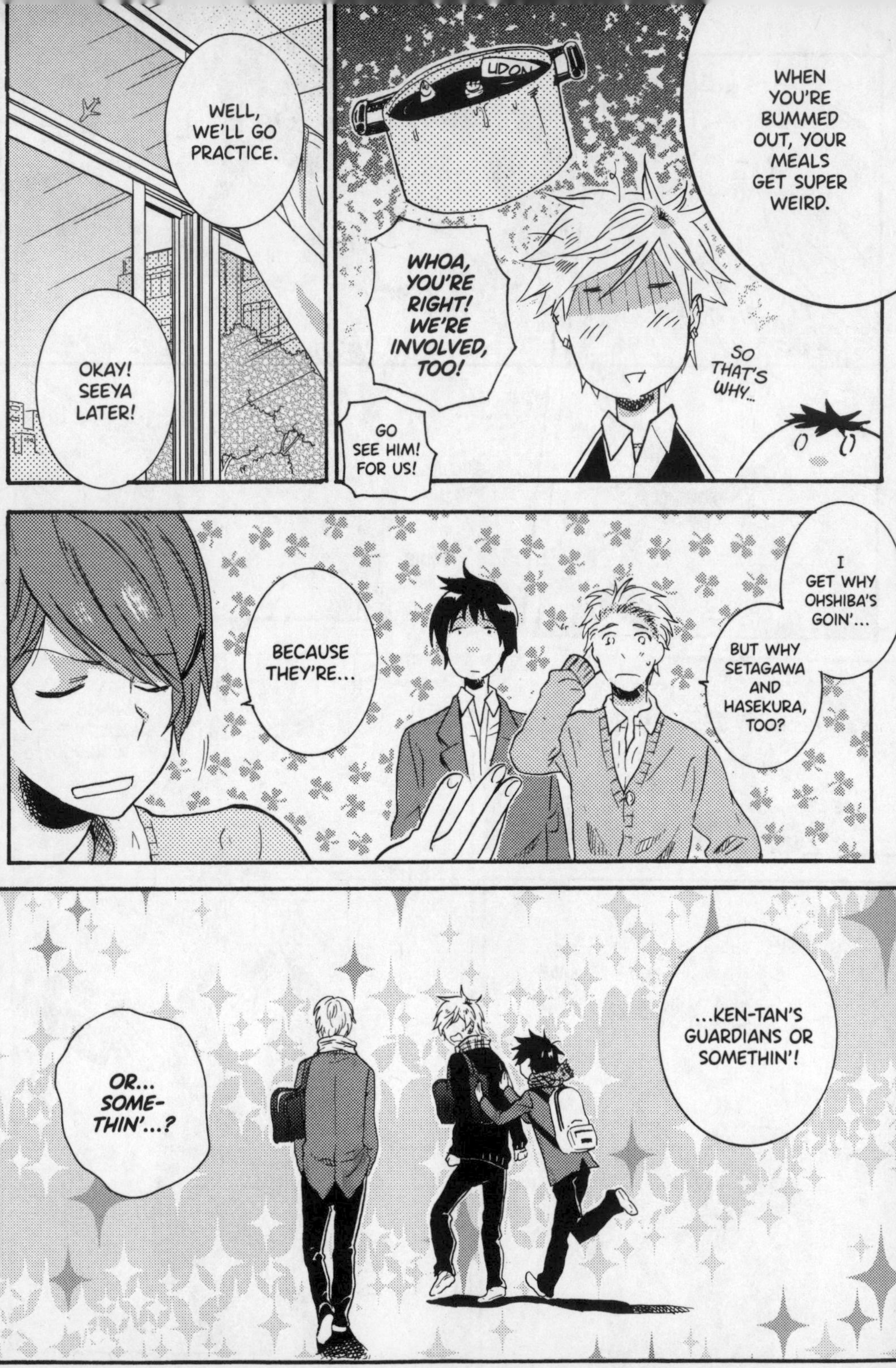
UDON
WHEN YOU'RE BUMMED OUT, YOUR MEALS GET SUPER WEIRD.
SO THAT'S WHY...
WHOA, YOU'RE RIGHT! WE'RE INVOLVED, TOO!
GO SEE HIM! FOR US!
WELL, WE'LL GO PRACTICE.
OKAY! SEEYA LATER!
I GET WHY OHSHIBA'S GOIN'...
BUT WHY SETAGAWA AND HASEKURA, TOO?
BECAUSE THEY'RE...
...KEN-TAN'S GUARDIANS OR SOMETHIN'!
OR... SOME-THIN'...?

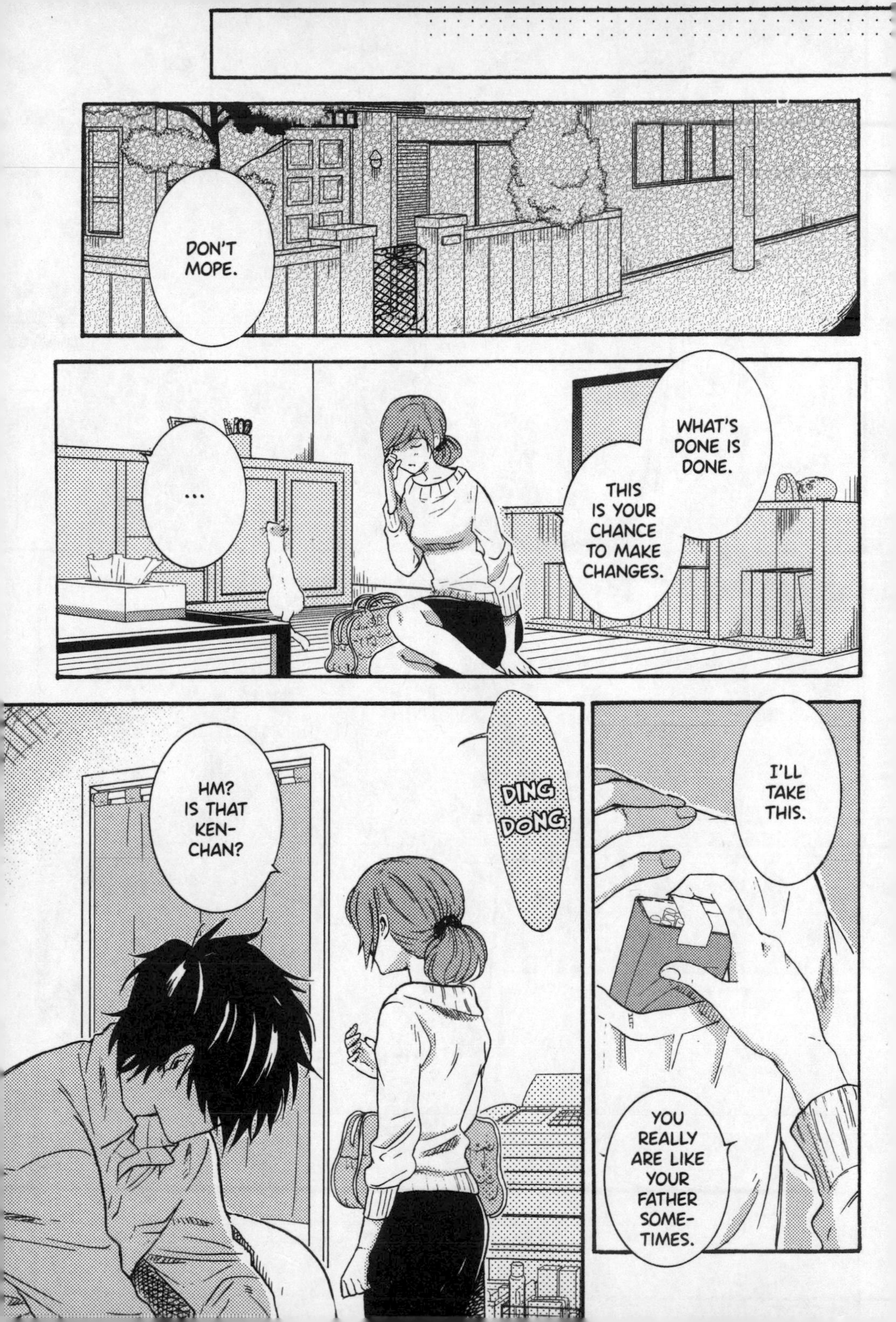
DON'T MOPE.
WHAT'S DONE IS DONE.
THIS IS YOUR CHANCE TO MAKE CHANGES.
...
I'LL TAKE THIS.
YOU REALLY ARE LIKE YOUR FATHER SOME-TIMES.
DING DONG
HM? IS THAT KEN-CHAN?

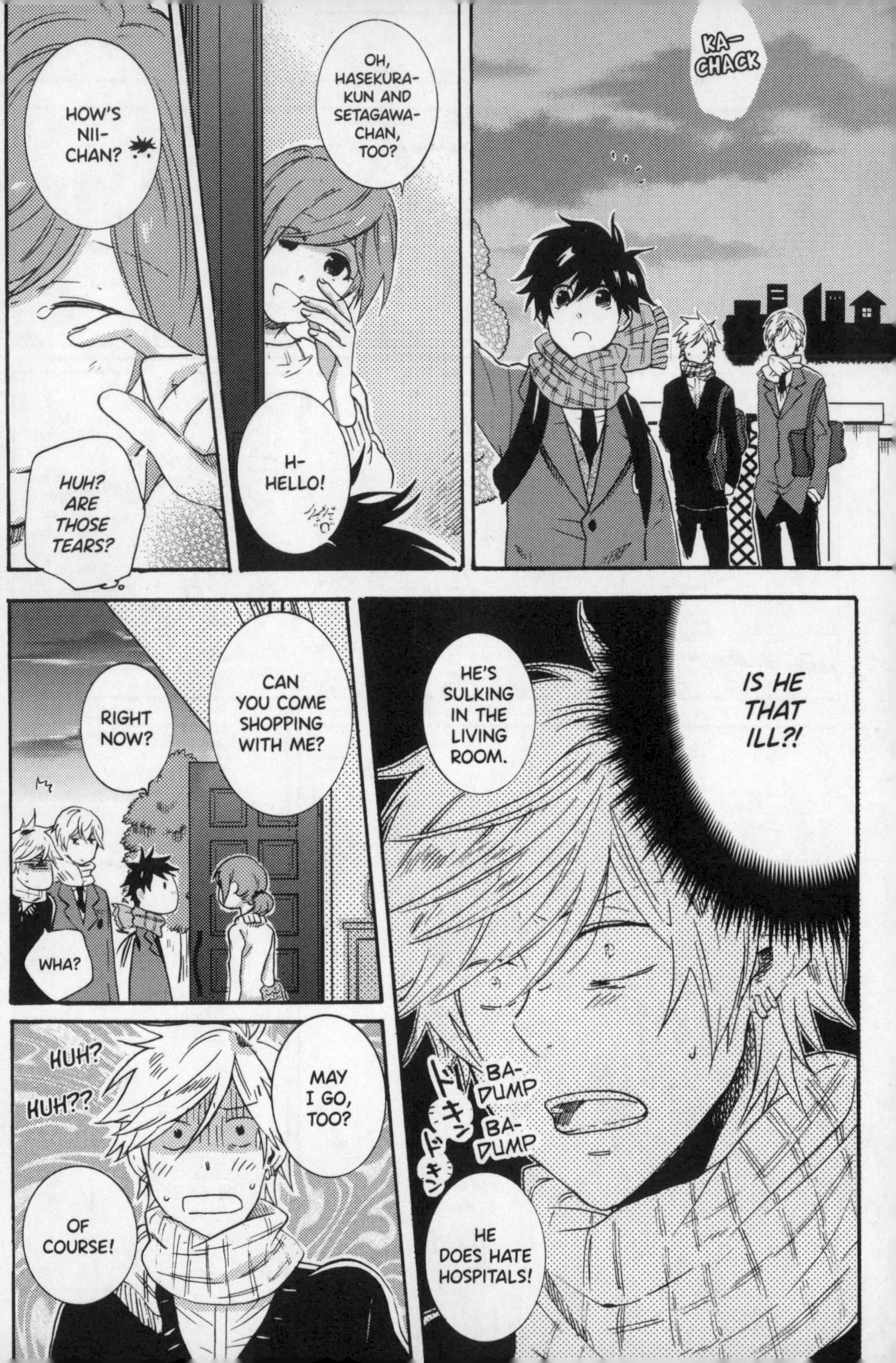
KA-CHACK
OH, HASEKURA-KUN AND SETAGAWA-CHAN, TOO?
H-HELLO!
HOW'S NII-CHAN?
HUH? ARE THOSE TEARS?
IS HE THAT ILL?!
HE'S SULKING IN THE LIVING ROOM.
BA-DUMP BA-DUMP
ドキン ドキン
HE DOES HATE HOSPITALS!
CAN YOU COME SHOPPING WITH ME?
RIGHT NOW?
WHA?
MAY I GO, TOO?
HUH?
HUH??
OF COURSE!

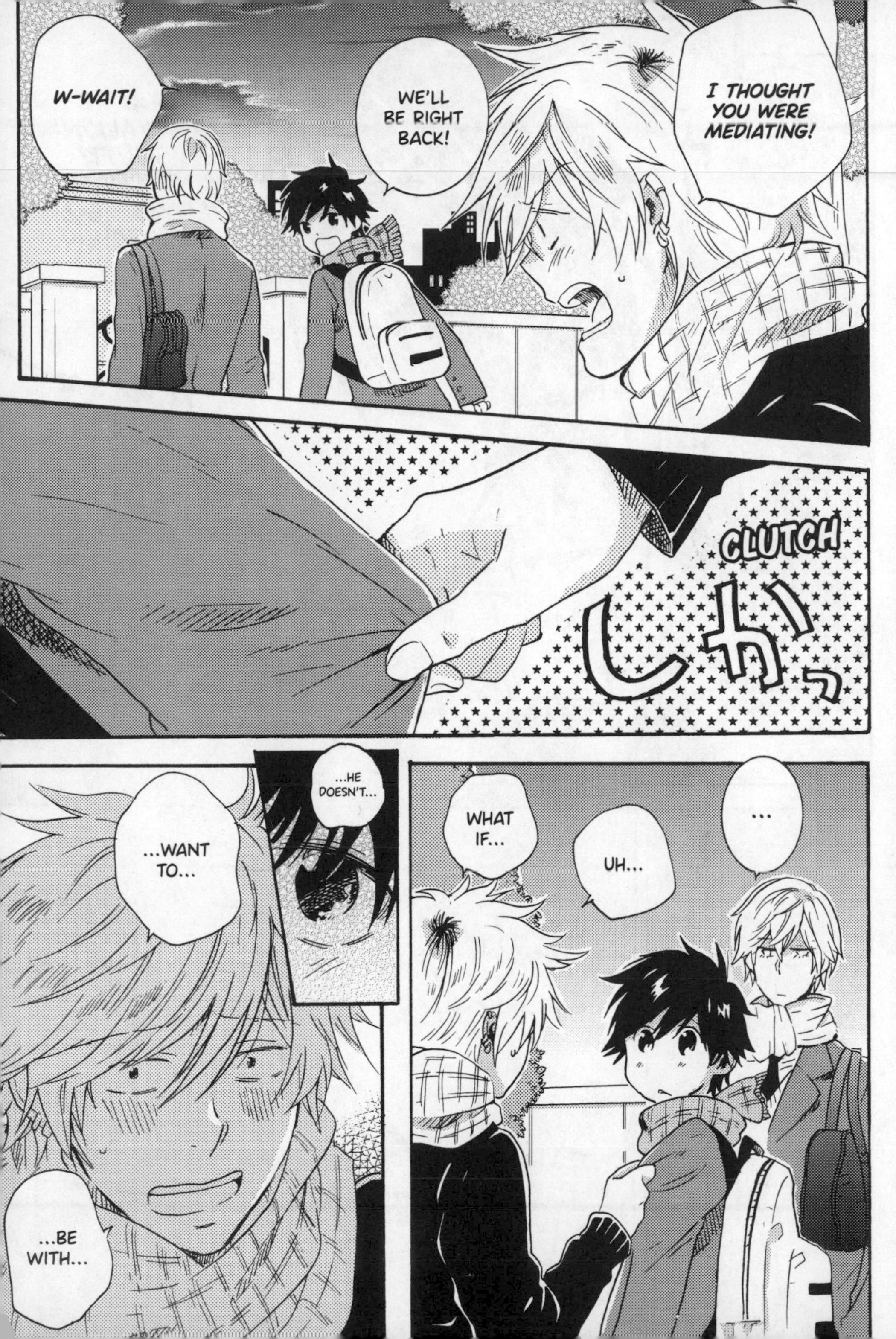
I THOUGHT YOU WERE MEDIATING!
WE'LL BE RIGHT BACK!
W-WAIT!
CLUTCH
しかっ
...
UH...
WHAT IF...
...HE DOESN'T...
...WANT TO...
...BE WITH...

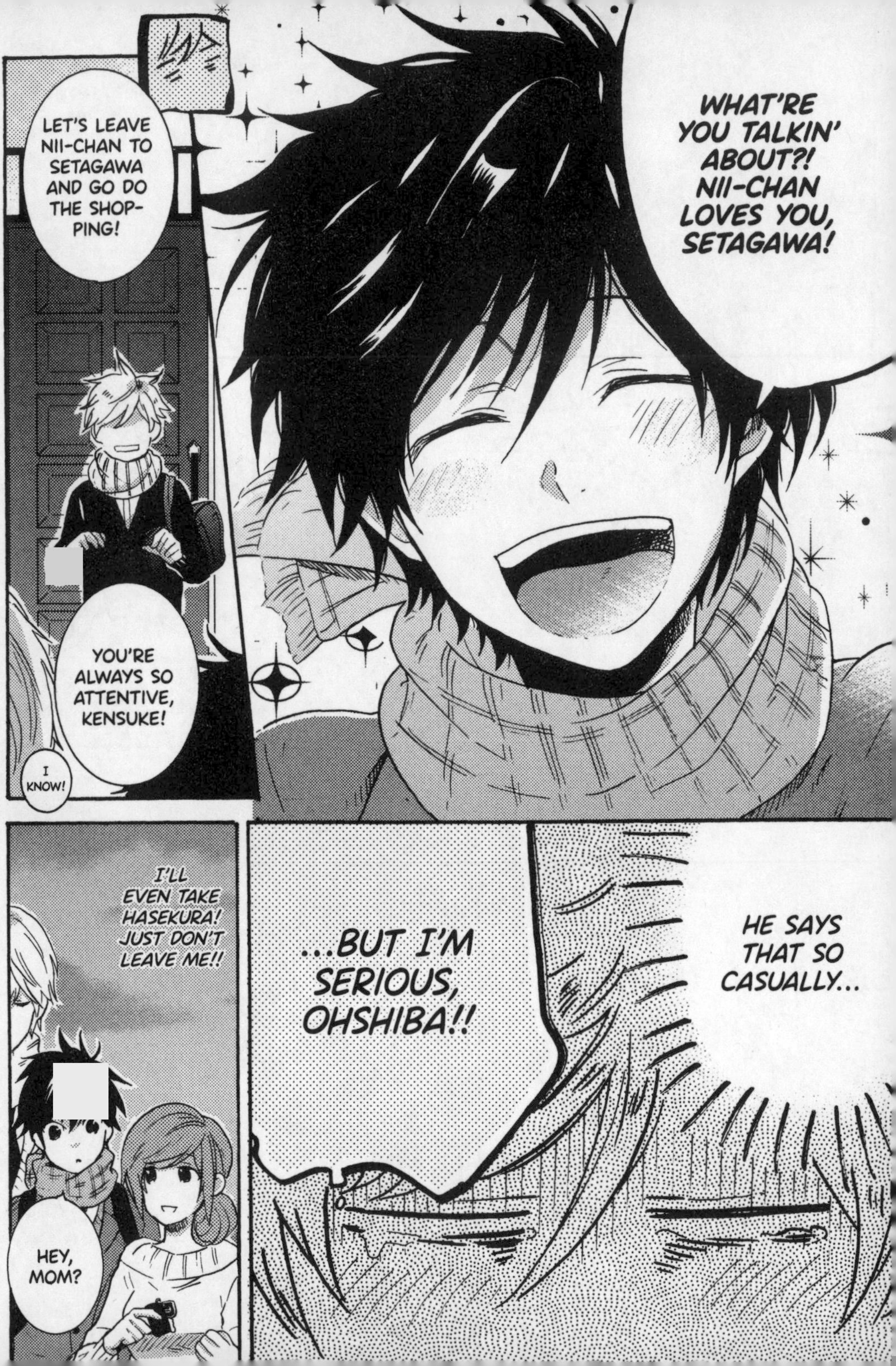
WHAT'RE YOU TALKIN' ABOUT?! NII-CHAN LOVES YOU, SETAGAWA!
LET'S LEAVE NII-CHAN TO SETAGAWA AND GO DO THE SHOP-PING!
YOU'RE ALWAYS SO ATTENTIVE, KENSUKE!
I KNOW!
HE SAYS THAT SO CASUALLY...
...BUT I'M SERIOUS, OHSHIBA!!
I'LL EVEN TAKE HASEKURA! JUST DON'T LEAVE ME!!
HEY, MOM?

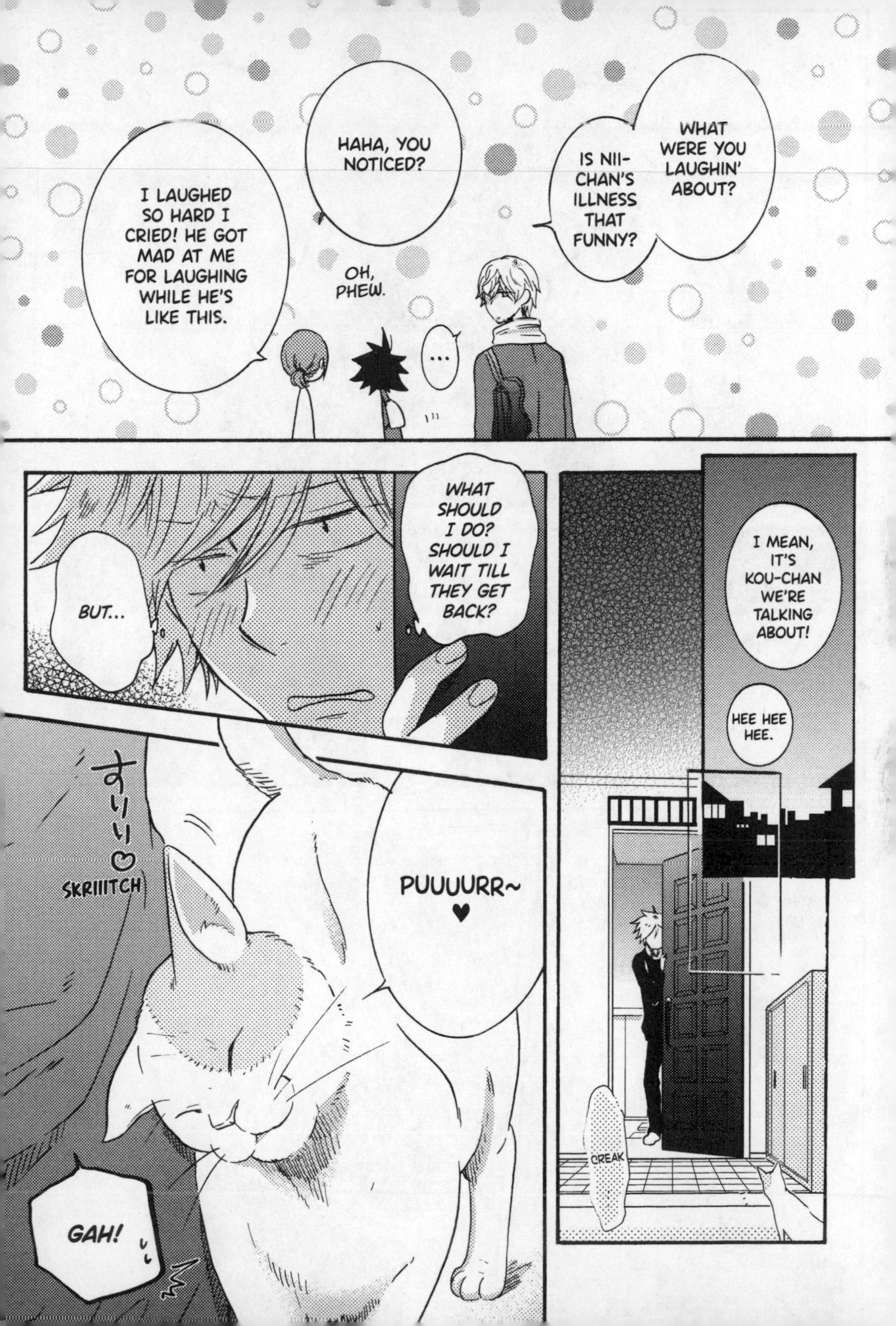
WHAT WERE YOU LAUGHIN' ABOUT?
IS NII-CHAN'S ILLNESS THAT FUNNY?
HAHA, YOU NOTICED?
...
OH, PHEW.
I LAUGHED SO HARD I CRIED! HE GOT MAD AT ME FOR LAUGHING WHILE HE'S LIKE THIS.
I MEAN, IT'S KOU-CHAN WE'RE TALKING ABOUT!
HEE HEE HEE.
CREAK
WHAT SHOULD I DO? SHOULD I WAIT TILL THEY GET BACK?
BUT...
PUUUURR~ ♥
すりりり♡
SKRIIITCH
GAH!

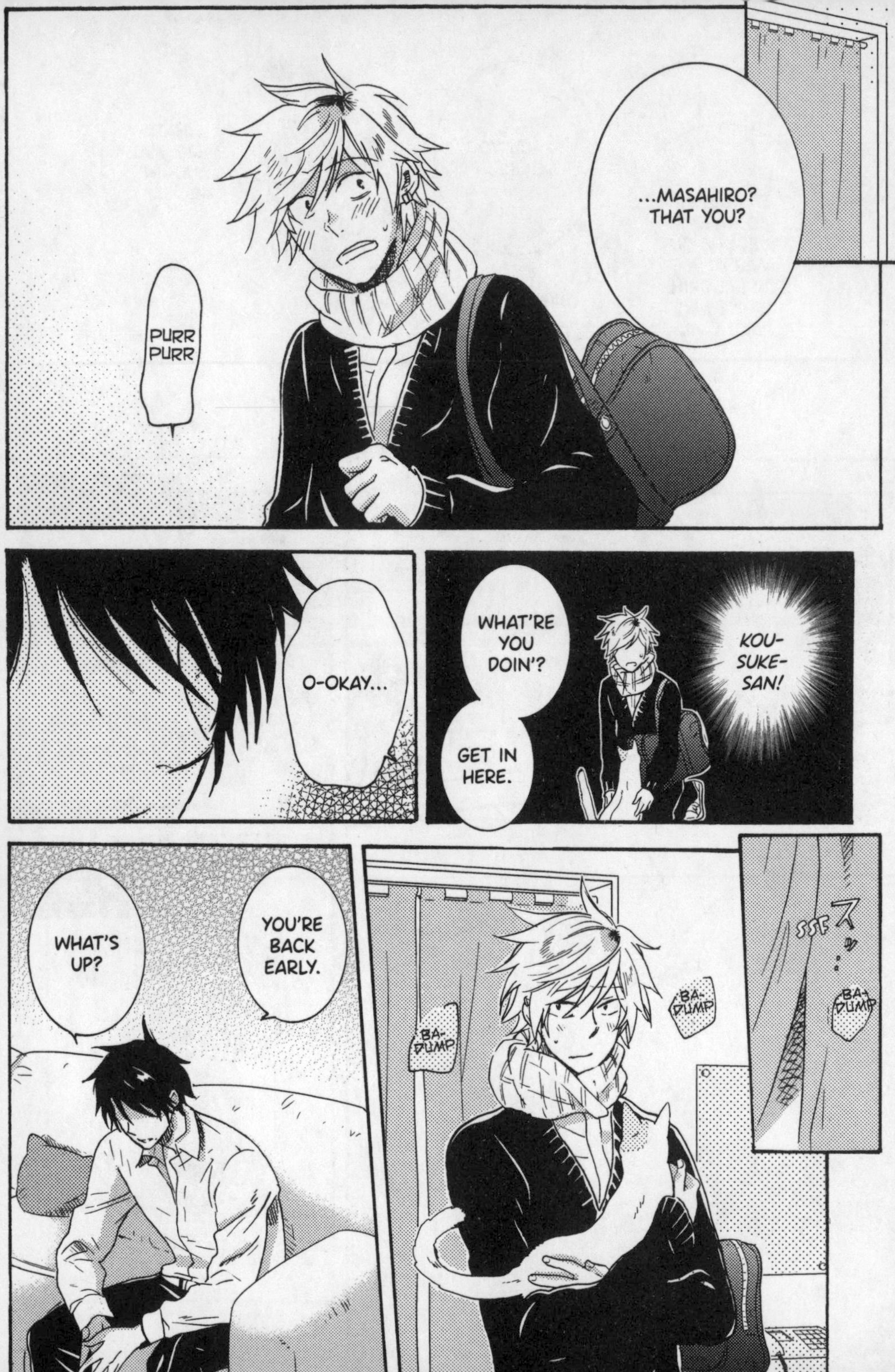
...MASAHIRO? THAT YOU?
PURR PURR
KOU-SUKE-SAN!
WHAT'RE YOU DOIN'?
GET IN HERE.
O-OKAY...
SSF
BA-DUMP
BA-DUMP
BA-DUMP
YOU'RE BACK EARLY.
WHAT'S UP?

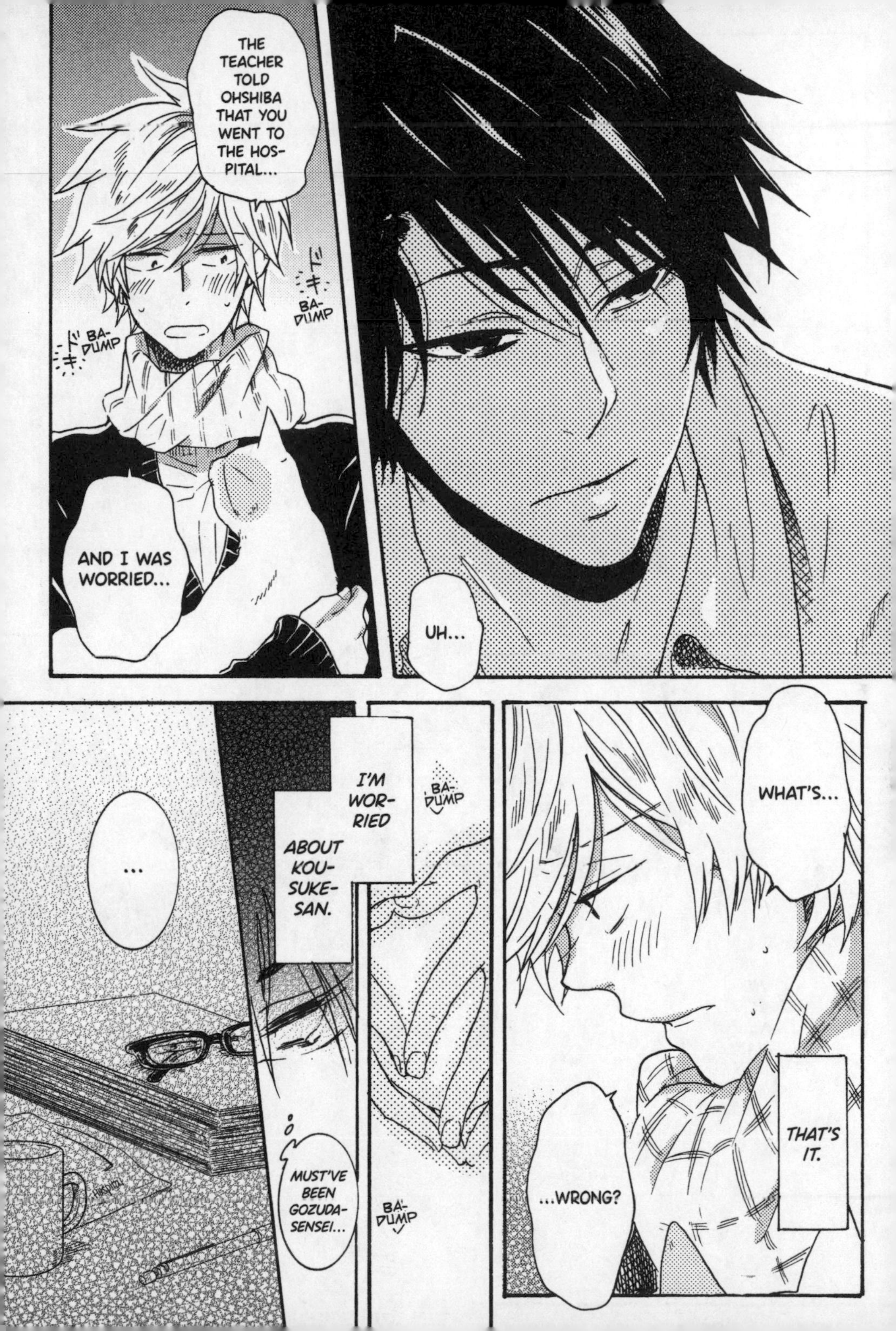
UH...
THE TEACHER TOLD OHSHIBA THAT YOU WENT TO THE HOS-PITAL...
ドキ
BA-DUMP
ドキ
BA-DUMP
AND I WAS WORRIED...
WHAT'S...
...WRONG?
THAT'S IT.
I'M WOR-RIED ABOUT KOU-SUKE-SAN.
BA-DUMP
MUST'VE BEEN GOZUDA-SENSEI...
BA-DUMP
...

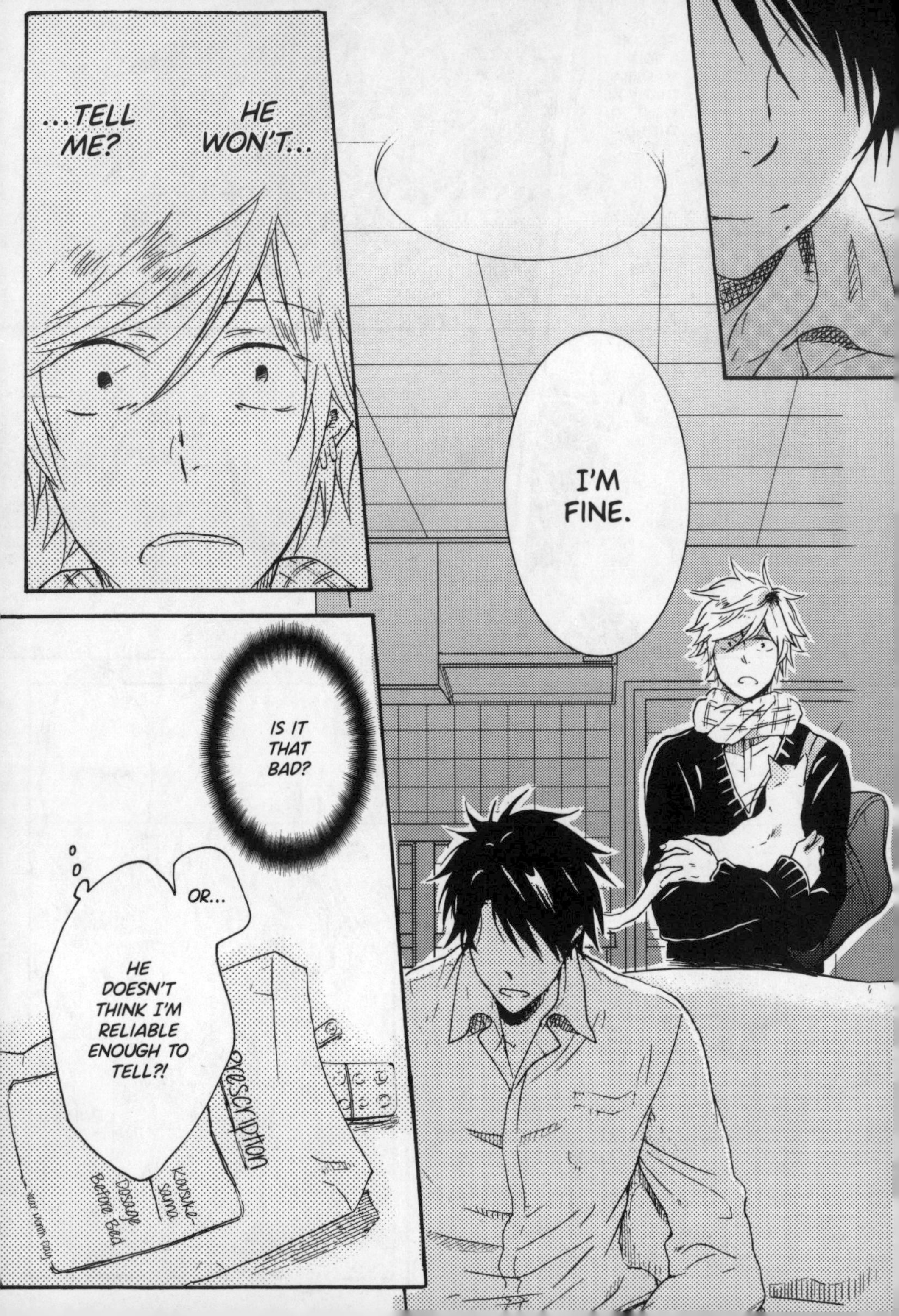
I'M FINE.
HE WON'T...
...TELL ME?
IS IT THAT BAD?
OR...
HE DOESN'T THINK I'M RELIABLE ENOUGH TO TELL?!
PRESCRIPTION
Kousuke-sama
Dosage Before Bed

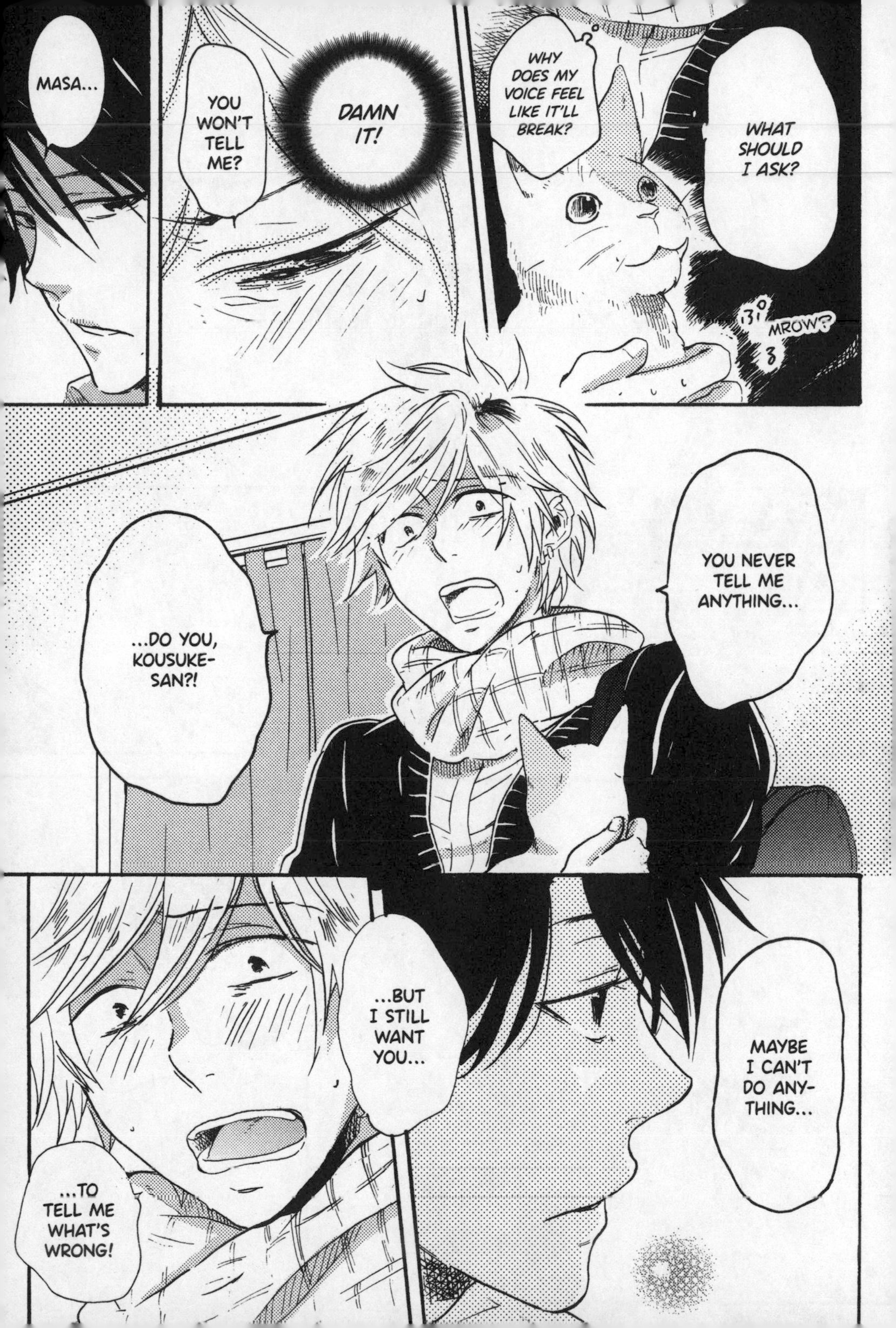

WHAT SHOULD I ASK?
WHY DOES MY VOICE FEEL LIKE IT'LL BREAK?
MROW?
DAMN IT!
YOU WON'T TELL ME?
MASA...
YOU NEVER TELL ME ANYTHING...
...DO YOU, KOUSUKE-SAN?!
MAYBE I CAN'T DO ANY-THING...
...BUT I STILL WANT YOU...
...TO TELL ME WHAT'S WRONG!

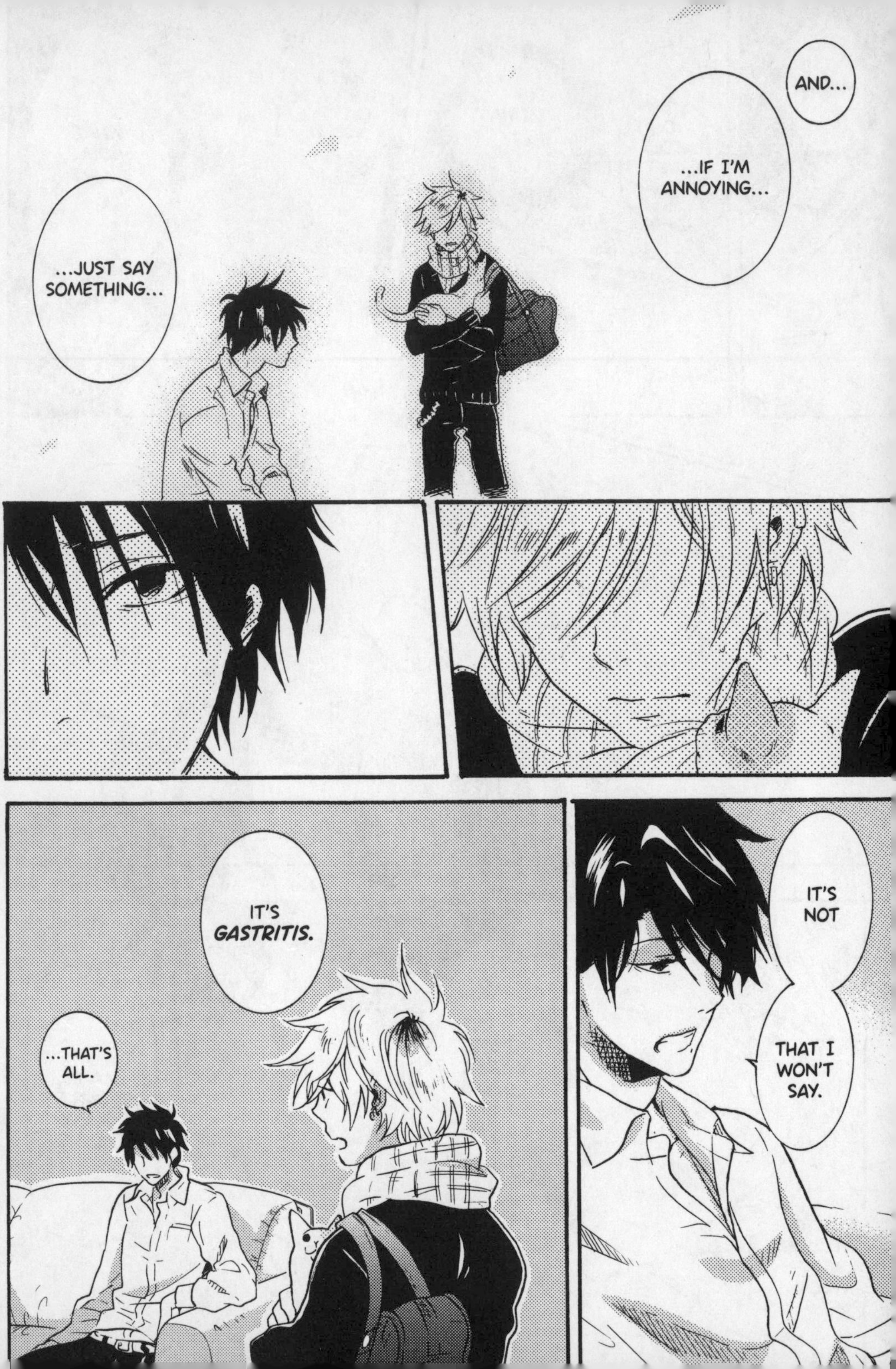
AND...
...IF I'M ANNOYING...
...JUST SAY SOMETHING...
IT'S NOT
THAT I WON'T SAY.
IT'S GASTRITIS.
...THAT'S ALL.

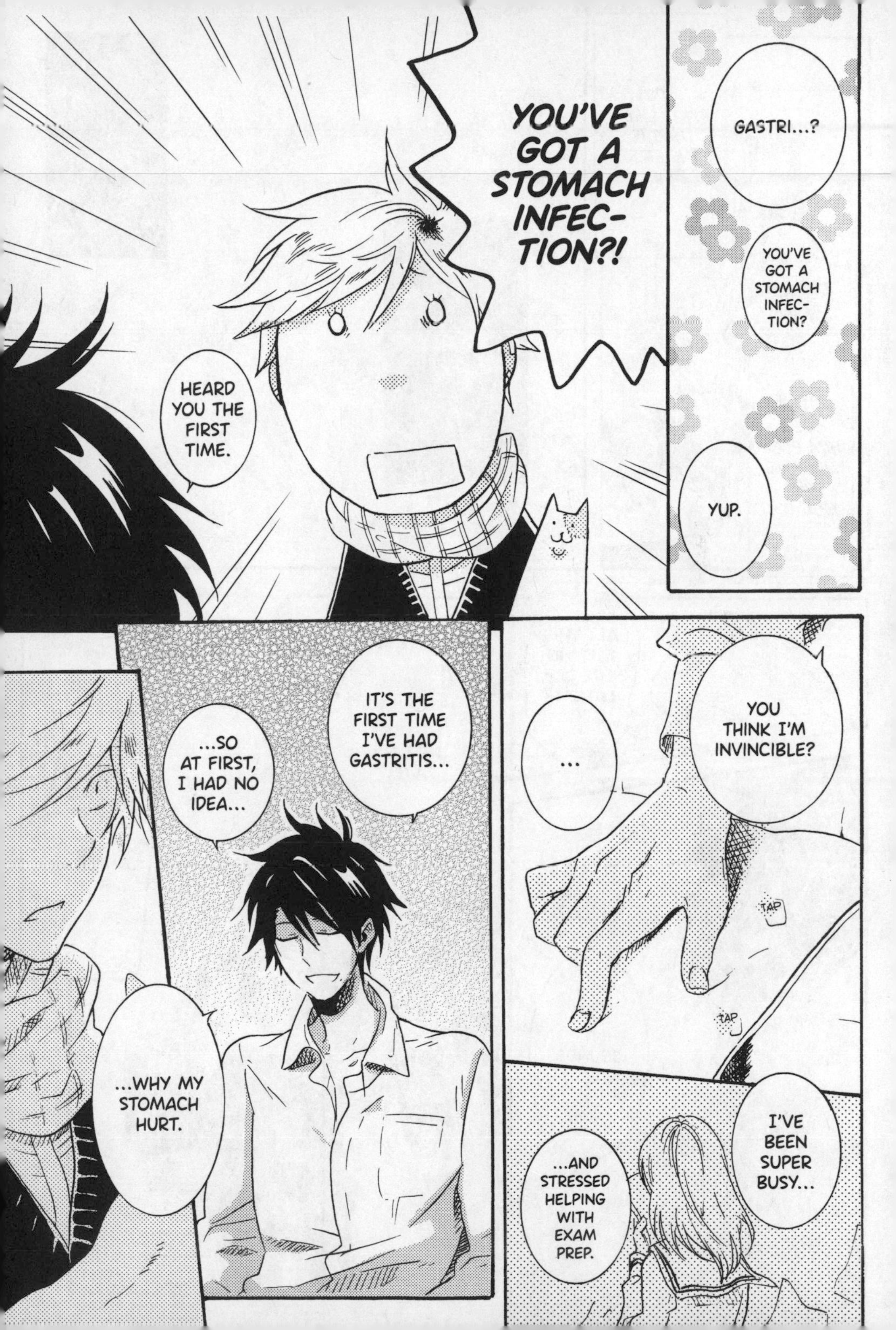
GASTRI...?
YOU'VE GOT A STOMACH INFECTION?
YUP.
YOU'VE GOT A STOMACH INFECTION?!
HEARD YOU THE FIRST TIME.
YOU THINK I'M INVINCIBLE?
...
TAP
TAP
I'VE BEEN SUPER BUSY...
...AND STRESSED HELPING WITH EXAM PREP.
IT'S THE FIRST TIME I'VE HAD GASTRITIS...
...SO AT FIRST, I HAD NO IDEA...
...WHY MY STOMACH HURT.

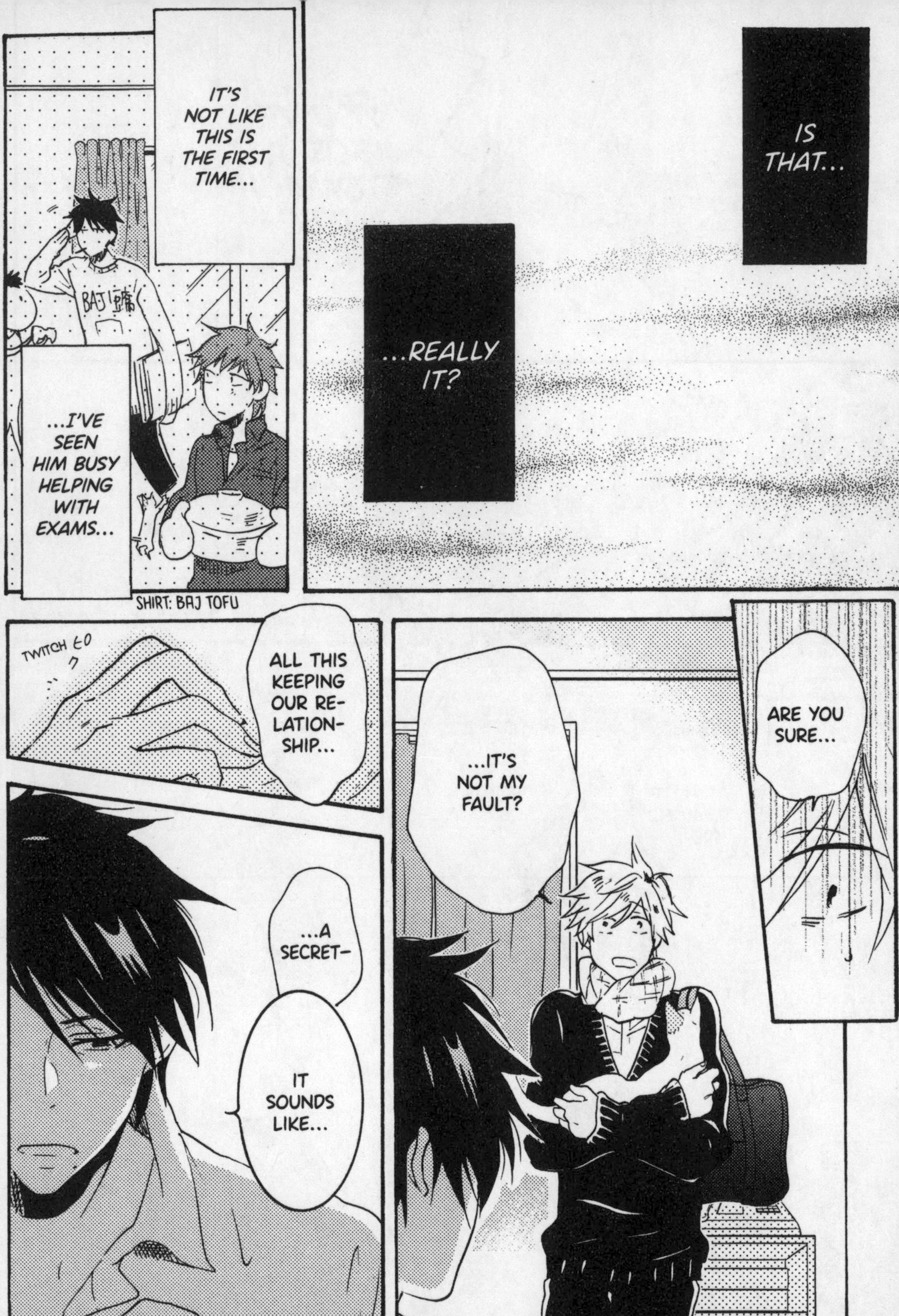
IS THAT...
...REALLY IT?
IT'S NOT LIKE THIS IS THE FIRST TIME...
...I'VE SEEN HIM BUSY HELPING WITH EXAMS...
SHIRT: BAJ TOFU
ARE YOU SURE...
...IT'S NOT MY FAULT?
ALL THIS KEEPING OUR RE-LATION-SHIP...
TWITCH
...A SECRET-
IT SOUNDS LIKE...

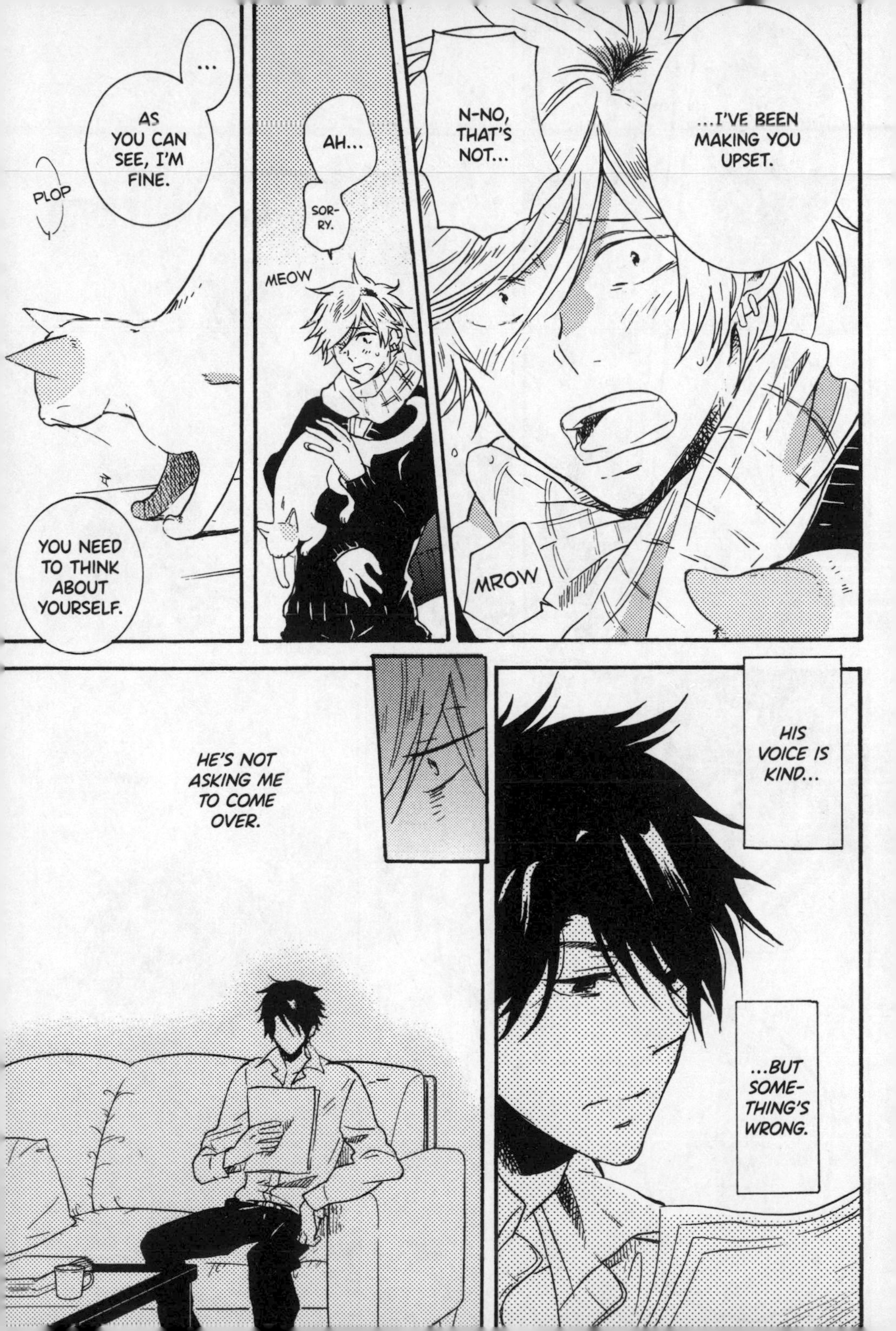
...I'VE BEEN MAKING YOU UPSET.
N-NO, THAT'S NOT...
MROW
AH...
SOR-RY.
MEOW
...
AS YOU CAN SEE, I'M FINE.
PLOP
YOU NEED TO THINK ABOUT YOURSELF.
HIS VOICE IS KIND...
...BUT SOME-THING'S WRONG.
HE'S NOT ASKING ME TO COME OVER.

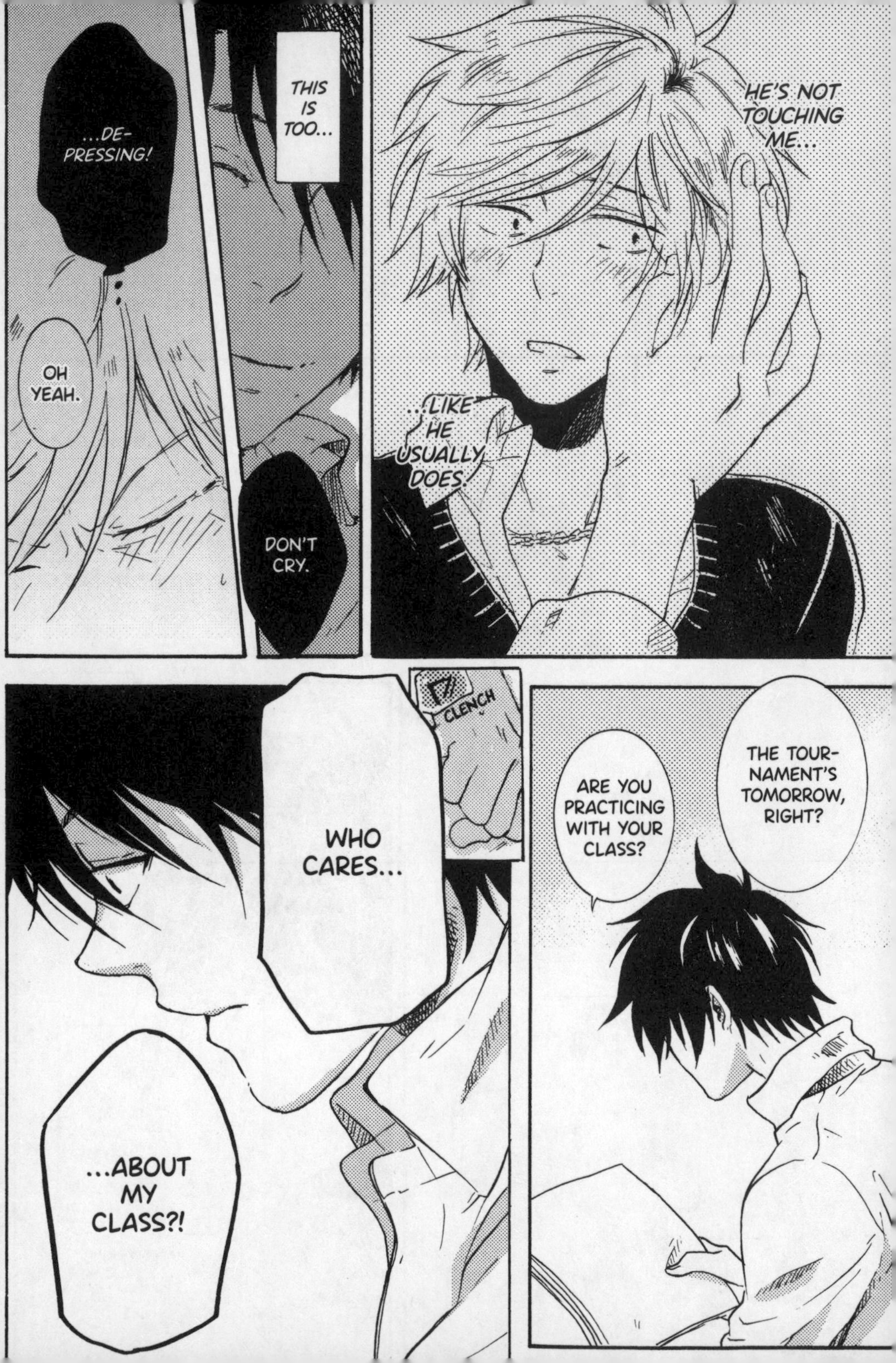
HE'S NOT TOUCHING ME...
...LIKE HE USUALLY DOES.
THIS IS TOO...
DON'T CRY.
...DE-PRESSING!
OH YEAH.
THE TOUR-NAMENT'S TOMORROW, RIGHT?
ARE YOU PRACTICING WITH YOUR CLASS?
CLENCH
WHO CARES...
...ABOUT MY CLASS?!

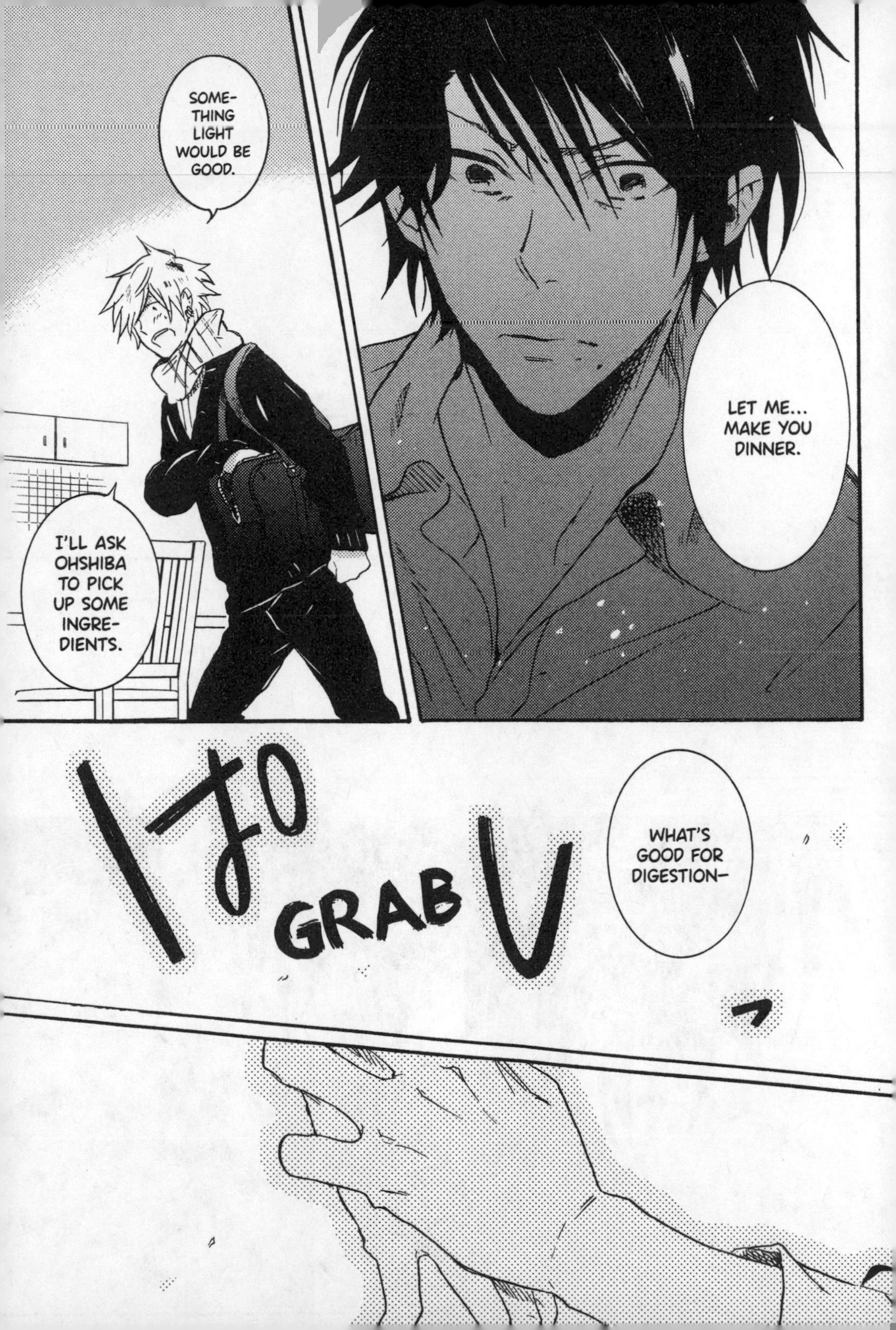
LET ME... MAKE YOU DINNER.
SOME-THING LIGHT WOULD BE GOOD.
I'LL ASK OHSHIBA TO PICK UP SOME INGRE-DIENTS.
WHAT'S GOOD FOR DIGESTION—
GRAB

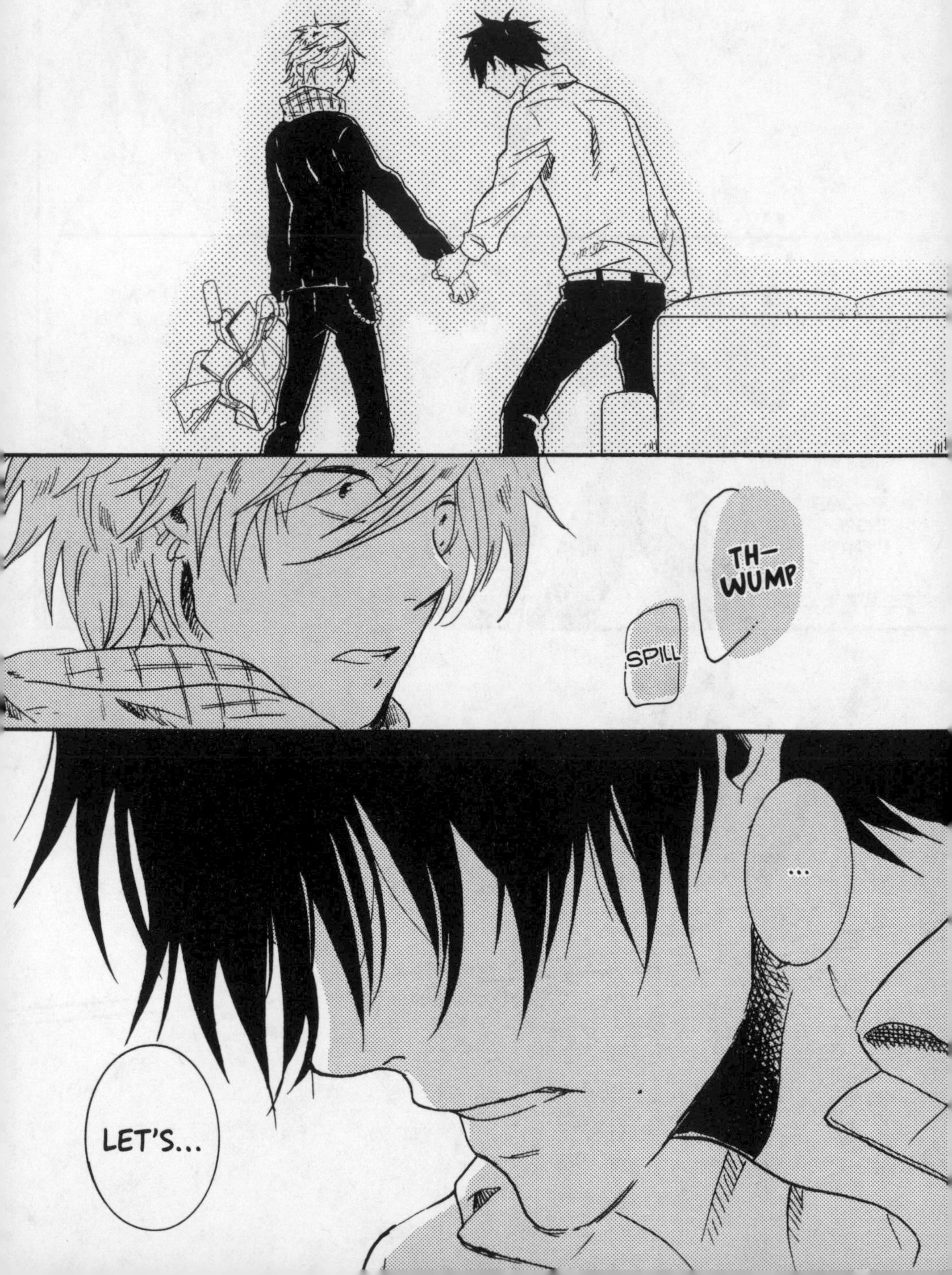
TH-WUMP
SPILL
...
LET'S...

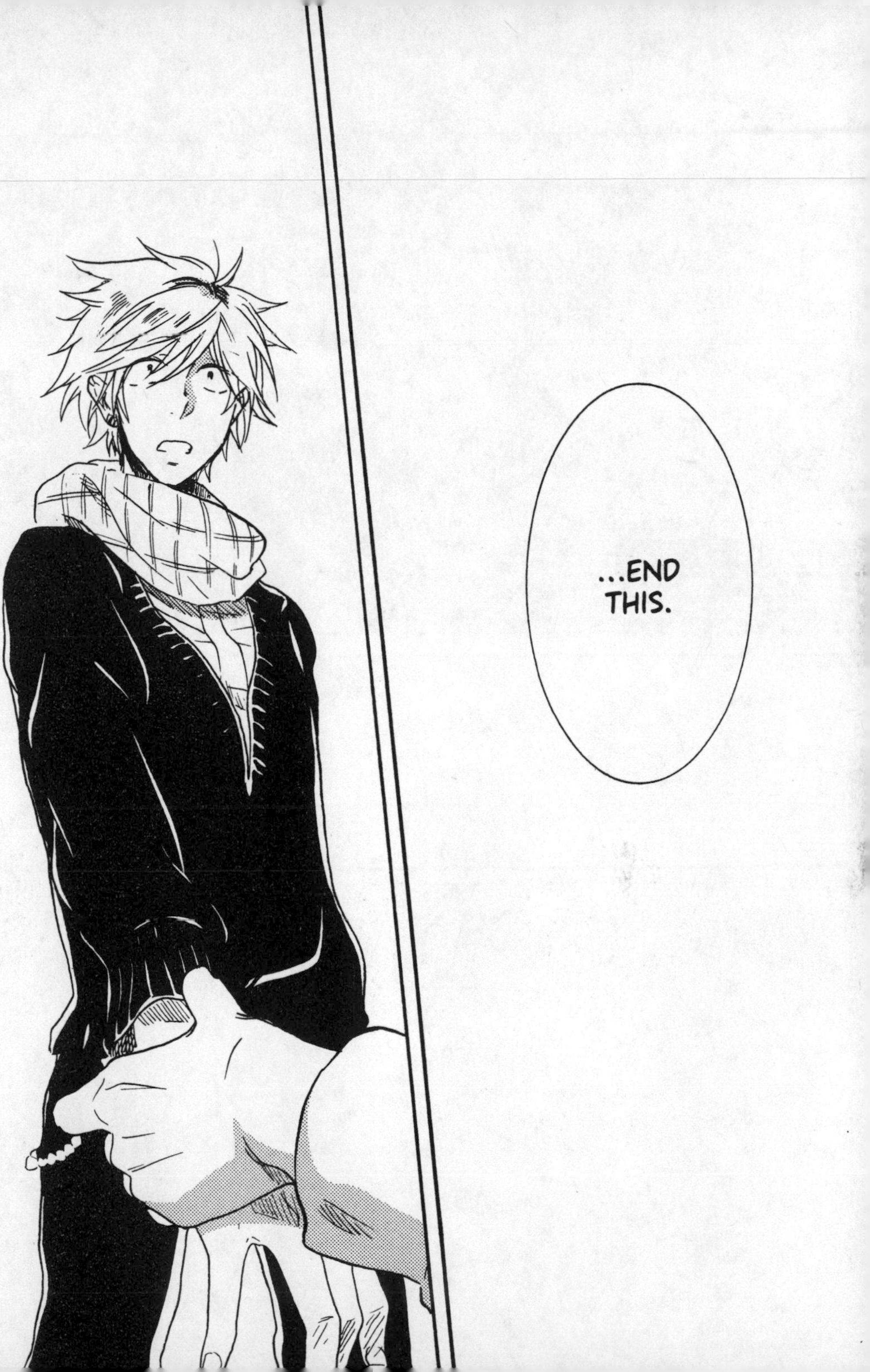
...END
THIS.

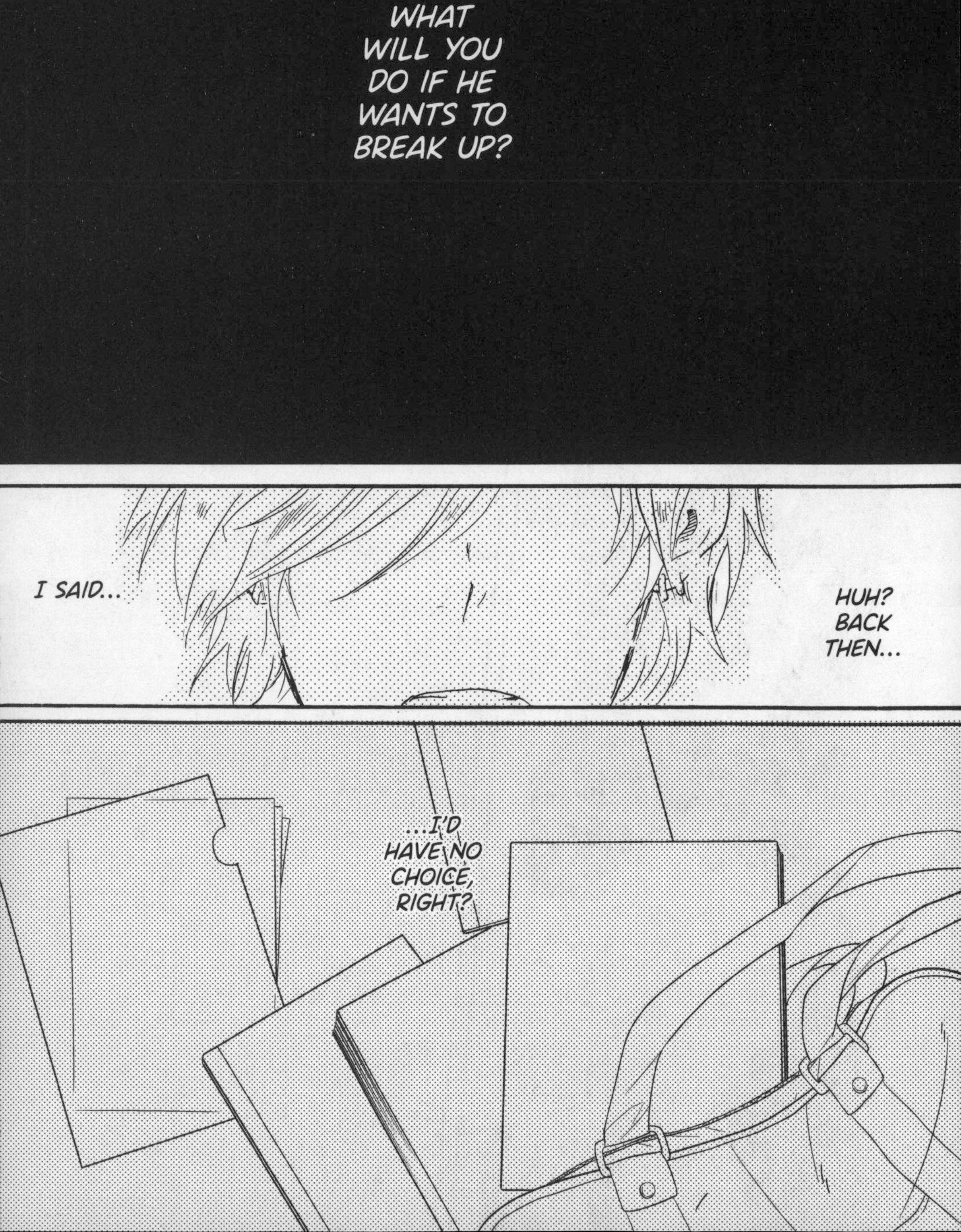
WHAT WILL YOU DO IF HE WANTS TO BREAK UP?
HUH? BACK THEN...
I SAID...
...I'D HAVE NO CHOICE, RIGHT?

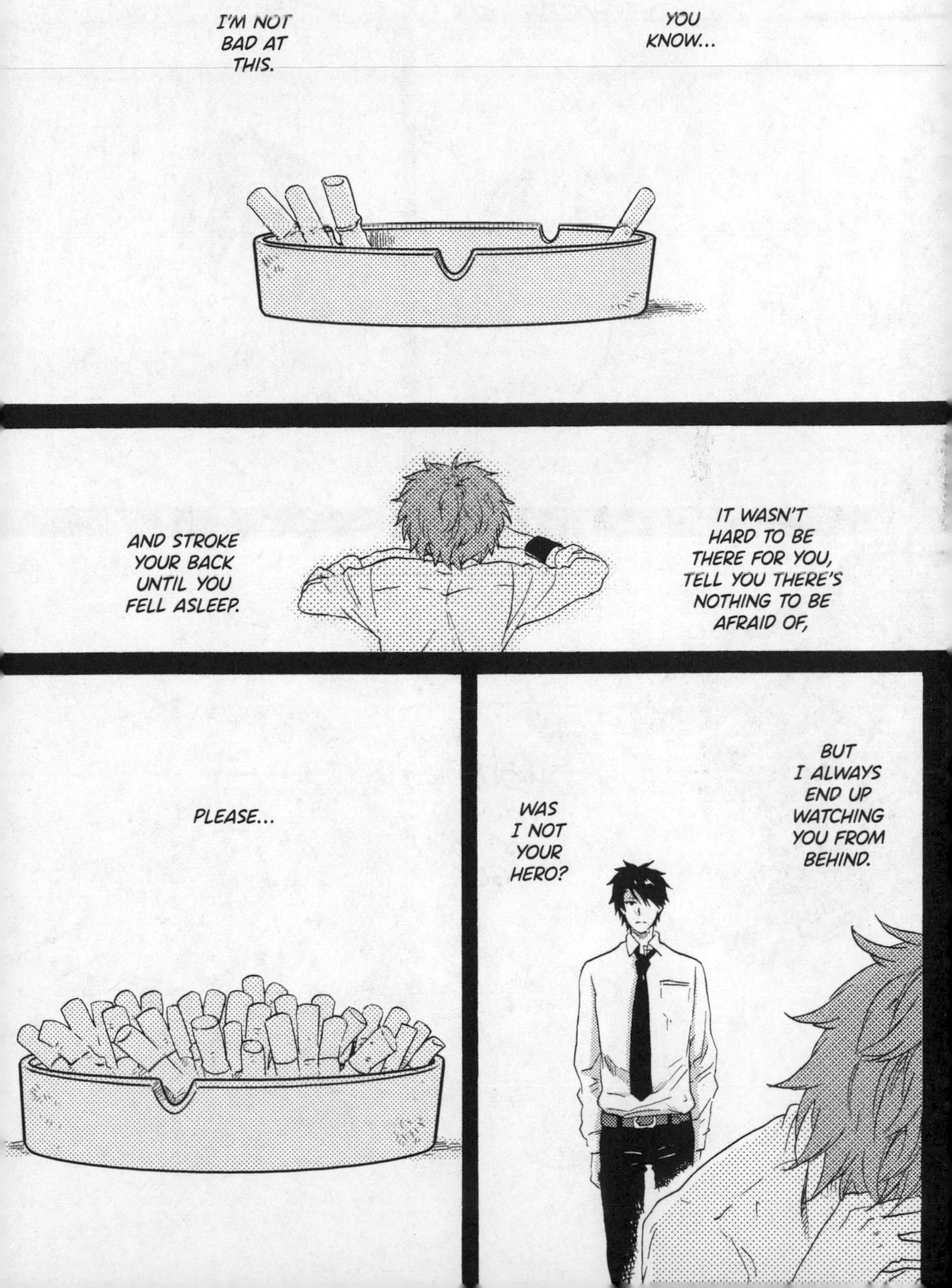
YOU KNOW...
I'M NOT BAD AT THIS.
IT WASN'T HARD TO BE THERE FOR YOU, TELL YOU THERE'S NOTHING TO BE AFRAID OF,
AND STROKE YOUR BACK UNTIL YOU FELL ASLEEP.
BUT I ALWAYS END UP WATCHING YOU FROM BEHIND.
WAS I NOT YOUR HERO?
PLEASE...

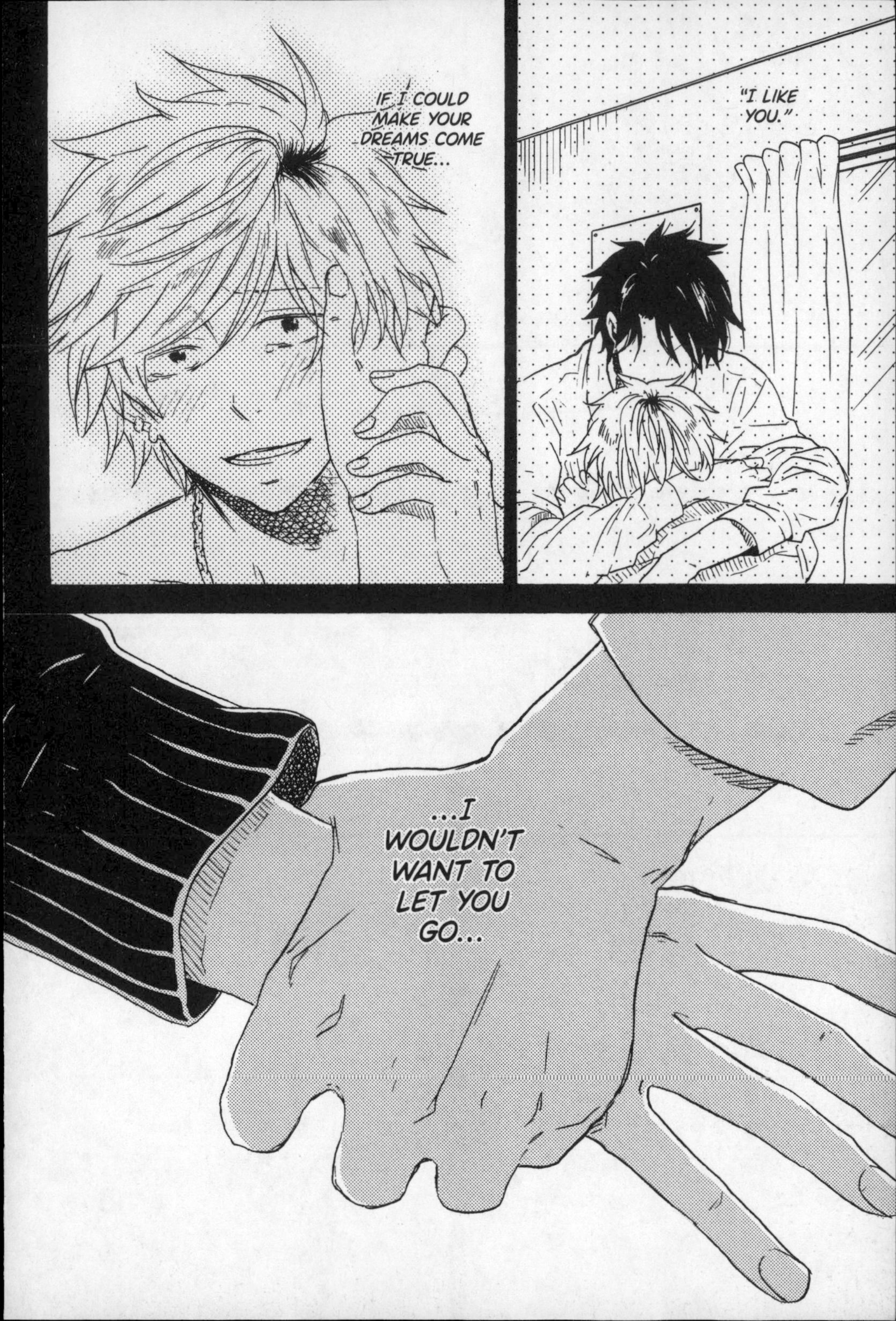
"I LIKE YOU."
IF I COULD MAKE YOUR DREAMS COME TRUE...
...I WOULDN'T WANT TO LET YOU GO...

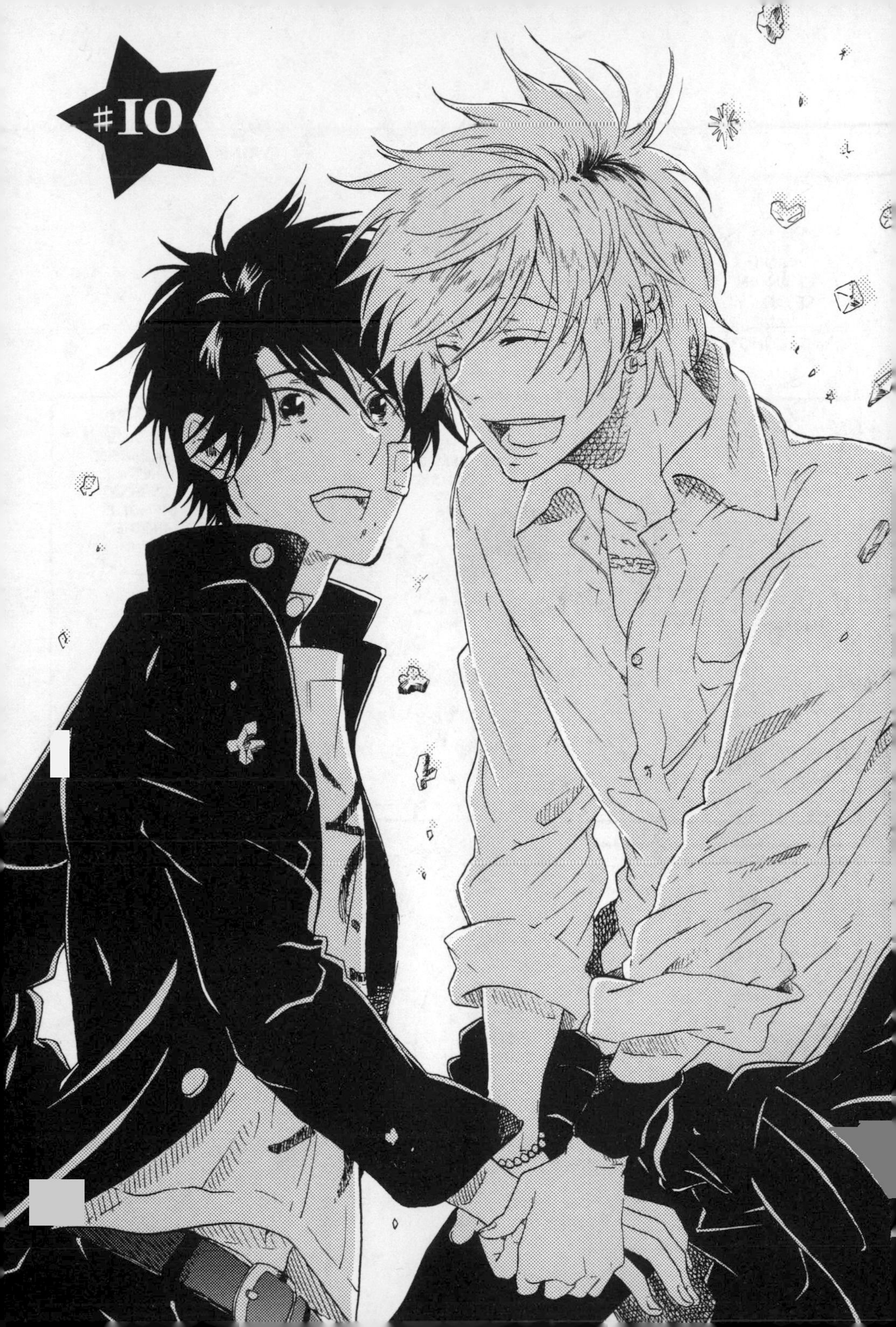
#10

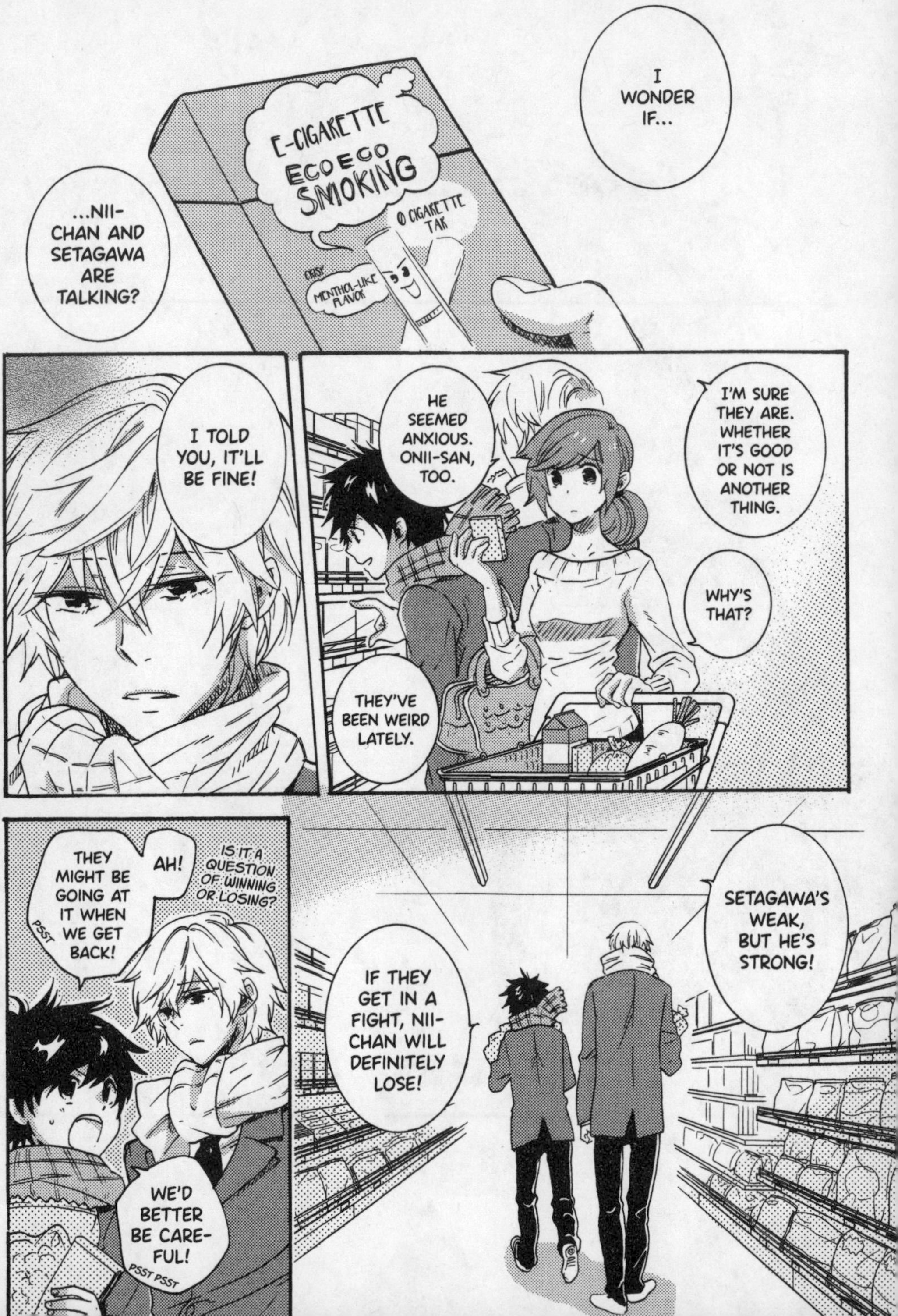
I WONDER IF...
E-CIGARETTE
ECO EGO
SMOKING
0 CIGARETTE TAR
CRISP
MENTHOL-LIKE FLAVOR
...NII-CHAN AND SETAGAWA ARE TALKING?
I'M SURE THEY ARE. WHETHER IT'S GOOD OR NOT IS ANOTHER THING.
HE SEEMED ANXIOUS. ONII-SAN, TOO.
WHY'S THAT?
THEY'VE BEEN WEIRD LATELY.
I TOLD YOU, IT'LL BE FINE!
SETAGAWA'S WEAK, BUT HE'S STRONG!
IF THEY GET IN A FIGHT, NII-CHAN WILL DEFINITELY LOSE!
IS IT A QUESTION OF WINNING OR LOSING?
AH!
THEY MIGHT BE GOING AT IT WHEN WE GET BACK!
PSST
WE'D BETTER BE CAREFUL!
PSST PSST

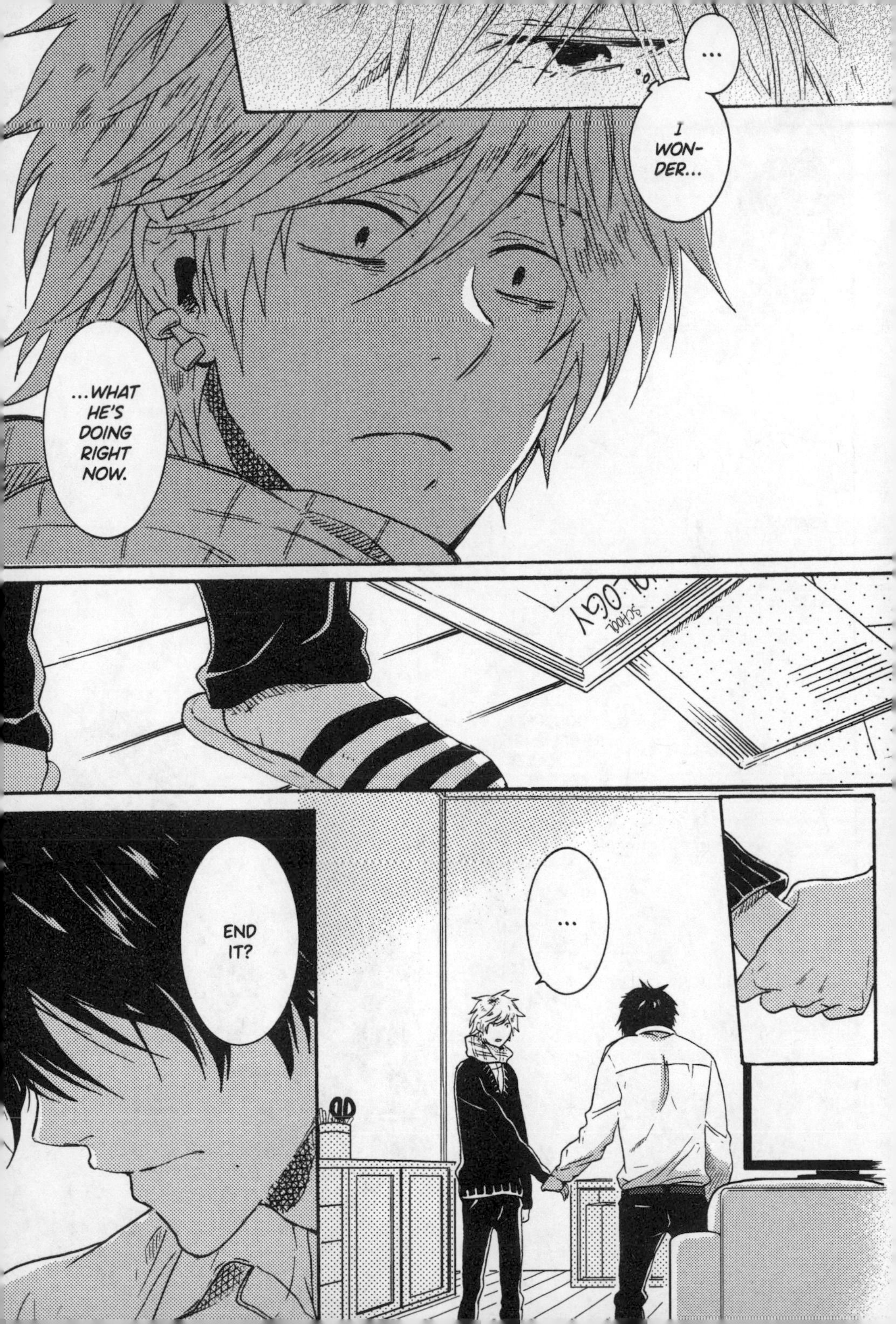
...
I WONDER...
...WHAT HE'S DOING RIGHT NOW.
...
END IT?

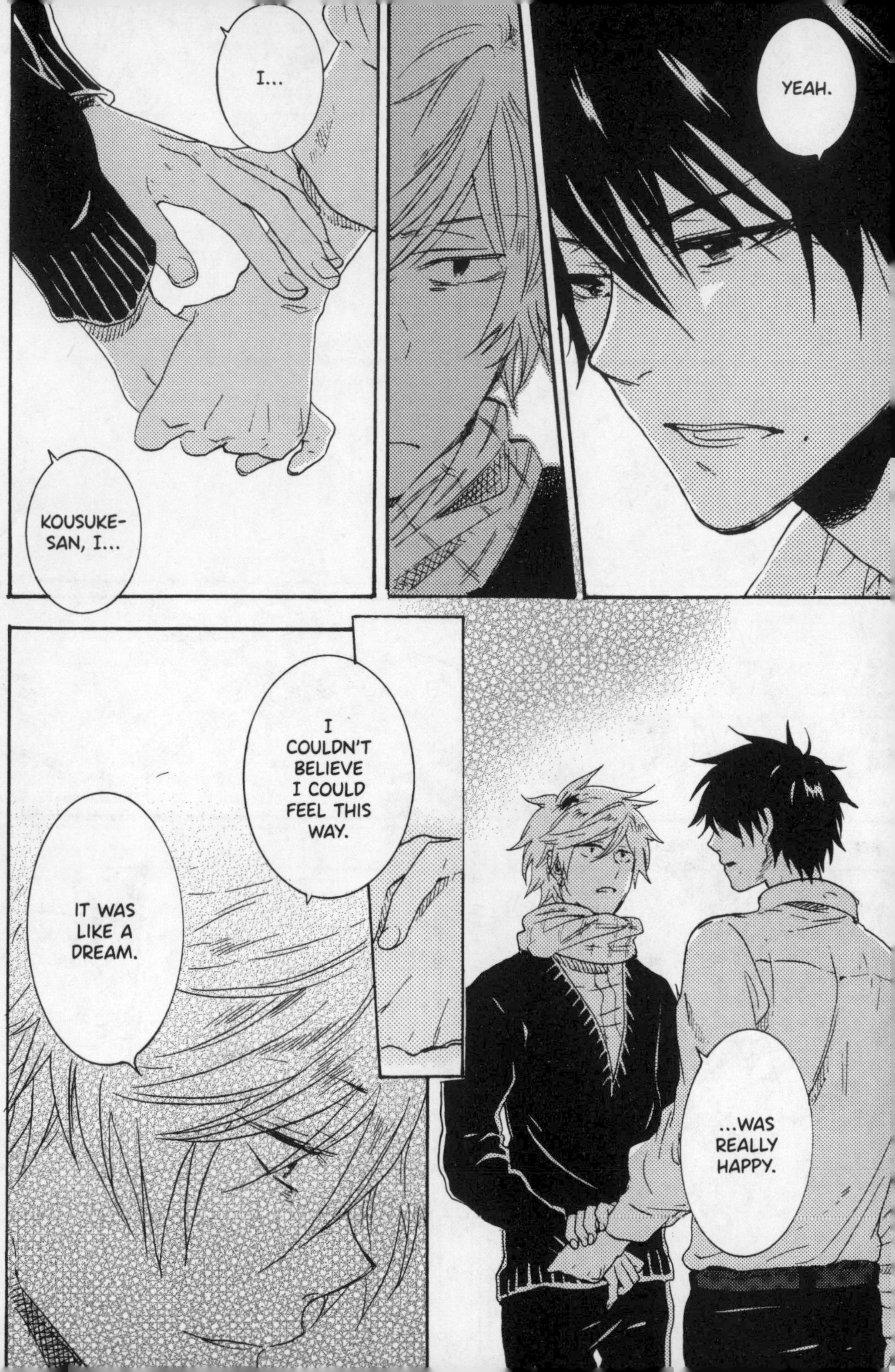
YEAH.
I...
KOUSUKE-SAN, I...
...WAS REALLY HAPPY.
I COULDN'T BELIEVE I COULD FEEL THIS WAY.
IT WAS LIKE A DREAM.

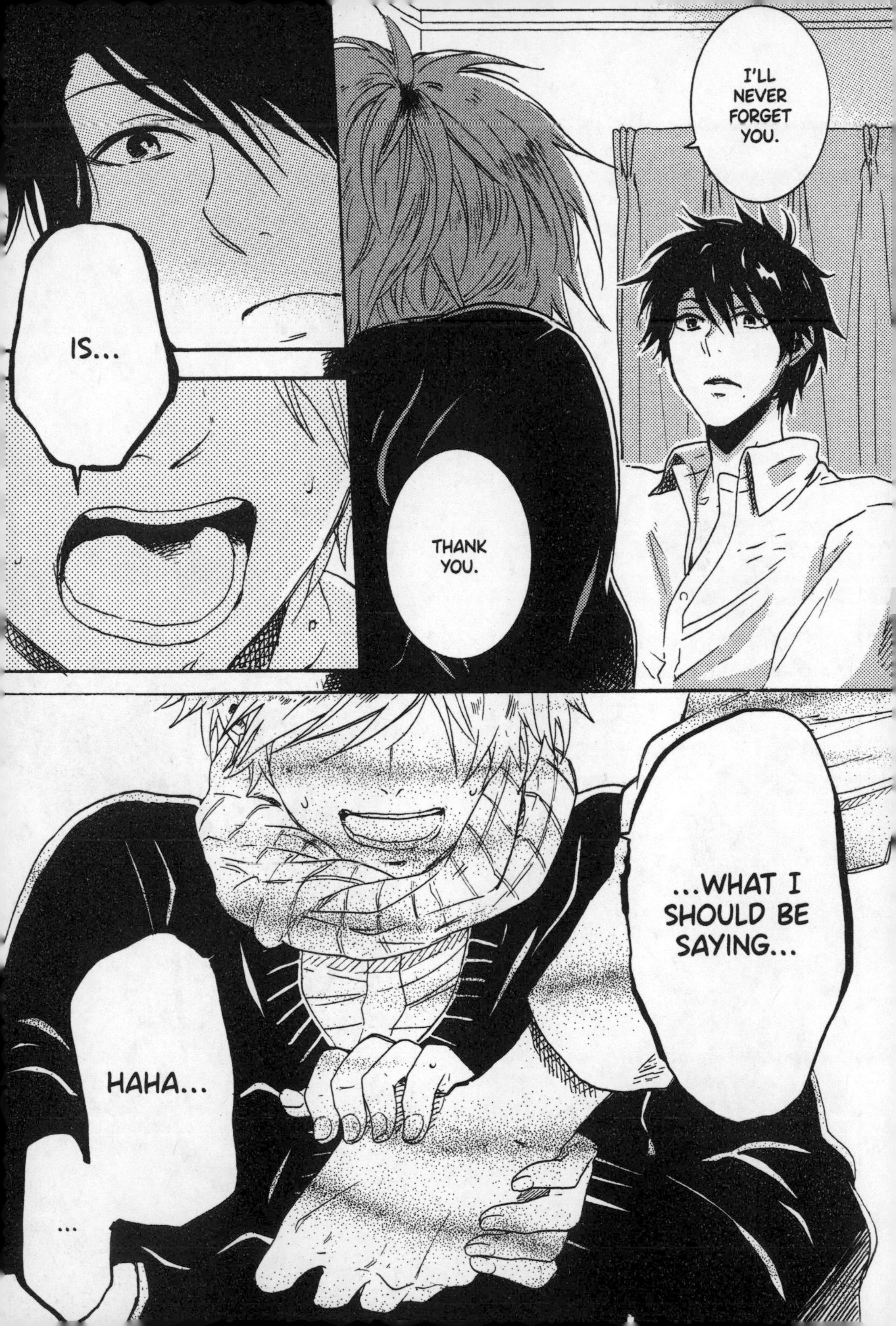
I'LL NEVER FORGET YOU.
THANK YOU.
IS...
...WHAT I SHOULD BE SAYING...
HAHA...
...

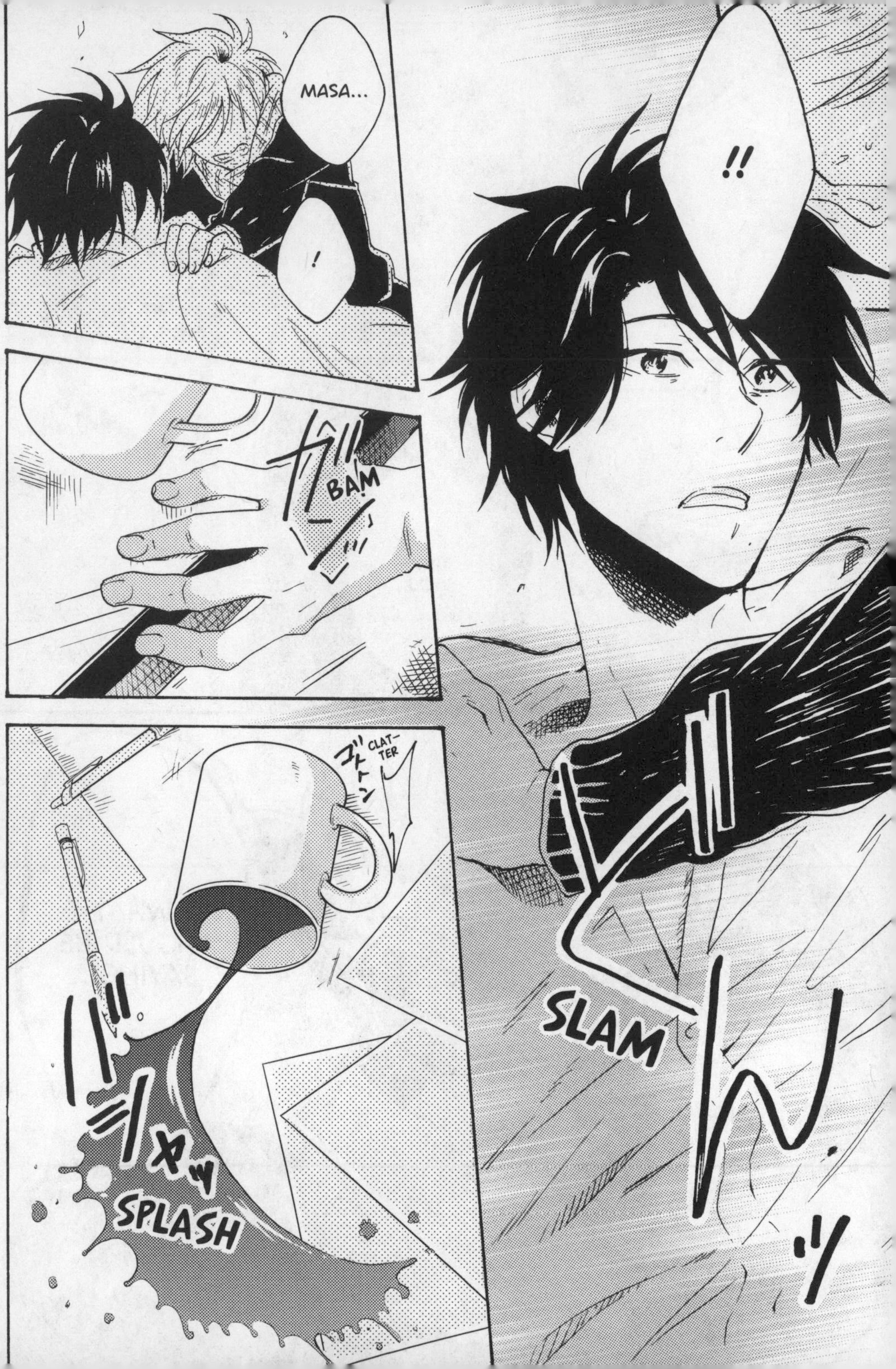
!!
SLAM
MASA...
!
BAM
CLATTER
SPLASH

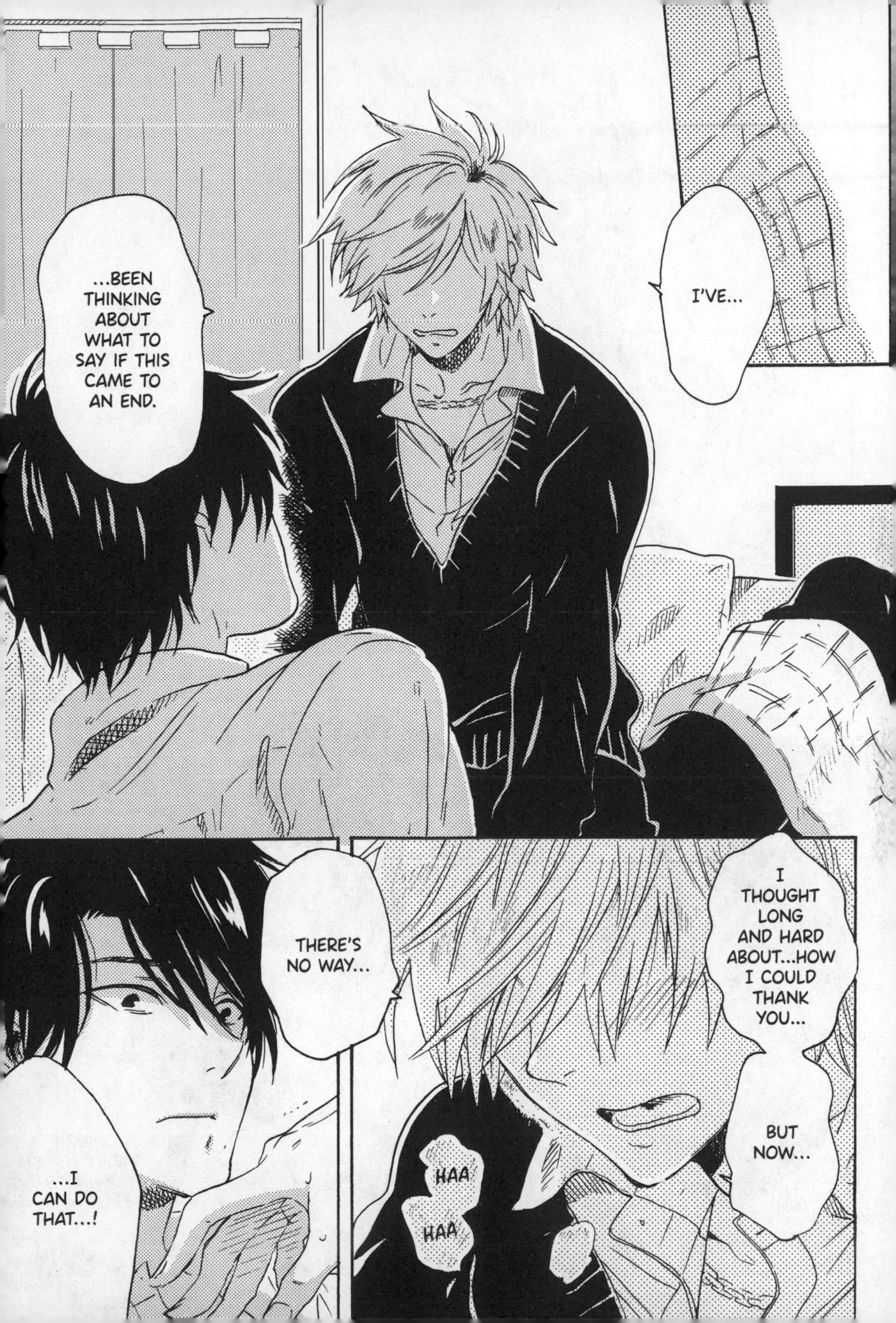
I'VE...
...BEEN THINKING ABOUT WHAT TO SAY IF THIS CAME TO AN END.
I THOUGHT LONG AND HARD ABOUT...HOW I COULD THANK YOU...
BUT NOW...
HAA
HAA
THERE'S NO WAY...
...I CAN DO THAT...!

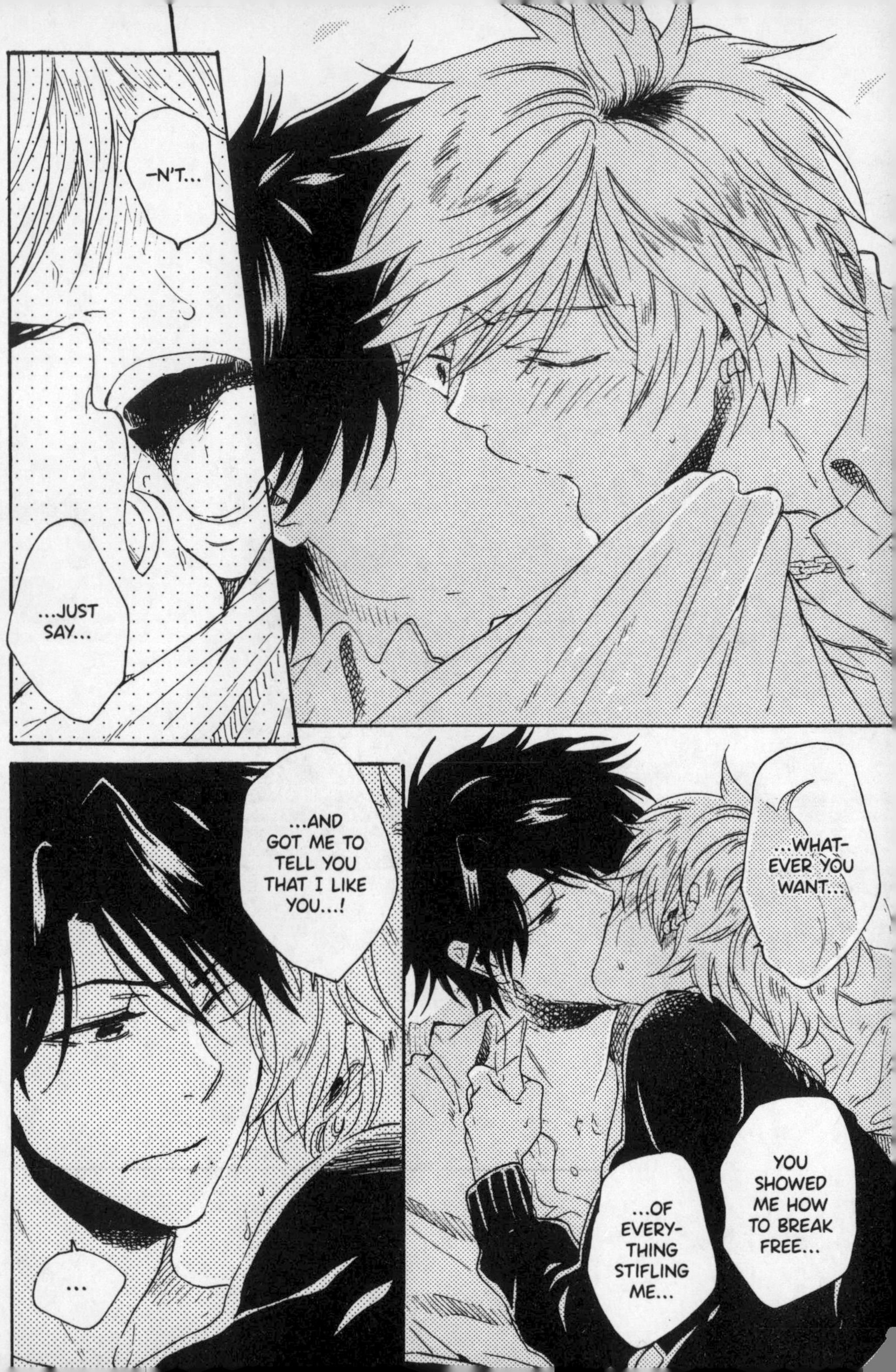
–N'T...
...JUST SAY...
...WHAT-EVER YOU WANT...
YOU SHOWED ME HOW TO BREAK FREE...
...OF EVERY-THING STIFLING ME...
...AND GOT ME TO TELL YOU THAT I LIKE YOU...!
...

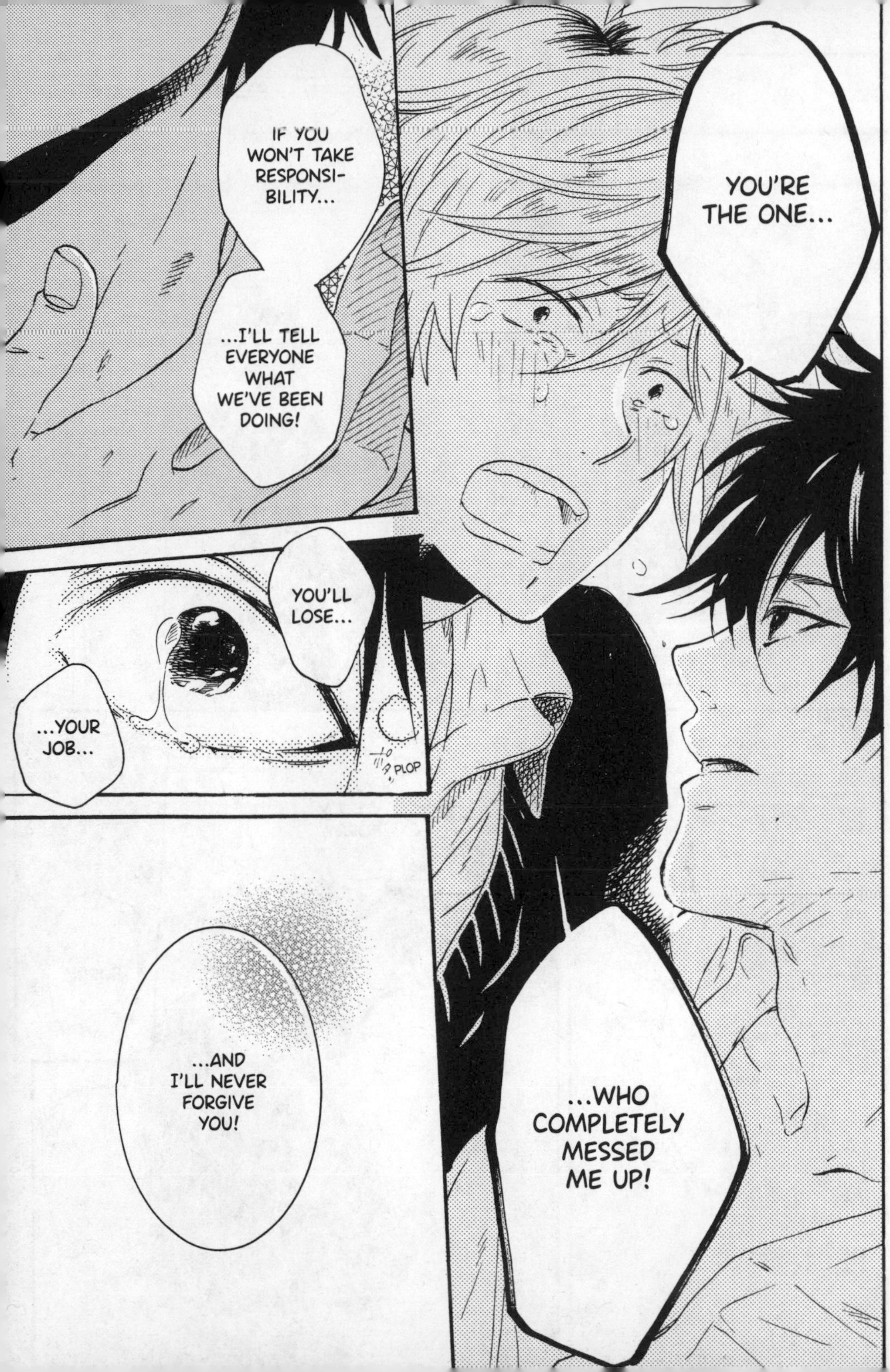
YOU'RE THE ONE...
...WHO COMPLETELY MESSED ME UP!
IF YOU WON'T TAKE RESPONSI-BILITY...
...I'LL TELL EVERYONE WHAT WE'VE BEEN DOING!
YOU'LL LOSE...
...YOUR JOB...
PLOP
...AND I'LL NEVER FORGIVE YOU!

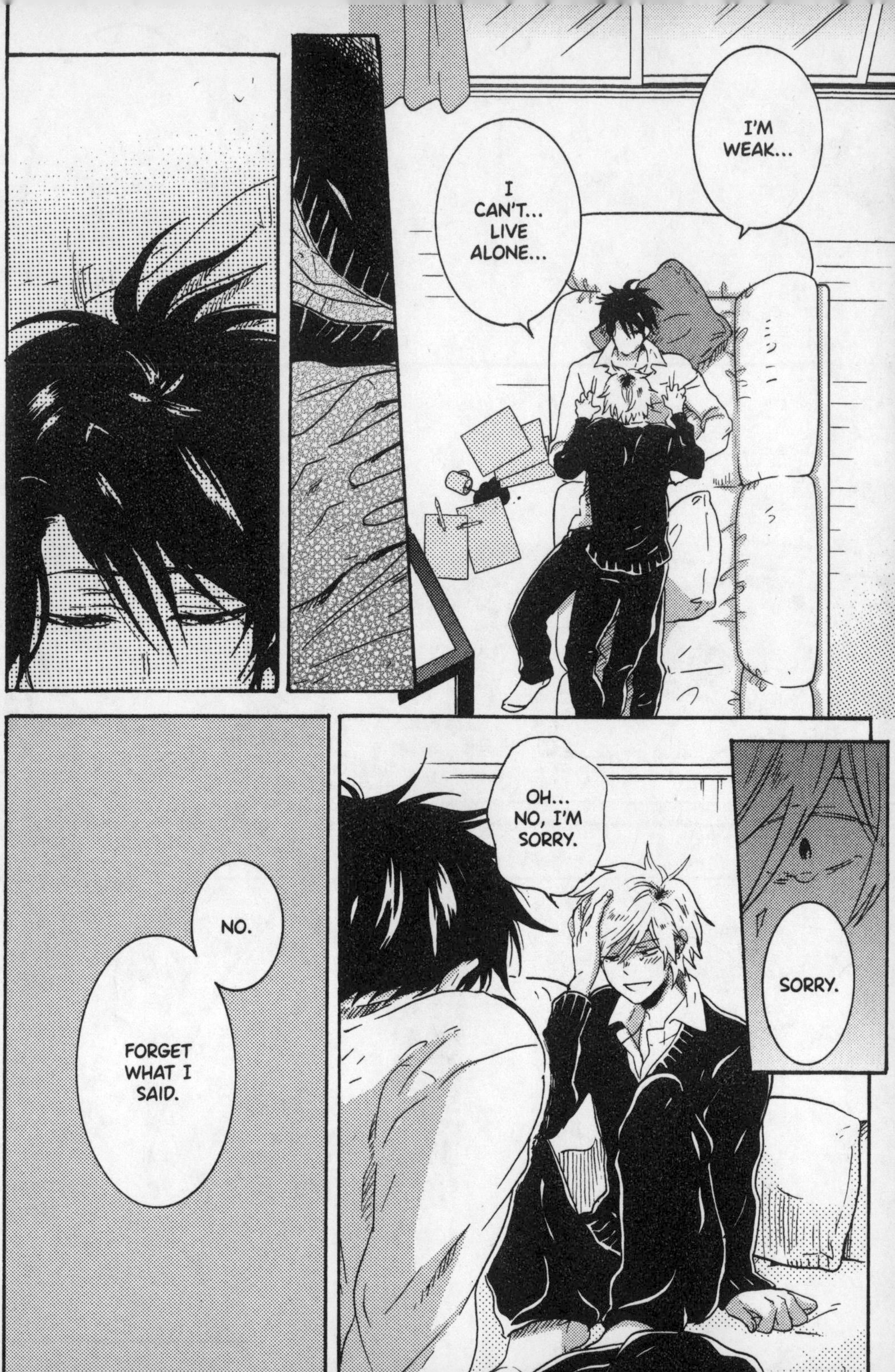
I'M WEAK...
I CAN'T... LIVE ALONE...
OH... NO, I'M SORRY.
SORRY.
NO.
FORGET WHAT I SAID.

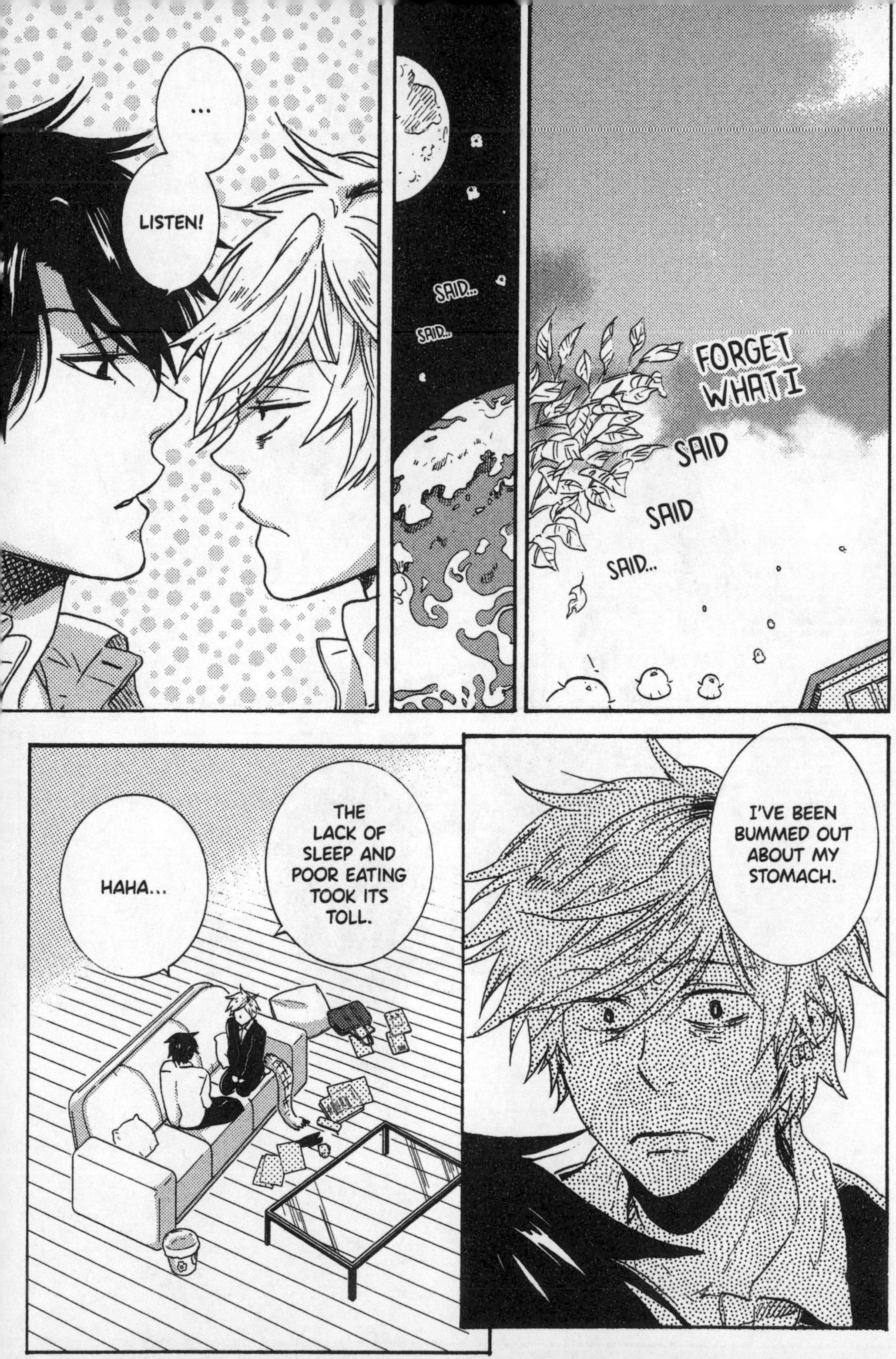
FORGET WHAT I
SAID
SAID
SAID...
SAID...
SAID...
...
LISTEN!
I'VE BEEN BUMMED OUT ABOUT MY STOMACH.
THE LACK OF SLEEP AND POOR EATING TOOK ITS TOLL.
HAHA...

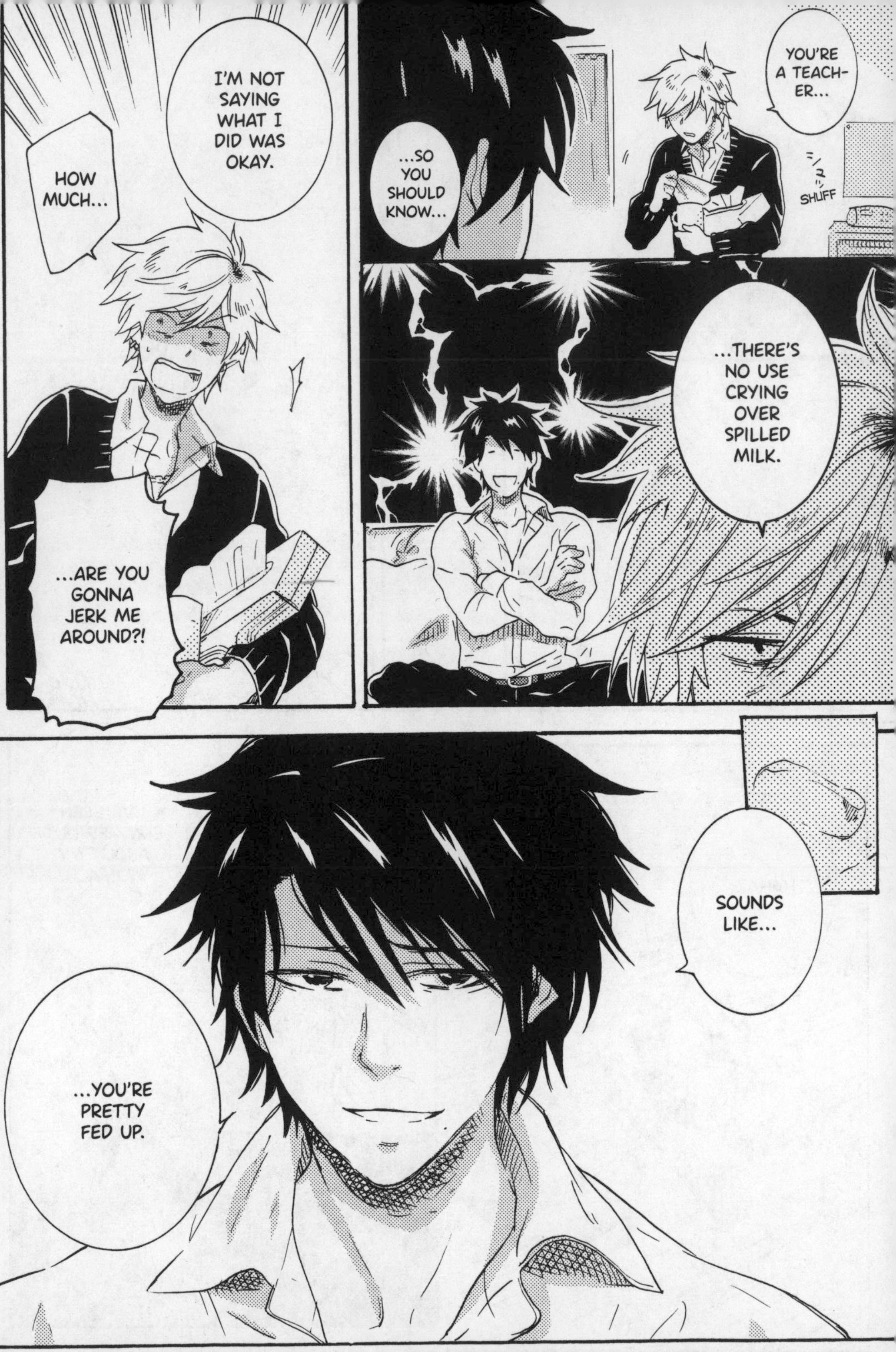
YOU'RE A TEACHER...
SHUFF
...SO YOU SHOULD KNOW...
...THERE'S NO USE CRYING OVER SPILLED MILK.
I'M NOT SAYING WHAT I DID WAS OKAY.
HOW MUCH...
...ARE YOU GONNA JERK ME AROUND?!
SOUNDS LIKE...
...YOU'RE PRETTY FED UP.

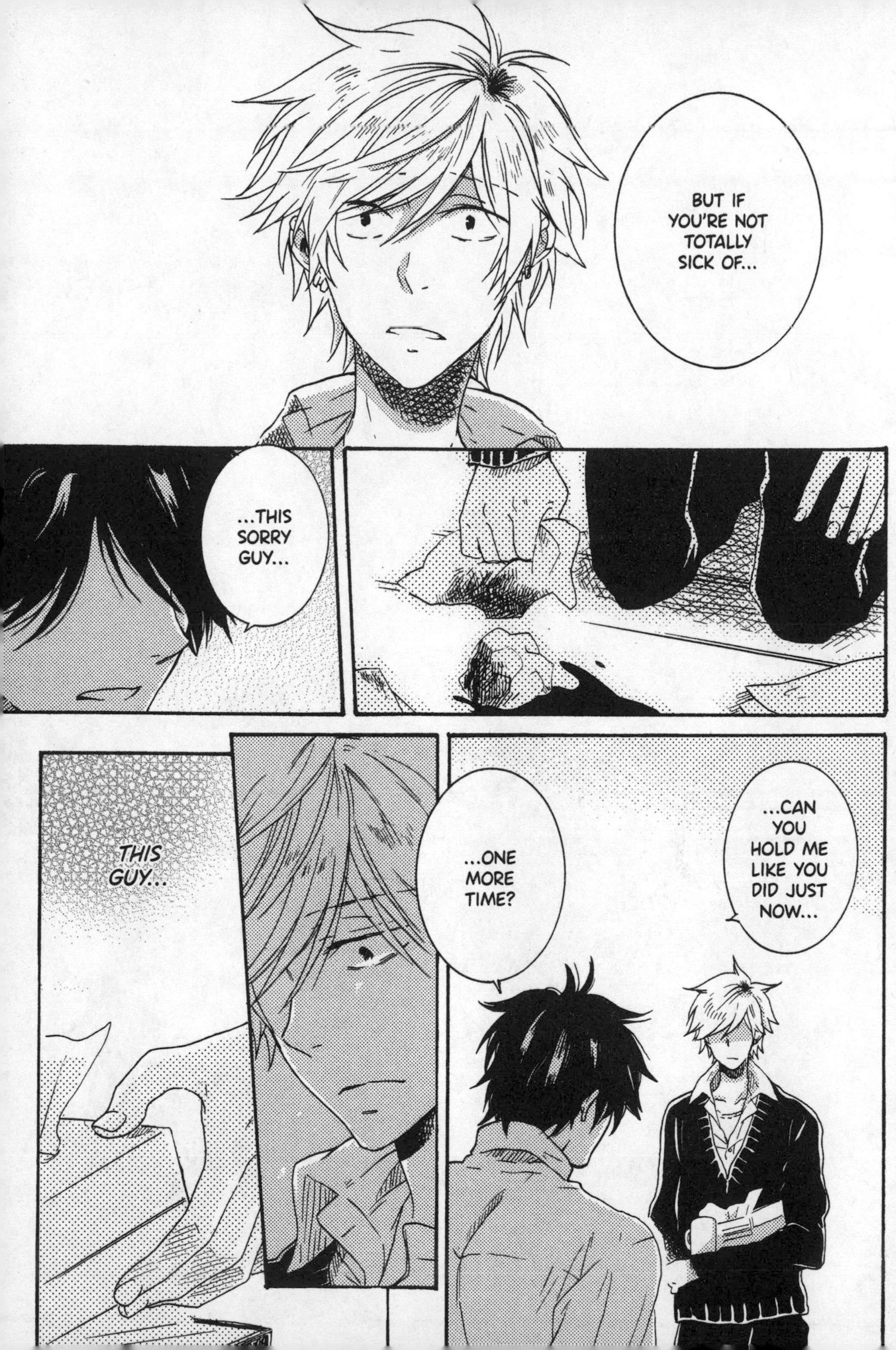
BUT IF YOU'RE NOT TOTALLY SICK OF...
...THIS SORRY GUY...
...CAN YOU HOLD ME LIKE YOU DID JUST NOW...
...ONE MORE TIME?
THIS GUY...

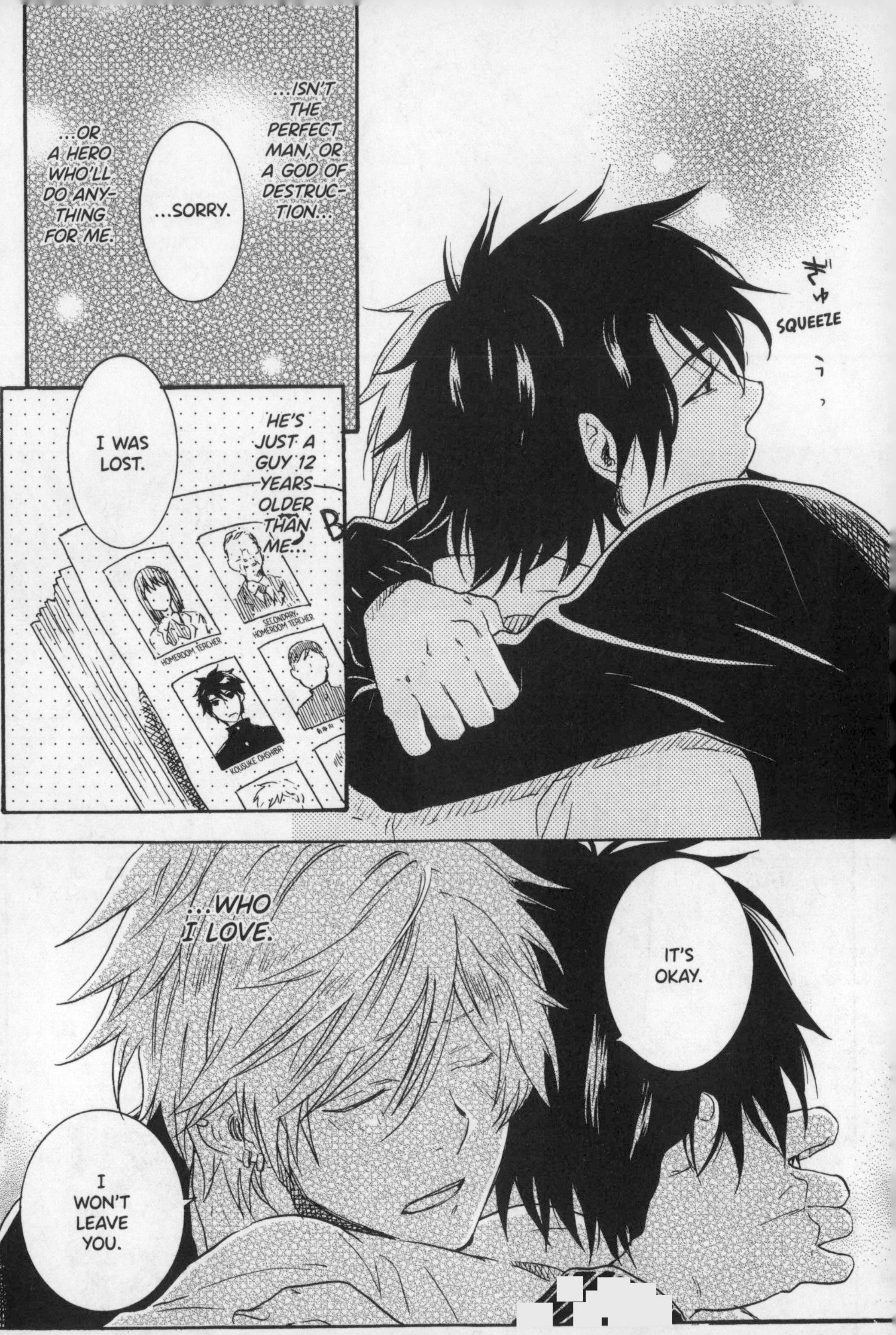
SQUEEZE
...ISN'T THE PERFECT MAN, OR A GOD OF DESTRUCTION...
...SORRY.
...OR A HERO WHO'LL DO ANY-THING FOR ME.
HE'S JUST A GUY 12 YEARS OLDER THAN ME...
I WAS LOST.
HOMEROOM TEACHER
SECONDARY HOMEROOM TEACHER
KOUSUKE OHSHIBA
...WHO I LOVE.
IT'S OKAY.
I WON'T LEAVE YOU.

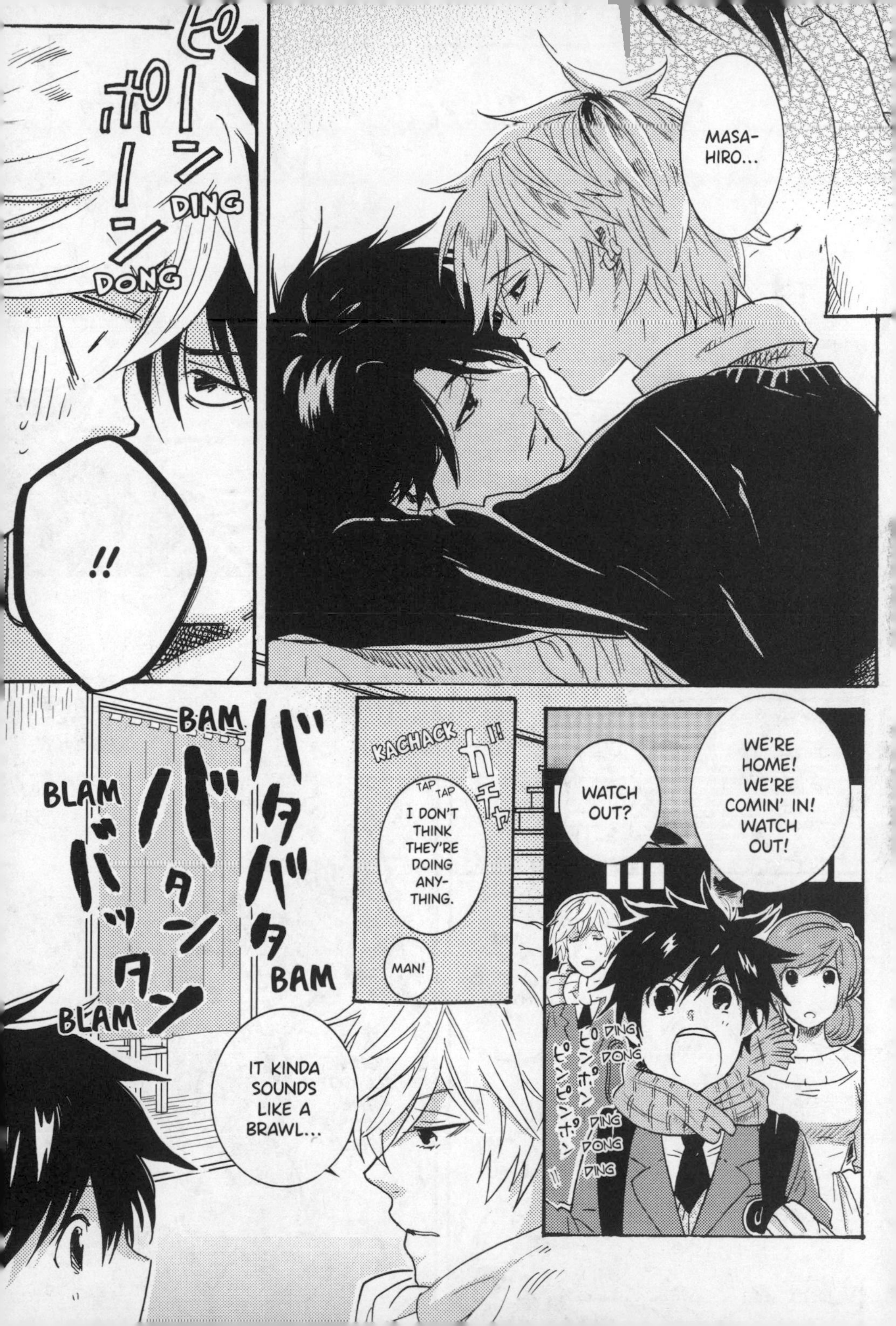

MASA-HIRO...
DING
DONG
!!
WE'RE HOME! WE'RE COMIN' IN! WATCH OUT!
WATCH OUT?
DING
DONG
DING
DONG
DING
KACHACK
TAP TAP
I DON'T THINK THEY'RE DOING ANY-THING.
MAN!
BAM
BLAM
BAM
BLAM
IT KINDA SOUNDS LIKE A BRAWL...

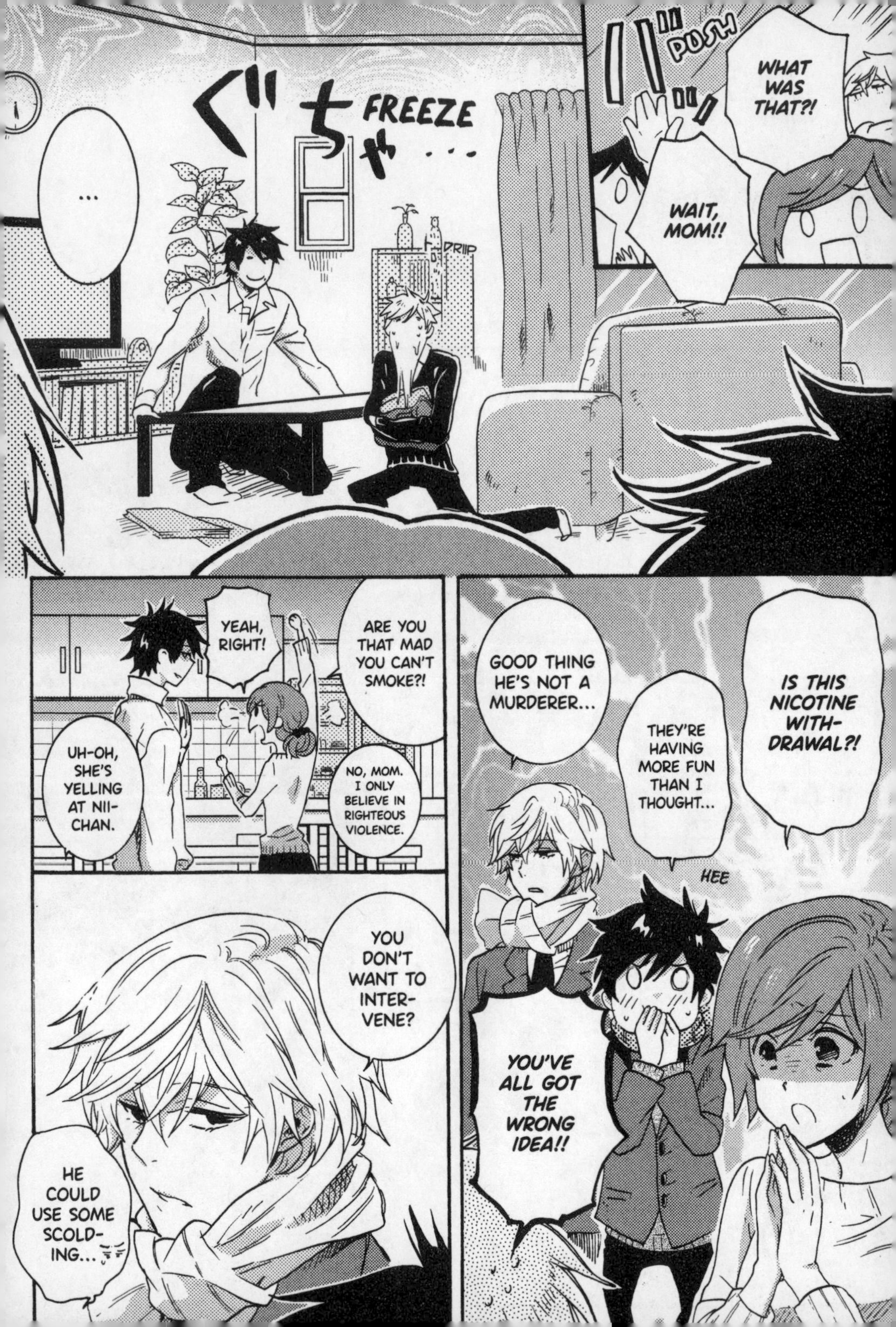
PUSH
WHAT WAS THAT?!
WAIT, MOM!!
ぐちゃ
FREEZE
...
...
DRIP
IS THIS NICOTINE WITH-DRAWAL?!
THEY'RE HAVING MORE FUN THAN I THOUGHT...
GOOD THING HE'S NOT A MURDERER...
HEE
YOU'VE ALL GOT THE WRONG IDEA!!
ARE YOU THAT MAD YOU CAN'T SMOKE?!
YEAH, RIGHT!
NO, MOM. I ONLY BELIEVE IN RIGHTEOUS VIOLENCE.
UH-OH, SHE'S YELLING AT NII-CHAN.
YOU DON'T WANT TO INTER-VENE?
HE COULD USE SOME SCOLD-ING...

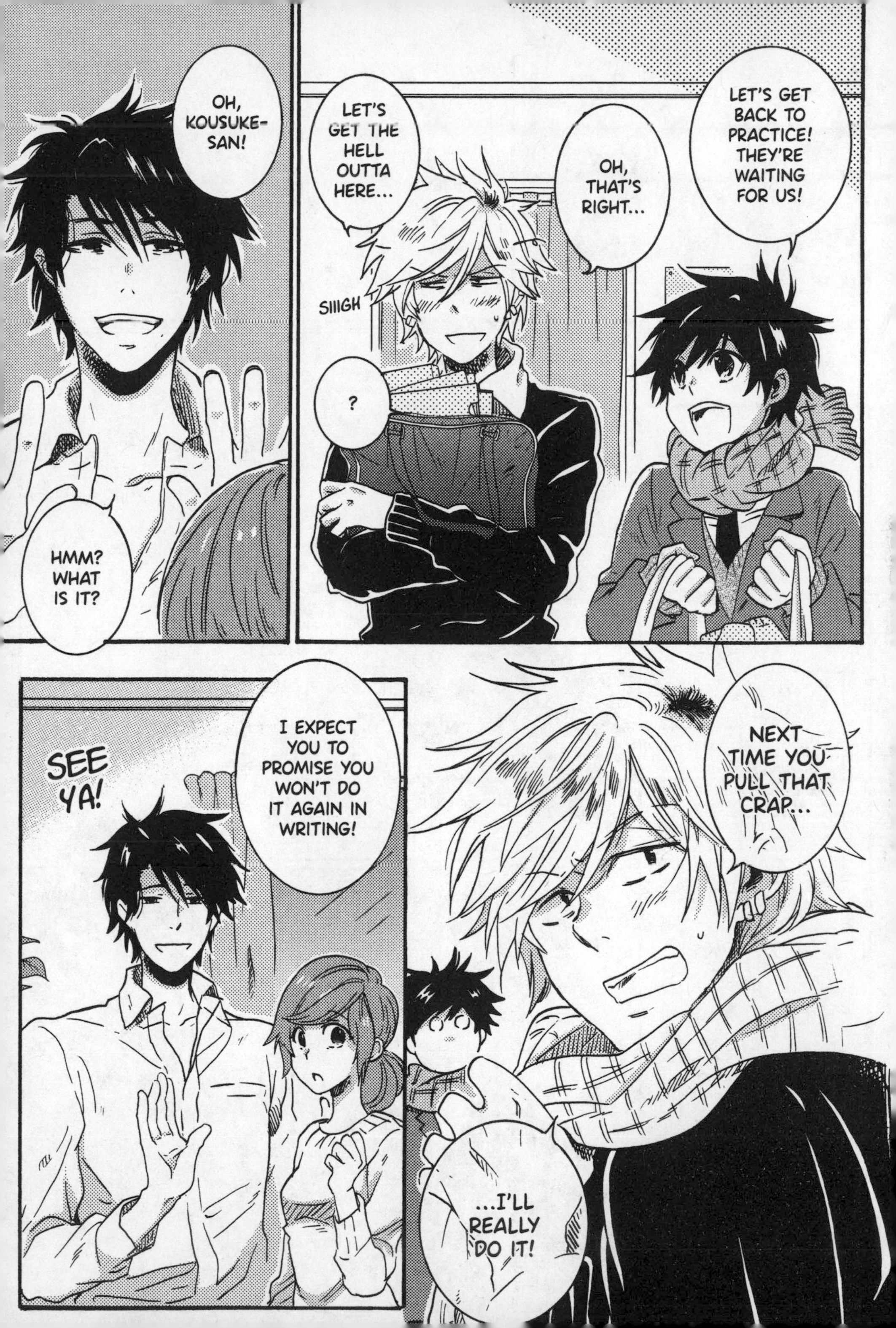
LET'S GET BACK TO PRACTICE! THEY'RE WAITING FOR US!
OH, THAT'S RIGHT...
LET'S GET THE HELL OUTTA HERE...
SIIIGH
?
OH, KOUSUKE-SAN!
HMM? WHAT IS IT?
NEXT TIME YOU PULL THAT CRAP...
...I'LL REALLY DO IT!
I EXPECT YOU TO PROMISE YOU WON'T DO IT AGAIN IN WRITING!
SEE YA!

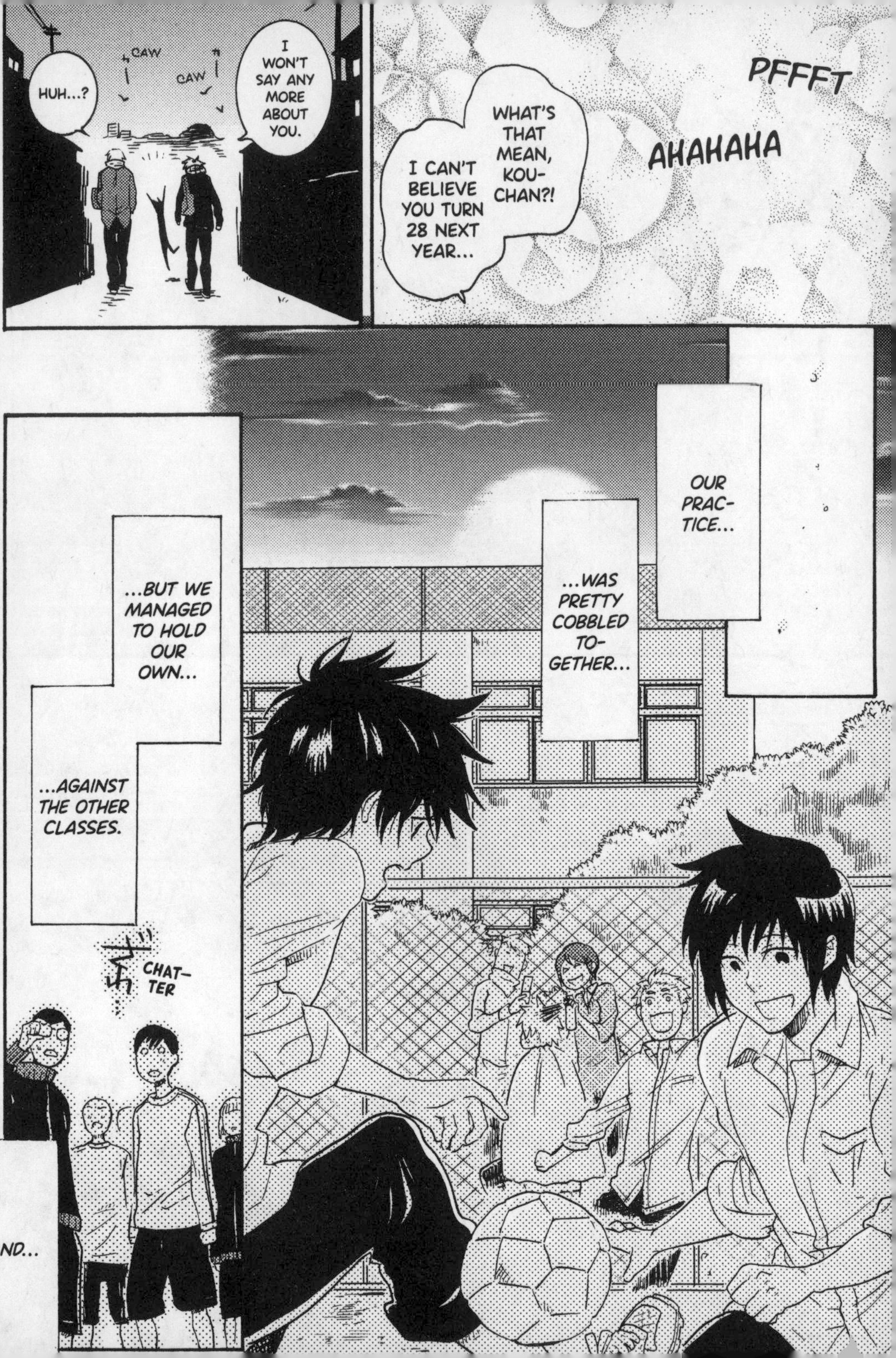
PFFFT
AHAHAHA
WHAT'S THAT MEAN, KOU-CHAN?!
I CAN'T BELIEVE YOU TURN 28 NEXT YEAR...
I WON'T SAY ANY MORE ABOUT YOU.
CAW
CAW
HUH...?
OUR PRAC-TICE...
...WAS PRETTY COBBLED TO-GETHER...
...BUT WE MANAGED TO HOLD OUR OWN...
...AGAINST THE OTHER CLASSES.
CHAT-TER
AND...

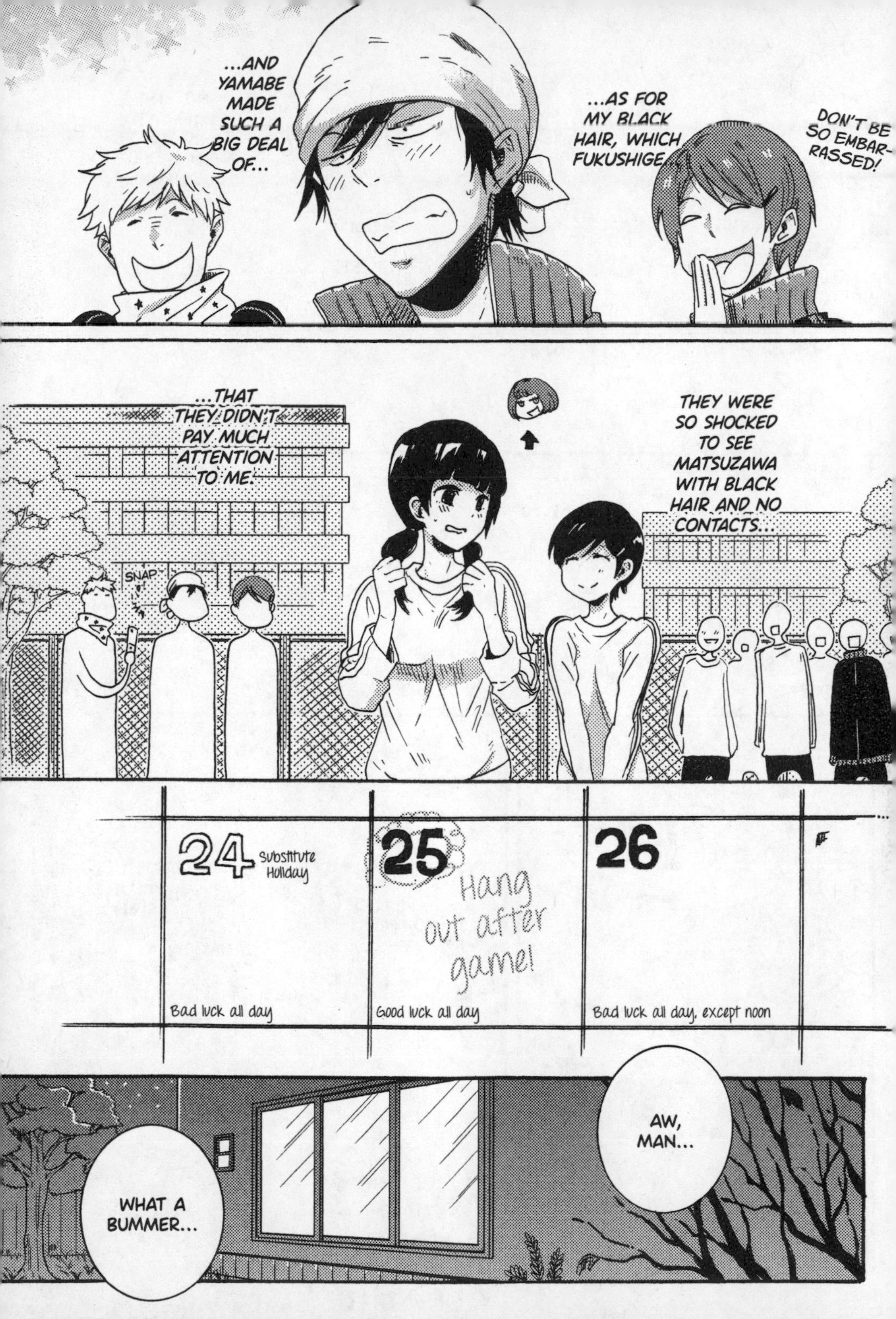
DON'T BE SO EMBARRASSED!
...AS FOR MY BLACK HAIR, WHICH FUKUSHIGE...
...AND YAMABE MADE SUCH A BIG DEAL OF...
THEY WERE SO SHOCKED TO SEE MATSUZAWA WITH BLACK HAIR AND NO CONTACTS...
...THAT THEY DIDN'T PAY MUCH ATTENTION TO ME.
SNAP
24 Substitute Holiday
Bad luck all day
25
Hang out after game!
Good luck all day
26
Bad luck all day, except noon
AW, MAN...
WHAT A BUMMER...

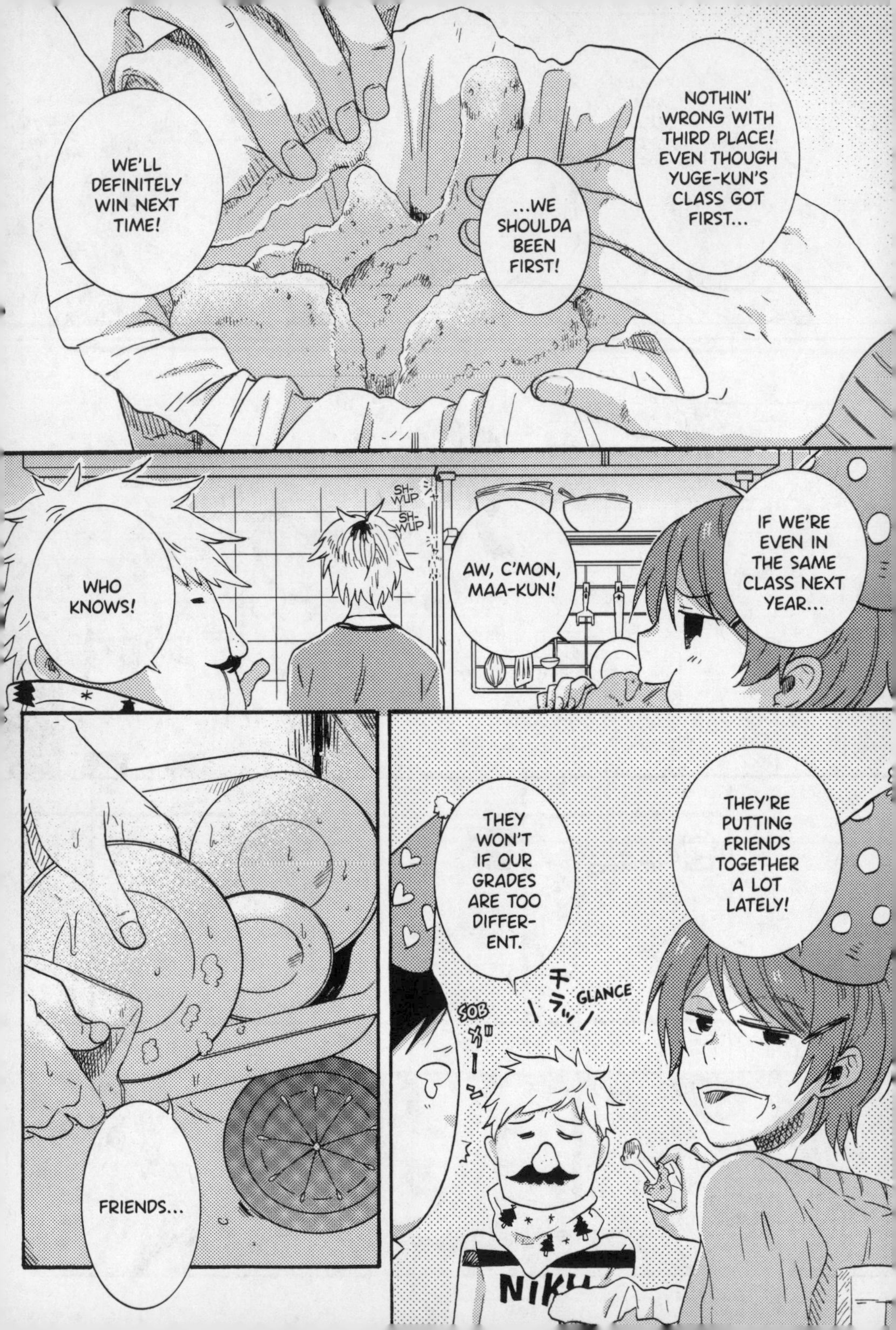
NOTHIN' WRONG WITH THIRD PLACE! EVEN THOUGH YUGE-KUN'S CLASS GOT FIRST...
...WE SHOULDA BEEN FIRST!
WE'LL DEFINITELY WIN NEXT TIME!
IF WE'RE EVEN IN THE SAME CLASS NEXT YEAR...
AW, C'MON, MAA-KUN!
SH-WUP
SH-WUP
WHO KNOWS!
THEY'RE PUTTING FRIENDS TOGETHER A LOT LATELY!
THEY WON'T IF OUR GRADES ARE TOO DIFFER-ENT.
チラッ
GLANCE
SOB
NIKU
FRIENDS...

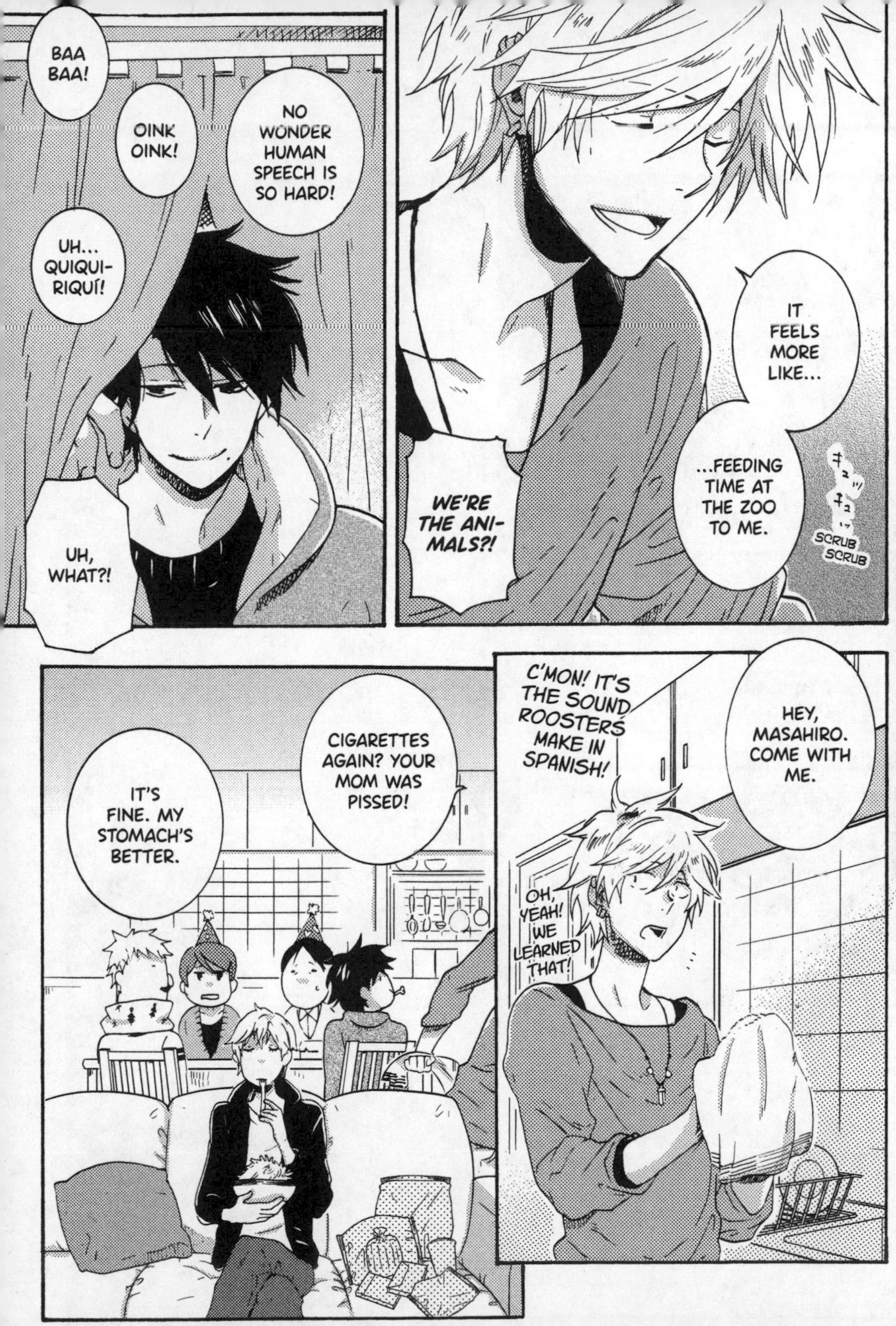
IT FEELS MORE LIKE...
...FEEDING TIME AT THE ZOO TO ME.
キュッ キュッ
SCRUB SCRUB
WE'RE THE ANIMALS?!
NO WONDER HUMAN SPEECH IS SO HARD!
OINK OINK!
BAA BAA!
UH... QUIQUIRIQUÍ!
UH, WHAT?!
HEY, MASAHIRO. COME WITH ME.
C'MON! IT'S THE SOUND ROOSTERS MAKE IN SPANISH!
OH, YEAH! WE LEARNED THAT!
CIGARETTES AGAIN? YOUR MOM WAS PISSED!
IT'S FINE. MY STOMACH'S BETTER.

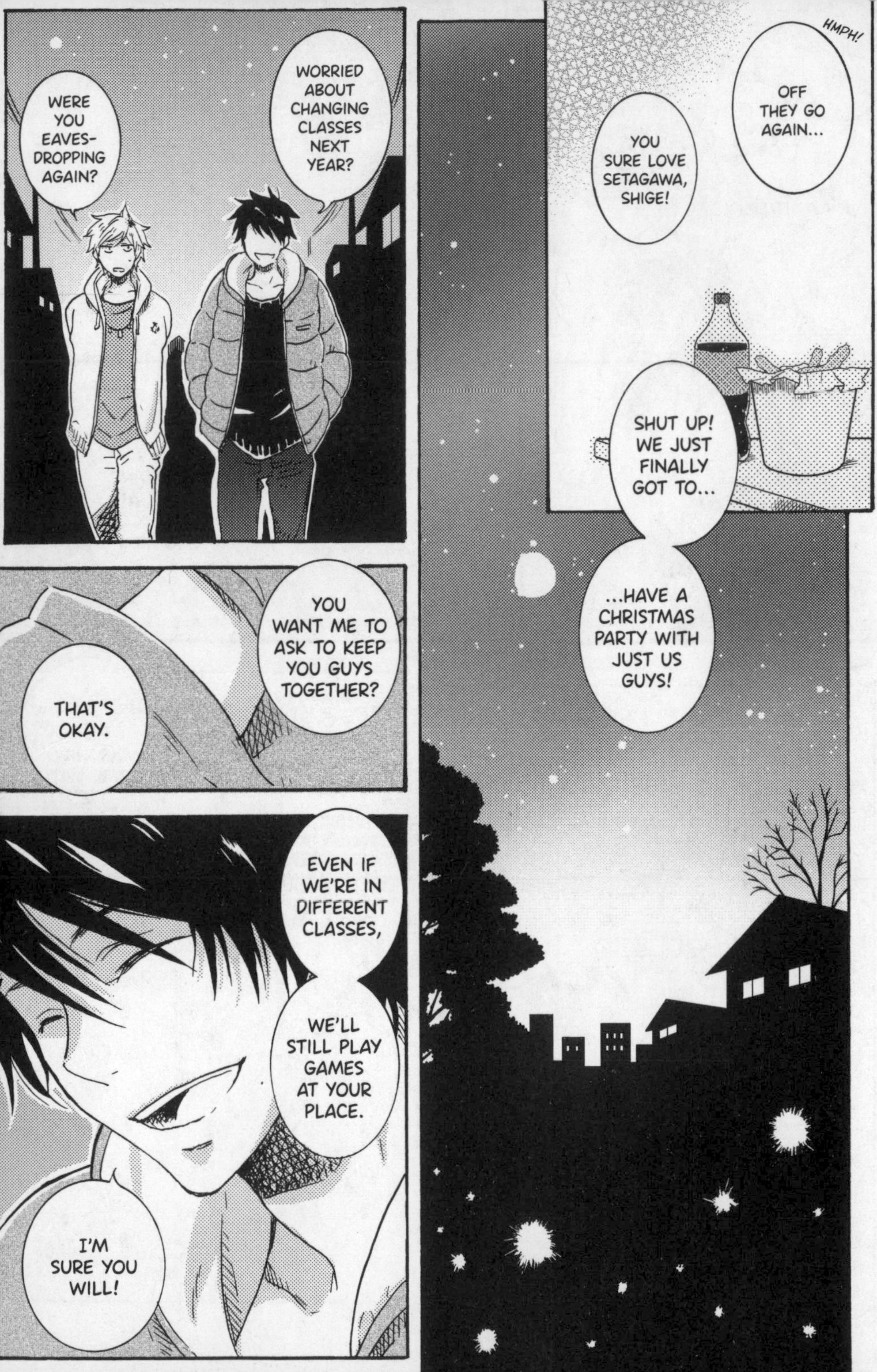
HMPH!
OFF THEY GO AGAIN...
YOU SURE LOVE SETAGAWA, SHIGE!
SHUT UP! WE JUST FINALLY GOT TO...
...HAVE A CHRISTMAS PARTY WITH JUST US GUYS!
WORRIED ABOUT CHANGING CLASSES NEXT YEAR?
WERE YOU EAVES-DROPPING AGAIN?
YOU WANT ME TO ASK TO KEEP YOU GUYS TOGETHER?
THAT'S OKAY.
EVEN IF WE'RE IN DIFFERENT CLASSES,
WE'LL STILL PLAY GAMES AT YOUR PLACE.
I'M SURE YOU WILL!

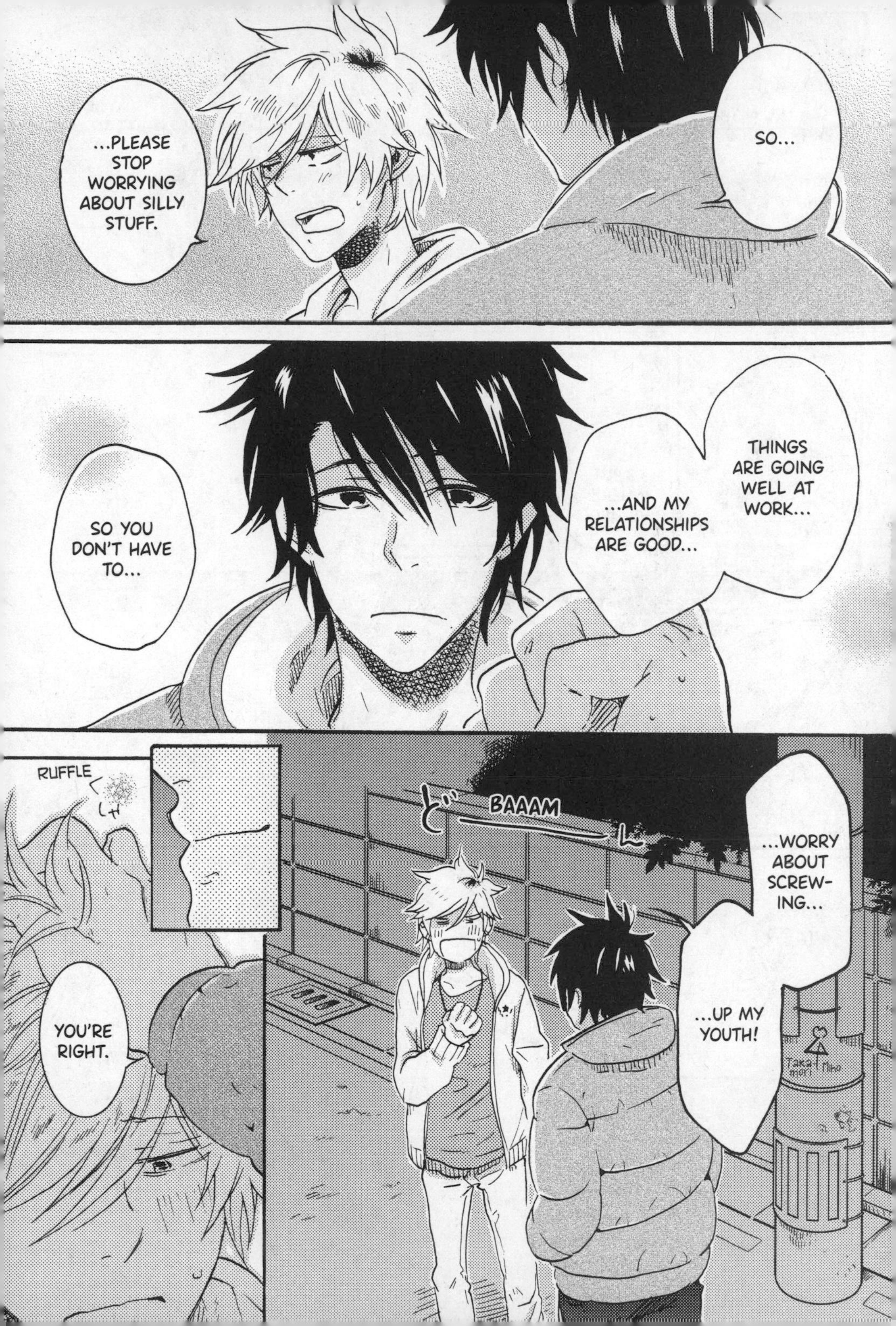
SO...
...PLEASE STOP WORRYING ABOUT SILLY STUFF.
THINGS ARE GOING WELL AT WORK...
...AND MY RELATIONSHIPS ARE GOOD...
SO YOU DON'T HAVE TO...
BAAAM
...WORRY ABOUT SCREWING...
...UP MY YOUTH!
Takamori
Miho
RUFFLE
YOU'RE RIGHT.

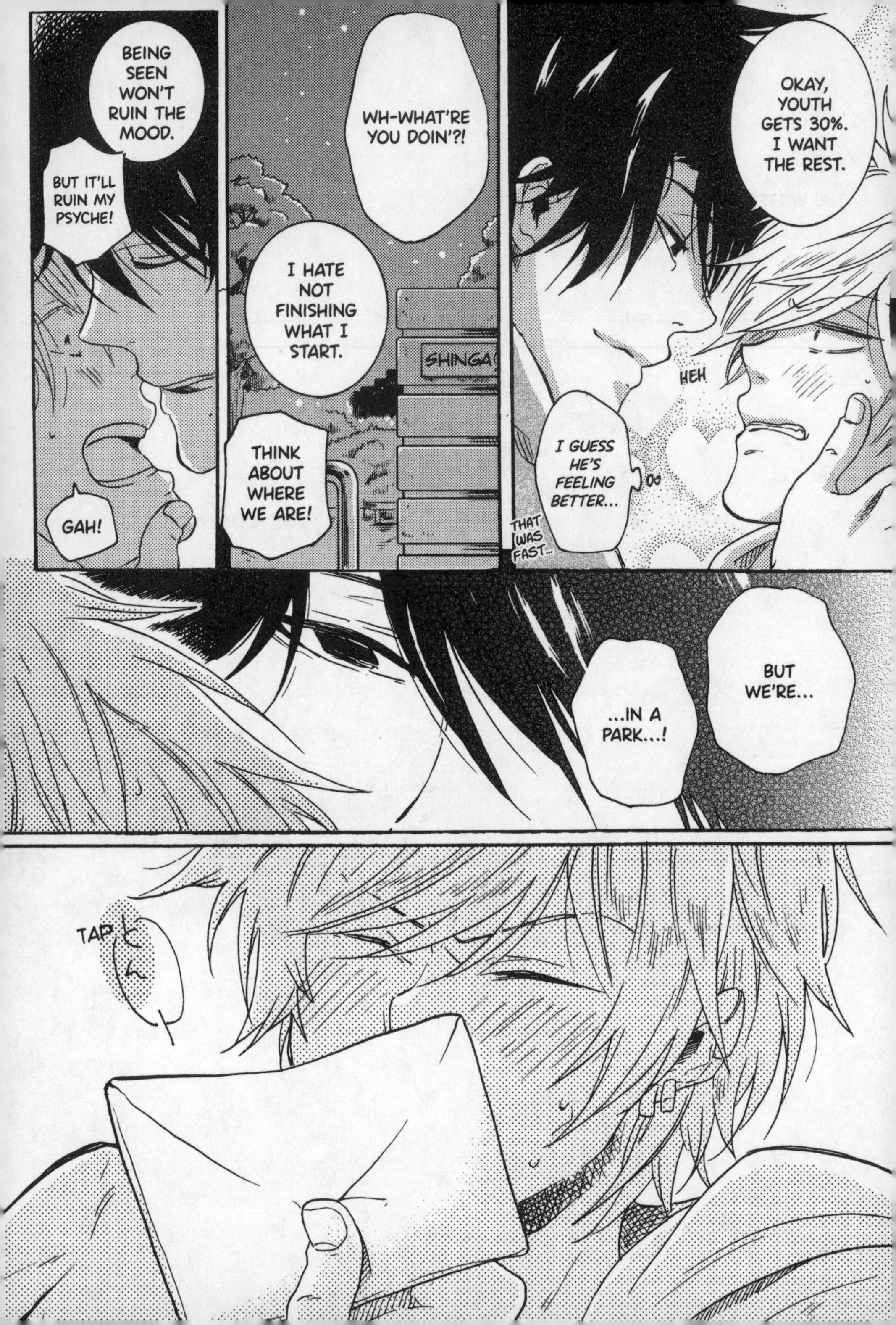
OKAY, YOUTH GETS 30%. I WANT THE REST.
HEH
I GUESS HE'S FEELING BETTER...
THAT WAS FAST...
WH-WHAT'RE YOU DOIN'?!
I HATE NOT FINISHING WHAT I START.
SHINGA
THINK ABOUT WHERE WE ARE!
BEING SEEN WON'T RUIN THE MOOD.
BUT IT'LL RUIN MY PSYCHE!
GAH!
BUT WE'RE...
...IN A PARK...!
TAP
とん

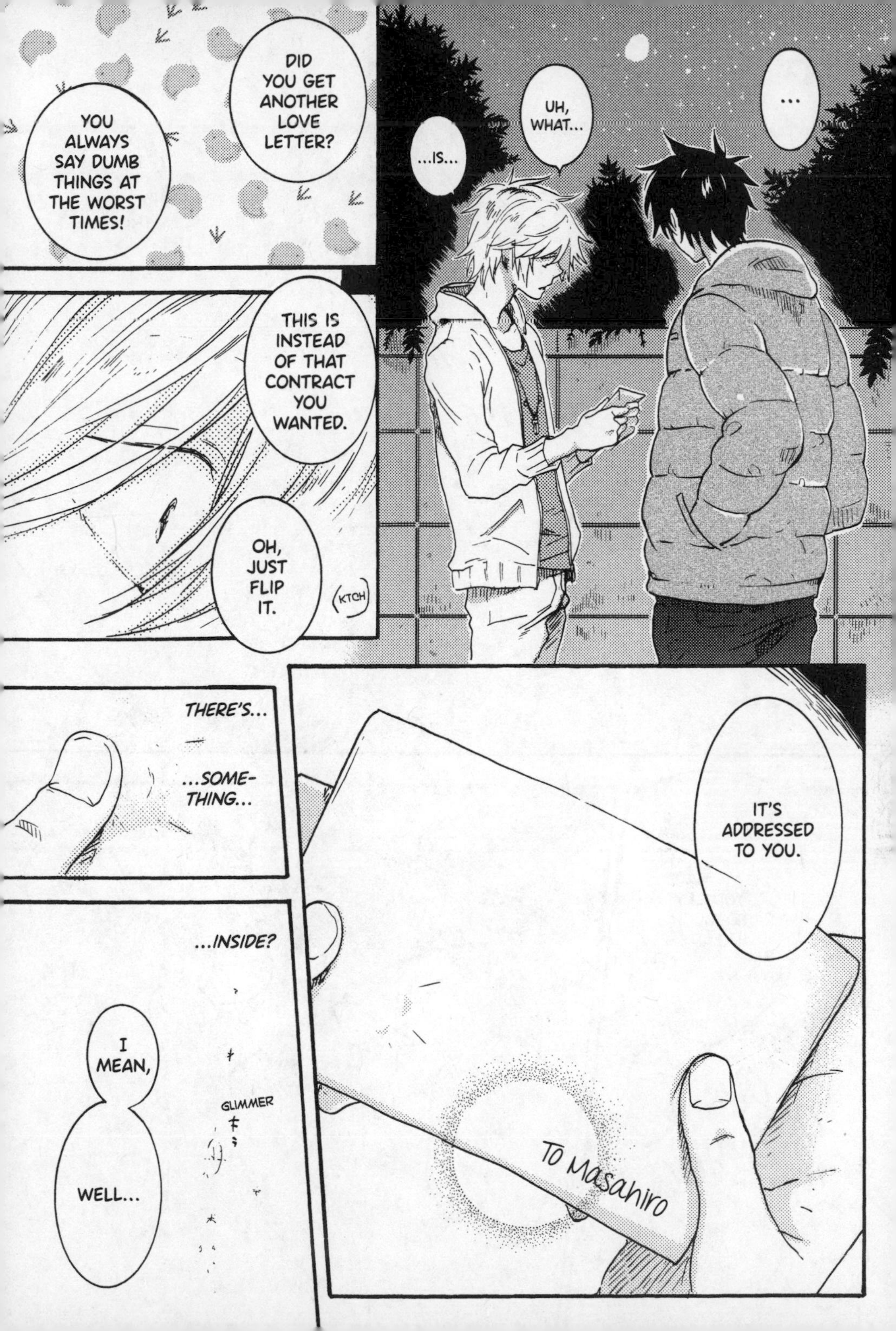
...
UH, WHAT...
...IS...
DID YOU GET ANOTHER LOVE LETTER?
YOU ALWAYS SAY DUMB THINGS AT THE WORST TIMES!
THIS IS INSTEAD OF THAT CONTRACT YOU WANTED.
OH, JUST FLIP IT.
KTCH
IT'S ADDRESSED TO YOU.
TO Masahiro
THERE'S...
...SOME-THING...
...INSIDE?
I MEAN,
WELL...
GLIMMER

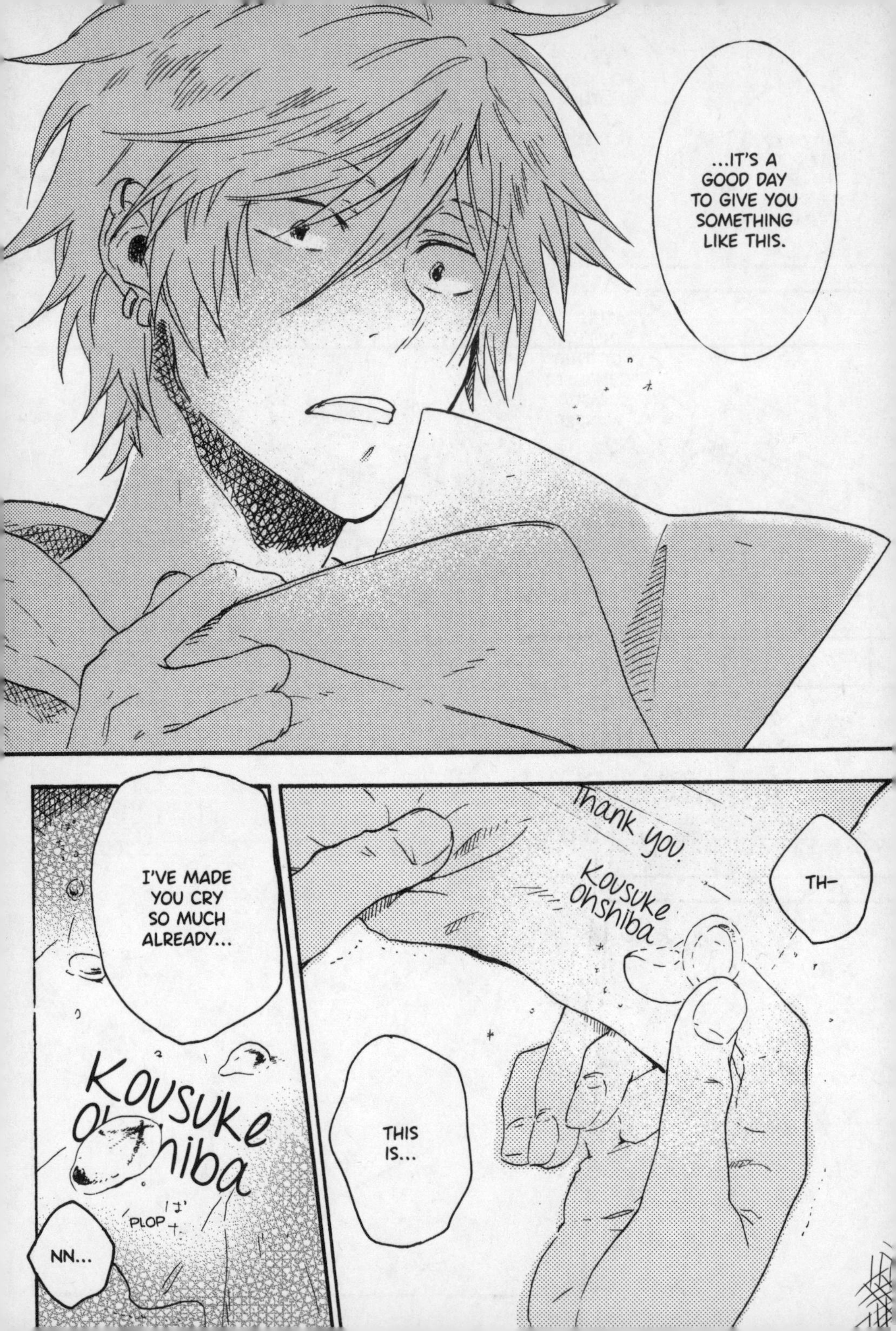
...IT'S A GOOD DAY TO GIVE YOU SOMETHING LIKE THIS.
TH-
Thank you. Kousuke Onshiba
THIS IS...
I'VE MADE YOU CRY SO MUCH ALREADY...
Kousuke Onshiba
PLOP
NN...

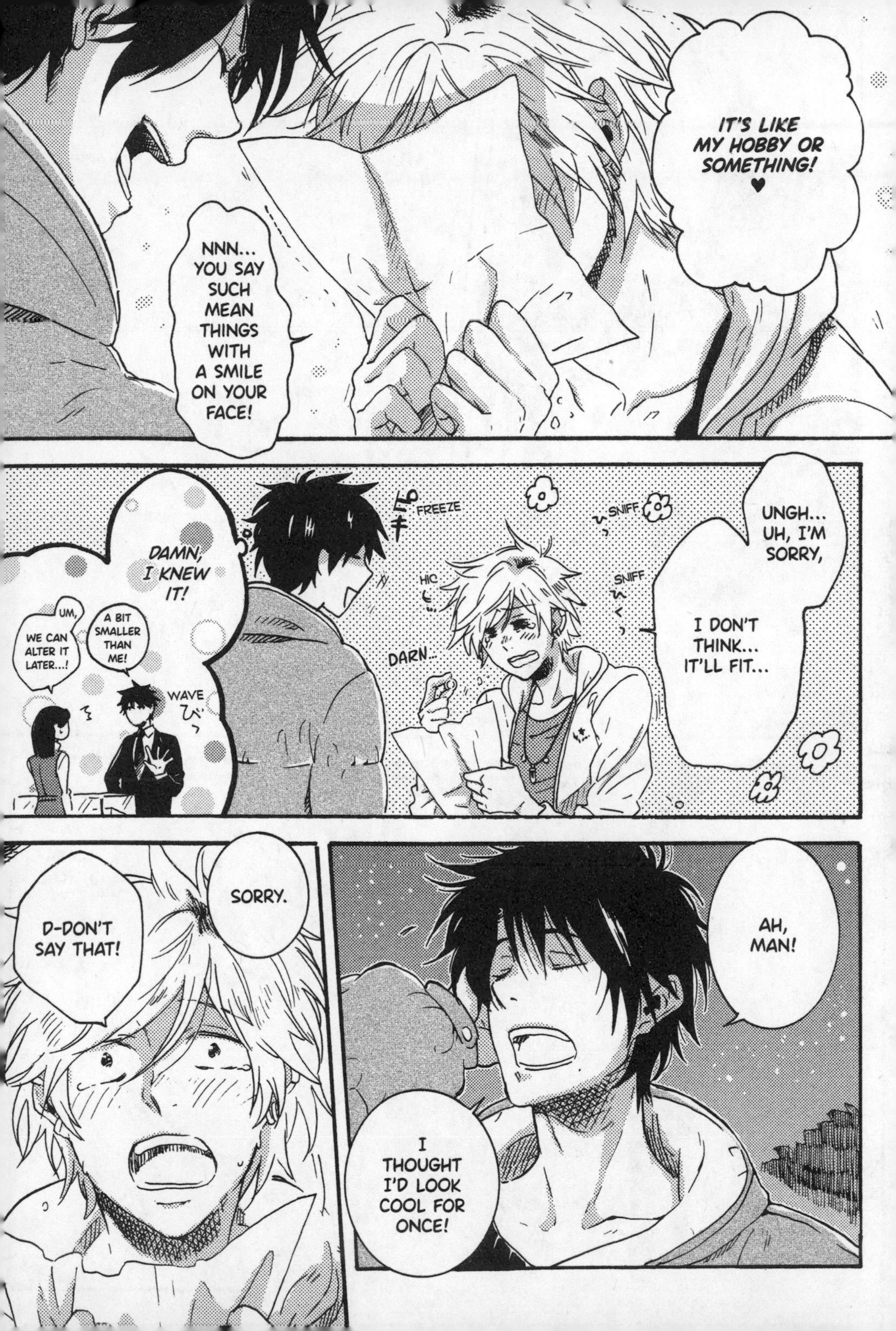
IT'S LIKE MY HOBBY OR SOMETHING! ♥
NNN... YOU SAY SUCH MEAN THINGS WITH A SMILE ON YOUR FACE!
UNGH... UH, I'M SORRY,
I DON'T THINK... IT'LL FIT...
SNIFF
SNIFF
HIC
DARN...
FREEZE
DAMN, I KNEW IT!
A BIT SMALLER THAN ME!
UM, WE CAN ALTER IT LATER...!
WAVE
AH, MAN!
I THOUGHT I'D LOOK COOL FOR ONCE!
SORRY.
D-DON'T SAY THAT!

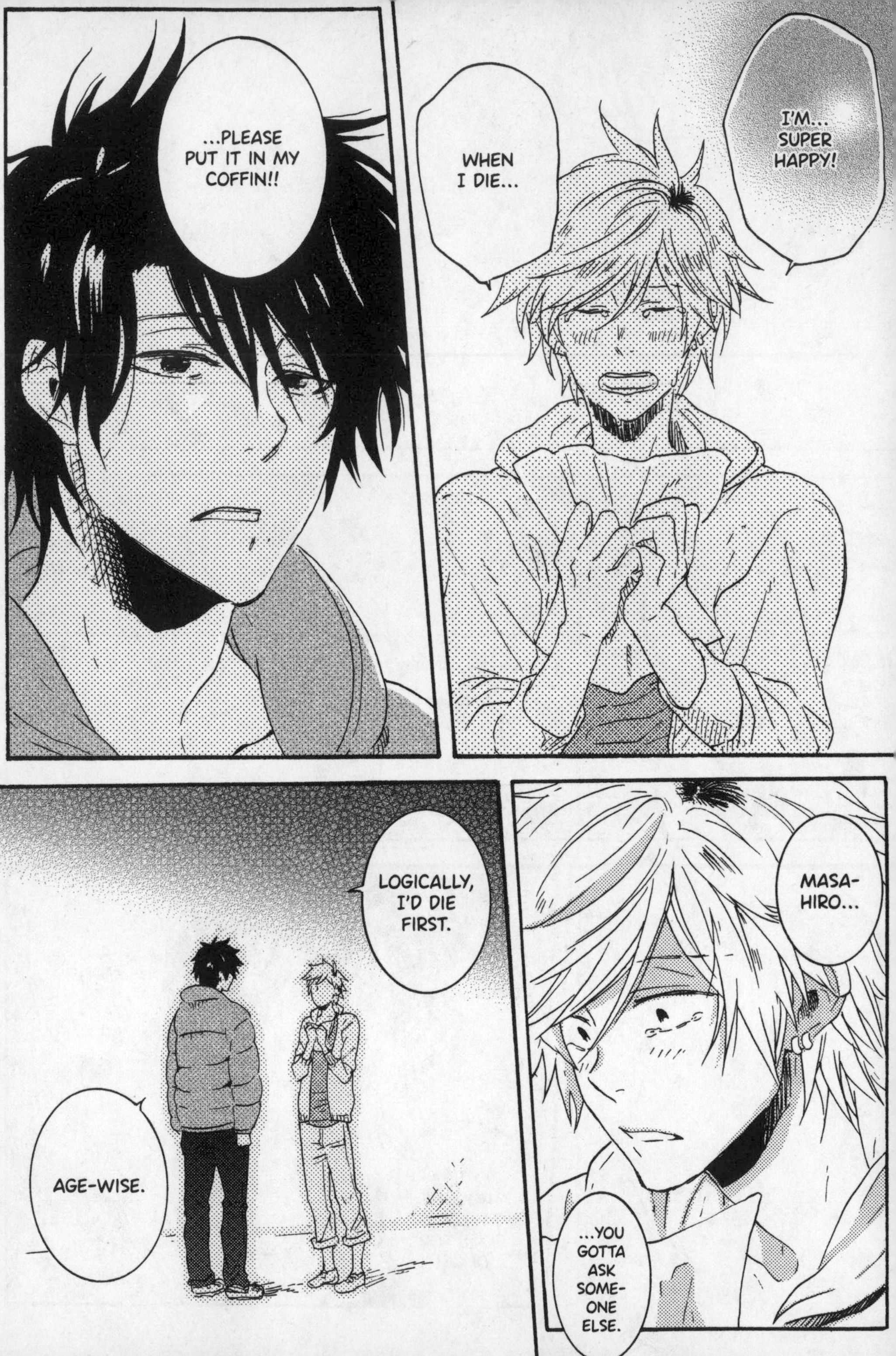
I'M... SUPER HAPPY!
WHEN I DIE...
...PLEASE PUT IT IN MY COFFIN!!
MASA-HIRO...
...YOU GOTTA ASK SOME-ONE ELSE.
LOGICALLY, I'D DIE FIRST.
AGE-WISE.

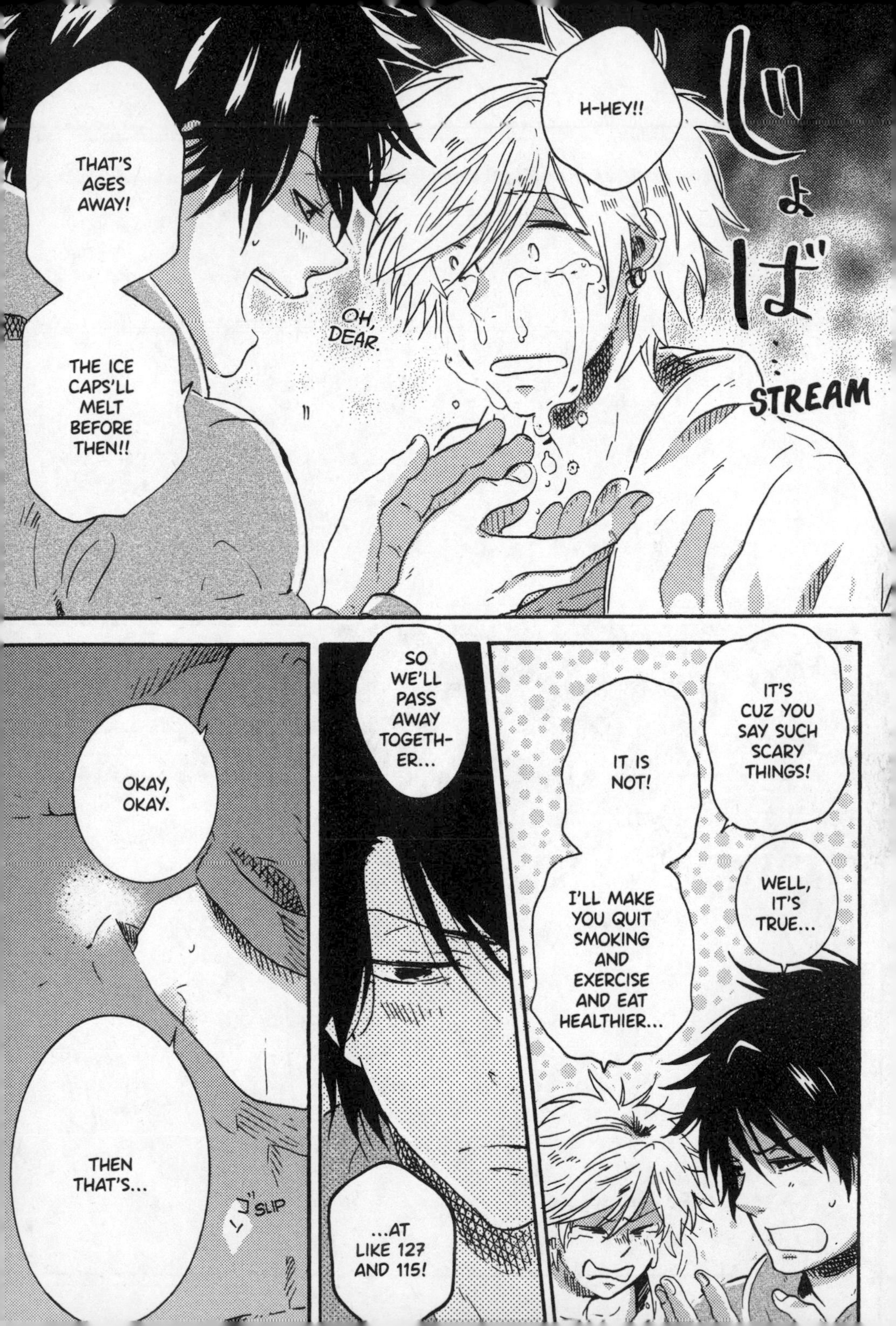
じょば
STREAM
H-HEY!!
OH, DEAR.
THAT'S AGES AWAY!
THE ICE CAPS'LL MELT BEFORE THEN!!
IT'S CUZ YOU SAY SUCH SCARY THINGS!
IT IS NOT!
WELL, IT'S TRUE...
I'LL MAKE YOU QUIT SMOKING AND EXERCISE AND EAT HEALTHIER...
SO WE'LL PASS AWAY TOGETH-ER...
...AT LIKE 127 AND 115!
OKAY, OKAY.
THEN THAT'S...
SLIP

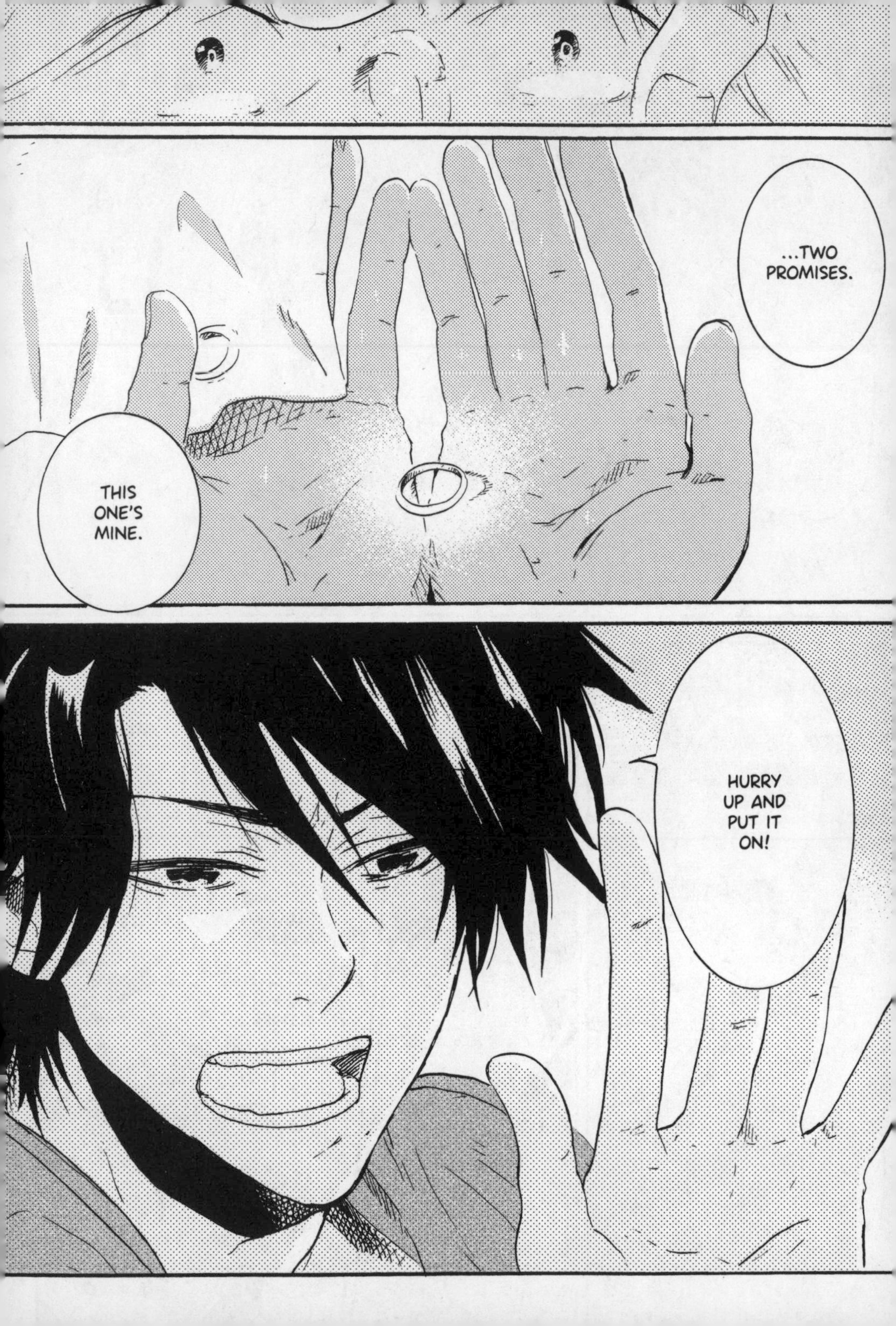
...TWO PROMISES.
THIS ONE'S MINE.
HURRY UP AND PUT IT ON!

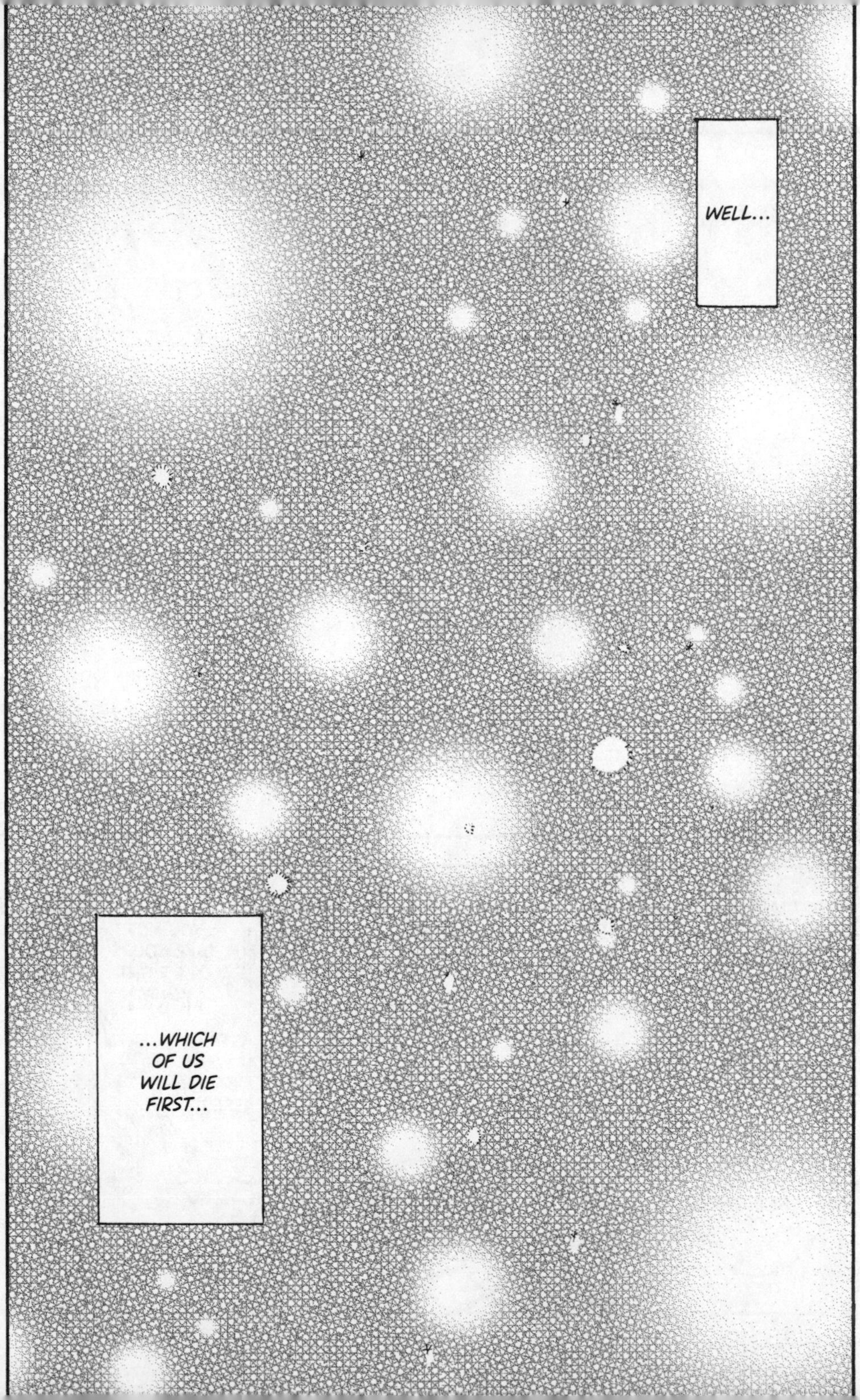
WELL...
...WHICH OF US WILL DIE FIRST...

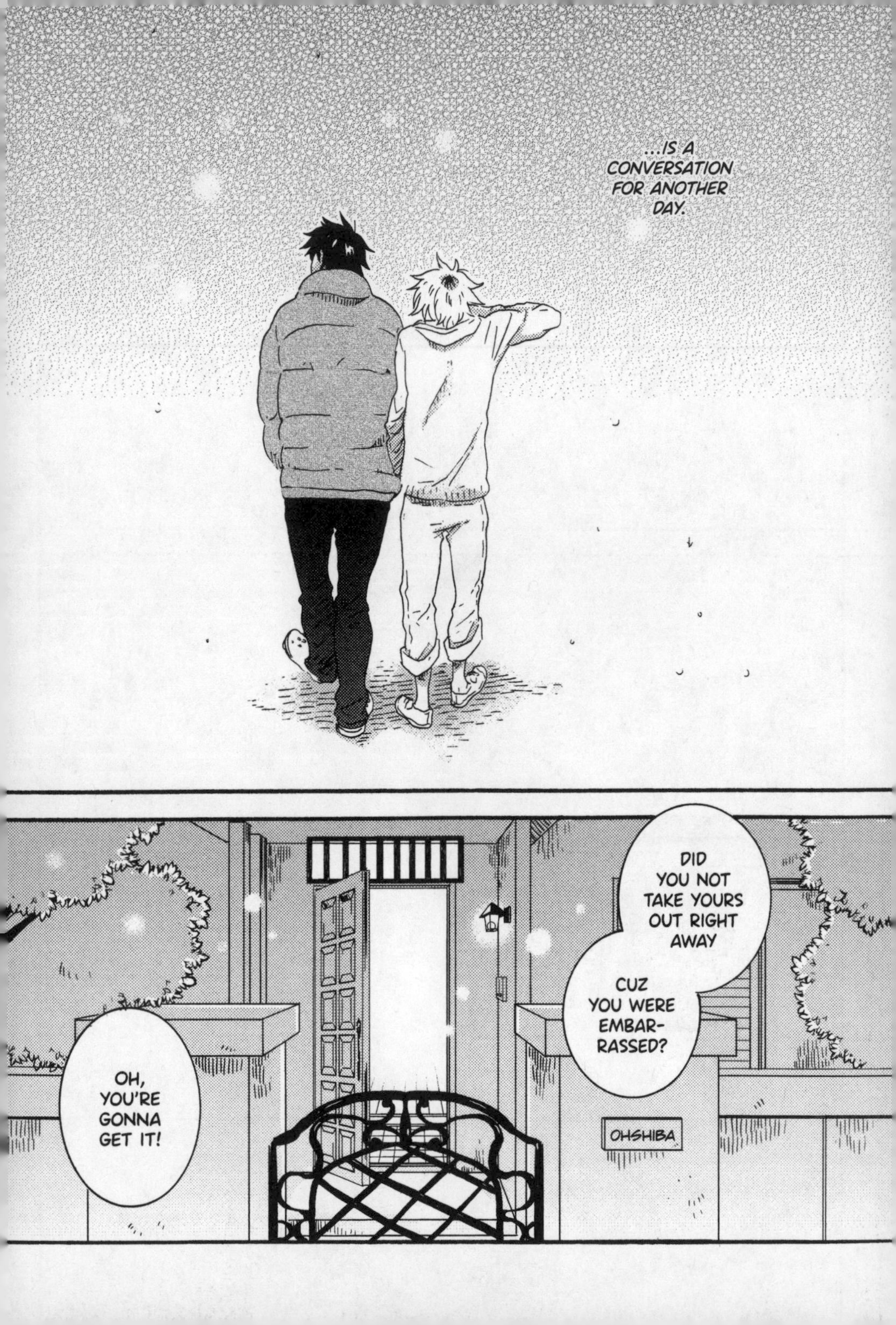
...IS A CONVERSATION FOR ANOTHER DAY.
DID YOU NOT TAKE YOURS OUT RIGHT AWAY
CUZ YOU WERE EMBAR-RASSED?
OHSHIBA
OH, YOU'RE GONNA GET IT!

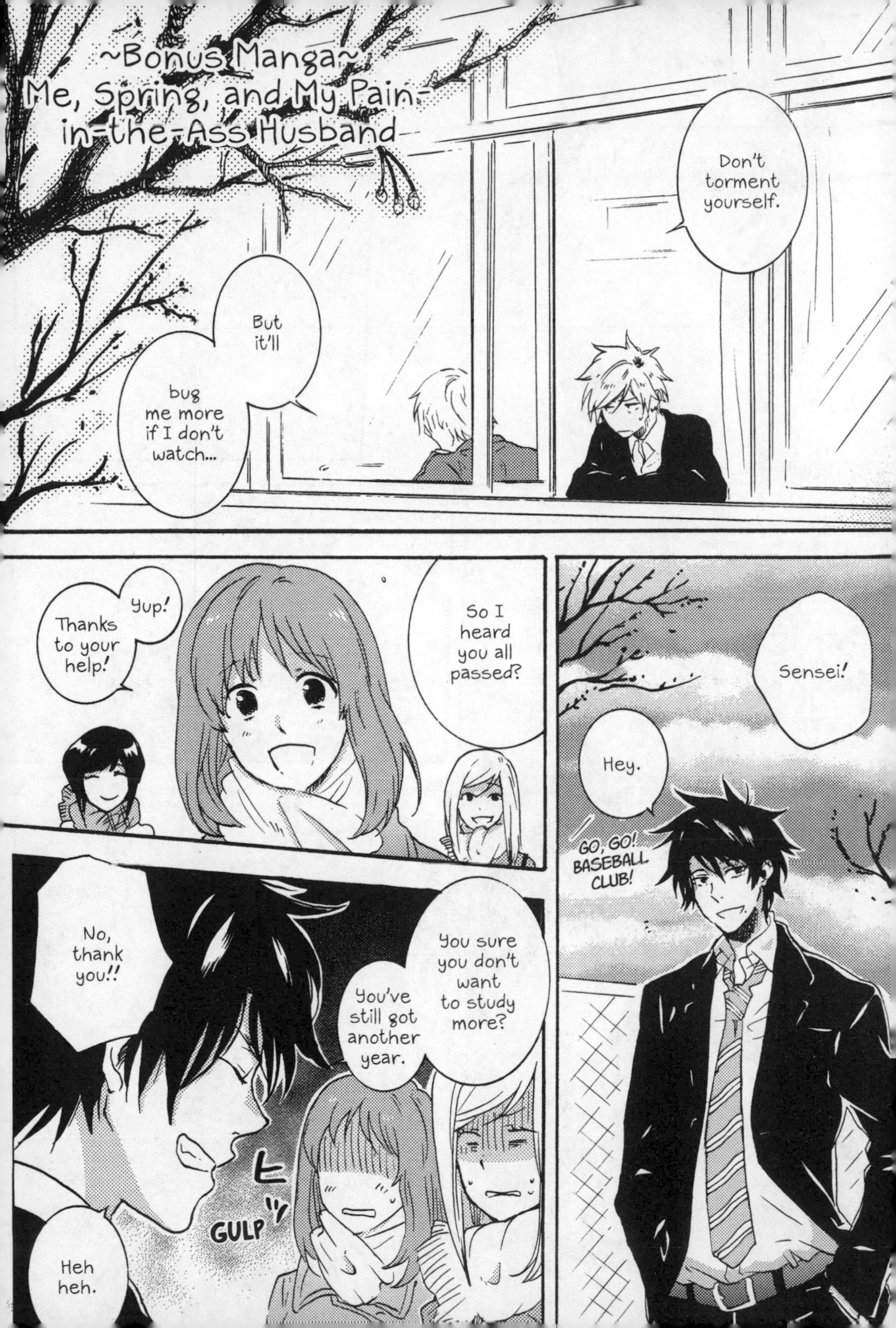
~Bonus Manga~
Me, Spring, and My Pain-in-the-Ass Husband
Don't torment yourself.
But it'll bug me more if I don't watch...
Sensei!
Hey.
GO, GO! BASEBALL CLUB!
So I heard you all passed?
Yup! Thanks to your help!
You sure you don't want to study more?
You've still got another year.
No, thank you!!
ヒッ
GULP
Heh heh.

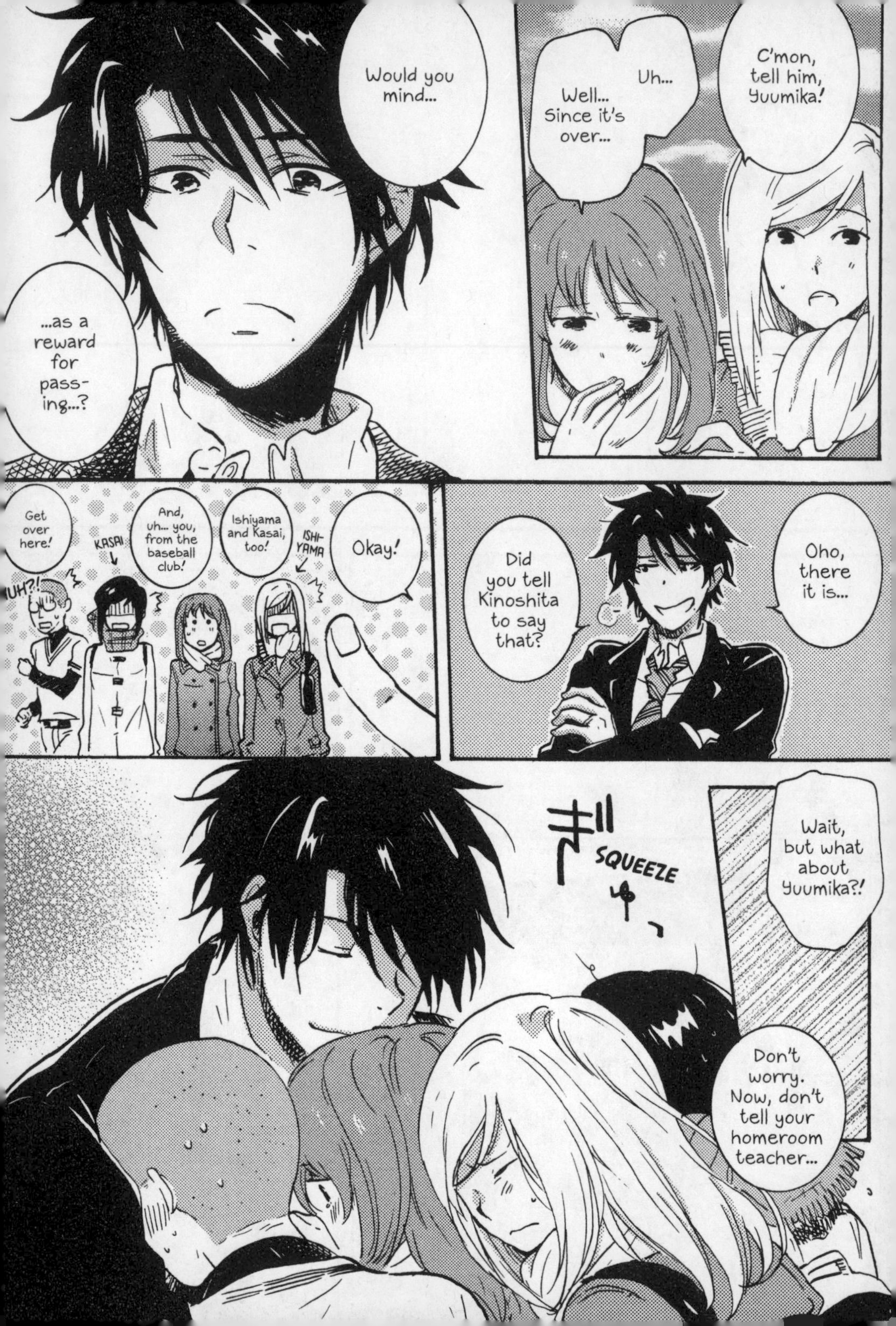
C'mon, tell him, Yuumika!
Uh...
Well... Since it's over...
Would you mind...
...as a reward for passing...?
Oho, there it is...
Did you tell Kinoshita to say that?
Okay!
ISHIYAMA
Ishiyama and Kasai, too!
And, uh... you, from the baseball club!
KASAI
Get over here!
UH?!
Wait, but what about Yuumika?!
SQUEEZE
Don't worry. Now, don't tell your homeroom teacher...

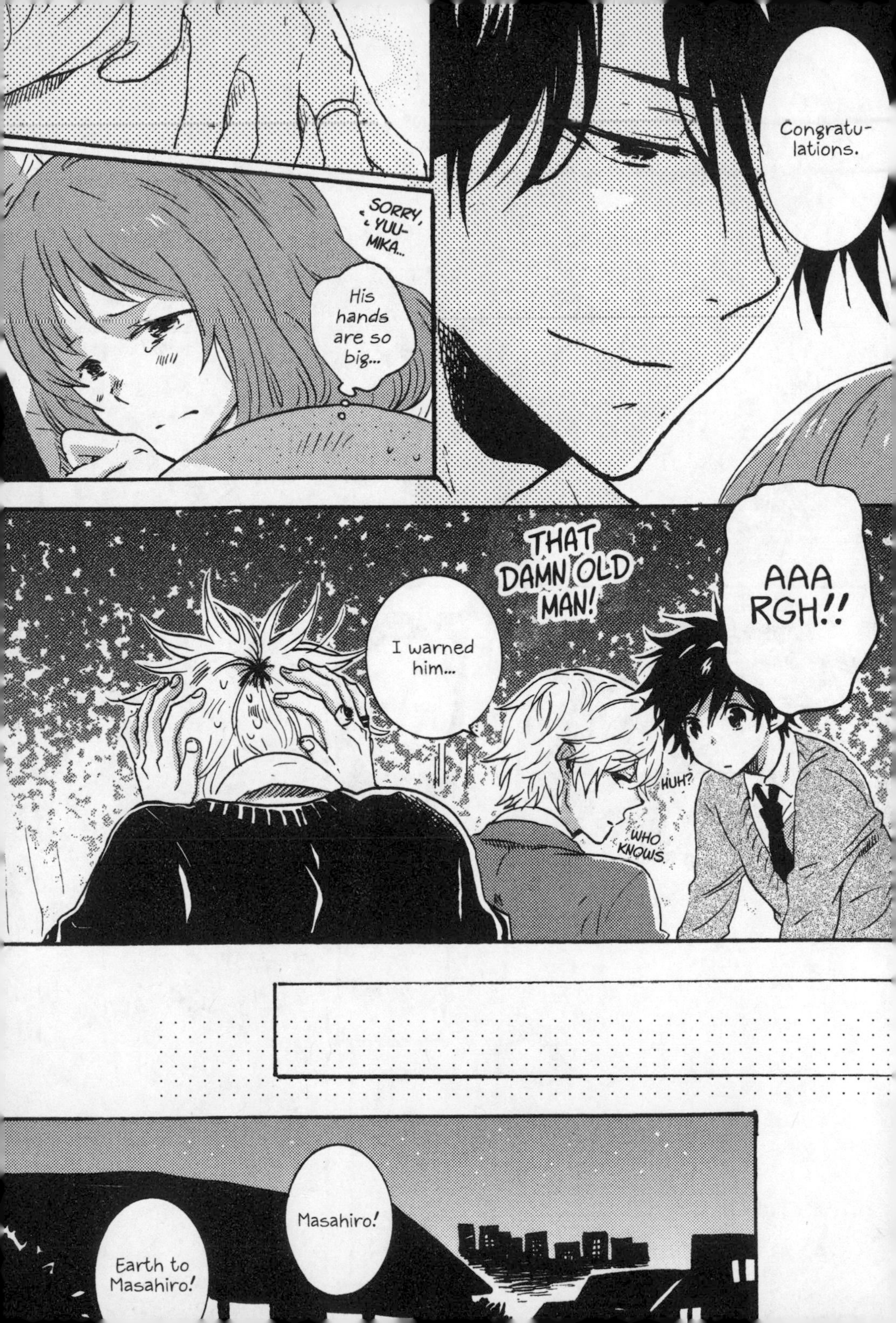
Congratu-
lations.
SORRY, YUUMIKA...
His hands are so big...
AAA RGH!!
THAT DAMN OLD MAN!
I warned him...
HUH?
WHO KNOWS.
Masahiro!
Earth to Masahiro!

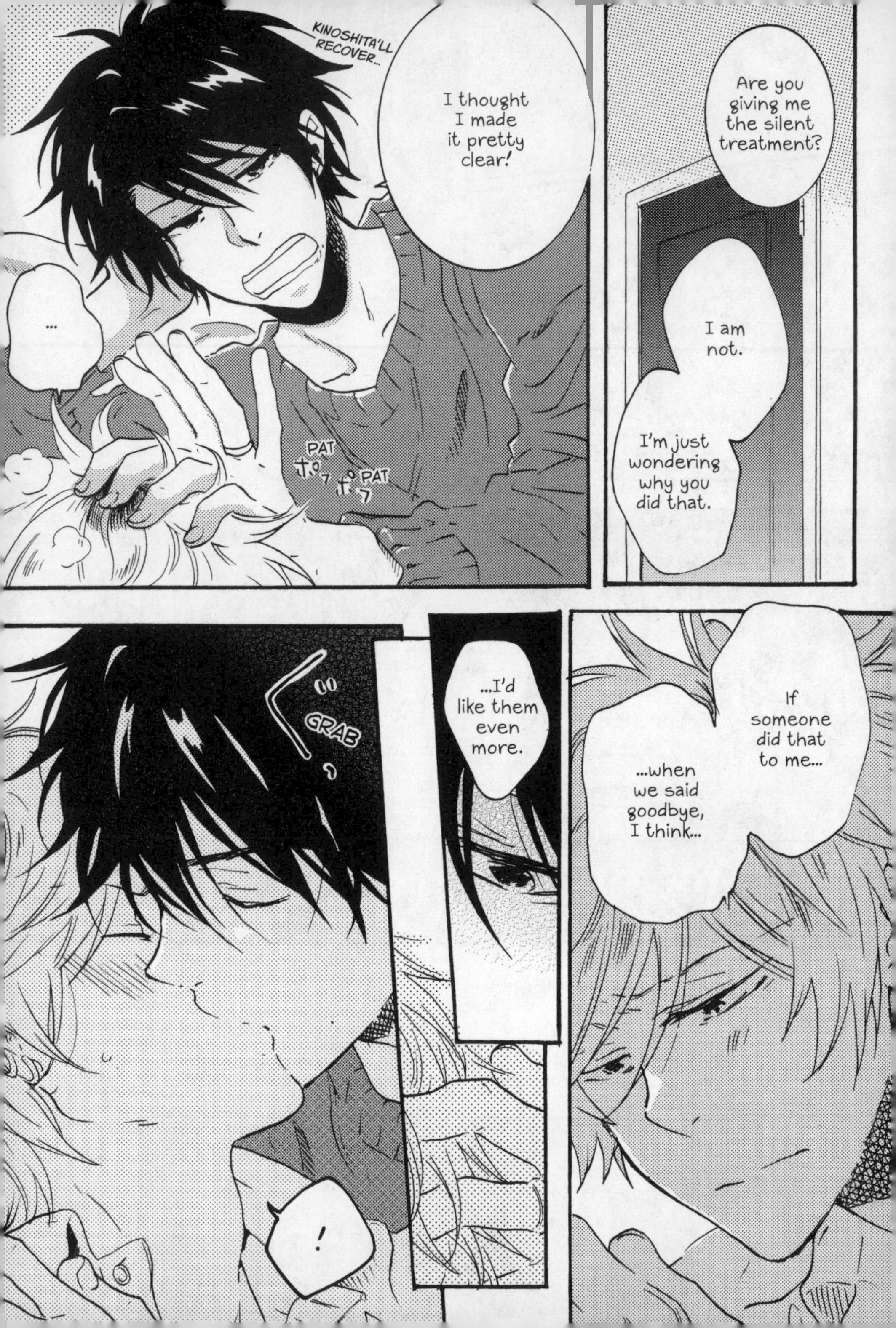
Are you giving me the silent treatment?
I am not.
I'm just wondering why you did that.
I thought I made it pretty clear!
KINOSHITA'LL RECOVER...
...
PAT PAT
If someone did that to me...
...when we said goodbye, I think...
...I'd like them even more.
GRAB
!

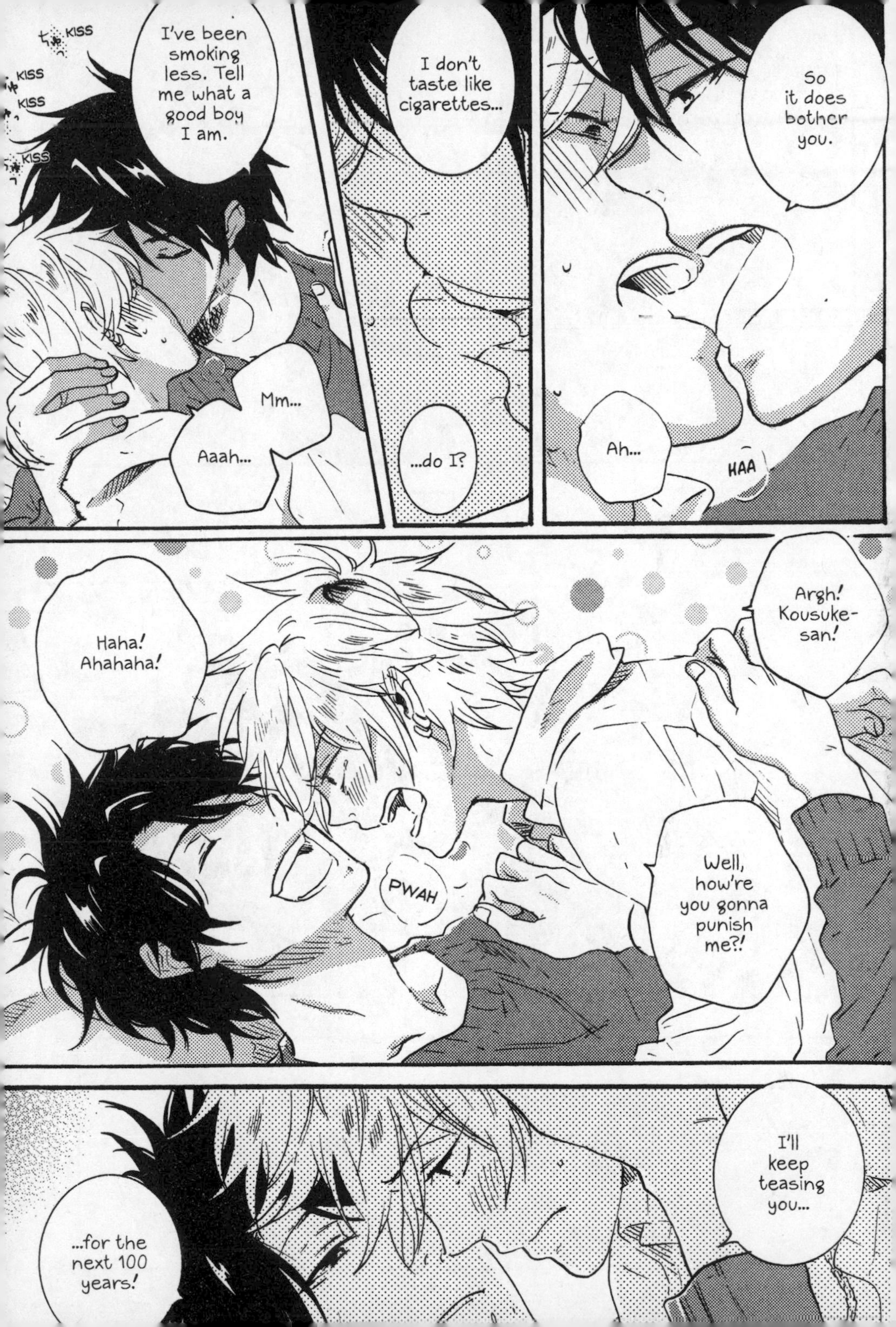
So it does bothcr you.
Ah...
HAA
I don't taste like cigarettes...
...do I?
I've been smoking less. Tell me what a good boy I am.
KISS
KISS
KISS
KISS
Mm...
Aaah...
Argh! Kousuke-san!
Well, how're you gonna punish me?!
Haha! Ahahaha!
PWAH
I'll keep teasing you...
...for the next 100 years!

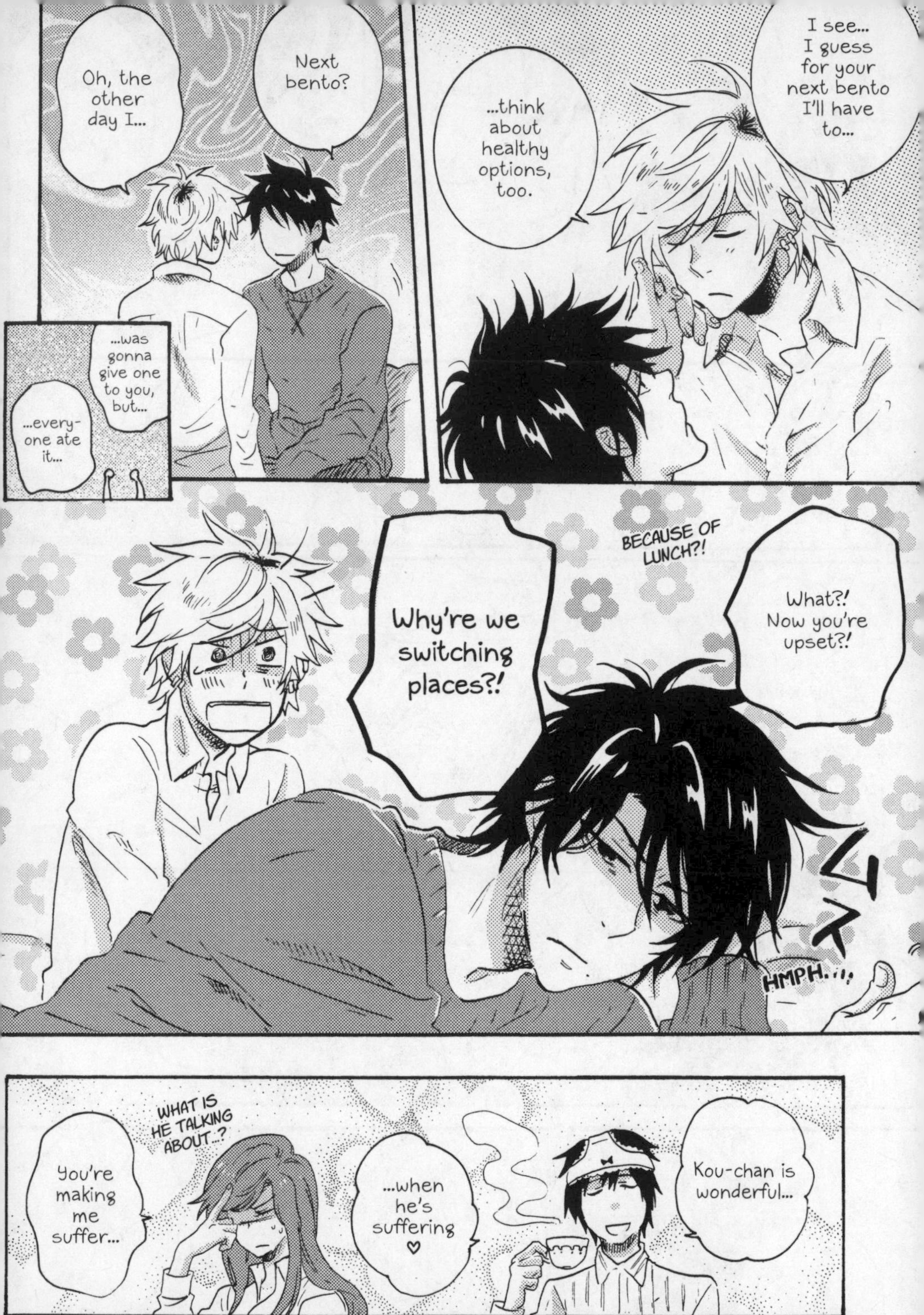
I see... I guess for your next bento I'll have to...
...think about healthy options, too.
Next bento?
Oh, the other day I...
...was gonna give one to you, but...
...every-one ate it...
What?! Now you're upset?!
BECAUSE OF LUNCH?!
Why're we switching places?!
ムス
HMPH...!
Kou-chan is wonderful...
...when he's suffering ♡
WHAT IS HE TALKING ABOUT...?
You're making me suffer...

♡ The End ♡

FIRST RUN

Hitorijime My Hero #5.5 → gateau vol. 9
Hitorijime My Hero #6 → gateau vol. 10
Hitorijime My Hero #6.5 → gateau vol. 11
Hitorijime My Hero #7 → gateau vol. 12
Hitorijime My Hero #8 → gateau vol. 13
Hitorijime My Hero #8.5 → gateau vol. 14
Hitorijime My Hero #9 → gateau vol. 15
Hitorijime My Hero #10 → gateau vol. 16

Thrilling and Suspenseful Afterword

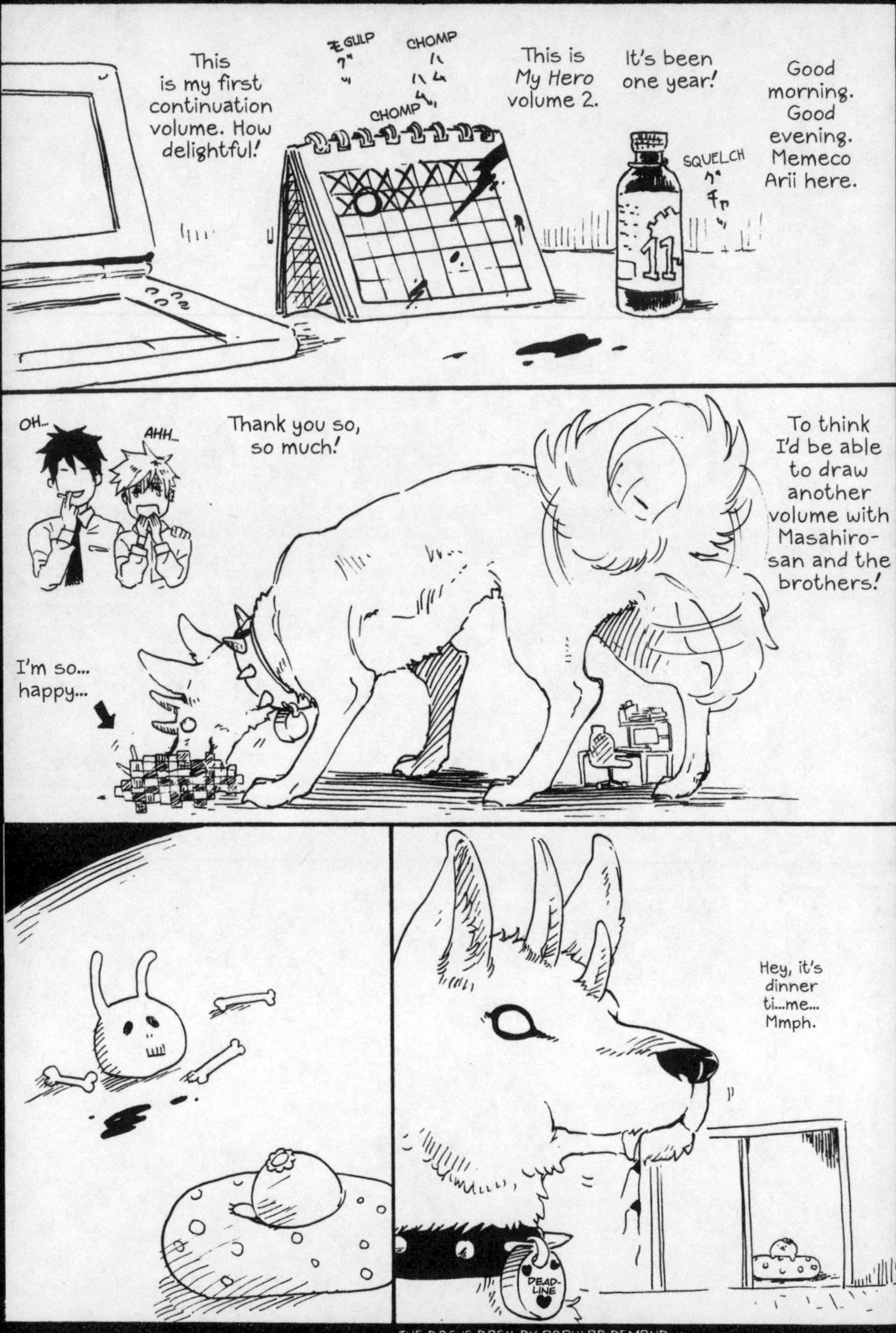
Good morning. Good evening. Memeco Arii here.
SQUELCH
It's been one year!
This is My Hero volume 2.
CHOMP
GULP
CHOMP
This is my first continuation volume. How delightful!
To think I'd be able to draw another volume with Masahiro-san and the brothers!
Thank you so, so much!
AHH...
OH...
I'm so... happy...
Hey, it's dinner ti...me... Mmph.
DEAD-LINE

THE DOG IS BACK BY POPULAR DEMAND

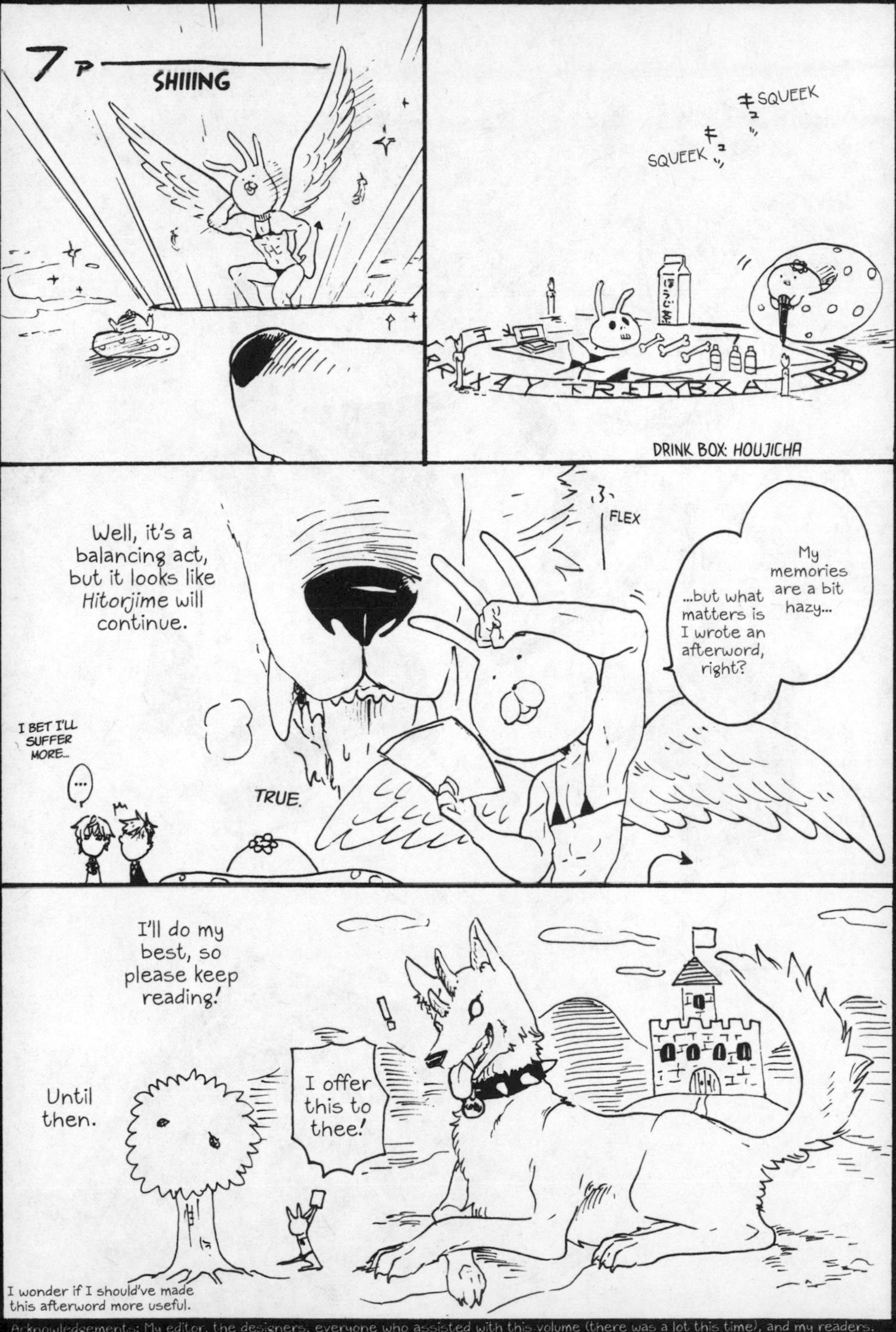
SQUEEK
SQUEEK
DRINK BOX: HOUJICHA
SHIIING
FLEX
My memories are a bit hazy...
...but what matters is I wrote an afterword, right?
Well, it's a balancing act, but it looks like Hitorjime will continue.
TRUE.
I BET I'LL SUFFER MORE...
...
I'll do my best, so please keep reading!
!
I offer this to thee!
Until then.
I wonder if I should've made this afterword more useful.

Acknowledgements: My editor, the designers, everyone who assisted with this volume (there was a lot this time), and my readers.
Thank you!

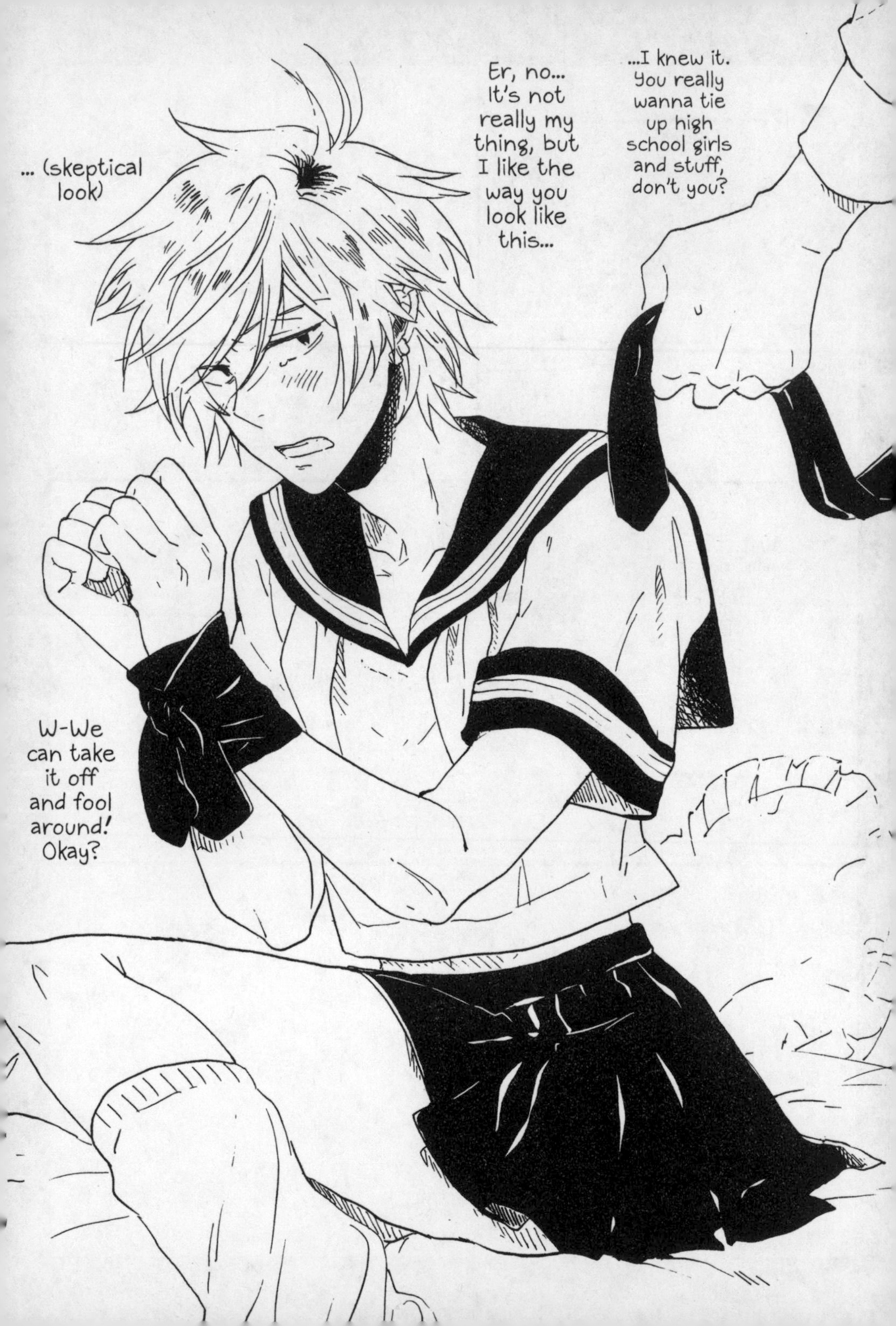
...I knew it. You really wanna tie up high school girls and stuff, don't you?
Er, no... It's not really my thing, but I like the way you look like this...
... (skeptical look)
W-We can take it off and fool around! Okay?

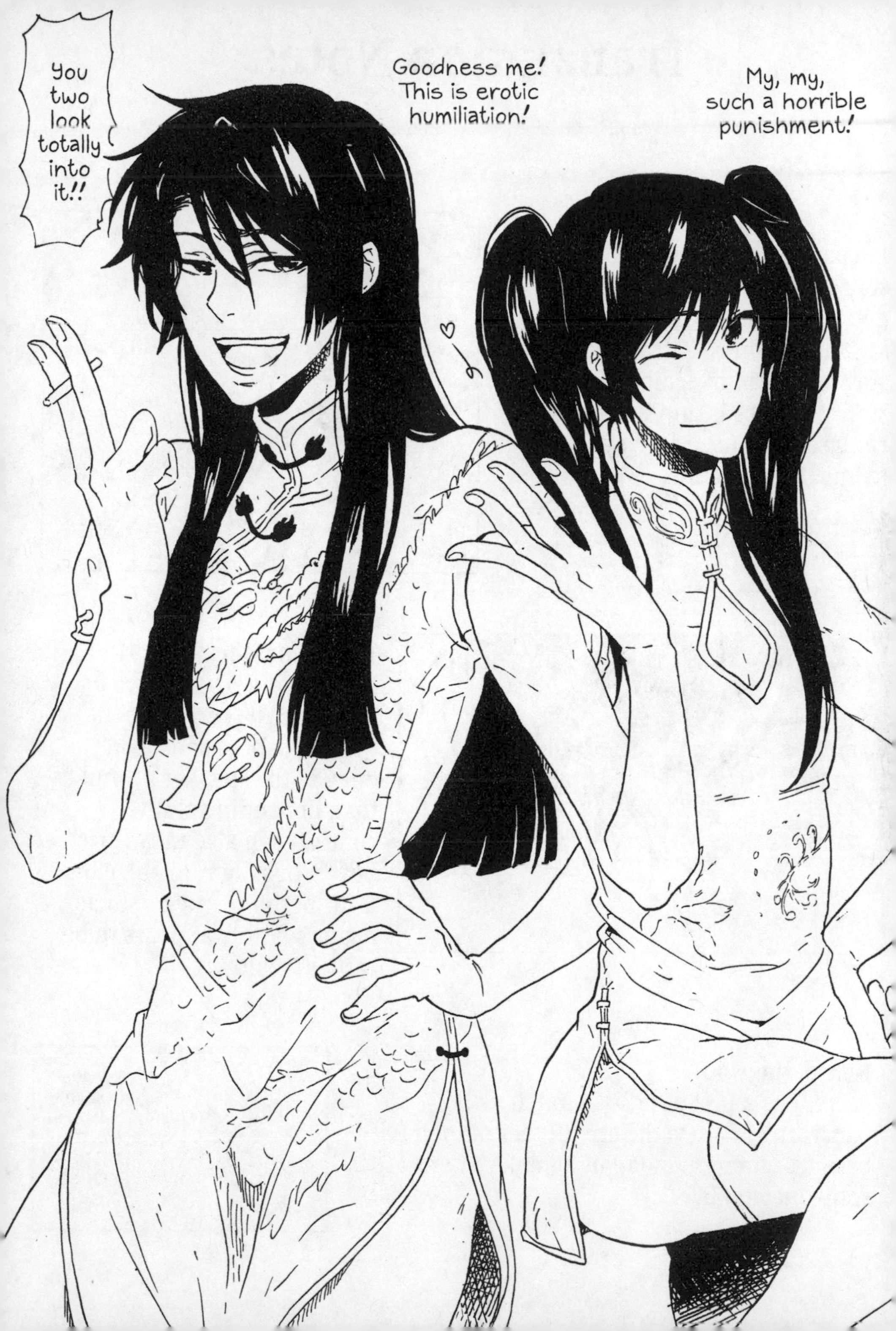
My, my, such a horrible punishment!
Goodness me! This is erotic humiliation!
You two look totally into it!!

Translation Notes

Love hotel, page 16
Love hotels are a form of short-stay accommodation where people usually go to engage in sexual activities. Patrons can stay hourly or overnight, and staff presence is minimized or replaced by automated systems to ensure discretion.

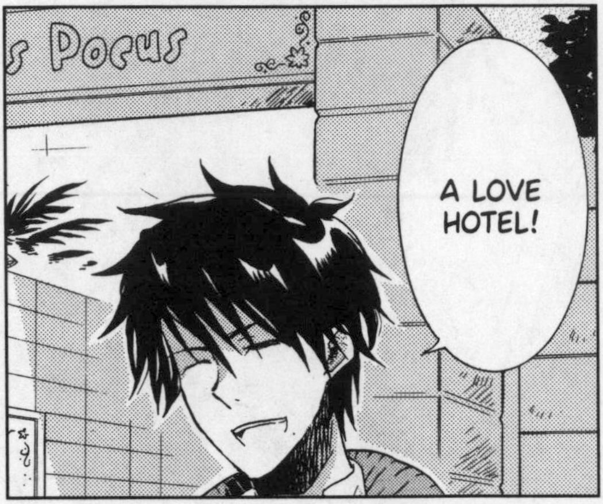
s Pocus
A LOVE HOTEL!

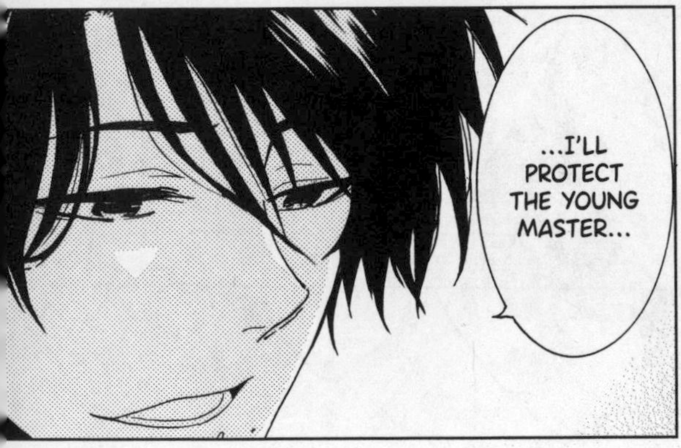
...I'LL PROTECT THE YOUNG MASTER...

Young Master, page 31
Kousuke refers to Asaya as *bocchan,* is a generic term used to denote sons from outside the speaker's family that, depending on the context, can also mean "rich boy." Kousuke is likely using it for both meanings, since Asaya's family appears to be rather wealthy.

Bento, page 40
A bento is a Japanese-style lunch usually consisting of a few different types of food with rice. It's common in Japan to make a bento for someone you like!

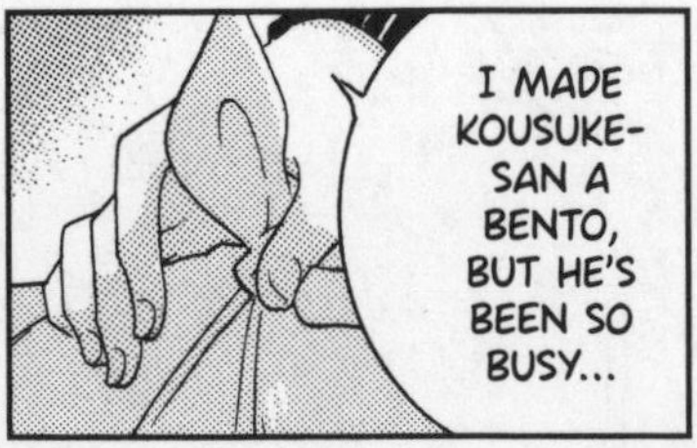
I MADE KOUSUKE-SAN A BENTO, BUT HE'S BEEN SO BUSY...

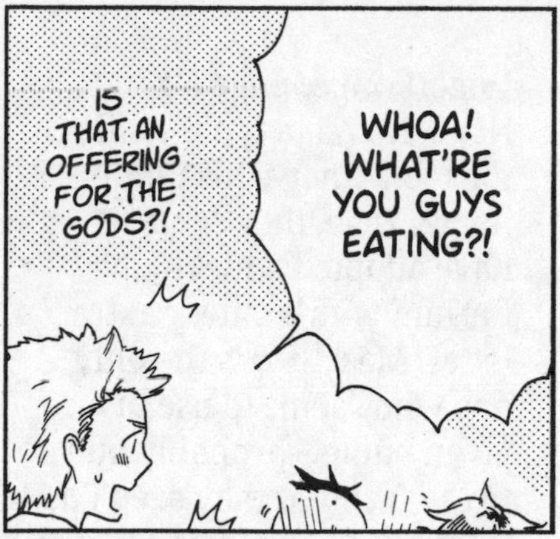
WHOA! WHAT'RE YOU GUYS EATING?!
IS THAT AN OFFERING FOR THE GODS?!

Offering for the gods, page 41
The student thinks Masahiro's bento looks like an offering to the gods because of its lavish and ornate nature. It also resembles the traditional New Year's food known as *osechi ryouri*, which, like bento, is made in boxes that can be stacked.

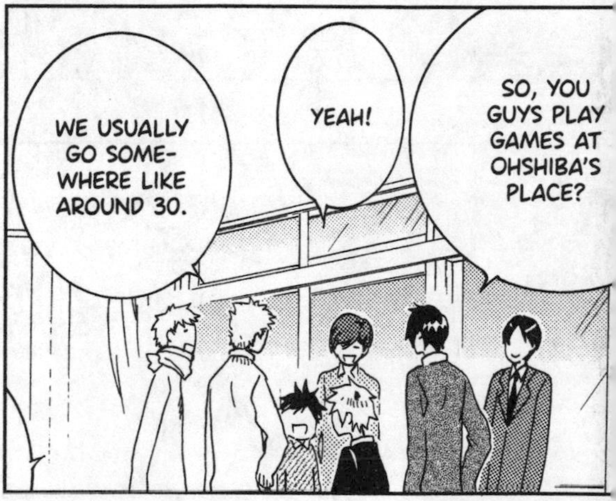
SO, YOU GUYS PLAY GAMES AT OHSHIBA'S PLACE?
YEAH!
WE USUALLY GO SOME-WHERE LIKE AROUND 30.

AROUND 30, page 42
AROUND 30 is likely a parody of ROUND1 Entertainment, an amusement-center chain that includes bowling, karaoke, pool, darts, and miniature versions of many sports. The name chosen here is likely a joke that while they go to AROUND 30, the Ohshiba gang go hang out with someone "around 30," too.

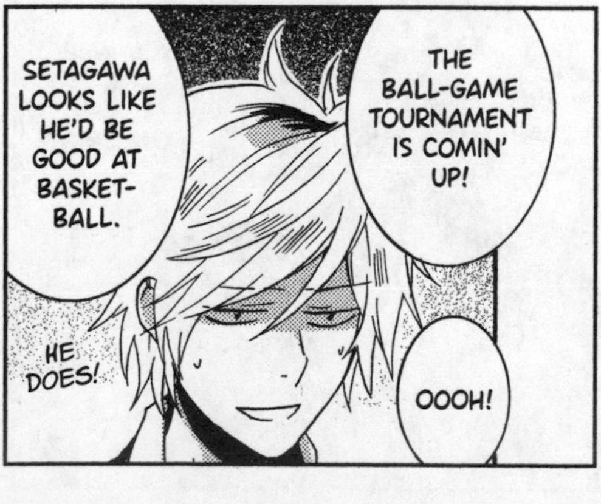
THE BALL-GAME TOURNAMENT IS COMIN' UP!
SETAGAWA LOOKS LIKE HE'D BE GOOD AT BASKET-BALL.
OOOH!
HE DOES!

Ball-game tournament, page 42
The ball-game tournament is just what it sounds like: a school-wide tournament for many kinds of ball games. Often, the games included are basketball, soccer, volleyball, and table tennis.

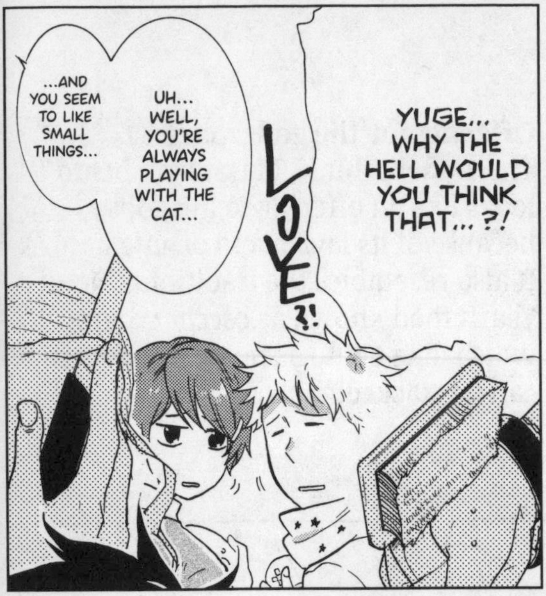
YUGE... WHY THE HELL WOULD YOU THINK THAT...?!
LOVE?!
UH... WELL, YOU'RE ALWAYS PLAYING WITH THE CAT...
...AND YOU SEEM TO LIKE SMALL THINGS...

Yuge/Yunge, page 52
Nope, it's not a typo. While the team knows his family name, Yuge, they seem to have adopted a nickname for him with a cutesy extra letter. Masahiro is the only one who seems to use his given name—probably due to the fact that they aren't as close (and have their cooking rivalry to boot!).

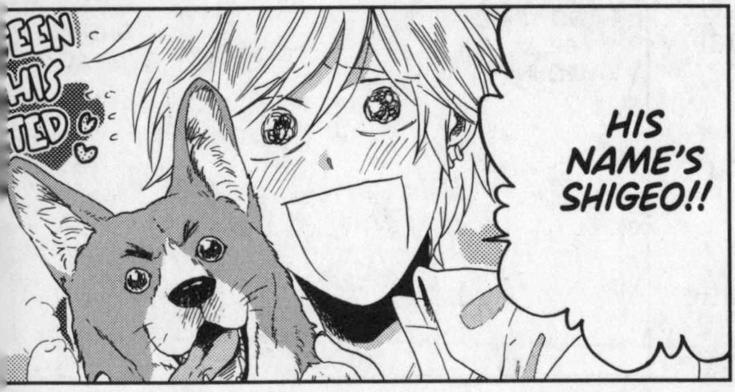
HIS NAME'S SHIGEO!!

Shigeo, page 60
This corgi's name is a reference to Shigeo Takamatsu, an actor and comedian with very distinctive eyebrows.

Romaneé-Conti, page 83
Wine from the Romaneé-Conti vineyard in France is the most expensive and sought-after wine in the world. A single bottle can go for thousands to hundreds of thousands of dollars depending on the vintage.

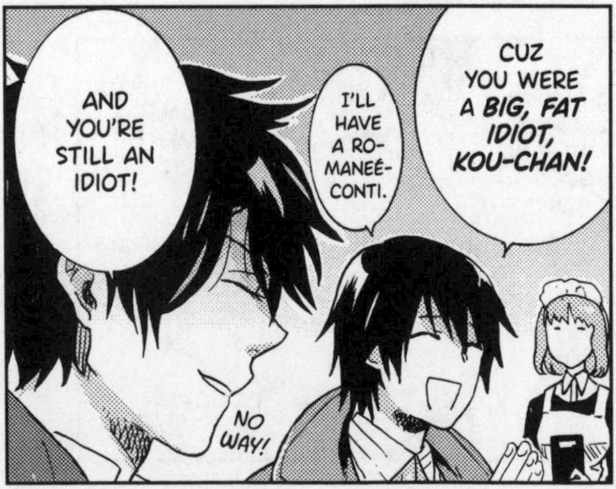
CUZ YOU WERE A BIG, FAT IDIOT, KOU-CHAN!
I'LL HAVE A RO-MANEÉ-CONTI.
AND YOU'RE STILL AN IDIOT!
NO WAY!

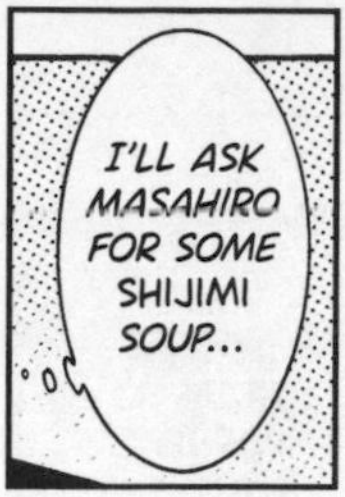
I'LL ASK MASAHIRO FOR SOME SHIJIMI SOUP...

Shijimi soup, page 98
Shijimi soup is a type of miso soup made with *shijimi* clams. It is a popular hangover cure.

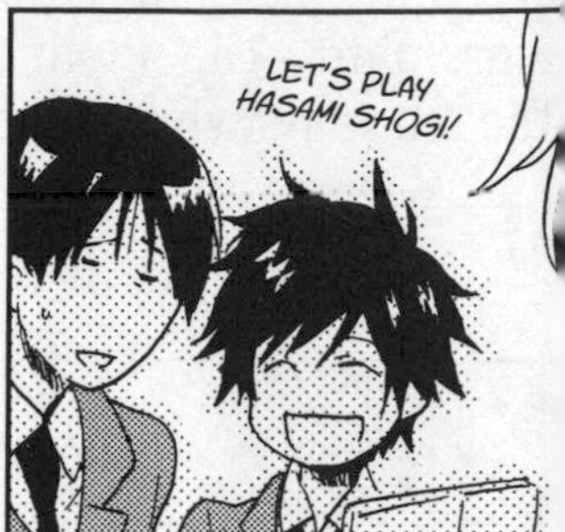
LET'S PLAY HASAMI SHOGI!

***Hasami shogi*, page 105**
Hasami shogi is a variant of *shogi,* or Japanese chess, that is popular with children.

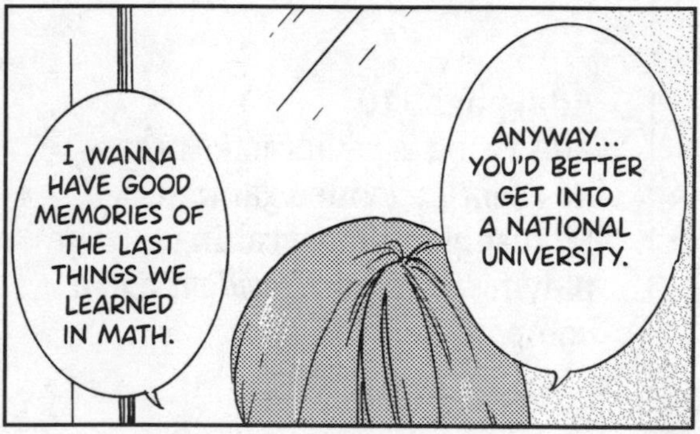
ANYWAY... YOU'D BETTER GET INTO A NATIONAL UNIVERSITY.
I WANNA HAVE GOOD MEMORIES OF THE LAST THINGS WE LEARNED IN MATH.

National university, page 107
National universities are generally more prestigious than private universities in Japan.

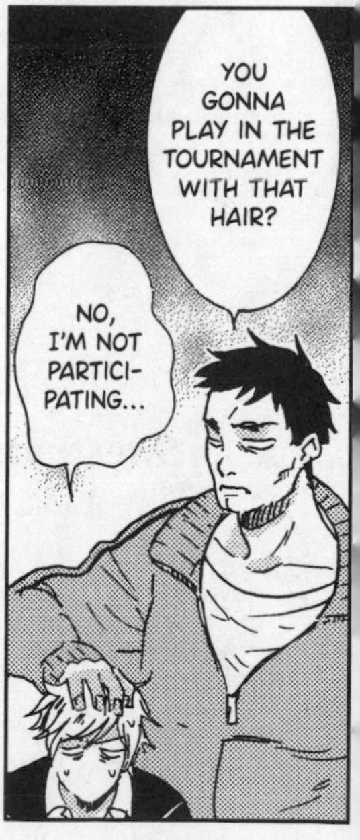
YOU GONNA PLAY IN THE TOURNAMENT WITH THAT HAIR?
NO, I'M NOT PARTICI-PATING...

That hair, page 108
The teacher is referring to Masahiro's bleached blond hair. It's often a violation of school regulations for Japanese high school students to have dyed hair. Bleached hair, in particular, is often associated with delinquents, which is why the teacher wants Masahiro to change it before the ball-game tournament.

Photo list, page 109
Students in Japanese high schools will sometimes sell photos of popular students to their classmates. The photo list refers to a list of all of the students whose photos are available for sale.

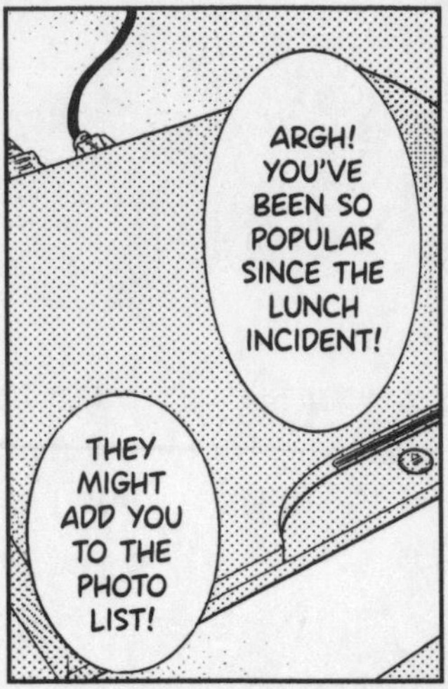
ARGH! YOU'VE BEEN SO POPULAR SINCE THE LUNCH INCIDENT!
THEY MIGHT ADD YOU TO THE PHOTO LIST!

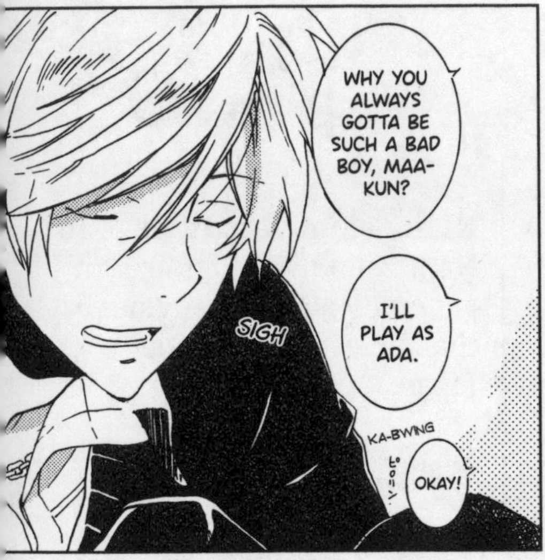
WHY YOU ALWAYS GOTTA BE SUCH A BAD BOY, MAA-KUN?
SIGH
I'LL PLAY AS ADA.
KA-BWING
OKAY!

Ada, page 110
Ada Wong is a character in the *Resident Evil* video game series. Fukushige is likely calling dibs on playing as Ada in *Resident Evil 6* co-op mode.

Pocari Sweat, page 129
Pocari Sweat is a popular Japanese sports drink, which boasts restorative electrolytes.

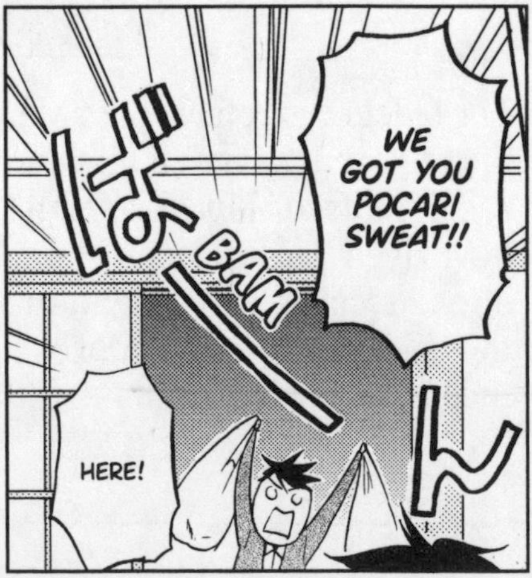
WE GOT YOU POCARI SWEAT!!
BAM
HERE!

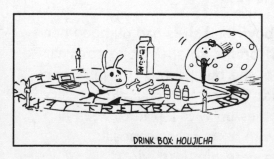

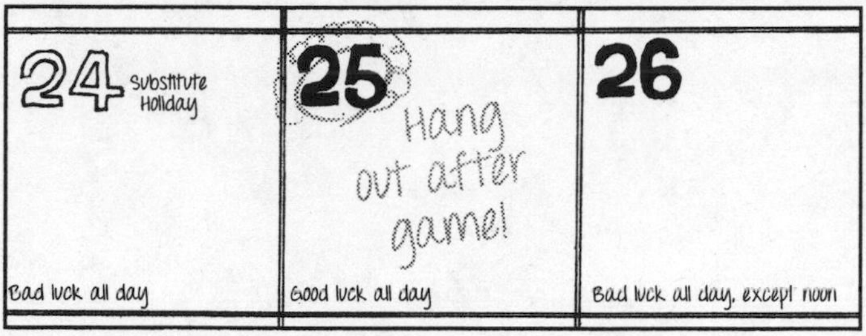
24
Substitute Holiday
Bad luck all day
25
Hang out after game!
Good luck all day
26
Bad luck all day, except noon

Japanese calendars, page 187
It is common for Japanese calendars to note how lucky each day is based on the *rokuyo* system, a 6-day cycle of auspicious and inauspicious days that reoccurs in a specific way throughout the year.

Good day, page 194
Kousuke is referring to the fact that it's Christmas day. Christmas in Japan is mostly celebrated by couples, who will often go on romantic dates and exchange gifts such as "pair rings," or rings worn by partners in a committed relationship.

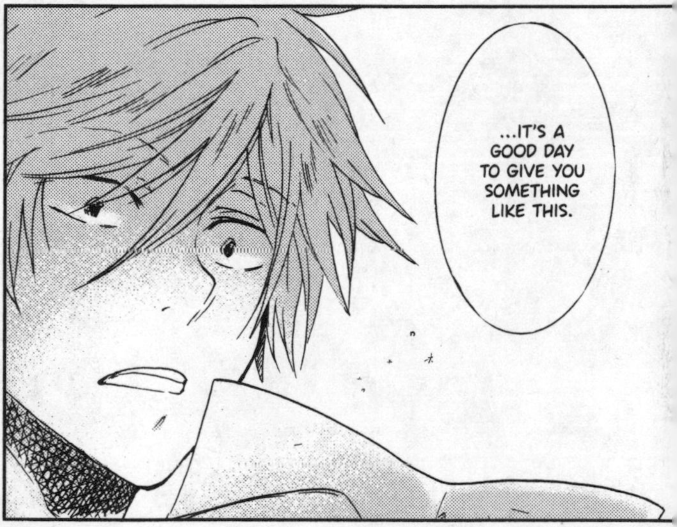
...IT'S A GOOD DAY TO GIVE YOU SOMETHING LIKE THIS.

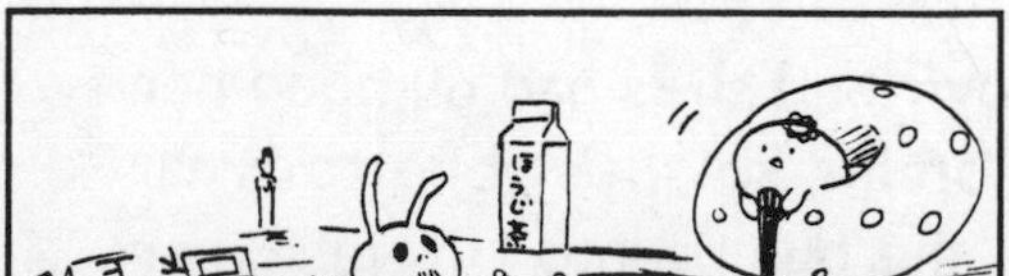
DRINK BOX: HOUJICHA

***Houjicha*, page 209**
Houjicha is a mild green tea that is made from roasted, rather than steamed, leaves.

In love, there are
no save points.

ヲタクに恋は難しい

WOTAKOI:
LOVE IS HARD FOR OTAKU
by FUJITA

Narumi has had it rough: Every boyfriend she's had dumped her
once they found out she was an otaku, so she's gone to great
lengths to hide it. At her new job, she bumps into Hirotaka, her
childhood friend and fellow otaku. When Hirotaka almost gets
her secret outed at work, she comes up with a plan to keep him
quiet. But he comes up with a counter-proposal:
Why doesn't she just date him instead?

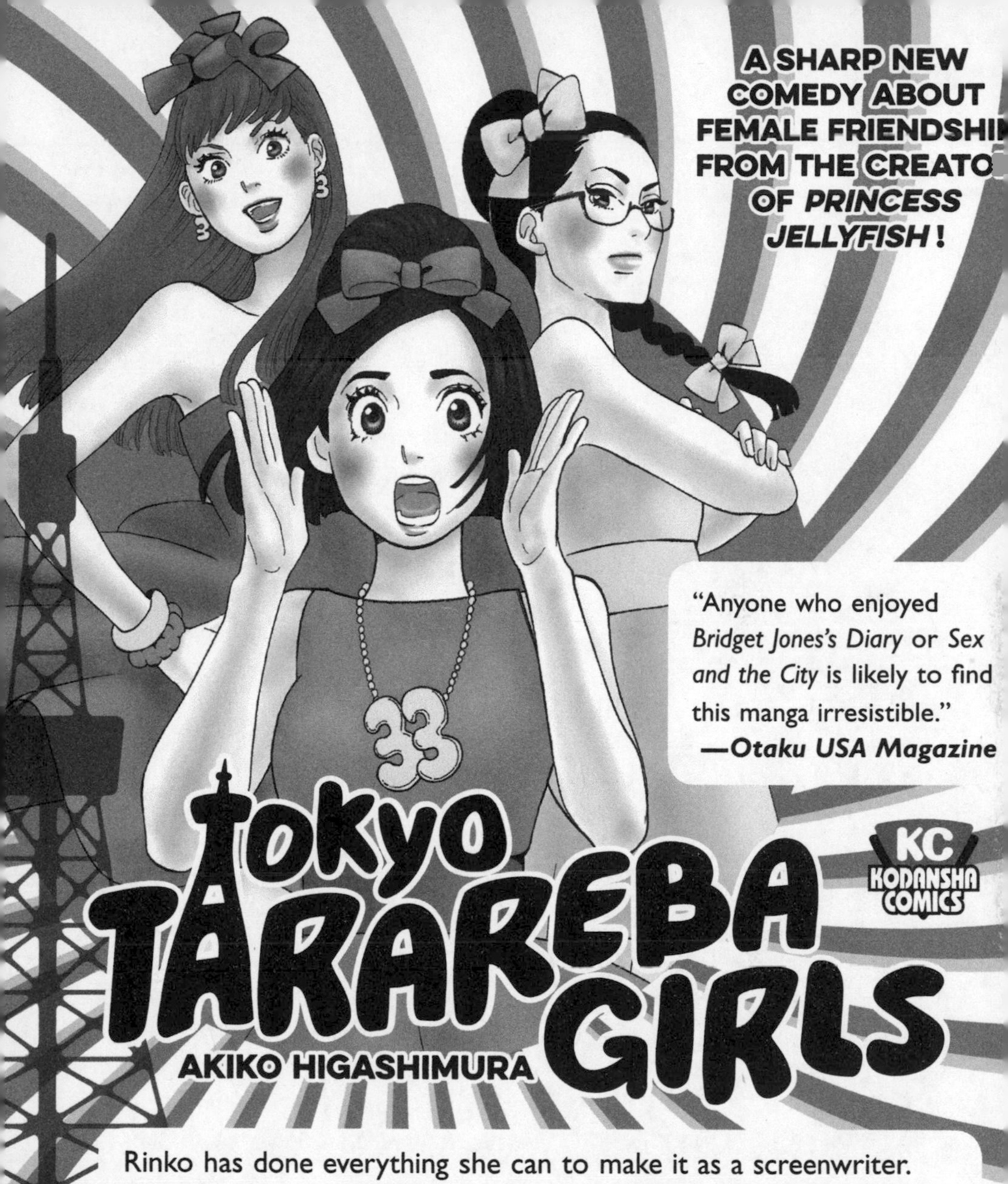

Tokyo TARAREBA GIRLS

AKIKO HIGASHIMURA

KC KODANSHA COMICS

Rinko has done everything she can to make it as a screenwriter.
So at 33, she can't help but lament over the fact that her career's
plateaued, she's still painfully single, and spends most of her nights
drinking with her two best friends. One night, drunk and delusional,
Rinko swears to get married by the time the Tokyo Olympics roll
around in 2020. But finding a man—or love—may be a cutthroat,
dirty job for a romantic at heart!

KC KODANSHA COMICS

Japan's most powerful spirit medium delves into the ghost world's greatest mysteries!

Story by Kyo Shirodaira, famed author of mystery fiction and creator of *Spiral*, *Blast of Tempest*, and *The Record of a Fallen Vampire*.

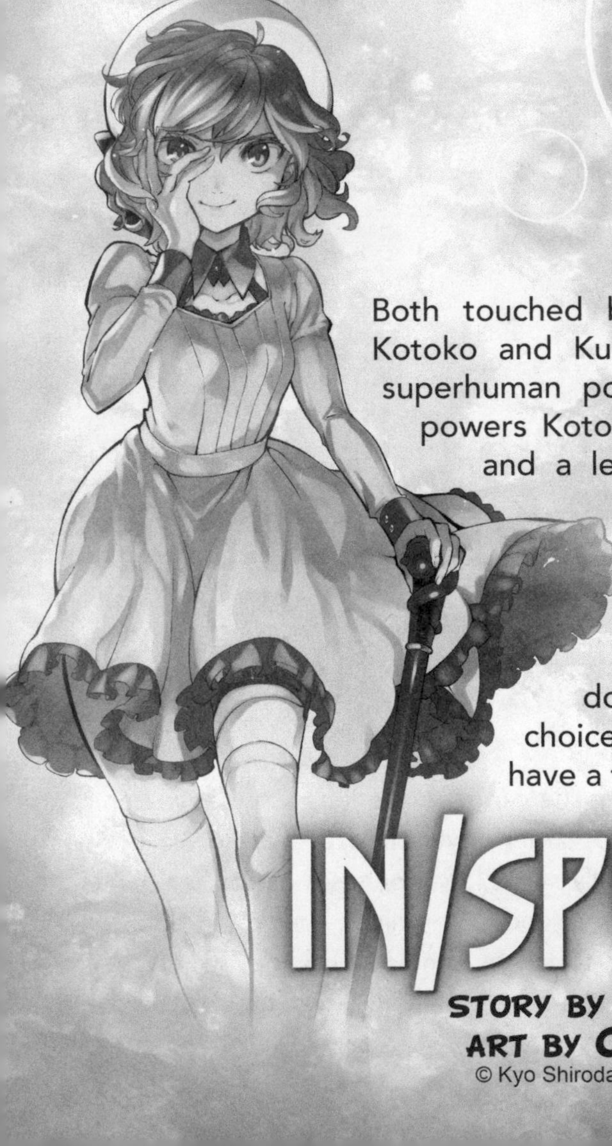

Both touched by spirits called yôkai, Kotoko and Kurô have gained unique superhuman powers. But to gain her powers Kotoko has given up an eye and a leg, and Kurô's personal life is in shambles. So when Kotoko suggests they team up to deal with renegades from the spirit world, Kurô doesn't have many other choices, but Kotoko might just have a few ulterior motives...

IN/SPECTRE

STORY BY KYO SHIRODAIRA
ART BY CHASHIBA KATASE

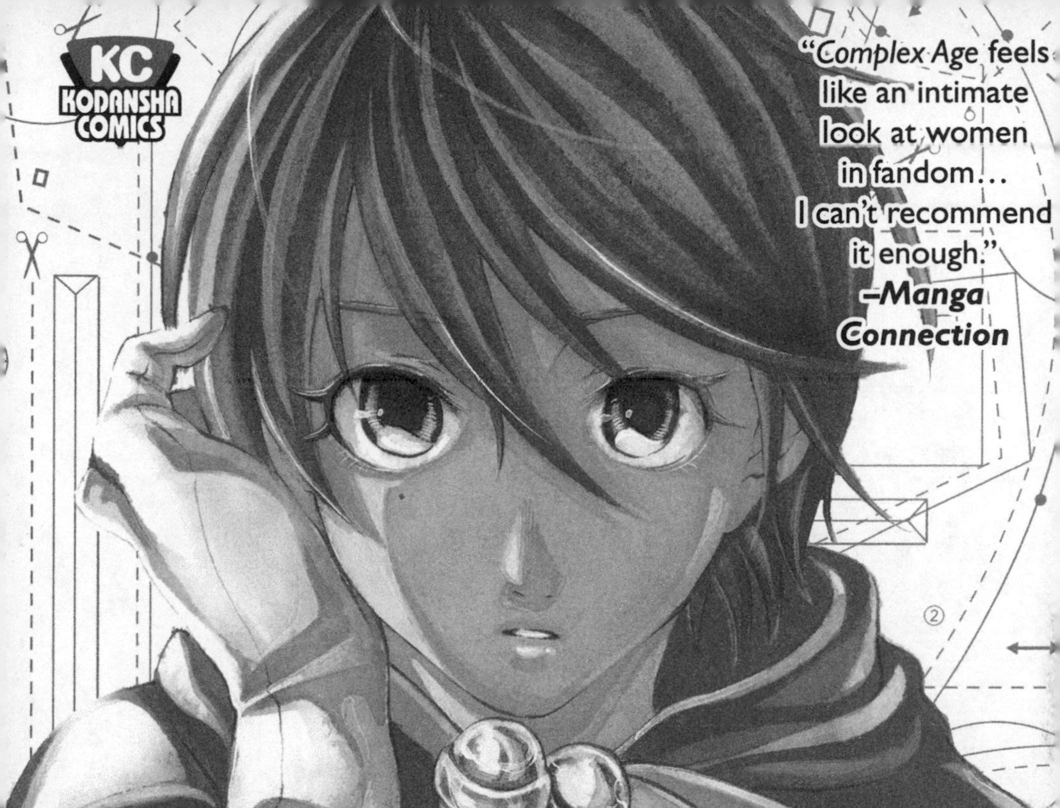
KC
KODANSHA COMICS
"*Complex Age* feels like an intimate look at women in fandom... I can't recommend it enough."
–Manga Connection
complex age
yui sakuma

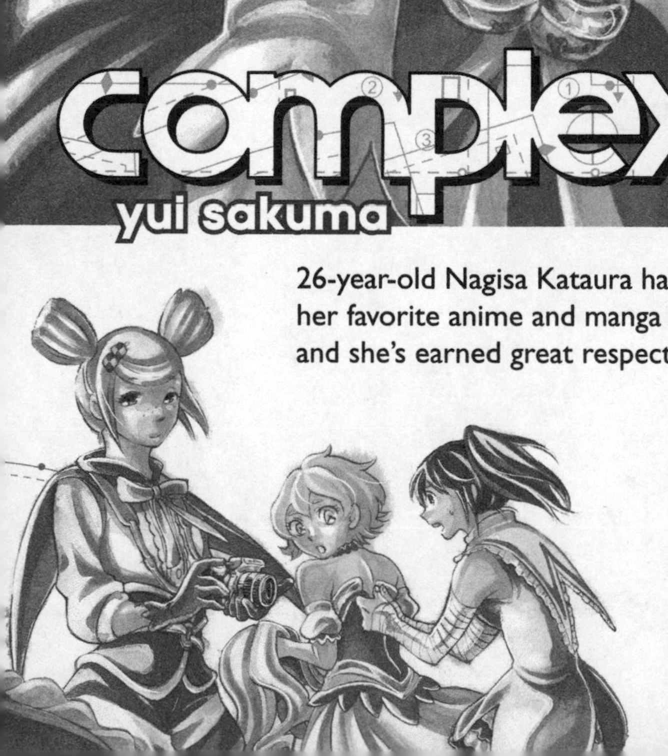

26-year-old Nagisa Kataura has a secret. Transforming into her favorite anime and manga characters is her passion in life, and she's earned great respect amongst her fellow cospayers. But to the rest of society, her hobby is a silly fantasy. As demands from both her office job and cosplaying begin to increase, she may one day have to make a tough choice—what's more important to her, cosplay or being "normal"?

"I'm pleasantly surprised to find modern shojo using cross-dressing as a dramatic device to deliver social commentary... Recommended."

-Otaku USA Magazine

The prince in his dark days

By **Hico Yamanaka**

A drunkard for a father, a household of poverty... For 17-year-old Atsuko, misfortune is all she knows and believes in. Until one day, a chance encounter with Itaru–the wealthy heir of a huge corporation–changes everything. The two look identical, uncannily so. When Itaru curiously goes missing, Atsuko is roped into being his stand-in. There, in his shoes, Atsuko must parade like a prince in a palace. She encounters many new experiences, but at what cost...?

Princess Jellyfish

Akiko Higashimura

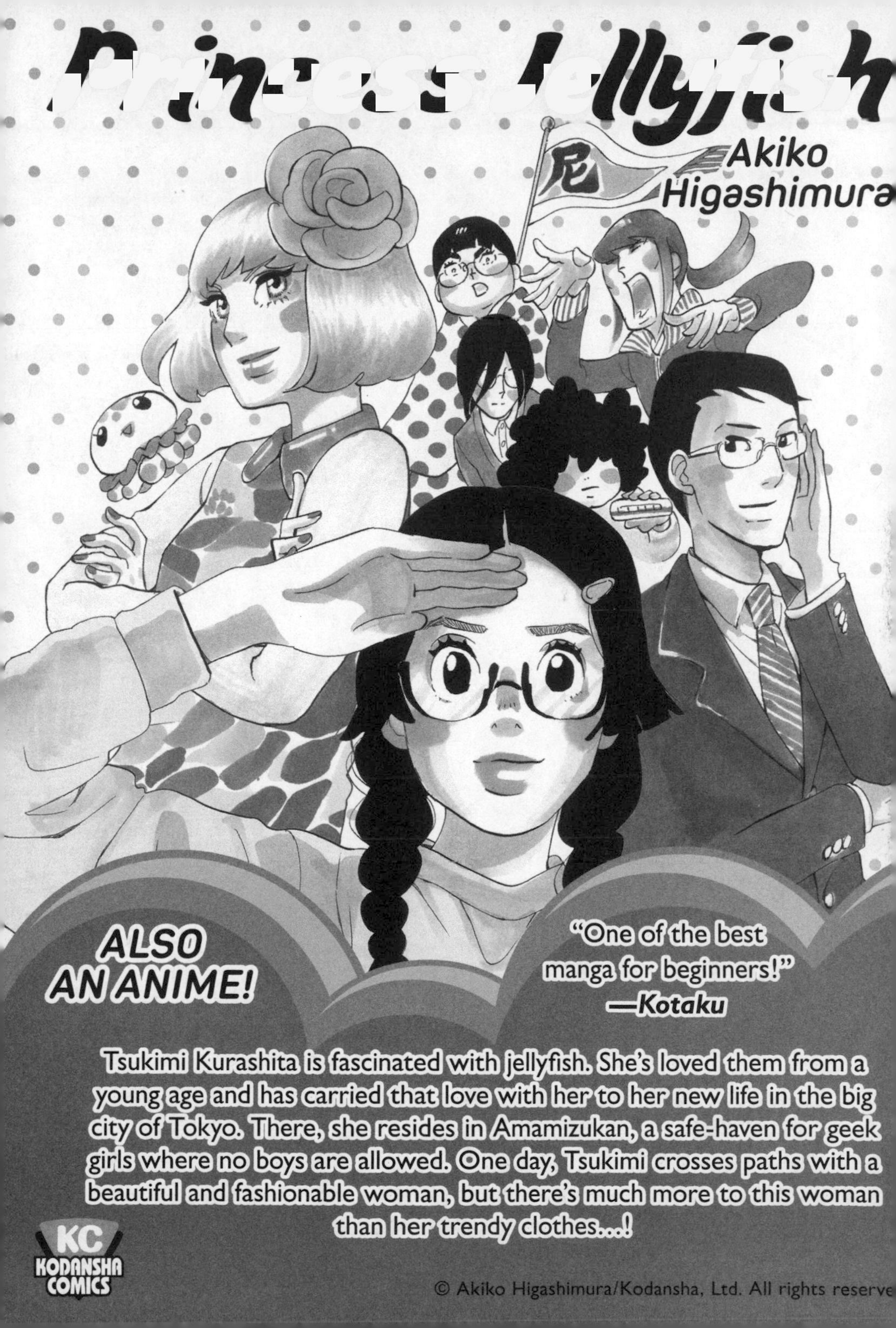
尼

ALSO AN ANIME!

"One of the best manga for beginners!"
—***Kotaku***

Tsukimi Kurashita is fascinated with jellyfish. She's loved them from a young age and has carried that love with her to her new life in the big city of Tokyo. There, she resides in Amamizukan, a safe-haven for geek girls where no boys are allowed. One day, Tsukimi crosses paths with a beautiful and fashionable woman, but there's much more to this woman than her trendy clothes...!

KC KODANSHA COMICS

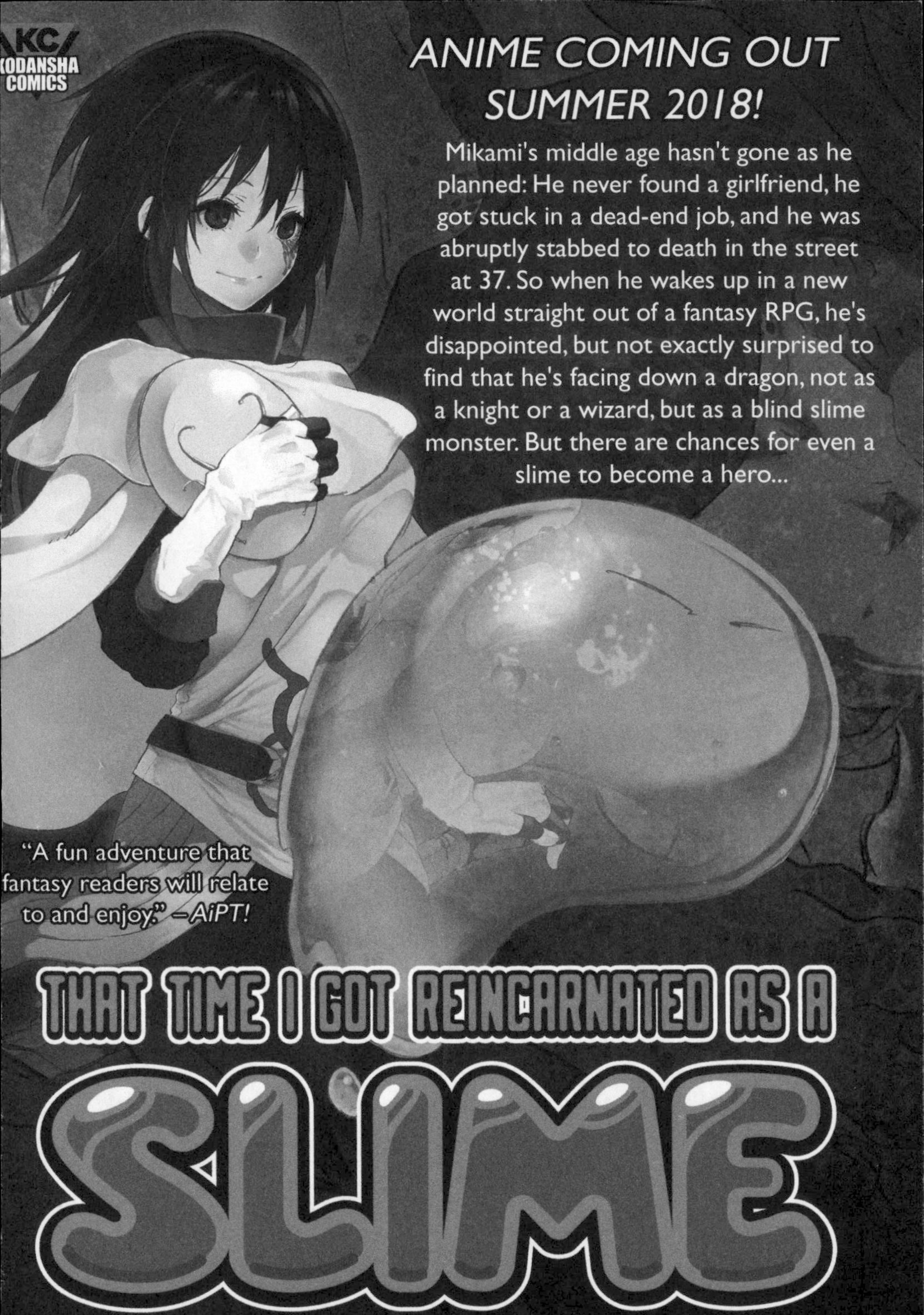
KC KODANSHA COMICS
ANIME COMING OUT SUMMER 2018!
Mikami's middle age hasn't gone as he planned: He never found a girlfriend, he got stuck in a dead-end job, and he was abruptly stabbed to death in the street at 37. So when he wakes up in a new world straight out of a fantasy RPG, he's disappointed, but not exactly surprised to find that he's facing down a dragon, not as a knight or a wizard, but as a blind slime monster. But there are chances for even a slime to become a hero...
"A fun adventure that fantasy readers will relate to and enjoy." –AiPT!
THAT TIME I GOT REINCARNATED AS A
SLIME

A new series from the creator of *Soul Eater*, the megahit manga and anime seen on Toonami!

"Fun and lively... a great start!"
-Adventures in Poor Taste

FIRE FORCE

By Atsushi Ohkubo

The city of Tokyo is plagued by a deadly phenomenon: spontaneous human combustion! Luckily, a special team is there to quench the inferno: The Fire Force! The fire soldiers at Special Fire Cathedral 8 are about to get a unique addition. Enter Shinra, a boy who possesses the power to run at the speed of a rocket, leaving behind the famous "devil's footprints" (and destroying his shoes in the process). Can Shinra and his colleagues discover the source of this strange epidemic before the city burns to ashes?

Hitorijime My Hero volume 2 is a work of fiction. Names, characters, places, and incidents are the products of the author's imagination or are used fictitiously. Any resemblance to actual events, locales, or persons, living or dead, is entirely coincidental.

A Kodansha Comics Trade Paperback Original.

Published in the United States by Kodansha Comics, an imprint of Kodansha USA Publishing, LLC, New York.

Publication rights for this English edition arranged through Kodansha Ltd., Tokyo.

First published in Japan in 2013 by Ichijinsha Inc., Tokyo.

ISBN 978-1-63236-772-3

Printed in the United States of America.

www.kodanshacomics.com

9 8 7 6 5 4

Translation: Anne Lee
Lettering: Michael Martin
Editing: Lauren Scanlan
Kodansha Comics Edition Cover Design: Phil Balsman